PRAISE FOR *THE WOMAN AT THE WASHINGTON ZOO*

"Truly bracing writing. There's no one I can think of producing that kind of raw, emotional essay . . . deeply honest, quite feminine in point of view, and ruthlessly clear."   —MARIE ARANA, editor, *Washington Post Book World*

"I never met Williams, but what this book reveals is a woman who was incapable of being a victim. She lives in the modern world of Halloween costumes and working mom quandaries, but the story she tells is straight out of Greek literature—of a person cheated by fate, but facing reality unflinchingly and asserting personal honor despite it all."

—DAVID BROOKS, *The New York Times*

"Williams's journalistic gifts include her delicious use of detail, wicked humor and a psychological insight so telling it raises the question of why anyone ever agreed to submit to her scrutiny. . . . It is the heart-rending "Hit by Lightning: A Cancer Memoir" that best displays Williams's to-the-core candor as she answers the macabre question everyone has probably indulged in: What would you do if you learned you had a short time to live?"

—*The Washington Post*

"Williams' sentences dance. They're acrobatic, graceful and sassy. . . . A call not to respectful tribute, but to pleasure and enlightenment."

—MAUREEN CORRIGAN, National Public Radio's "Fresh Air"

"Dramatic and analytic . . . meticulously walks readers through both the agony and the uplift."

—citation for a National Magazine Award given posthumously to *Vanity Fair* for "A Matter of Life and Death," a longer version of which appears in this volume as "Hit by Lightning: A Cancer Memoir"

"Like Joan Didion . . . Ms. Williams had a privileged perch from which to write about life's most universal experience: death itself. She earned it the hard way, with meticulous profiles that, as she once put it, worked the 'seam between the accepted narrative, usually hammered out between the Washington press corps and its sources, and the grubby human nature stuff.'"

—TODD PURDUM, *New York Times*

"[Williams] had a clear-eyed way of seeing two sides of an issue, or of a person's character, an insightfulness she brought even to her intimates. . . . It is this book of essays and columns, which have the strengths of a great novel: insight, wit, and a fierce refusal to accept anything that struck her as too reliably orthodox. . . ." —MEGHAN O'ROURKE, *Slate*

"By itself, ['Hit by Lightning'] is worth the price of the book. . . . For those who have never read Williams' work, *The Woman at the Washington Zoo* offers many pleasures and surprises. For those already familiar with her writing, this collection is a splendid memorial to an elegant prose stylist." —*The Los Angeles Times*

"Even if you didn't know Marjorie Williams through her columns and profiles in *The Washington Post* and *Vanity Fair*, you'll still be moved by this posthumous collection—and finish it with a sense of loss. . . in describing scenes like wrestling a doctor for her medical chart, she offers a glimpse of her steel-gut gumption—a quality that served her well right until the end." —*People Magazine*

"I'm biased by friendship, but hardly alone in believing that our era's Henry Adams is Marjorie Williams. . . . *The Woman at the Washington Zoo* combines peerless political anthropology with heartbreaking insight into the complexities of family life and her own struggle with cancer. . . . And in writing about Mary McGrory, Williams summed up her own gift: 'There was no divining the difference between Mary's talent and her ease at being indelibly herself.'" —JONATHAN ALTER, *Newsweek*

"Every once in a while a writer's voice is presented to you and it sinks into your brain, and you think: I'd like to have some more of that, please. . . . Williams' inward-seeking pieces are, not surprisingly, her most poignant. Her cancer, as she raises two young children, is almost unbearable to contemplate. . . . You can find all of this very sad. Or you can find all of this very brave and learn from it. I choose the latter." —JENNIFER WELLS, *Toronto Star*

"Marjorie Williams' posthumous collection is both sharp and sad, revealing with equal skill public figures and the most personal moments of a private life." —*The New York Post*

"This uncanny, insightful book contains revelatory pieces. . . . It tells the truth and breaks our hearts. There is nothing more a reader could ask." —*The Cleveland Plain Dealer*

"Williams was known as an unsparing portraitist of the Washington elite in profiles she wrote for *The Washington Post* and *Vanity Fair* magazine. You knew you had arrived when Marjorie Williams called for an interview. . . . Her reporting was exhaustive, but it was her wit and insight and her effortless way with language that made her such a pleasure to read."

—*The Baltimore Sun*

"Marjorie Williams . . . had the ability to infuse her journalism with the sort of psychological acuity usually found only in the best fiction . . . an astoundingly good collection of her writings edited by her husband, Timothy Noah . . . In his moving introduction, Noah pays homage to 'the intense pleasure' of his wife's company. Dipping into this compelling collection, we see what he means."

—*O, The Oprah Magazine*

"With her intellect and perception, the late *Washington Post* columnist Marjorie Williams possessed a kind of X-ray vision that Superman would envy. . . . I have not enjoyed a book about politicians and the issues that engage them so much since Richard Ben Cramer's famous campaign account, 'What It Takes.' Williams set an Olympian standard for profiles, which unfold in a smooth, effortless style. . . . In her analysis of national politicians, Williams was, indeed, fierce with reality. In the face of her impending death, she exhibited a bravery that bordered on the fierce."

—*Pittsburgh Post-Gazette*

"[Williams's] profiles are rich with personal details and insight too often passed over in stories about the powerful. . . . Williams's elegant style is at the same time so breezy and casual that you can imagine her writing her columns as notes to friends. . . Particularly moving are her writings on parenthood, marriage, and family."

—*The Washingtonian*

"As a seasoned Washington writer, Williams was both one of the pack and anomalous. . . . Her writing also stands out for what simmers just beneath, whether it's a passage of excavatory reporting or a personal, painful insight. . . . Whether she was writing about presidents, changing mores or her own primal fears, Williams was artful, original and above all, honest."

—*The Minneapolis Star-Tribune*

"Long ago, when we were children, I sat next to Marjorie Williams at *The Washington Post*. I say this in the same spirit that someone might be lucky enough to say they once worked in the same office as Dorothy Parker. She was an incredible wit with x-ray eyes and a voice, in print and in person, that was unmistakable. As you read these piece on Washington life and, then, on her own life, you also begin to see that she was a writer of intelligence, courage, and soul. We were lucky to have had her and lucky, too, to have this book."

—DAVID REMNICK

"Marjorie saw inside what the rest of us only see the outside of—and about the most opaque subjects—family, relationships and Washington pols. . . . What a gift to the world she was."

—MARGARET CARLSON, political analyst,
CNN and editor at large, *The Week*

"Marjorie Williams never shied from what she described as 'the inconvenient argument, the longing to know what was real,' even as she held a mirror unsparingly to her own life. She had a kind of literary intuition that allowed her to see what others could not, and in this collection she lays bare the characters and culture of Washington with remarkable originality. Marjorie lived as she wrote, with warmth, wit, and effortless style."

—SALLY BEDELL SMITH, author of *Grace and Power:
The Private World of the Kennedy White House*

"A master of the political profile, Marjorie had that rare combination of old-school reporting smarts and newer-school social psychological insight. On top of this she was a witty and graceful stylist. . . . As a journalist, and as a lunch companion, she had few peers and no betters."

—GRAYDON CARTER, *Vanity Fair*

"What a tragedy that this superb writer—and woman—is no longer with us, but how lucky we are that she left us these marvelous writings. This is a book to treasure, as we did her."

—CHRISTOPHER BUCKLEY, author of *Thank You For Smoking*

"There are many memoirs of illness, but the one included here stands apart for its extraordinary insight and artistry. Marjorie Williams shows us how our spirit need not succumb to even the most terrible maladies. Her writing comforts and inspires us all."

—JEROME GROOPMAN, M.D., author of *The Anatomy of Hope*
and professor, Harvard Medical School

"Marjorie Williams put her whole best self into everything she wrote—wit, high spirits, honesty, heart, and brilliant literary gifts. She was not just the best Washington journalist of her generation, she was one of the best journalists, period." —KATHA POLLITT, columnist, *The Nation*

"Someday the great Washington novel of power and scheming, of campaign hacks and backroom deals will be written. But until that day comes, my key to that world will be the collected journalism of Marjorie Williams." —JACK SHAFER, *Slate*

THE WOMAN AT
THE
WASHINGTON
ZOO

Writings on Politics, Family, and Fate

BY MARJORIE WILLIAMS
EDITED BY TIMOTHY NOAH

PUBLICAFFAIRS
New York

Book Design by Janet Tingey

The Library of Congress has catalogued the hardcover edition as follows:
Williams, Marjorie, 1958–2005.
The woman at the Washington Zoo : writings on politics, family, and fate /
    Marjorie Williams.
p.   cm.
Includes index.
ISBN-13 978-1-58648-363-0
ISBN-10 1-58648-363-3
1. Washington (D.C.)—Social Life and customs—1951—Anecdotes. 2.
    Political culture—Washington (D.C.)—Anecdotes. 3. Political cul-
    ture—United States—Anecdotes. 4. Politicians—United States—
    Biography—Anecdotes. 5. United States—Politics and
    government—1945–1989—Anecdotes. 6. United States—Politics
    and government—1989—Anecdotes. 7. United States—Social
    conditions—1980—Anecdotes. 8. Williams, Marjorie—1958–2005—
    Anecdotes. 9. Women journalists—United States—Biography—
    Anecdotes. I. Title.
F201.W55 2005
975.3'041—dc22
                                                        2005050050

Paperback: ISBN-13 978-1-58648-457-6; ISBN-10 1-58648-457-5

10 9 8 7 6 5 4 3 2 1

FOR WILL AND ALICE

CONTENTS

The saris go by me from the embassies.
Cloth from the moon. Cloth from another planet.
They look back at the leopard like the leopard.
And I . . .
                this print of mine, that has kept its color
Alive through so many cleanings; this dull null
Navy I wear to work, and wear from work, and so
To my bed, so to my grave, with no
Complaints, no comment: neither from my chief,
The Deputy Chief Assistant, nor his chief—
Only I complain . . . this serviceable
Body that no sunlight dyes, no hand suffuses
But, dome-shadowed, withering among columns,
Wavy beneath fountains—small, far-off, shining
In the eyes of animals, these beings trapped
As I am trapped but not, themselves, the trap,
Aging, but without knowledge of their age,
Kept safe here, knowing not of death, for death—
Oh, bars of my own body, open, open!
The world goes by my cage and never sees me.
And there come not to me, as come to these,
The wild beasts, sparrows pecking the llamas' grain,
Pigeons settling on the bears' bread, buzzards
Tearing the meat the flies have clouded. . . .
                                        Vulture,
When you come for the white rat that the foxes left,
Take off the red helmet of your head, the black
Wings that have shadowed me, and step to me as man:
The wild brother at whose feet the white wolves fawn,
To whose hand of power the great lioness
Stalks, purring. . . .
                You know what I was,
You see what I am: change me, change me!

                                —*Randall Jarrell,*
                        "The Woman at the Washington Zoo" (1956)

INTRODUCTION
BY TIMOTHY NOAH

Before me is a faded clipping from the *Washington Weekly*, an alternative paper that enjoyed a brief life in our nation's capital during the mid-1980s. It's a column on the publishing industry, and the fourth item announces that one Marjorie Williams will open a Washington office for Simon & Schuster. She "will be aggressively acquiring Washington properties from her Dupont Circle office starting this week." The date is July 2, 1984.

The item (written by Margaret Carlson, now a well-known political commentator) didn't explain that Marjorie Williams was all of twenty-six, and that the office in question was really an apartment shared with a boyfriend, from which Marjorie continued to perform the editing duties she'd previously executed in New York. The boyfriend lasted a few months, the publishing career (in which she'd invested seven years after dropping out of Harvard, rising to a level of some influence) about a year. What endured was Washington.

Washington became Marjorie's subject as expressed through the lives of the people within it who sought and exercised power. She wangled an editing job at the *Washington Post* ("I've been a news junkie since I was twelve," she wrote the *Post*'s personnel chief), then leveraged an offer to run the Book-of-the-Month Club into a writing job in the paper's marquee features section, Style. Within five years she'd established herself, among her professional peers, as the country's most perceptive writer of political profiles, writing first for the Style section, then for the *Post*'s Sunday magazine, then for *Vanity Fair*, then for *Talk*, and finally once again for *Vanity Fair*. A Marjorie Williams profile was conspicuous for its almost frightening psychological acuity, its painstaking accumulation of reportorial detail, and its elegant prose. "Try to be one of the people on whom nothing is lost," Henry James famously advised aspiring writers. Marjorie didn't just try; she embodied the ideal.

The Washington that Marjorie wrote about was mostly that of presidents George H.W. Bush and Bill Clinton. The decade of the 1990s was a period of relative moderation in politics, bookended by two eras of ideological fervor—the presidencies of Ronald Reagan at one end and George W. Bush at the other. Most of the people Marjorie profiled were political technicians who liked to think of themselves as visionaries or idealists; some of them perhaps were. But always there was tension between quotidian, usually partisan or commercial priorities and the vague, long-term goal to apply government muscle to beneficial ends.

Marjorie liked to point out that partisan and commercial self-interest almost always got the upper hand, and when that happened Washington's power players typically looked away. That's very much the theme of "The Pragmatist" and "The Rainmaker," Marjorie's profiles of Richard Darman and Vernon Jordan. "The Hack," her profile of Tony Coelho—whom she credits as inadvertent architect of the congressional Democrats' catastrophic electoral losses in 1994—illustrates what happens when the pretense of idealism is dispensed with altogether.

Once Marjorie had perfected the political profile, she started sharpening her skills at personal observation, and within a few years she had produced a corpus of essays whose brilliance, I believe, exceeds that of the profiles. (Two of these essays, "The Alchemist" and "Hit by Lightning: A Cancer Memoir," are published here for the first time.) By the end of the 1990s, Marjorie was writing exquisitely crafted columns blending the personal and the political for the *Post*'s op-ed page. She never lost her passionate interest in the psychology of political leadership, but increasingly Marjorie's attention shifted to the subtler and more intimate dynamics of family life, including her own. Or rather, I should say, "our own," because in 1990 Marjorie had become my wife. She subjected my marriage proposal to textual analysis in a *Post* magazine cover story reprinted here as "Reader, I Married." Our two young children, Will and Alice, play leading roles in "Entomophobia" and "The Halloween of My Dreams," respectively, and make other, briefer appearances throughout this volume.

Marjorie's journalism career reached its peak in July 2001, when she began syndicating her *Post* column to other newspapers around the country through the Washington Post Writers Group. A long piece for *Vanity Fair* about the rocky relationship between former president Bill Clinton and his vice president, Al Gore, had just been published, and it was getting a lot of favorable attention. (Titled "Scenes from a Marriage," the joint profile concludes the first section of this book.) Marjorie was getting ready to tackle her next assignment for *Slate*'s Book Club, which paired off for email exchanges members of a distinguished stable of critics that Marjorie had felt flattered to join. She had also taken up running with characteristic intensity, and looked forward to entering her first marathon. Meanwhile, she was furiously refurbishing the spacious Victorian on the "wrong" side of Rock Creek Park that we'd purchased the year before. Everything was falling into place. Then everything came crashing down.

There was a lump in Marjorie's lower abdomen. It was probably a fibroid tumor, her gynecologist said, a minor annoyance. But he sent her out for a sonogram immediately, and the lump turned out to be one of several metastases. Marjorie, who hadn't felt healthier or more excited by her work in years, had an advanced case of liver cancer, one of the deadliest of all cancers, and (in the United States) a somewhat rare one. Marjorie relates the shock of her diagnosis in "Hit by Lightning: A Cancer Memoir," the first and longest chapter in the third section. She was assured that she only had a few months to live, but in fact Marjorie went on to live three and a half years more before she died in January 2005. She was forty-seven.

What made Marjorie the extraordinary writer she was? I think it was her unrelenting refusal to accept fraudulent surface reality and her remarkable skill at finding the hidden truth that lay beneath. Washington journalists tend to exaggerate the difficulty of becoming an "insider" to the political subculture, and to deny the willed blindness that is often the price of admission. Marjorie showed that you could burrow into Washington's power culture without surrendering to its deceptions, on the one hand, or embitterment, on the other. "Of course," Marjorie writes in "Flying to L.A.," Washington is "a hive of conformity and caution, but that's part of what I like about it—about covering it, anyway."

> The mixture of that brittle, conservative set of social conventions and all the messy human stuff that goes on inside and among the people who try to climb to the top of the heap makes for such rich material. . . . I love working this seam between the accepted narrative, usually hammered out between the Washington press corps and its

sources, and the grubby human nature stuff that is nearly always as plain as the nose on your face.

Marjorie's dispassionate assessments of her subjects and her authoritative classifications according to social type inspired this book's title, which I borrow from Randall Jarrell's poem of the same name. Jarrell was a favorite of Marjorie's, and she quoted the poem in "A Woman Who Knew Her Due," her tribute to her late *Post* colleague Mary McGrory, which closes the second section. I plead guilty to subverting Jarrell's meaning by casting Marjorie as the Woman of the poem's title, and by implying that this book's organization by phylum of the Washington menagerie ("The Philanthropist," "The Pragmatist," and so on) somehow mimics Jarrell. It does not. Jarrell's poem, to the small extent that it addresses politics at all, does so by casting the Woman at Washington's National Zoo as a government bureaucrat clad in "dull null/ Navy," in stark contrast to the colorful saris worn by embassy wives from the Indian subcontinent ("cloth from the moon") and to the caged animals ("white wolves," a vulture's "red helmet"). Jarrell himself, in a commentary on the poem, called the Woman an "aging machine part." McGrory, however, had (Marjorie wrote) "the heart of a buccaneer." She was no machine part. Neither was Marjorie.

But there's another way to read the poem. William Pritchard, in a literary biography of Jarrell, noted that the Woman's rage against repression, as expressed by Jarrell, "belies the woman's powerlessness" and constitutes "a sound of strength and mastery rather than weakness and confusion"— so much so that the poem "has been adopted as a rallying point . . . for liberation or 'empowerment.'" In that sense, Marjorie seems very much like the Woman at the Washington Zoo. A strong feminist streak runs through the essays collected here, from Marjorie's exasperation when *Ms.* magazine decided to accept cosmetics advertorials ("Makeup and *Ms.*"), through her sympathetic exploration of the idea of a "marriage sabbatical" ("Run for Your Life"), and on to her disgust when the feminist establishment gave Bill Clinton a free pass about Monica Lewinsky ("Bill Clinton, Feminist"). To observe Marjorie's "strength and mastery" as a writer and a human being, you need look no further than "Hit by Lightning: A Cancer Memoir." (I assembled this essay, after Marjorie's death, from fragments of a book she had started to write about her illness.) Marjorie was furious that she had to think endlessly about her coming death while you, dear reader, might be lucky enough never to "catch sight of the blade assigned to you." It made her furious when doctors treated her like a child, and (in her essay "The Doctor Factor") she exposed their arrogance and their petty vanities. Above all, Marjorie was furious that her body was failing her. In this context, Jarrell's concluding lines—"You know what I was,/ You see what I am: change me, change me!"—seem right on the money.

Marjorie overflowed with love for her family and her friends, but, even before her illness, she never accepted less than she thought she deserved, which was quite a lot. Self-denial was, to Marjorie's mind, a form of self-neglect, something not to admire but to mistrust. The greatest piece of writing Marjorie ever produced, I believe, is "The Alchemist," a portrait of the self-denying figure in Marjorie's life: her late mother, Beverly Williams. I had no idea, when Marjorie died, that she had written the essay; I found it when I was going through her files to compile this book. Why did she never publish it during her lifetime? My best guess is that it felt too close to the bone.

The house on Maple Street in Princeton, NJ, where Marjorie grew up, was part salon and part five-star restaurant. The salon's host was Marjorie's father, Alan Williams, a learned and gregarious editor at Viking Press. His authors included Nadine Gordimer, Shirley Hazzard, and Stephen King, and literary figures were forever passing through the Williams living room. Filling the stomachs of these luminaries fell to Beverly, a somewhat reserved woman whose self-effacing demeanor masked a razor-sharp wit. It was from her mother, and not her more conspicuously literary father, that Marjorie inherited the remarkable acuity about human character that makes her profiles so memorable. In "The Alchemist," Marjorie describes forever positioning herself, as a child, by the back stairs separating the living room, where Alan held court, and the kitchen, where Beverly lost herself in preparing exquisite meals for near-strangers. It was an ambivalence that haunted her the rest of her life. Eventually, though, "between my mother's moon and my father's sun, I made my choice." She planted herself in the sun; she chose to be hungry and alive. That choice radiates from every page of this book.

What follows is a small fraction of Marjorie's work. Although the selections tend to represent what I felt was her very best journalism, the scheme I chose imposed some limitations. As I noted earlier, the first and longest section, "Profiles," presents the reader with a sampling of distinct social types in Washington. That ruled out inclusion of some great profiles of non-Washingtonians; her *Vanity Fair* portraits of Anna Quindlen and Patricia Duff come to mind. The profile subjects whom I did include are not necessarily the most significant figures Marjorie profiled. Rather, they are the people Marjorie wrote about in a particularly insightful or entertaining way. An extreme example is "Protocol," a profile of Archie and Selwa Roosevelt, two utterly forgotten Reagan-era personages. The piece is included here because of the deft comedy Marjorie employed to describe one Washington power couple's particularly clumsy pas de deux. It felt like a good curtain-raiser. Gwendolyn Cafritz, the Washington-area philanthropist profiled in the book's second chapter, wasn't a political person at all, but I included her for variety, and because it's simply too much fun to rubberneck a big fight over a rich person's last will and testament.

The book's second section, "Essays," contains a mixture of magazine essays, newspaper columns, book reviews, and email exchanges published in *Slate*. In choosing items to include here, I tended to winnow out anything that didn't relate in some way to family or women's issues, which were Marjorie's principal concerns during her last active years. Consequently, very few of Marjorie's fine columns on the 2000 election made the cut.

The final section, "Time and Chance," is about Marjorie's fight with cancer. It includes her narrative about being a cancer patient as well as a few columns that Marjorie managed to produce during (and about) her illness. It's the book's most personal section, and the one that most clearly makes my editing of this book, in the first months after Marjorie's death, an act of mourning. Marjorie and I never discussed publishing a collection of her writings after her death; she barely weighed in on the more immediate question of what to include in her memorial service. I do know that, before Marjorie got sick, she dismissed the idea of making her debut between covers anything but a single, original, previously unpublished work of nonfiction, or perhaps even fiction. So in a very narrow sense, I wish this anthology were not being published. Its publication is a painful reminder that Marjorie never lived to write even one of the many books she had inside her. On balance, though, I am very glad this anthology *is* being published. The insight and effervescence and sweet sadness and tart humor of Marjorie's words will always keep part of her alive. The mere fact that you never knew her and loved her as I did is no reason to deny you the intense pleasure of her company.

PART I

PROFILES

PROTOCOL
(ARCHIE AND LUCKY ROOSEVELT)

The U.S. chief of protocol begins by threatening to cry.

The interview has been arranged for a dual profile of Ambassador Selwa (Lucky) Roosevelt and her husband Archie, a retired Central Intelligence Agency officer who has just published his memoirs. Most of it will take place at the couple's house in Georgetown, but the reporter has asked first to meet Mrs. Roosevelt at her office in Foggy Bottom. To catch her, as it were, in her habitat. She has agreed to this much, but says first and firmly, "This is Archie's hour." He deserves the limelight for his book, she says. She gets far too much attention as it is, she says. Don't, she pleads, make it a story about her. "I'll burst into tears if you do that," she says.

Protocol demands fair warning.

"Darling Gracie," wrote Theodore Roosevelt to his daughter-in-law in July 1918, the year his grandson was born, "the picture of darling wee bunny Archikins made me so dreadfully homesick for him. I long for him, and shall croon every kind of aboriginal nursery song to the blessed wee person. . . . " That is the extraordinary heritage of Archibald Bulloch Roosevelt Jr. His pedigree is there to hear in his voice, a dry emanation from the very back of his nose; it is there more faintly to see in his looks—in the sly smile that goes with a wit as dry as the voice. But *For Lust of Knowing: Memoirs of an Intelligence Officer* is largely the story of how Archie, then seventy, saved himself from the wretched fate of being a Roosevelt.

"I've always been attracted by the exotic," Archie says. "I didn't want to fall into the mold: I was brought up as a Groton-Harvard-Long Island-New York type, and I didn't want to fall into that." According to former CIA Director Richard Helms, Roosevelt is the real McCoy, "an uncommonly good intelligence officer." The subtitle of his book is something of a misnomer, however; it is discreet to a fault about his CIA activities. More than anything, Archie Roosevelt's memoir is a romance in the tradition of the British Arabists, an account of his love affair with the East. "When I speak of an intelligence officer," he writes tellingly, "it is in the old-fashioned sense, perhaps best exemplified in fiction by Kipling's British political officers in India." With an initial leaning toward academia, he learned at one time or another twenty different languages, from Arabic to Old Norse to Middle High German. (Being a Roosevelt had its advantages after all: "I learned Russian at home," he says. "I taught myself the grammar, and I learned how to speak by talking to the Polish gardener.")

World War II was the welcome disruption that turned him toward his passion. Sent to North Africa and the Middle East as an army intelligence officer, he came away with strong opinions about French colonialism and Soviet expansionism in those regions—and about American myopia toward them. He also came away confirmed in his lust for the East. At war's end he joined the CIA, and served, until 1974, as chief of stations including Istanbul, London, and Madrid, and later in Washington as a high-level administrator.

In the course of events, he married properly (to Katharine Tweed, daughter of Wall Street lawyer Harrison Tweed) and, improperly, divorced. After the 1950 divorce, "I pondered it night after night," he writes,

> and concluded that perhaps my nature was too different from that of the New Englanders with whom I had spent my youth. My next wife would not be a Yankee, but perhaps a warm, smiling Southerner with a softer nature, or even an Arab girl, a black-eyed Houri like many I had seen—but never touched!—over the last few years. I had known a few married to British and Americans in the Middle East and their husbands all appeared to be serenely happy.

Only a few months later, Roosevelt found Southern belle and black-eyed Arab rolled into one twenty-one-year-old Vassar student. He was then on loan to the Voice of America, where Selwa Showker, who was about to graduate, was referred for a job interview. "The minute Archie saw me," she says, "he understood me. He knew my history practically from one look at my face." They were married three months later. "I took this little thing right out of Vassar," he says, and suddenly you can see generations of Roosevelt males behind him. "I didn't want anyone else to see her first."

"May I call you Barbara?" The question, an hour into the interview, is delivered in her low, nearly husky tones, with standard Southern ebullience. It seems peculiar only because it is addressed to someone named Marjorie, and asked by someone who is paid $77,500 a year to be the best-mannered person in America.

Washington, of course, produces lots of attractive, well-married ladies in slim Chanel suits and smiles of businesslike sociability. Some of them work for salaries and some of them serve their husbands' careers; and a few, lately, do both. But Lucky Roosevelt, who has the accoutrements down so completely that she could give lessons in the type, is yet too extravagant a personality to belong to it.

Like many others, Selwa Roosevelt reflexively salutes both her lord and her master at every turn, as in: "You know how darling Ronald Reagan is, I mean he's the most adorable man, he's so sweet and nice. And Archie's just like that." Like others, she has been known to drop a name or two. "I could never ask someone I know socially," she told *House & Garden*'s John Duka about her fund-raising for the renovation of Blair House. "Take John Kluge. Now he really hides his light under a bushel, but it wouldn't have been kosher to ask him, especially since we were both on safari with Malcolm Forbes."

But she is not like others. She has, first, the distinctive, dark good looks of her parents' native Lebanon. And with Middle Eastern parents, a Southern upbringing, and a patina of Roosevelt reserve, at fifty-nine, Selwa has the air of struggling to fit too many parts into too small a container; of Bette Davis auditioning to be Joan Fontaine. Her parents, both of the Druze sect, raised their two daughters in conservative Kingsport, TN. Her father—who immigrated at sixteen and started as a peddler—built up a dry goods business, only to lose it in the Depression and then have to start over. "We never were well off," says Lucky, "but we were very rich in love and warmth and a happy home." Although Selwa is a common name in Lebanon ("It's like Ann, or Jane or something"), people in the South thought it "the most exotic thing in the world." Over time, the nickname "Lucky" evolved. "I was lucky at cards," she says.

Lucky first worked at age thirteen, earning Christmas money by selling perfume in a department store. Later, she saved money toward her college education, which was mostly paid for by scholarships she earned with her top grades. "If I had as a child any experience of sadness, I suppose it was because I wasn't blond and blue-eyed and the girl next door," she once told *Interview* magazine. But as time went on, she says, she came to "love the fact of my background . . . . I have always basically found that I was an object of interest to people. I think it's also given me some more empathy with people."

"The difference between [Archie's] background and mine is huge," she continues, saying of her own family's boisterous warmth, "My mother-in-law thought it very, very *de trop*. I think Archie's family taught me something of the dignity of restraint. There is a dignity maybe I would not have had, just being ethnic me."

After decades of fudging what he did for a living—pretending to work for the State Department, answering questions about his career with vague generalities—Archie Roosevelt seems to enjoy the mild exhibitionism of authorship. But in this interview, he doesn't get to enjoy much of it. He is asked about the great discretion he used in writing the book—whether it was his choice, the CIA's, or both. "Well, the thing is," he says, "I can say by the contract I wrote [upon retirement] that I served overseas for the agency, always as chief of station. But I couldn't say what stations I was chief of. But if you read the book—"

"Now, Archie," Lucky interjects. "You have to be very careful."

He improvises. "Well, no, I think what you can say is I wasn't allowed to say where I was chief of station. So what you'll have to do is read *Who's Who*—"

Lucky breaks in again. "I don't think you should say *anything* about that. I'm sorry."

"All right," he says, "all right."

To the reporter, she says, "I just think he's going to get into trouble."

"I'll get into trouble," repeats Archie. "All right. Well, I—"

"Skip that."

"Well, what *can* I say, then?"

Lucky smiles. "Well, what was the question?"

She is more afraid, it develops, that he will get *her* into trouble. Minutes later, Archie is warming to a description of his old craft. "Now, intelligence—its function is to get the intelligence and find out what's going on in all the countries of the world, and of course the number one intelligence target is the Soviet Union—"

"Now, *Aaar-chie*," says Lucky.

"That is *perfectly* all right to say," he asserts with some asperity.

"No, but you're—I'm the chief of protocol." She turns to the visitor and smiles, points to the tape recorder on the tea table. "Turn this thing off," she says sweetly.

These four words, and variations on them, will get a workout in the next two hours. Each time, she indicates that she had not sufficiently thought out the delicate problems that might arise in a joint interview. Given her position, she cannot countenance any slurs on other countries or their leaders. "Archie," she says, "is an innocent where the press is concerned."

The conversation goes more smoothly when she is invited to talk about her husband's attributes. "I still think I'm married to the most brilliant man that I've ever met," she says. "I always wanted to be married to a man whose mind was exciting and different . . . . Archie will not remember the name of someone I've just introduced him to. But he can remember esoteric things about Roman history or—or the Visigoths. Or the Uzbeks."

As soon as the conversation returns to more recent history, however, her brow furrows. Archie brings up former CIA director William Colby, whom he castigates in the book as one of the worst directors he worked for.

"Now, Archie. I can't—"

"I've said it in my *boo-oook*," he points out plaintively.

"I've told you," she responds tartly: "You can have your controversial things, but not with me."

She objects to talk about former CIA agent Philip Agee.* She rules out his routine description of security procedures in foreign missions.

"But that's got nothing to do with your job, or politics," he objects.

---

* Agee created a furor in 1975 by publishing a book, *Inside the Company* (Simon & Schuster), in which he revealed the identities of CIA operatives around the world.

"I know, but I don't—I find it difficult."

Archie is asked about the defections, twenty-seven years earlier, of British intelligence officers Kim Philby and Donald Maclean.

"Aaaaaaah," Lucky moans. "I think Archie ought to talk about something other than specific things to do with the agency, when he's being interviewed with me," she says. "I don't really care what he says when we're separate."

He is trying in vain to explain that he wasn't even in London at the time.

"Archie, please!" she says. "You have to be careful!"

What has he said that has hurt her, he asks. Has he said anything compromising about a foreign government?

"Well, I know," she answers, "but I just, I mean, it's very hard for me."

"Well, you tell me when I've said anything that's difficult. . . ." His voice is beginning to rise.

"Remember," Lucky admonishes her husband, "we're being recorded as we're discussing this."

Could you turn that off a minute?

Several times she reiterates her concern, and the next morning she will call and say,

> I didn't ever want to stop him from saying what was on his mind, but there were times when I thought he was on thin ice. I can't be associated with something about foreign leaders or countries that might be pejorative, I just never would in this job. I just might as well quit as do that.

The obvious solution—that she might leave the room while he is being interviewed—never seems to cross her mind.

"It didn't bother me," Archie says of the anonymity that inevitably accompanies intelligence work,

> because I had self-confidence. But we'd have friends from the foreign community who'd say, "Why doesn't Archie ever make ambassador? At his age, shouldn't he be an ambassador? He seems to know quite a lot about the countries, and to be doing a good job, and why does he never get promoted?"

In the end, of course, it was his wife who made ambassador. While the Roosevelts were moving around the world, returning to Washington for occasional stretches, Lucky worked as a writer. In the mid-1950s she wrote a column for Washington's *Evening Star* titled "Diplomatically Speaking," and later she freelanced for a number of magazines and newspapers, including *Town & Country, McCall's, Family Circle,* and the *Washington Post.* "All my life," she says, "I was a housewife first, a journalist second."

In November 1981, when Nancy Reagan was being widely criticized as extravagant, Lucky wrote a rousing defense on the op-ed page of the *Washington Post* asking, "When is the press going to give the first lady a break?" She made this appealing diagnosis of Nancy Reagan's difficulties: "Mrs. Reagan is shy, sensitive and vulnerable. . . . She cannot dissemble. She is so honest she cannot 'stage' events to make her look good." Two months later, President Reagan's first chief of protocol, Leonore Annenberg, resigned after only a year in office. White House Deputy Chief of Staff Michael K. Deaver suggested that Lucky Roosevelt replace her—an idea prompted in large part, according to several former White House staffers, by her article. "The name Roosevelt didn't hurt any, either," added one.

The protocol chief's office is responsible for, among other things, coordinating visits from foreign dignitaries; the purchase and presentation of gifts to foreign leaders; accrediting foreign diplomats; and the maintenance of Blair House (the official guest residence across the street from the White House). When Lucky Roosevelt leaves office with Ronald Reagan, she'll be one of the longest-serving chiefs of protocol in history. It is a physically demanding job, calling for early hours and late ones, and for endless smiling visits to embassy functions. But it confers a redoubtable social standing.

In the words of Henry Catto, who served as chief of protocol under President Lyndon B. Johnson: "It's a little bit like being the captain of a mine sweeper. If you do your job well, nobody notices. If you don't, there's a hell of an explosion."

In 1974, when he retired from the CIA, Archie took a job with the Chase Manhattan Bank as director of international relations. When mentioned chiefly as Mr. Lucky Roosevelt, he would take that, too, in stride. "He has been so supportive of me in this job," Lucky says.

"He's totally secure in himself," says their longtime friend Ina Ginsburg, "and he wants her to shine." "She is very lucky to have a husband like Archie," says another old friend, "because many husbands would hate being dragged around like that. . . . When you have a strong woman like Lucky, who does come on strong and tend to dominate, well, Archie is a very strong man, he's at peace with himself. It would drive some men crazy, but it doesn't bother him."

"Well, I have no insecurities about myself," Archie says. "So I don't mind playing second fiddle and being a prince consort, and picking up her train. I mean, after all, she spent her life following me around . . . I think she's got this coming to her." He does point out, with some glee, that diplomatic practice—which has long had an established role for the wife of an ambassador—has not yet come to a universal decision about what to do with the "husband of." "So let's say I go to an embassy dinner," he continues, "I never know how I'm going to be treated. If the ambassador—"

"*Aaar-chie-*" Lucky begins.

"I don't see—do you think this is bad, to say this?"

"Not—yeah. I mean, you can say it, but I don't think you care," she says.

"I don't care, it's just that—"

"It's just that it amuses him," she explains.

"—it amuses me," he finishes. "Because sometimes I'm treated as if I'm of ambassadorial rank, you know, next to two lovely ladies. Other times, I'm next to the pantry."

When they walk their visitor downstairs, Archie lags slightly behind. "He's so precious to me," Lucky half-whispers, her hand over her heart. As the Roosevelts stand on the stoop of their house waiting for the visitor's cab to arrive, Lucky grasps her husband's chin and pushes until his left profile is toward the visitor. He pulls his chin up and protests mildly, but again she grasps, and pushes. "There," she says, stroking back his hair and indicating his forehead. "This part looks so much like his grandfather, doesn't it?"

In the end, she may sense that the reporter is having difficulty seeing this as "Archie's hour." A week after the interview, she calls again. "I realized there was one thing I hadn't commented on, about Archie's book," she says breathlessly. "I just wanted to tell you. The first time I read it, when I got to the part where I read that epilogue, the last two pages, I burst into tears I was so touched." The passage in question describes her, his "companion on the Road," as having "Arabian eyes and a smile that lights up the world," and says, ". . . long ago she took my heart within her hand and joined me on the caravan."

There is a pause. "In fact, I cry when I try to talk about it." There is a sniffle. "Even now." Another. "Oh, dear. I'm sorry," she whispers. But she presses on. "And the *second* time I read it I burst into tears. I thought that was such a lovely thing to say after 38 years of marriage."

—March 22, 1988

THE PHILANTHROPIST
(GWENDOLYN CAFRITZ)

On June 10, 1986, Gwendolyn D. Cafritz gave her last party. She had not given a party for eight years, and even then, she had been memorializing the past; the real tradition, the old wine being decanted on this lambent June evening, had been decades in storage. But it was a heady enough wine to call out 300 guests and the ghosts of many more who had preceded them.

To slip out of the speedy traffic on Foxhall Road into the half-circle driveway was to slip back in time. Here, still, was the art moderne house, nearly as startling in 1986 as it had been when Morris Cafritz built it for his young family almost fifty years earlier. Here, beyond the threshold, was the stunning circular entrance hall, dramatic enough to live up to the woman who once swept down the stairs to greet her guests.

The house was not so much well-tended as beautifully preserved, arrested in time; and the party duplicated the past in every anachronistic detail. As the hostess had asked, Ridgewell's Caterers heaped the silver platters and chafing dishes with the same filling, fusty food—the whole poached salmon, the ham and turkey, and carved tenderloin; none of the pastas or blackened seafood or grilled vegetables then in fashion. Waiters passed shrimp with cocktail sauce, while full bars offered prehistoric spirits such as bourbon and gin, defiant holdouts in the age of chardonnay and bottled water. The same plain white damask draped the table, with plain white damask napkins tied around settings of her heavy Georg Jensen flatware.

It was an invitation to stroll around the house and remember: When Gwen Cafritz, with her nineteen-inch waist and Balmain gowns, her raven hair and regal air, had won constant publicity for her parties—twenty-two to dinner, with toasts over champagne, and enormous receptions like this one each spring and fall. When the Duke and Duchess of Windsor came and danced downstairs in "the Club," with the dance floor lighted from below. When the Cafritzes' back terrace offered the most celebrated view of the city, southeast, past the swimming pool and rolling lawn, all the way to the Capitol.

She could no longer make an entrance, of course. This time, the receiving line snaked across the long, low living room to the far wall, where the hostess was displayed in a yellow silk armchair. Ridgewell's had produced, out of retirement, the same waiter who had announced the guests eight years before. As he stood by her chair, he could name at a glance quite a few of the guests—*Chief Justice and Mrs. Warren Burger . . . Senator Barry Goldwater . . . Baron and Baroness Constantine Stackelberg. . . .* From the others he solicited their names, bending to murmur prompts into the ear of the star. Her hair was still a lacquered black, heavily dressed (as always) at the back of her head. Her gown, as in the past, was spectacularly formal: folds of purple satin sweeping to her ankles beneath a fitted bodice. But it was hard to remember, here, the titanic social ambition that had made her what she was. Her skin had an unhealthy, pouchy pallor; extending an uncertain hand, she had the air of a dreamer deploying remembered charms.

No one needed to be told that this was Gwendolyn Cafritz's last hurrah. So if some of these nostalgic callers had once doubted or mocked her, with her grand house and her grand airs and her husband's enormous fortune, it was surely too late, in 1986, for any of these social acquaintances to want to shatter this fading legend. That task was left to her closest relatives.

Among the guests that June evening were her three sons, Calvin, Carter, and Conrad. Recognizably brothers, the youngest of them nearing his fifties, they were a striking presence at the party. All three had become local real estate developers, successful, if less spectacular, emulators of their father. Yet, in Morris's absence, the family was anything but the tight-knit dynasty he had paved the way for. All three sons were rumored to have difficult relationships with their mother, and it was rare to find them together, bearing in unison the family standard.

Two and a half years later, Gwendolyn Cafritz was dead of cancer, at age seventy-eight, and the following summer—three years after that final party—her two younger sons filed suit in D.C. Superior Court to have her will overturned and her estate, worth at least $140 million, divided among her children. Their complaint challenges her wish to leave all she owned, except for minor bequests, to the Morris and Gwendolyn Cafritz Foundation, a charitable trust her husband had established forty years before. Implicitly, Carter and Conrad Cafritz are also challenging her designation of Calvin, the eldest, as the only son who would have a future role in running the foundation, which already controls assets of more than $220 million.

Named in the lawsuit, besides Calvin, is everyone to whom Gwendolyn Cafritz made a bequest, including her former servants and grandchildren, two nephews, and an old escort. But its true targets are two longtime advisers who are executors of her estate: Martin Atlas, for decades the closest business associate of both Morris and Gwendolyn Cafritz, and William P. Rogers, the former attorney general and secretary of state who was Gwendolyn's personal attorney. These two, according to the complaint by Carter and Conrad Cafritz, "exerted undue influence" in Gwendolyn's decision to leave her entire estate to the foundation, of which they are both trustees. The complaint further asserts that "when Decedent allegedly executed the purported Will and Codicil that have been offered for probate herein, Decedent lacked a sound and disposing mind and was not capable of executing a valid deed or contract. Decedent lacked sufficient capacity to, and did not, dispose of her property with judgment and understanding, considering the nature, character and extent of her estate." In plain English, Gwendolyn Cafritz's two younger sons are contending in court that their mother was too feebleminded to write her will; document requests filed in court suggest they may try to prove she was incapacitated by alcoholism.

What do Conrad and Carter Cafritz hope to gain from an arduous legal proceeding that already involves at least twelve law firms and threatens to stretch on for years? None of the Cafritz sons can be said to need the money that is at stake. All are multimillionaires and Conrad Cafritz, by most accounts the prime instigator of the lawsuit, has spun his inheritance from his father into a vast personal fortune of, at minimum, $100 million. But like all wills, the one now known in probate court as 3035–88 offers more than one legacy, and thus more than one motive. There is, for example, the very palpable legacy of real estate developed by Morris Cafritz, including several downtown lots and office buildings. The majority of this property was already owned by the Cafritz Foundation, but Gwendolyn was partial owner of many of the buildings; even a limited power to control their disposition would presumably attract men with ambitions in Washington real estate.

Then there is the charitable legacy. The foundation is Washington's largest source of private funds earmarked exclusively for local projects, large enough to give the person who controls it a potentially shaping influence on the city. Morris had one vision and Gwendolyn another; whoever now gains control might offer still a third. Finally, there is the legacy contained in any will: The power to reward or to punish the living, to define or rearrange the narrative of a family's history. For the sons of Gwendolyn Cafritz, to accept her last will and testament would be to allow her, in more than one sense, the last word.

Morris and Gwendolyn Cafritz were oil and water, a marriage forged out of surprisingly dissonant elements. Their differences were, in fact, a part of their legend, for they were one of the earliest families to bring together the two cities on the Potomac. On the one hand was the ethereal world of social and political Washington—her world, which venerated either good birth or a seat in the Senate. On the other hand was his world, the corporeal city of sewers and streets and buildings and real citizens, men and women who grew up above grocery stores the way Morris Cafritz had.

Cafritz developed real estate for more than four decades, until his death in 1964, and by the sheer volume and variety of his building activities was for a time the undisputed king of his field. He had emigrated from Russia as a boy with his family, which stopped briefly in New York before settling down to run a grocery store at Twenty-fourth and P streets NW. Morris grew up working in the store, stalking the Maine Avenue wharf for the freshest fish sold there, and learning to love the adolescent city he saw around him. In 1904, with a $1,400 loan from his father, he started out running first a coal yard at Fourth and K streets NW, and then a saloon near Fourth and O. Gradually, he branched into entertainment, operating the first open-air movies in Washington (a matter of setting up chairs in vacant lots), and then a bowling alley and pool hall in Southeast, near the Navy Yard. By 1915, he was known locally as "The Bowling King" but still restlessly sought an opportunity that would truly engage him. So he began buying real estate speculatively and, in 1920, opened a real estate office on Fifteenth Street in DC's northwest quadrant.

Beginning with single-family houses and moving on to apartment houses and office buildings, he managed to dodge the Depression and was well positioned to preside over the city's transforming boom during and after World War II. In the process, he amassed one of the first great fortunes to be carved out of Washington itself. When he died, his estate would be the largest ever probated in the District of Columbia; it would take teams of lawyers and IRS agents four years to settle the estate, finally valued in 1968 at $66 million. Small wonder that, as he approached his forties unmarried, he was one of the most eligible bachelors within the small, closed circle of Washington's Jewish society.

But he reached outside that circle when he finally married. It is not clear how old he was when he fell for a nineteen-year-old Hungarian-American beauty named Gwendolyn Detre de Surany; perhaps because she was so much younger than he—Cafritz appears to have habitually understated his age by six or eight years. Papers filed in court by his sons' lawyers say that he was born in 1888; his gravestone says 1890, which would have made him only fourteen when he started his business career. In any case, he was at least twenty years older than his bride when they married in 1929.

The daughter of a Hungarian immunologist who had a role in devising the early Wasserman test to detect syphilis, Gwen Cafritz was the opposite of her husband. He was meat and potatoes, earnest frugality, and civic pride; she was flashing dark beauty, mercurial moods, and social ambition. The house on Foxhall Road, completed in 1938, was explicitly designed to fulfill that ambition.

Even as the chaos of wartime Washington started to loosen social strictures, Washington's leading hostess, Evalyn Walsh McLean, stopped entertaining; this opening, together with a boost from Eleanor "Cissy" Patterson, publisher of the *Washington Times-Herald*, gave Gwendolyn her opportunity. Throughout the '40s and '50s, it was Gwen's custom to give a large cocktail reception each spring and to mark the opening of every fall season with a party honoring the start of the Supreme Court term. At seated dinners for twenty-two, she entertained ambassadors and justices, senators, and Cabinet secretaries.

Gwen Cafritz and her chief rival, Perle Mesta, were in fact the first of a new breed—celebrity hostesses who openly courted the press and saw no shame in self-promotion. Old press notices, written in the uncritical fashion of the day, recount her summers in Monte Carlo; her typical day in Washington (beginning with a ride in her limousine—license number 2301, to match her address—to the Supreme Court or the Capitol, to take in a decision or an interesting hearing); her winter trips to Palm Beach; her shopping trips in Paris; her ladies lunches at the Mayflower Hotel. Only between the lines or in conversations with old friends can one make out how nakedly she wore her ambitions, and how hard she was working to measure up.

"She was not, as they say, invited anywhere at the beginning," recalls Gore Vidal, whose novel *Washington, D.C.* includes a character "suggested," he says, by Gwendolyn Cafritz. Irene Bloch, as she is called, is a wealthy department store owner's wife who mounts a relentless campaign for acceptance in Washington society. "Old Washington was very anti-Semitic, as you know," continues Vidal, whose childhood here as the stepson of lawyer and investor Hugh D. Auchincloss and the grandson of Oklahoma Senator Thomas Gore gave him an intimate education in Washington society.

> Jews in general just didn't figure. There were of course the grand exceptions like the Warburgs, and Walter Lippmann, and Arthur Krock. . . . And even then, there was always fussing. And [Gwendolyn] was just considered comical, and there were a lot of jokes about her. That's why her final victory rather delighted me.

High culture was one of her chosen routes to acceptance. She was multilingual and had studied art history at the University of Budapest. But she had a disconcertingly self-serious way of advertising it. To one interviewer she said that art was "the theme, you might say" of her life, "as in a Wagnerian opera." To Edward R. Murrow, in a 1956 interview, she said that to speak of Washington cocktail parties was "unfair to Washington. They're more like the French salons."

Vidal wrote, "Irene's evening dress was much too vivid, too personal, too fashionable for the calculated dowdiness" of a dinner in old-line Washington. And to the publicity-loathing cave dwellers, the Georgetown hostesses who were society leaders by birth, Gwendolyn's so-visible efforts made her a figure of fun. Ymelda Dixon, who covered many of her parties for the *Evening Star*, recalls, "They were great parties, because she had the means and the imagination. But they also sort of outraged people." There was no one she would not invite to dinner, sometimes calling the offices of Cabinet secretaries to ask for any day in the next year when the secretary would be free. Even her friends laughed at the way she would seat herself intently in the lobby of the Paris Hotel in Monte Carlo, at a table "very strategically placed," in the words of one, to court the passing society.

Morris was a famously frugal man who used to tell friends he couldn't afford to rent office space in the best of his buildings, and his major vanity, beyond lying about his age, appears to have been combing his pomaded hair over a bald spot at the back. Yet he uncomplainingly supported all of Gwendolyn's efforts, and was said to adore his colorful bride. "I think he went along," says a longtime business associate, Irwin Altman. "He wasn't overly enthused about it, but those were her wishes, and he sort of enjoyed it in a quiet way."

While she cultivated the mighty, Morris looked closer to home, helping to found the Washington Community Chest and becoming an activist in local Jewish groups. He was, for years, the president of the Jewish Community Center and donated the land for its first headquarters on Q Street NW. He was "greatly respected and liked, even in an anti-Semitic society," recalls Dixon. Yet Morris made little impression on Gwendolyn's social world, and she often went out or took vacations alone. In Vidal's *Washington, D.C.*, when Irene Bloch's husband dies, a character says, "We should build him a monument, and dedicate it to the Unknown Husband."

The Cafritzes slept in separate bedrooms, with Morris rising at dawn to get to the office. He may sometimes have yearned for recognition: One night, after one of the glamorous dinners, he drew a friend of Gwendolyn's away from the dining room and into the kitchen. "He took me into the kitchen and showed me how the cook would leave coffee for him in the morning," remembers the friend. "He got up at 5 or 5:30, and he wanted to show me what a hard-working man he was." The family observed Jewish holidays, and the sons attended religious school, at Washington Hebrew Congregation, on weekends. But Gwendolyn sometimes took pains to tell friends that she herself was not Jewish. The strange paradox of her marriage was that Morris's money enabled her to carry out her lavish social dreams, while the family's being Jewish also placed limits on her chances of realizing them.

But in the end, her siege of Washington society outlasted most of those limits. "She was a classic case," summarizes Vidal. "She wanted something, and she put up with a lot of shit, and she got it. That's what we call a success story. That what she wanted was pointless is not for us to judge."

Nor, apparently, is it for us to judge what her sons now want from a DC Superior Court judge: All three declined to be interviewed. The suit was filed by the middle and youngest Cafritz sons, Carter, fifty-three, and Conrad, fifty-one. But almost no one seems to doubt that Conrad is the main force behind it. "When I heard about it, I wrote Conrad and told him I thought it was a horrible thing he and his brother were doing to his mother," says Dorothy L. Casey, a retired secretary who worked for the Cafritz Co. for decades, reflecting a widespread tendency to speak of Carter as his brother's satellite.

Certainly it is Conrad who seems to embody, in one slight frame, the polarities of his parents' lives and personalities. For better or worse, he is the son who has tried to live out both their ambitions—to build on a scale that will make an impact on the city, and to develop a persona that will make him an actor in the capital. "He's part of a legendary family, and he's the only one who seems interested in keeping up the legend," says one friend. There are, superficially, great similarities among the three brothers, who all share their mother's dark coloring. All three stayed in Washington to work at some variation of their father's trade. Each is in his second marriage; each is in some way involved in the arts.

Calvin, fifty-eight, who finds himself a defendant in this lawsuit, is usually described as gentlemanly, methodical, and reserved. "Calvin is a very sweet, very nice person," says local lawyer Max N. Berry. "Very sort of philosophic, sort of honorable." Operating under his own banner, Calvin Cafritz Enterprises, he has built both residential and commercial buildings in DC and Virginia.

Carter Cafritz, who sits on the board of WETA, a Washington public television station, began his career in partnership with Conrad, building apartments and town houses in and around the city. Today, he shares office space and support staff with Conrad's growing interests, but for the most part pursues his own deals. Carter appears something of a cipher even to old family associates. "Carter, he always did what the other two did," says Casey. "Carter Cafritz is just a genuine nice fellow," says Raymond Carter, a former vice president of the Cafritz Co. "Conrad is more in the father's mold. He's truly out to make a big impact on the city, I think."

Conrad Cafritz is, in a word fondly used by friends, weird. "Conrad is really an anomaly," says lawyer and real estate developer Donald Brown. "He's creative, he's smart, also ambitious, like his father. But he's much different from his father, in a lot of ways. Conrad's strange, and doesn't mind people thinking that he's strange; he kind of encourages it." For one thing, he has a dark, avowedly cynical sense of humor. For another, he is said to alternate in seconds between a manic intensity and a mumbling diffidence. "Right at the moment he could be most charming, he does something to undercut it," says one friend. "That black sense of humor asserts itself, or he'll do something outrageous." Several friends read this changeability as part of a larger ambivalence about whether he wants to be an insider or a maverick, an heir to a famous tradition or the rebel who subverts it.

All of their lives, the Cafritz boys have been aware of their status as the sons of Morris and Gwendolyn. In high school, for example, Conrad stood out even among his privileged classmates at St. Albans. His class yearbook is littered with references to his family's money; in a list at the back of "most likely" candidates, the last two entries read, "Most Likely to Succeed: Johnson, Clague," and "Doesn't Have To: Cafritz." Today, he still combats a version of that assumption, pithily summed up by one detractor in this way: "You don't have to be Albert Einstein to take money and make additional money in real estate." Conrad is angrily aware, say friends, that his success will always be explained away. Of the three Cafritz sons, says restaurateur Herb White, "Conrad seems to be the one who has something to prove to himself." Perhaps as a result, he works hard, with much of Morris's old drive. "Maybe we try a little harder because our family name is well-known," he told a reporter in 1965.

He also still fights his battles with a surprising intensity, rarely bothering with the shake-hands-and-forget-it bonhomie common in Washington business. In particular, he has carried on an epic feud with Herbert S. Miller, chairman of Western Development Corp. Western won a city contract in 1985 to develop the so-called Portals site at the foot of the Fourteenth Street Bridge, potentially the largest commercial development in the city. Conrad, who was a losing bidder for the job, waged a lengthy challenge, arguing that Western was giving short shrift to the minority partners whose participation qualified the partnership for the contract award; though he finally lost, he succeeded in forcing a renegotiation of terms between Western and the Redevelopment Land Agency. The entire time, he fought with gloves off, publicly charging his rivals with bad faith.

Then, in 1988, came the announcement that Conrad Cafritz, with Japanese partners, had bought Washington Harbour, the glitzy development below K Street in Georgetown that had been troubled from its opening; the original developer of Washington Harbour was Western. "Conrad was persistent as hell in getting that project," says one person familiar with Conrad's business. "I'm sure part of it was to show Herb Miller he was serious."

Conrad's strategy has been diversity. Through a number of different companies, he both invests in and develops all kinds of properties—commercial, residential, retail, and even industrial. He has assembled a group of about fourteen local hotels, including the Georgetown Inn and One Washington Circle. He also has interests in a booming brokerage firm that he helped bankroll, and in a Midwestern shopping-center conglomerate. Conrad has always been involved in the bread and butter real estate of housing, from building single-family homes in Prince William County to renovating apartment complexes in Alexandria; he was a major beneficiary of the Washington condo boom. The Washington Harbour purchase, along with a joint venture to develop a riverfront office and hotel project in Rosslyn, has caused speculation that Conrad Cafritz is increasingly eager to be identified with high-quality, high-profile projects that might bring him more notice.

There also are hints that he has social ambitions on Gwendolyn's scale, if not exactly of her type. Conrad and his first wife entertained often in their Georgetown house in the 1960s, giving parties—often liberal fundraisers—that offered cozy intimations of radical chic. (His first wife, Jennifer, later married Laughlin Phillips, son of Duncan and Marjorie Phillips and president of the Phillips Collection.) Conrad then married Peggy Cooper Cafritz, a local power in the arts and in liberal political causes—and the only Cafritz listed in *Who's Who*. Peggy, the product of a well-to-do black family from Mobile, AL, has worked especially at promoting arts in the black community: She almost single-handedly founded the Duke Ellington School for the Arts and was Marion Barry's first chairman of the D.C. Commission on the Arts and Humanities. (Conrad and Peggy were both involved in Barry's first election campaign, and Peggy is the godmother of Barry's son, Christopher.) She appears every week on the WETA-TV arts show *Around Town*. She pressured the Smithsonian to increase the number of minorities in high-ranking positions, and has been arrested outside the South African Embassy as a leader of Mother's Day protests there. Through her advocacy, Peggy established a high profile—and raised a lot of hackles among the old guard that runs most of the city's major cultural institutions.*

After their marriage in 1981, Conrad and Peggy bought Senator Stuart Symington's house in the Foxhall Road area, studied it for a while, then tore it down to build a new house. They had a large fund-raiser for Jesse Jackson in 1988, and for Conrad's fiftieth birthday, Peggy gave him an enormous black-tie dinner at home. "There were moments when you wanted to go around and have everybody wear not just a name tag, but a bio," says their good friend Margaret Lenzner.

Conrad has six children—three adopted sons, who were Jennifer's from a previous marriage; two daughters with Jennifer; and, with Peggy, five-year-old Zachary. Perhaps the most remarkable member of this third generation is his daughter Julia, who dropped out of Brown University to found a band named Pussy Galore with a classmate. It has been variously reviewed as "one of the more important bands to emerge from the new head-slamming school of American guitar/noise bands" and "the gnarliest, most scuzzed out molotov to hit the streets since the heady days of Teenage Jesus and The Jerks." Most of the band's song titles are too profane for citation in mainstream reviews; one, a song that would surely have outraged the vocalist/guitarist's grandparents, is titled "You Look Like a Jew." It is a jolting reminder that Peggy and Conrad—a black woman married to a white Jewish millionaire in a racially divided city—represent a fascinating reshuffling of the social deck that produced the polarized marriage of Morris and Gwendolyn.

There is a poignant moment in Gwendolyn's 1956 interview with Murrow when she points out a portrait of herself that hangs on the wall. "I think it has the clean linear design of a Botticelli, and the elegance of an English portrait," she burbles, in her faintly accented great-lady voice, "and that's the way I would like my children to remember me. I hope they will." Conrad and Carter Cafritz have chosen instead the purgatory of probate court, where their complaints suggest less lovely memories. "Getting along with her," says one developer who knows the family, "was some-

*The couple divorced in 1998. Two years later, Peggy Cooper Cafritz was elected president of DC's Board of Education.

thing none of them ever mastered."

Gwendolyn reportedly raised her children according to the dictates of her European background—under the aegis of servants, to be seen and not heard. Her statements in the press, even the adoring press of yore, suggest at the least a daunting mother. Asked in 1954 why all her sons bore two-syllable names beginning with "C," she replied, "Morris names all children, horses, dogs, apartment houses and everything around here. I just make speeches."

To those who thronged to the parties, the children were rarely in evidence. An old friend remembers a Fourth of July party at which one or more of the boys stood in a window above the path that led indoors from the pool to the cocktail area, throwing firecrackers down onto the guests. Once grown, the sons established limited, perfunctory contacts with their mother. One possible reason for that—and for any bitterness that might motivate the lawsuit—is suggested by the suit's underlying argument: "For many years, beginning at a time not precisely known to plaintiffs, but at least by the time of the death of the late Morris Cafritz, the Decedent began suffering from a number of conditions that resulted in physical and mental debilitation," reads the complaint. "Decedent's condition deteriorated after the death of her husband in 1964 and grew worse in the following years."

Other documents filed in court indicate that the sons argue that their mother was incapacitated by alcoholism. One interrogatory demands that Riggs National Bank, which was Gwendolyn's bank, "identify all individuals or facilities that, from 1954 until Gwendolyn Cafritz' death, provided to Gwendolyn Cafritz any care, advice, counseling, or treatment relating to her consumption of alcohol . . . including, but not limited to, any facilities located in Washington, DC; Palm Beach, Florida; or Monte Carlo, Monaco." Another asks the bank to produce "all documents relating to purchase or provision of wine, champagne, or liquor on behalf of or for Gwendolyn Cafritz or for delivery to or consumption at 2301 Foxhall Road."

Interviews suggest that the sons will not lack evidence to support their argument. Michael J. Dowling, who became the Cafritzes' butler in the early '60s, describes a tragically common decline. "She was good to me, and she was a good woman in my eyes," he says. But he believes her drinking was a source of family discord. "The boys used to make a joke of their mother. If she gave them an order, they took it lightly, because she liked to drink." Her drinking got out of control, he agrees, shortly after Morris

Cafritz's sudden death of a heart attack in 1964. "Lots of times she could drink and she knew exactly what she was doing. And other times she didn't. As time went on, she lost complete control, and she had to drink more." She kept up appearances even in the privacy of her home, where she drank Scotch from a decanter in the living room. "The decanter always had to be full," Dowling says. "Those were her orders: The Scotch should never be let go beneath the neck of the decanter."

As is often true when the secretive disease of alcoholism is combined with the see-no-evil sociability of Washington, Gwendolyn's problem was rarely recognized. It is, as always, unclear where her inborn quirkiness shaded into the effects of alcoholism; but many of her friends, in later years, simply came to think of her as "difficult" or "eccentric." Nearly everyone has a story about her forgetting their names, or making some sudden comment of shocking rudeness. But almost no one noticed what seemed apparent to Gore Vidal, in brief glimpses of her during the 1960s: "Toward the end [of the decade], she was always drunk whenever I saw her. She was forever trying to tell me some long story I could never make head or tail of."

According to friends, her confidence was badly shaken when she was robbed at home in 1969 by gunmen who bound and beat her, stealing most of the spectacular jewelry Morris had given her. In the 1970s she became a near-recluse. Given the life she had lived and the kind of friends she had cultivated, few people were close enough to her to understand why. "I used to call up the house and get her maid, and her maid would talk to me about her, and say that she was completely worn out and simply couldn't get up and get herself ready to go on the warpath," says socialite Polly Logan. "I just thought she maybe had had enough of running around, and she was maybe going to stay in a while."

Gwendolyn gave only two parties in the last fifteen years of her life— one in 1978, her first in five years, and the final party in 1986. "With so-called friends all around her, she was a very lonely woman," says Dowling. "She felt that was the end, when she couldn't function socially."

She carried her isolation to her grave. Her husband, along with her parents, was buried in Washington Hebrew Cemetery, in Southeast Washington, in a nicely landscaped, square plot designed for four under a monumental headstone reading CAFRITZ. But the fourth square in the plot remains empty; Gwendolyn Cafritz was memorialized in a Presbyterian church and had herself buried far north in Rockville's Parklawn Cemetery, among strangers.

* * *

Of the three sons, Calvin seems to have had the best relationship with his mother. Upon Morris Cafritz's death in 1964, he became president of the Cafritz Co.; and in the first will Gwendolyn wrote, in 1969, which included all three sons, she made Calvin an executor and left him the Foxhall Road house. In 1971, he resigned from the company amid reports of conflict with his mother, and by the time she wrote a 1977 will, all three sons, including Calvin, had been dealt out of any inheritance. By the time of her death, however, Calvin was still the son closest to his mother. When she drafted her third and last will in 1981, she wrote a final clause that reads almost like an afterthought, but resounds in the lawsuit now underway: "It is my wish that our descendents [sic] shall maintain an interest in the affairs of THE MORRIS AND GWENDOLYN CAFRITZ FOUNDATION and its philanthropic purposes and I desire that, following my death, CALVIN CAFRITZ be elected to serve on the board of the Foundation." Today, Calvin is foundation chairman. And it is over the foundation, established to memorialize the name and works of the Cafritz family, that the Cafritz family is now at war.

Morris Cafritz incorporated the foundation in 1948 to give money to Washington-area charities, and when he died sixteen years later, he left it half his estate, mostly as stock in dozens of closely held corporations; as the new majority owner of most of these companies, and with Gwendolyn owning most of the rest, the foundation became in essence the owner of the Cafritz Co., its subsidiaries, and its assets.

After Morris Cafritz died, his close associate Martin Atlas became executive vice president of the company, and vice president and treasurer of the Cafritz Foundation, while Gwendolyn Cafritz ultimately became president of both. The foundation's board of trustees consisted of Gwendolyn Cafritz and the two men who would become her executors—Atlas and William P. Rogers, her attorney.

Conrad and Carter Cafritz claim that Rogers and Atlas "secured domination and control" over Gwendolyn, controlling all of her assets and making her the figurehead president of both the foundation and the real estate businesses, "notwithstanding that she was, and Defendants Atlas and Rogers knew she was, incapable of discharging the duties incumbent upon her in such positions." They charge in their suit that Rogers and

Atlas influenced her to leave all the property she controlled to the foundation.

Rogers, an attorney general under President Eisenhower and secretary of state under Richard Nixon, declined to be interviewed for this story; he has denied the allegations in papers filed in court. Atlas too declined to comment, but he issued a statement when the suit was filed saying that he had no role in drafting the will, and no advance knowledge of its contents. He also has denied the sons' allegations in his formal answer to their complaint. "I know Atlas hates publicity like poison," says Raymond Carter, a former Cafritz Co. vice president. "He's always very, very protective of the Cafritz name, as if it were his own."

Gwendolyn's estate is worth at least $140 million, including both her personal holdings and a trust passed on from Morris Cafritz's will. Under the terms of an old agreement, each of the sons will automatically receive $7 million, tax-free, in recompense for having forfeited, in the late '60s, some money from a different trust. But of the property over which she had control, Gwendolyn left her children only "such photographs, family mementos, and similar objects of domestic use or ornamentation as my executors, in their absolute discretion, shall determine that I would wish to have preserved for my children."

And Gwendolyn's estate is not, in the end, the only—or even the main—thing at stake. At the heart of the lawsuit is a quest to gain at least partial control over the whole empire of which Gwendolyn's estate is an integral piece, over the whole legacy that Morris Cafritz created.

Some observers speculate that Conrad, hardheaded real estate man that he is, simply wants some say in the disposition of the real estate owned—in many cases, co-owned—by the foundation and Gwendolyn's estate. In real estate, especially within the constricting borders of DC, power isn't limited to those who own the land; controlling the land can be almost as good. The holdings in downtown Washington include buildings in the 1700 and 1800 blocks of K Street and a parking lot at Twelfth and K; buildings in the 1300 and 1600 blocks of L Street; and property in the 1600, 1700, and 1800 blocks of I Street. The holdings also include a major share of the two Universal buildings at the intersection of Connecticut and Florida avenues, and shares of the massive River House apartment

---

* Excepting this last, these are all located in downtown Washington, DC. Morris Cafritz was instrumental in developing the newer part of Washington's downtown, which follows K Street west toward Georgetown, extending north to Dupont Circle.

buildings in Pentagon City, VA.* In addition, there are at least ten apartment buildings in DC.

Conrad, say friends, has watched in frustration as downtown Washington boomed and the foundation failed to take maximum advantage of its holdings. Says one friend, "He thinks they're a lot of fuddy-duddies living in the 17th century." It is easy to imagine that, for a son of Morris Cafritz, watching great deals go unmade is a kind of hell. The only thing that might be worse would be to watch deals go on without him.

Calvin Cafritz has taken the helm of the old Cafritz Co. and is reportedly trying to bring it to new life, and also has become chairman of the Morris and Gwendolyn Cafritz Foundation. The foundation itself, with its powerful endowment for the city and with its more than $220 million in assets, is the largest source of private funds earmarked for the District of Columbia. It also is a secretive organization: The foundation would answer no questions for this article.

Public records, however, show that—like any organization privately controlled by a very small number of people—it is very susceptible to change spearheaded by a determined leader. In 1962, when it was the product of Morris Cafritz's vision, the largest grants went to the United Jewish Appeal and the Community Chest Federation. Small grants went to fifteen more Jewish charities, and the rest to such local charities as boys clubs and hospital funds. Gradually, as Gwendolyn took command of it, its character changed. By 1967, records show a sprinkling of grants to highbrow cultural causes: the Committee to Rescue Italian Art, the Opera Society of Washington, the Corcoran Gallery. By 1970, arts and humanities took the largest share of the funding.

Of the $54 million that the foundation has given away since 1970, $32 million has gone to the arts and humanities, almost $9 million to community services, $8 million to education, and nearly $5 million to health. Its annual reports list a fairly traditional, staid set of beneficiaries, and its grants are studied by an advisory board heavily weighted toward the kind of high-profile, high-society arts philanthropy that Gwendolyn favored. Among the members are National Gallery of Art Director J. Carter Brown, retired Smithsonian Secretary S. Dillon Ripley, and retired Librarian of Congress Daniel Boorstin, as well as Carolyn Deaver, wife of former White House deputy chief of staff Michael K. Deaver, and a social friend of Gwendolyn's, Mrs. Tazewell Shepard. The control of so much money, especially in a city with limited corporate philanthropy, brings enormous power. It is intriguing to imagine what different directions Conrad Cafritz might urge—and how much they would draw from the activism of his wife, who has likely pondered what difference the Cafritz endowment might make to her lifelong campaign to wrest the arts from Washington's white upper classes.

Finally, there is an emotional legacy to be earned—or perhaps shed. It is hard not to wonder what the effect might have been of hearing Gwendolyn Cafritz's will read for the first time.

To Martin Atlas, Gwendolyn left $50,000 and a Chagall painting. She set aside bequests for two nephews ($35,000 each); a former company employee, Dorothy Casey ($10,000); and four former servants (two bequests of $50,000 and two of $25,000). She left $25,000 to a favorite former escort, a Brazilian former employee of the Inter-American Development Bank. She also made bequests of $100,000 each to ten of her thirteen grandchildren—excluding the children that Conrad adopted, to whom he has remained a committed father.

To Calvin Cafritz, she left the symbolic role of family chief, Morris Cafritz's successor in a world of primogeniture. But Carter and Conrad Cafritz are not named in their mother's will. "I make no other provision in this will for the benefit of my children," it states, "as their financial needs are adequately provided for" by the old agreement giving them $7 million each. Of other needs, the will says nothing.

The outcome of the lawsuit is unpredictable, though clearly it will be an uphill fight: Showing that someone was alcoholic is very different from demonstrating that she was incapable of writing a will. It is also different from proving that a respected lawyer and former Cabinet member, in league with a longtime family associate, unfairly loaded the dice. Conrad has rolled out impressive legal artillery, however, captained by former White House counsel Lloyd N. Cutler, and seems prepared to dig in for a long siege—at least long enough, perhaps, to wring a settlement from his opponents.*

* The parties finally settled in 1996, six years after this article was published. Each Cafritz son received $7 million, and Carter and Conrad received an additional $5 million to create charitable foundations of their own. The rest of Gwendolyn's estate—about $50 million, the *Washington Post* reported—went to the Cafritz Foundation, of which Calvin is chairman, president, and chief executive officer.

Meanwhile, for as long as it takes, Conrad's childhood home turns a sleeping face to Foxhall Road, drapes drawn at all the windows. Gwendolyn left the $14 million landmark to the foundation, with the very Gwendolyn-like wish that it become "a center in which scholars, statesmen and civic leaders may conduct research, conferences, seminars and other functions relating to issues of interest to mankind."*

For now, the house is tended by at least two servants, who are listed in court documents as living there, and the grass is beautifully clipped, the pachysandra well-tended. There is still a sign directing deliveries to the back of the house, as if tradesmen were still streaming up to the front door to importune the lady of the house and Ridgewell's were due at any moment with more shrimp and cocktail sauce. But it has that air of a property just turning past ripeness, toward seed. As you draw close to the famous burgundy front door, with its surrounding marble, you can see that the paint is cracking and fading to pink, and greenish stains from metal window fixtures are starting to weep down the white brick walls. If you could walk around to the back, you might look out at the famous view; and you might almost see as far as southeast DC, where Morris lies with his in-laws, still waiting. Perhaps one day Calvin, or Conrad, or some Cafritz now unknown, will find a way to bring together the opposite forms of ambition that thrived in this house, and give a second start to the dynasty that never was.

—February 25, 1990

* Instead, it became home to The Field School, a tony private school.

THE PRAGMATIST
(RICHARD DARMAN)

Never mind, for the time being, the Freudian slip that brought us to Dick Darman's rec room at 9 on a Wednesday night in June; that's another, more complicated part of the story. At the moment, the man who presides over the world's largest budget is hunting for another set of Ping-Pong paddles—the *good* paddles.

Having found them, he prepares to serve. Of course, he says, this basement room of his is too small to play in properly. The real way to play is to set up the table out of doors, and—*Wham!* Cramped quarters notwithstanding, he is quite good at this. Ah, but not as good as he would be, he points out, if he were properly warmed up.

Plock. . . . He has this devious little serve that loops leftward into the court and then bolts right, off the table; you might call the serve, as one senator called this man's characteristic way of approaching a problem, Darmanesque. Worse is what he says, pityingly, as the ball passes under my paddle: "I'm sorry."

Don't apologize, he is told—I'll return that serve yet.

"You won't." It's a statement of fact, delivered with a tinge of adolescent pride.

We continue, rallying back and forth. He hits a number of sharp, fast shots, mixing them up with spins—and he also hits a fair number of flashy shots that miss the end of the table. "If we kept playing," he says, again matter-of-factly, "those would all go in."

I propose that we play an actual game. "You don't want to play with me," he warns, straight-faced. Besides, we haven't had dinner, and there's still an interview to do. "It'll be too late," he says, "by the time we warm up enough to play decently." Before we stop, the tricky serve makes a last appearance. "Oh, *sooorrry*."

A glimpse of Dick Darman at play is enough to make you believe many of the stories about Richard G. Darman, master gamesman, at work. George Bush's director of the Office of Management and Budget is an object of endless fascination and debate in Washington. He is said to be arrogant and abrasive, competitive and driven; he is said to be one of the smartest men in government, and—at long last, after years of the galling shame of being mistaken for a mere aide—one of the most important. Almost everyone agrees that he combines a rare intellectual grasp of government with a bare-knuckles skill at power politics. Almost no one doubts that he is, from one motive or another, passionate about his work. But beyond that, there is little accord. Dick Darman, the man who knows all the numbers, just doesn't add up.

He's one of the few non-elected career government officials to be found in top Republican circles—yet he gave years of important service to the Reagan administration, which was dedicated to "getting off the backs of the people" the government Darman has committed his life to. This wily bureaucrat was a willing participant in the Reagan policies that spawned an unprecedented federal budget deficit—yet he's now the man who, in the name of cutting the deficit, has steadily nudged President Bush toward the political castor oil of higher taxes.

In some quarters, Darman is seen as a committed, even idealistic, public servant capable of a laudable pragmatism in the name of "getting from here to there." Elliot L. Richardson, the mentor under whom Darman served in five Cabinet departments, says, "I know him to be a person who is, who really is, committed to trying to discern and serve the public interest. He has no other real motivation." But others, of all ideological stripes, see him as a deep-dyed cynic who is addicted to the action and power of being at the center of government, and who masks his expediency with grandiose speeches about long-term ambitions for the country. "I think he would do anything to advance himself," says one former colleague. "If the cavalry is winning, he's for Custer," says another. "And if the Indians are winning, he's for Sitting Bull."

The debate over Darman extends to his personal qualities. Fans describe someone whose only faults are the rough edges of a man who knows how smart he is, and has a no-nonsense love for his work. Detractors depict a petty tyrant who is disdainful of others and prone to temper tantrums—especially toward his staff. He is, they say, vindictive, and capable of systematically planning the fall of a rival or enemy. The curious thing is that even some of his oldest friends and associates seem unsure which is the real Dick Darman, pointing to incidents and qualities that support both views.

In truth, each view of Dick Darman is alone too simple. Darman is properly seen not as unique but as typical: as the classic protagonist in democracy's most familiar tale. He may be spinning his narrative more skillfully and colorfully than anyone since Henry Kissinger. But his is, finally, just a very subtle rendering of Washington's old, old story: of the man with conflicting impulses, toward service on the one hand, and status on the other; toward the long-term pursuit of policy, and the short-term thrill of the game.

The federal budget, and Darman's efforts over nearly a decade both to address and to paper over the deficit—to address simultaneously the warring imperatives of the long and short terms—are the perfect expressions of his struggle. Just as his choice of two mentors, one for each decade of his government career and each facet of his ambition, reflects his divided nature. "I think he's trying to have it both ways," says Tony Aldrich, who was one of Darman's best friends at Harvard's business school and who views politicians with asperity.

> There's not a one of them who can't make you an argument that this is what you need to do for the short term. And he's more comfortable with that argument than I would have expected him to be . . . . I didn't think he was that pragmatic. I didn't think he was that cynical.

Darman's fans—the most prominent being Darman himself—believe him to be smart enough, complex enough, and honorable enough to juggle his two impulses indefinitely. He has called himself "a long-term idealist and a short-term realist," as if these definitions posed no conflict. But the record, and common sense, suggest otherwise.

The only way to make Darman's years in government add up is to consider the life and character of the man himself, keeping in mind one thing: Even if it is true that government needs men like Dick Darman, the great probability is that Dick Darman needs government more.

An old friend summarizes Darman by paraphrasing what was once said about Theodore Roosevelt: "They said that every time he goes to a wedding he wants to be the bride, and every time he goes to a funeral, he wants to be the corpse. That's Dick Darman." Edward J. Rollins, who served with Darman in the first-term Reagan White House, says, "Certainly Dick was probably the most brilliant guy in there, but he had an ego to match his IQ . . . He's the kind of guy who writes his own part bigger than anybody else's part, and wants to be the star."

Darman was born into money, and his wife inherited a large fortune in trust. In his few brief forays into the private sector, Darman has shown (if proof were needed) that he could prosper in any sphere he chose. But the sphere he has chosen is government, and for two decades Darman has conducted a steady march toward Washington's center stage.

Beginning as an analyst in the Department of Health, Education and Welfare, he spent the '70s working for Elliot Richardson, the very definition of traditional moderate Republicanism. Even in the Democratic years of Jimmy Carter, he and his first mentor were able to keep their hands in at the State Department, helping negotiate the Law of the Sea treaty. Although GOP moderates went into eclipse with Ronald Reagan's 1980 victory, Darman offered his experience to the newcomers from California. With his Richardsonian background—not to mention two degrees from Harvard and a period teaching at Harvard's John F. Kennedy School of Government—he was the White House aide conservatives most loved to hate, yet he dodged their bullets to become an indispensable strategist of Reagan's presidency.

Early in Reagan's second term, Darman followed his second patron, White House Chief of Staff James A. Baker III, to the Treasury Department, and to the title of deputy secretary. It is widely said that his only real mistake of the Reagan years was to underrate the political prospects of Vice President George Bush. Bush suspected Darman (rightly) of being a champion leaker, and blamed him for several leaks that reflected poorly on the vice president. Bush had "very strong reservations" about Darman's loyalty, according to a senior administration official. Nonetheless, Bush was eventually persuaded to give him a second chance—and, after a model performance by Darman during the general election campaign, the job of OMB (Office of Management and Budget) director. In little more than a year, Darman again consolidated his power, placing himself at the center of George Bush's domestic policy and becoming the president's chief adviser on economic affairs.

How has Darman overcome so many political liabilities? Partly through the old-fashioned virtues of hard work and a specific, disciplined knowledge of his field. He works six or seven days a week, twelve or fourteen hours a day. Having experience at HEW, Defense, Justice, State, Commerce, and Treasury, as well as four years at the center of White House decision making, Darman has to a rare degree been willing to engage the machinery of federal policy: the whole constellation of laws, programs, rules, budget accounts, regulations, sub-agencies, and sub-sub-departments that some of the most important people in Washington describe, with a faint air of dismissal, as "the substance."

Today, standing for even a few minutes in Darman's office to watch the in-and-out traffic of staff members, it is clear he has an encyclopedic overall grasp of the behemoth. It is also, suddenly, easy to understand that abstract compliment widely paid to Darman: He has an uncanny analytic quickness, an ability immediately to spot the problem, the drawback, the inconsistency. Says one staffer, "If you're talking about something that you know really well, and he knows about 18 percent of what you do, he can just take you apart analytically."

If Darman earned his way to the table the old-fashioned way, however, it is his supple political instincts that have raised him to such a powerful position. "Darman has the best raw understanding of power of anyone I've ever run across since Henry Kissinger," says Rollins, now co-chairman of the National Republican Congressional Committee. "He's the ultimate insider. He understands everything from office locations to controlling the mail to people being invited to meetings to always making sure your draft is the draft that gets marked up. He just has great instincts for the jugular."

Ask people what Dick Darman has done in his years in government and they tend to describe not specific achievements, but processes: He devised the *process* by which Reagan's legislative agenda would be sold. He devised the *process* through which congressional negotiators compromised to make the Social Security system solvent. Today, he hopes he is managing the process by which Congress and the White House, Democrats, and Republicans can together take the risks required to cut the deficit.

A man with a gift for process, however, is by definition a man who works best behind the scenes. Here, Darman's talents and ambitions are out of step: For years, he has felt unrecognized, unheralded for his finest sleights of hand. During the Reagan years, Darman's staff was instructed to keep a bibliography, with separate sections for mentions of Darman in books, in periodicals, and in newspapers; at times when Darman was in the news, the bibliography was updated often—weekly or even every few days. As for the morning newspapers, secretaries were told to clip headlines and only the portions of the stories that dealt with Darman; those would be pasted up together on a plain sheet of paper, and then the clips would be assembled in batches, by newspaper and subject. The stories that described Darman as an "aide" to Baker would not be saved at all.

Our first interview is scheduled for 6 o'clock on a Wednesday evening, but with Darman nothing is simple. The phone rings late that morning: He has a string of amendments to propose. He has to go to a meeting at 7, he says. It's likely to be very boring, but if I'd care to—he can't think why I would, but if I'd care to—I could come along and see him in action. Then we can have our interview. Except, well, first there's something else. "My parents are—" Darman catches his slip, and starts again. "I mean, my wife and children are out of town, temporarily, in Boston." So Darman, a multimillionaire who employs a housekeeper, a wily sophisticate in shaping his public image through the press, proposes to divert the interview from downtown DC to McLean—*because he has to feed the pets*. We'll stop at his house, then talk over dinner at a local restaurant.

It's easy to understand why a man would want to show off this house, a modern affair of clapboard and bricks and expansive windows tucked away down a long, hilly lane, on five and a half acres that overlook the Potomac. Standing on one of a series of terraces descending toward the river behind the house, you are surrounded by trees, and can see and hear almost nothing but the rushing of Little Falls just below.

"Have you ever seen anything like it?" he asks, not waiting for an answer, or hearing the one that comes. "Not 12 minutes from downtown, you haven't. There are *no* houses like this one anymore. Not *this* close."

But there is no stopping to admire the view. Restlessly, Darman leads on, conducting a tour. Through the sliding doors into the living room, up into a wing the Darmans added to house a series of studies—more high ceilings, more bookshelves, more sweeping vistas. But before I can pause to admire anything, Darman is on the move again, flipping on lights, narrating all the while.

Darman doesn't drink or smoke, and professes indifference to food; this asceticism is apparent in the furnishings, which are tasteful but spare. Climbing the stairs at the opposite end of the house, he hurries past the wall of photos in the stairwell, pictures of him and his wife, Kathleen, in childhood, his brothers and sister and family, brushing off all questions about them; but he lingers upstairs to admire the enormous color photos he has taken of his two boys, Willy and Jonathan. "I guess," he says more than once, "this is a very child-centered house." Into the bedroom, sparsely furnished with a joined pair of four-poster twin beds swathed in navy, and the simple antique desk at which Darman sometimes works. (Showing the bedroom, like showing the house, is entirely Darman's idea.) Scanning the desktop, I note, aloud, that he is reading T.S. Eliot's *Four Quartets*.

"*Re*-reading," he amends sharply.

Next door, the boys' bedrooms. Darman designed these rooms, he says proudly, and any child might envy them: There are loft beds recessed into the wall, under the eaves of the house ("The boys think we never look up there, so that's where the mess is") and skylights you can open and stand up in, to look out over the roof. Willy, the thirteen-year-old, has on and around his dresser an impressive collection of athletic credentials—trophies, plaques, team photos. Darman acknowledges pride that his son is, as he was, an athlete, but soon focuses on the one disorderly element in the display: a summer camp trophy that hangs on the wall, a distinctly unsleek plank of wood with roughly painted letters and a green baseball glued to it. "That's got to be the ugliest trophy ever," Darman says.

It is a habit with him, constantly seizing on the discordant detail, always beating you to the punch he seems braced for—pointing out the mess that lurks just out of view. "Isn't that a beautiful picture?" he will say, pointing at a photo of Kath cradling one of their babies. He took a lot of those, he says. "Of course," he then adds dismissively, "maternity is a very conventional subject."

We move back downstairs to the small, stark-white kitchen, and the breakfast room where the children's finger paintings are framed and hung on the wall. Still he is going at a near-jog, as photos, books, personal artifacts—the revelatory details that are red meat to a journalist writing about personality—flash by. He points out what he wishes, and waves away questions about attractions that are not on the tour. The message seems to be that he would like to display his pride in this house, this family; but he would like also to control what is seen. This tension in the evening seems emblematic of a larger tension in his life. Despite a clear hunger for recognition, he shelters his privacy carefully—especially the events of his life before college.

Years ago he asked family members not to speak to the press about him, a request they honor ("Dick pretty much firmly has insisted on his right to keep his private life out of the public eye," says his brother John). He speaks as if his life began when he entered government. In early conversations about this article, Darman offered a list of possible sources—all of them past and present professional associates, none dating back further than 1971. Explaining the absence of personal friends, he said that with the exception of his wife and children, his work life is his life. "There ain't no more of me to get." On learning that I was interviewing old high school classmates of his, Darman scoffed at the idea. "Of course, this stuff is of no relevance," he said during a phone conversation. He said he assumed, however, that I would check with him about the trustworthiness of anyone I spoke to

> For instance, there's a man from high school who's made a sort of career of talking to reporters about me. Don't say this to him if you do speak to him, of course, but as far as I can tell he's a near-complete kook. . . . I hardly even knew him.

He mentioned a name—the name of a man who had shared extensive and credibly detailed memories of Darman, a classmate in a class of only seventeen boys.

Darman's cooperation for this article will finally end over the question of control. After the house tour, which concludes with Ping-Pong, Darman is pressed over dinner to proceed with the formal interview he has promised—sitting down, with the tape recorder running. No, he says, he will only talk "on background," meaning that anything he says may be quoted, but not attributed to him. He doesn't want to do it for the tape recorder—oh, and also, he doesn't really want to talk about his early life; that's all just tedious detail. We are at an impasse, neither willing to abide by the other's ground rules. For now, a tour of his house is as close as we may get to a tour of his mind.

The enduring image of the evening will have to be this one: of Darman, unprompted, flinging open the door of a closet to illustrate something he is saying about his marriage—then quickly instructing me that the closet's contents are off the record, not to be written about.

Look at me, he says. But do not see.

At first it is hard to understand why Darman is so reticent about his childhood. In high school, he possessed "the cardinal virtues of the late '50s," according to his classmate Joe Scott. "My impression was, here was the all-around boy. The girls. The sports. The academics. And depending on what company you were in, the order of importance changed."

He was captain and quarterback of the football team at the Rivers School, a small progressive prep school then located in the Boston suburb of Chestnut Hill; he was also captain of the wrestling squad and lacrosse team. He aced his studies (at least the ones he cared to), was a big wheel in student government and knew a lot about cars. To make his social success complete, he sometimes hung out with the kids from the local public high school, and belonged to their hot rod club, the "De-fenders." Even then, he was competitive and somewhat cocksure. His motto, as recorded in his 1960 Rivers yearbook, was "I don't mind telling you."

Says F. Ervin Prince, a former math teacher at Rivers, "I would have had to describe him as being somewhat arrogant in his attitude in class. But I think it's largely because he knew the work so well. He could do it so well he wasn't what I'd call a pleasant student to teach." Prince gave frequent quizzes, writing the questions on the blackboard, and remembers that on one occasion, moments after the quiz began, Darman raised his hand to ask the teacher to clarify a word in question number eight. He told Prince later that he was trying to get "a little psychological edge" by convincing the class's other star student that he was almost through with the test. "He was about the only one I ever had who did something like that," says Prince.

"He had an incredible awareness of how smart people were," says Walter Channing, who met him years later at business school.

> You know how some people are aware of the net worth of everyone around them? They just have a way of sifting all data for that information? Well, Darman used to have that for IQ. Any kind of information that might tell him how smart people were—where they went to school, what their parents were like, how they talked—he paid attention to.

His competitiveness also extended to "getting" the best women, according to several friends. As a Harvard freshman, he picked out two women he was interested in: They were, by general acclaim, two of the most sought-after women at Radcliffe—bright, beautiful WASP legends. Waiting until the last moment to sign up for a required freshman course, he lurked by the bulletin board to find out which section they would choose. He dated one of them seriously for several years; the other, Kathleen Emmett, he never succeeded in meeting as an undergraduate—but eventually married. To this day, says Ed Rollins, he talks about her being "the most beautiful woman on the Radcliffe campus. So I'm sure getting her was a contest too."

Almost anyone from Darman's past who is asked about the source of his drive offers the same speculation: Darman, the oldest of four children, was under enormous pressure to live up to the paternal legacy of Morton H. Darman. "There was some sort of very unrelenting, competitive relationship he had with his father," says Rivers classmate Rich Williams. "You could always get a rise out of him by suggesting that snazzy car he drove around the parking lot was a gift from his father."

Darman's parents, who are retired today in Lincoln, MA, abide by the family's no-comment policy. But Mort Darman is, by most accounts, a formidable figure. A textile executive, he raised his family in Woonsocket, RI, and later in the wealthy Boston suburb of Wellesley Hills in an imposing red-brick house that is set up and back on a manicured lawn. Mort had joined his own father's business, and eventually became president of the Top Co., for a time the nation's largest maker of wool top (an early stage in the processing of wool, after it is cleaned but before it is dyed). He also spent considerable time in Washington, as president of the American Textile Manufacturers Institute, but was a canny enough businessman to diversify out of the fading textile industry into real estate and oil distribution. He is said to have been a soft-spoken but authoritarian father. Darman himself has said, "My grandfather was a perfectionist and made one of my father. It was expected that I would succeed in everything I did. I expected it too."

Two old friends of Darman's, from two different phases of his life, independently arrived at an unusual adjective to describe Mort Darman: *seamless*. "That would be a big factor in your life, being worthy of that man," says Robert C. Lea, a former college roommate. "The relationship with his father is really critical." It wasn't only a matter of exalted expectations, according to some old friends; it was also that Mort Darman, for whatever reason, was slow to offer his son approval when those expectations were met. "I knew for a fact he found the expectations from his father hard to deal with," says Tony Aldrich. "His father was not a warm guy. In any encounter, you had the feeling your performance had not measured up."

When his father fell seriously ill in the early '80s, Darman told Laurence I. Barrett of *Time* magazine, it was painful in part because "I still wasn't successful in a way that really meant something to him." The contrasts between father and son are interesting. Mort Darman is remembered by one of his son's old friends as the kind of man who always wore a coat and tie and "must have had his hair cut once a week." Dick Darman, on the other hand, affects a casual disregard for appearances. He cuts his own hair, and does it badly: Swept back from his forehead, his straight brown hair ends, above his collar, at a miscellany of lengths. Staff members say he sometimes comes to work in scuffed loafers whose tassels are long gone. His collars are frayed, his suits are shiny with wear, his neckties are the kind that never run any danger of being in or out of fashion.

But do not be fooled. Dick Darman cares terribly for appearances, though of a different kind. He's very credential-conscious, according to people who work closely with him: "He wants people who went to the best schools around him," says one White House colleague. "He's aware of who went where, and how they did there." In interviews he often mentions having studied literature for a year at Oxford, but almost never mentions that he has a master's degree in education—from Boston University. Without disguising that he spent the first thirteen years of his life in Woonsocket, RI, he emphasizes his later upbringing in the far tonier Wellesley Hills. And he has de-emphasized the colorful reality of the Darman family background.

"The way he describes it is as this Brahmin family," says a former White House colleague. Over the years, the one- or two-line description of Darman's patrimony that appears in most press accounts has portrayed the family as a generations-old textile dynasty, all Yankee rectitude and Bostonian reserve.

In fact, the family is more extravagantly interesting than Darman usually lets on—especially his grandfather, who first staked out the family fortune. Arthur Isaac Darman was born in 1889 in Kurelvitz, Russia, and, after emigrating to Rhode Island with his parents at the turn of the century, ran away, at age fourteen, to join a pantomime company, George Adams's Humpty-Dumpty Show. He worked as a peanut vendor and an actor, and ultimately, had to work his way back across the country—often as a dishwasher. Returning home at age twenty, Arthur developed his father's modest business into the Arthur I. Darman Co., a small but lucrative firm that manufactured and traded in wool top. His love of vaudeville never died. As a sideline he developed and ran theaters; his kindness to actors was recorded in a 1945 article in the *Saturday Evening Post* about Woonsocket's Park Theater.

Arthur Darman loved living well, with gold-plated dishes and a house with a theater that seated 300; just before Prohibition went into effect, he bought more than sixty cases of liquor from the head chef at New York's Ritz-Carlton, and he often entertained Rhode Island's governor. Sometimes known as "The Little Napoleon," he was a short, dapper man who conducted negotiations from atop a throne of telephone books, according to former labor leader Larry Spitz, who organized the workers of the Arthur I. Darman Co.

Old friends of Dick Darman's remember that he used to describe his grandfather fondly, but with a sense of some embarrassment: He was definitely not the proper Bostonian character Morton would become. And Arthur was, among other things, a devout Jew. He was for thirty years the president of Woonsocket's Congregation B'nai Israel, whose synagogue— the first in Woonsocket—he was instrumental in building. He was a tireless fund-raiser for Jewish philanthropies; and his son, Morton Darman, also was religiously active. When the family moved to Wellesley, it too lacked a synagogue, and Morton became a founder and first president of Temple Beth Elohim, as well as a promoter of Jewish charities. He was more the restrained Yankee than his father, and quieter—without being secretive—in his religious activities. "I would have said he was an Episcopalian," says Wellesley resident Frank Conway, who worked with Mort Darman in civic affairs. The family was still religiously active enough to see to it that just before the family left Woonsocket, in May 1956, Dick Darman was bar mitzvahed at Congregation B'nai Israel. True to form, he was awarded a plaque as "outstanding student" in Hebrew school.

Today, Dick Darman belongs to an Episcopal church in McLean. Charlotte Hays has reported in the *Washington Times* that Darman grew touchy when asked about his grandfather and his religion, explaining that his background is "complex," including Jewish and Catholic forebears. He is, he said, "a mongrel and currently a practicing Episcopalian." But the biggest part of Darman's inheritance was inescapable. "I have a feeling something was being handed on here, from his grandfather to his father, and Dick was the one it was being given to," recalls Lea, the college roommate. "Both of these men were very successful people. And the thing that was to be handed on was for Dick to be successful in some unusual way."

Hanging on Darman's office wall is a photo, clipped from his Harvard class of '64 yearbook, of President John F. Kennedy at a Harvard football game in the last autumn of his life. Behind him in the crowd you can make out, dimly, the undergraduate Dick Darman. Darman has spoken often about being inspired to public service by JFK—a fellow son of Massachusetts and Harvard who was elected the same fall that Darman came to Harvard Yard. "JFK was an enormous influence on all of us," says Scott Harshbarger, another college roommate of Darman's who is now the district attorney of Middlesex County, MA.* When Darman graduated from college, Harshbarger says, "He really did feel that a very active part of his life was going to be a role in public affairs." A look at Darman's early career casts some doubt on this inspirational account of his ambitions. For it was only after seven years of graduate work at five universities that Darman would seriously pursue his life's passion. "Dick was never starry-eyed. He never struck me as the type," says Tony Aldrich.

If anything about the Kennedy administration inspired him, it was probably less the bear-any-burden zeal of the young president than the rationalist spirit of the hotshot young technocrats who were brought into government to work on the New Frontier. Walter Channing remembers Darman's fascination during a visit to the business school by Alain Enthoven, one of the "whiz kids" who headed Defense Secretary Robert S. McNamara's civilian brain trust, the Office of Systems Analysis. "Darman was turned on by his reputation, his aura," recalls Channing. But his first move right out of college was to spend a year in France with another Harvard roommate, Richard Keyes. The two audited a hodgepodge of subjects—French history, philosophy, art—for a term each at the Universite d'Aix-en-Provence and at the Universite de Paris. He had majored in government in college but, according to several friends, was also drawn toward a career in liberal arts—as a writer, perhaps, or teaching literature. But at the end of the year Darman returned to Harvard for the two-year business program. "I think he envisioned himself going into business,"

* Subsequently Harshbarger, a Democrat, would be the Democratic nominee for Massachusetts governor (he lost to the Republican incumbent, Paul Cellucci, in 1998) and president of Common Cause.

Keyes recalls. "At the same time, I think he wasn't sure whether the business world was going to be wide enough for him."

By the end of business school, Tony Aldrich says, Darman seemed depressed and withdrawn. "I think he had a hard time figuring out what to do. And I think he was pretty pessimistic about finding something he'd be interested in." After graduation, Darman took a job in the Washington office of McKinsey & Co., the management consulting firm—and didn't last the summer before quitting in boredom. In September he married Kath Emmett. While she did graduate work in English literature at Tufts, he pursued his master's degree in education at Boston University. Then he followed her to Oxford, where she had a fellowship, and spent a year studying literature. In 1969, Darman again returned to Harvard, for a Ph.D. program in education. It was this that would finally pull him off the path of the perpetual graduate student. He got involved in a consulting project for what was then the Department of Health, Education and Welfare and, in 1971, was hired by HEW as a deputy assistant secretary in the Office of Planning and Evaluation. He never finished his Ph.D., and never looked back.

"He struck me in some respects as a guy who got lucky," recalls Tony Aldrich. "After that, he seemed really charged up. . . . It was a quick shift, from being depressed about his career to being unleashed. . . . It's kind of like he had to get out of town to get going."

In Washington, Darman quickly formed one of the two relationships that would most advance and influence his career: with Elliot L. Richardson, who was Richard Nixon's HEW secretary. Richardson was a true son of Brahmin Boston, and also someone who had found in government a personal way of dealing with high expectations. With a background as a crusading prosecutor and a Harvard–East Coast establishment pedigree, he stood, in the early 1970s, for the moderate, centrist tradition in the GOP. "Richardson was, among Cabinet officers, unusual," says John Palmer, a former HEW colleague who is now dean of Syracuse University's Maxwell Graduate School of Citizenship and Public Affairs. "He had a very powerful intellect, and liked to think about the issues that were in his domain in very conceptual, abstract and principled terms. And then work back from that, to think about specific programs and policies."

For Darman, with his natural analytic abilities and rationalist approach to life, this was a perfect fit. "They were kindred spirits, I think," says Palmer. The young analyst first came to Richardson's notice, the former secretary remembers, when he wrote a memorandum that "struck me by its incisiveness and clarity." The subject, as Richardson recalls it, was a proposed framework for identifying the level of government at which a given problem could most appropriately be addressed—precisely the kind of abstract question that engaged both Richardson and Darman. Richardson asked Darman for further memos, and gradually came to rely on him as a sort of one-man think tank.

By 1973, Darman had moved from the policy shop into the role of special assistant, joining the coterie of smart young aides—"Richardson's mafia"—who stayed with him from one assignment to the next. Increasingly, his analytical skills were turned toward temporal problem solving. When Richardson was moved to secretary of defense, in Nixon's post-election Cabinet shake-up, Darman moved too. Their time at Defense lasted only a few months, however, before Richardson was nominated attorney general, following Richard Kleindienst's Watergate-related resignation. Here, too, Darman followed as a special assistant.

Richardson entertained elegant visions of reforming the criminal justice system, but he and his mafia were immediately mired in the problem of Vice President Spiro Agnew. Darman was one of a small group that hammered out a deal in which Agnew agreed to resign, pleading no contest to one count of tax evasion. Immediately after Agnew resigned, the Justice Department was plunged full force into President Nixon's constitutional struggle with special prosecutor Archibald Cox. When the conflict reached its climax in the so-called "Saturday Night Massacre," with the president's demand that Cox be fired, Darman and several other aides joined Richardson in resigning.

But, in the ensuing years, Darman never strayed far from government—or from Elliot Richardson. He joined Richardson at the Woodrow Wilson International Center for Scholars, while also entering a consulting business, ICF Inc., that performed mostly government-related and policy-consulting work. When Gerald Ford nominated Richardson to be secretary of commerce in late 1975, Richardson immediately created for Darman the role of assistant secretary for policy. With Ford's loss to Jimmy Carter in 1976, Richardson became Carter's ambassador to the United Nations Conference on the Law of the Sea; Darman went with him. At the same time, Darman returned to ICF, and also—again, with

Richardson's support—commuted to Harvard's John F. Kennedy School of Government as a lecturer in public policy.

The end of the '70s marked the eclipse, within the GOP, of Elliot Richardson's brand of moderate Republicanism. The man who had once been thought a presidential contender, who had been lionized for standing up to Richard Nixon, would spend the next decade more or less on the sidelines, working in law firms. In the '80s, his most prominent protege would go on to ever-greater success in a world made new by the landslide victory of Ronald Reagan's conservatism.

For this, Darman would need a new patron. He carried with him, into the 1980s, some of the lessons of Elliot Richardson, especially his literacy in institutional subtleties and levers of power—the paper flow, the role of language, the importance of job description over title. It was probably from Richardson that Darman acquired too his talent for casting anything controversial, including himself, in terms so abstract as to dissipate their friction.

But Darman would far outstrip his first protector, who was known, finally, as something of a naif. Richardson didn't win many battles within the Nixon administration—partly, of course, because he spent so little time in any one Cabinet seat, but partly because his talents leaned so strongly to the abstract. On Capitol Hill he was seen as reserved, aloof, and a little otherworldly. Playing against the John Ehrlichmans, he lost graciously—but he lost. He was a man who spoke lovingly of a career "working a margin" outside the center of power—a statement impossible to imagine, today, from the mouth of Dick Darman. And no matter how greatly Richardson is appreciated as a student of institutions, the one act of his government career that will long be remembered is his principled decision to quit it.

Today Richardson speaks somewhat wonderingly of Darman's ascent, and his analysis of Darman's talents is revealing. Darman's thinking is distinguished by three attributes, Richardson says in his measured, rather Victorian way:

One, wishful thinking never distorts his view of anything. It's fair to say that non-rational factors do not distort his view of anything. . . .

The second is that he is much less prone than other people to allow his view of a situation to fall into a pattern or a mold imposed by convention. . . . He instinctively understands the fallacy of believing that there is a real thing behind every label.

The third asset he has in addressing problems is that he knows that he is dealing with a dynamic, and not a frozen cross section. That the impact of what he's doing is downstream, and that he needs to try to sense the direction of the forces that comprise the current, and the ways in which they interact.

Richardson and Darman are neighbors, and over the years they have often shared the morning drive into Washington. But lately, Richardson says, "I don't see Darman very often . . . I know he's so busy, I know he needs time with his family." It is hard to know whether, under his patrician humility, a note of irony lurks: "I just try to—you know, I don't want to bother him."

James A. Baker III, the smooth Texas outsider who was recruited to be Reagan's first White House chief of staff, has next to no interest in the theory of governance, and little passion for the pursuit of innovative domestic policy. While obviously smart, he is not at all intellectual. The only things Baker has in common with Richardson are the Republican Party, a good WASP pedigree, and a hand in promoting Richard G. Darman. Baker had known Darman slightly in 1976 when the two briefly overlapped in Commerce Department jobs. Still, he didn't know much about this man who suddenly, in the fall of 1980, sought him out in Houston with proposals, plans, offers of help—both on the phone and by Federal Express.

But Baker is a quick study, and it was soon obvious that Darman was offering him gold—an intimate knowledge of the levers and man traps that determine power and survival in Washington. In return, Baker offered Darman a chance to join the inner circle of the new administration, and had the political capacities to sell the schemes of his more abrasive junior partner. Over the next six years, the two would form an almost perfect symbiosis. And it was with Baker that Darman's political, short-term, game-playing skills—his more cynical side—reached full flower.

Darman quickly became the administration's jack of all trades. Initially bearing the humble title of deputy assistant to the president, Darman became the channel for all paper that reached the Oval Office; among other things, he decided each evening what the president should read that night. In a presidency as passive as Reagan's, that was tantamount to controlling the president's information. It was also Darman who devised the legislative strategy group, a small (six or seven people) circle that met each evening to plan the advancement of Reagan's agenda. While Baker rival Edwin C. Meese III was swimming in Cabinet council meetings and position papers, Darman's group effectively seized control of administration decision-making in the crucial policy battles that are played out between the White House and Capitol Hill. "Darman did a lot of the best thinking in the group," recalls David R. Gergen, former White House communications director. He came to each meeting with a single-page agenda, Gergen says, which served as the starting point for "an intensive effort to strategize everything down to the last detail. What could go wrong. What your fallback position was going to be . . . the pros and cons, upside, downside, around-the-corner questions." For the risk-averse Baker, Darman was the political equivalent of a minesweeper.

The White House was the perfect venue for Darman's fascination with process, with making the pieces—the policy, the personalities, the press, the politics—fit together. Especially Baker's White House, where the trick was to advance a revolutionary new economic policy while restraining what Darman and Baker privately thought of as the amateurs and right-wingers who had done so much to elect Ronald Reagan. Inevitably, working in the White House emphasized the expedient side of Darman's nature. "He certainly got thrust into positions where it would be harder and harder to be effective, and be seen as a loyal participant, if you didn't increasingly emphasize the short-term pragmatism," says one former colleague. "You have to be weighing the president's short-term political interests in everything you do."

Darman's success also required a careful compartmentalization of his life. As he freely admitted, his wife took a dim view of politics and government—especially the politics of the Reagan administration. Several old friends believe Kath Darman voted for George McGovern in 1972. The Darmans dealt—and still deal—with their differences in part by avoiding the Washington social scene; Kath, who has taught at several local universities, avoids even the quasi-mandatory social events her husband attends.

After Baker and Darman moved to the Treasury Department in 1985, as secretary and deputy secretary, the department was routinely described as "the Baker-Darman Treasury." Here, Darman had a chance to show his capacities as an initiator of policy—most notably in the Treasury's activism in driving down the dollar and coordinating economic policies with major allies. "Dick was certainly the intellectual driving force behind moving towards international economic policy coordination," says Robert Zoellick, a former Darman aide who now works as counselor to Secretary of State Baker.* But in some important respects, the pair remained cautiously tied to political accomplishment. Their major domestic preoccupation was tax reform. When Darman and Baker moved to Treasury, they were scornful of the politically inflammatory reform bill that Donald Regan's Treasury Department had produced, but they concluded that, with the president solidly on record favoring tax reform, they had to produce something that could be called a tax-reform victory on Capitol Hill.

It was Darman at his best and his worst. He made himself the bride at the wedding, learning the ins and outs of the tax code and nudging aside the assistant secretary for tax policy to become the Treasury's chief tax operative. Most observers were convinced that Darman truly favored tax reform, and worked tirelessly toward it. But he was never one of those who, at various points, took political risks in its pursuit. When Senator Robert Packwood moved to save tax reform by burying a loophole-laden version his Finance Committee had been horse-trading over for days, proposing instead a radically stripped-down bill with almost no special-interest deductions and far lower rates, Darman immediately gave it the administration's support; but he had been equally ready to push the special-interest extravaganza that was on the table the day before. The professional tax-writing staffs of the Treasury Department and the congressional committees involved, long accustomed to Washington maneuverings, were nonetheless shocked by some of the ways Darman proposed in conference to make sure the bill did not lose revenue. Since the Senate bill phased out the deduction of sales taxes, for instance, why not publish new charts upping the deductions—thereby boosting the "savings" that appeared to come from eliminating them? "He would come in with anything he thought he might be able to make a case for without smiling," recalls one veteran of the tax wars.

In the end, Darman was credited as a major strategist for one of the

---

* During the presidency of George W. Bush, Zoellick would become U.S. trade representative and, subsequently, deputy secretary of state (to Secretary Condoleezza Rice).

Reagan era's most important legislative achievements. The credit he got, however, was never enough. Throughout his Reagan years, Darman rankled at not being recognized for his central role in the web of administration policy making. It wasn't for lack of cultivating admirers in the press corps. But as often as not, he was known by the galling shorthand "aide" or "staffer." His sensitivity on this point was so well known that, during Reagan's second inauguration, mischievous colleagues arranged to have Darman's special inaugural license plate say "BAKER AIDE." Darman was "livid," remembers one of the participants. "He went out and bent it in half."

He could not truly get his due, he felt, until he ceased being, in Washington argot, "Richardson's guy" or "Baker's guy"; until he had a Cabinet seat of his own. Thus, he was reportedly furious not to be asked to succeed David Stockman in 1985; worse still was to be passed over for someone like James C. Miller III, who became such a bland budget director that Hill staffers nicknamed him "Miller Lite."

Darman resigned from the Treasury in 1987 to become a managing director at the investment banking firm Shearson Lehman Hutton. He has told friends that there was simply not much challenge left in the Reagan administration—no real agenda, no real will to pursue one. But even as he left, his interest may have been rising. Darman is canny enough to know that, in the conservative GOP circles that have dominated the executive branch for the past decade, a desire to work full time in government is slightly suspect. Frederick N. Khedouri, formerly a top Stockman aide at OMB, says, "I always assumed, though he never said this to me, that his period of private service was—this sounds crass—but that it was a kind of laundering process. Republicans can't be professional public servants."

The good news for Darman is that, at last, he has a seat of his own in the president's Cabinet. By some accounts, his accession to real power—like proof that the snazzy car was not a gift from his father—has relaxed him, taken the anxious, abrasive edge off his personality. The Office of Management and Budget, especially in the hands of a shrewd executive, has many powers beyond the simple accounting of government funds, and Darman has already brought the agency back to its Stockman-era heights as the central nervous system of domestic policy. The bad news is that

Darman's perceived success or failure will depend on whether he can "solve" the intractable budget deficit. Darman's critics see a kind of justice here, for Darman was among those most responsible for creating the Reagan-era legacy of red ink.

David Stockman's book, *The Triumph of Politics*, records Darman's knowing complicity in the deficit pileup—especially in the passage of the Conable-Hance version of the supply-side tax cut originally proposed as Kemp-Roth. The book effectively climaxes on July 23, 1981, when Reagan and his top circle met with congressional Republicans to pile onto the tax-cut bill enough expensive "incentives" that it could beat out a rival, similarly ornamented Democratic bill. The result of the negotiating session on that day, according to Stockman, was a bill that would reduce the federal revenue base by $2 trillion over the following decade.

Late that afternoon, the "numb" Darman and Stockman, the two men who best understood the numbers, stood talking in the West Executive parking lot. "I don't know which is worse," Stockman quotes Darman as saying, "winning now and fixing up the budget mess later, or losing now and facing a political mess immediately." After a moment of uncharacteristically somber meditation, Darman pulled himself together. "Let's get at it," he urged. "We win it now, we fix it later. I can think of worse choices."

Darman and other White House moderates did try at several later points to fix the imbalance, and even succeeded more than once in selling Reagan on tax hikes. But they were not enough to avert the years of budgetary stalemate. Small wonder that congressional Democrats look on Darman's present incarnation with some skepticism. He did nothing to dampen that skepticism with his submission, in January, of Bush's first full budget, which included many of the (by now) standard accounting gimmicks—imaginary "savings" and over-optimistic economic assumptions—commonly used to disguise the true enormity of the deficit. Instead of the standard boilerplate introduction, Darman submitted a wide-ranging discussion of federal budgeting and future liabilities, full of punchy, rather cloying imagery: the budget as Cookie Monster, future liabilities as unseen "PACMEN" that threaten to gobble up resources. The playful tone annoyed some. But more offensive, to many Democrats, was what they saw as Darman's hypocrisy. "*At some point,*" he wrote in passionate italics, "*there is an obligation to be serious. At some point, partisan posturing must yield to the responsibility to govern . . . to complete the job of fiscal policy correction.*"

Democrats denounced the document as a thoroughly disingenuous piece of work—the same old budget, wrapped in a masterpiece of finger-pointing. "There are two Dick Darmans," thundered New York Representative Charles Schumer. "There is Dr. Jekyll-Darman the pamphleteer and Mr. Hyde-Darman the budgeteer—and the two don't add up." Senate Majority Leader George Mitchell of Maine called it "the ultimate example of the old saying, 'Do as I say, not as I do.' I know of no person more responsible for the practices of the past decade, spanning two administrations, than Mr. Darman." In other words, here again were the two Dick Darmans—the long-term idealist and the short-term realist, happily ignoring the improbability of their partnership.

But, as this year wears on, it seems that the two are finally merging, for the simple reason that the country's long-term interest in eliminating the deficit coincides more and more with Darman's short-term interest in pulling off a heroic "big fix." Increasingly, as the economic risks of delay have risen, the potential political payoffs to Darman for action have increased. Darman has long believed the deficit can be addressed only through a bipartisan agreement that essentially "handcuffs" politicians together in a nonaggression pact: Republicans won't go after Democrats for raising taxes, in other words, and Democrats won't go after Republicans for cuts in entitlement programs like Social Security. It is "the political equivalent of an immaculate conception: a compromise that materializes without any politician having to take the blame," as Darman described it in a 1987 op-ed piece. This is what Darman has tried to promote in the budget summit that has met over the past two and a half months. And he is widely credited (or reviled, depending on your point of view) as the administration strategist most responsible for persuading the president to renounce his anti-tax pledge—a move Democrats called a vital precondition for any further progress in the talks. Bush's willingness to do so has been widely taken as a sign that the administration—and Darman—are serious about deficit-cutting this year.

In fact, a confluence of circumstances—including slower-than-anticipated growth and the multibillion-dollar weight of the savings and loan crisis—may have made it impossible to slide through another year without making real change. The Gramm-Rudman-Hollings deficit reduction law sets a deficit target of $64 billion for the 1991 fiscal year; at present, OMB's sunniest analysis—not counting, of course, the exploding cost of the S&L bailout—predicts a deficit of more than $168 billion.

For the first time, allowing the ax of Gramm-Rudman's mandated across-the-board cuts to fall in October would result in genuine cutbacks of vital government services. Even if negotiators could finesse the problem for one more year, that would only push it into 1991—and George Bush's reelection effort.

So Darman has been working in a pressured, now-or-never atmosphere. At this writing, it isn't clear whether the strategy can work: As of mid-July, congressional negotiators were still far apart, on both what taxes might be raised and what domestic spending might be cut.* In the meantime, Darman must walk a fine line between scaring Congress into action and scaring the financial markets into panic. It doesn't help that, despite his careful efforts to develop a mellower manner, he is widely mistrusted on the Hill. Even House Budget Committee Chairman Leon Panetta, said to be one of the Democrats most appreciative of Darman's efforts, says, "You deal with Dick Darman, but you always watch your back."

Darman can't be seen to fail at this if, as is widely believed, he hopes to rise higher politically—to treasury secretary or even, one day, to secretary of state. But, despite the pressures of his predicament, Dick Darman is savoring the limelight. "I think he enjoys this sort of situation, which places an enormous premium on cleverness, and coming up with formulas that satisfy everyone's problem," says Fred Khedouri. "That was the thing he was always really good at."

The man who holds the nation's purse strings does not bother to buckle his seat belt. Fitting his key, with its Batman keychain, into the ignition, he settles impatiently into his Mercedes (license DD–20) and takes off. As he drives, he talks. Dinner, like Ping-Pong, has come to a desultory end, with no official score. Now, having promised to drive me back from our hours-long detour into northern Virginia, he has a last few minutes in which to convince me of the existence of Dick Darman, idealist.

* In the end, the strategy succeeded, in the sense that a budget deal was struck that, at long last, set the deficit on a downward path; continuing this effort, President Clinton would eventually eliminate the budget deficit altogether. (Clinton's successor, George W. Bush, pumped it right back up again.)

Politically, though, it was a bust. Clinton beat George H.W. Bush in the 1992 election amid widespread disenchantment within Bush's political base over Bush's violation of his anti-tax pledge at the 1988 Republican National Convention ("Read my lips, no new taxes").

Darman can be a persuasive man. He has a great talent for making people feel that he, better than anyone, understands their dilemmas, their positions, their problems. Representative Barney Frank has aptly summarized Darman's modus operandi: "He's very good at giving people the impression he really agrees with them," Frank told reporters in March. "There are people always in this town that let you know that they're the secret good guy. They're really fighting hard inside against these other people for the right things. . . . And I think Darman is a master at being a secret good guy."

He has convinced supporters of supply-side economics that he agrees with their views; he has convinced sympathetic journalists that he is a man who treasures words, a fellow observer of the scene; he has made old friends see him as a closet liberal who will one day, given enough power, allow his compassion to flower. He has made many, many people believe that under the armor of the bureaucrat beats the heart of an optimistic idealist.

Over weeks of interviews for this story, friends and former colleagues made passionate cases for this Dick Darman. It is, they argue, the Darman who gives controversial speeches, which he writes himself, denouncing the "corpocracy" of shortsighted businesses and the greedy "now-nowism" that makes Americans such champion consumers and poor savers. It is the Darman who is nuts about the space program, who is shoring up the NASA budget and sending his kids to space camp. It is the Darman who talks up a needed transformation in American values. It may have been the Darman who, earlier this evening, slowed his headlong house tour long enough to show me his photo album, bound in rich blue leather. Outside, it was characteristically literal: RICHARD G. DARMAN/ PORTFOLIO, it said, spelled out in gold lettering. But its contents were testament to a certain innocence. With a very few exceptions, the pictures were all of two subjects—his boys and what could only be called Americana: an off-track betting parlor on Labor Day . . . flags and fireworks on the Fourth of July . . . a lone Marine playing taps. "Isn't that quintess*entially* American?" he'd said, again and again, as he flipped through the book.

Now, as Darman drives down the George Washington Parkway toward the Roosevelt Bridge, he continues to talk, excitedly, animatedly. By speaking off the record, in the nighttime intimacy of a car ride, he may hope to do what public officials always hope to do in the phony frankness of their confidential chats with reporters: convince me that he is dropping his guard, showing the one true Darman.

As always, the vapor of self-certainty leaks off him like rocket fuel, but his customary air of irony is gone. He is unconstrained now by the senior official's need for sanctimony, and free to explain his great visions. While he talks, he begins gesturing—with his right hand, with his left, with both at once. At crucial points, he looks from the road to his passenger, to be sure he is understood. The car meanders across the center line . . . then back . . . and again over the line. Darman has slowed down, though not nearly as much as he should have; driving has become one of those muzzy details that his busy brain, in its own thrall, tunes out. No one could drive this badly without sincerity. It is real (if hair-raising) proof that the well-meaning, earnest Dick Darman is in there somewhere. The one who really believes he could fix the problems of the inner cities (that he will!); that when he has finally risen far enough to amount to something, he will be free to turn all his energy and intelligence to the important goals.

It is possible, then, to believe in the existence of both the cynic and the idealist. Darman does: He really believes that he can operate at two speeds. That government operates at two speeds. One is the fast, day-to-day whirl of the Washington game, in which all that matters is the reputation of this week; the other is the lofty, long-term, incremental pace at which true creeping change takes place in a democracy, over periods far longer than most actors' attention spans. As I cower in the plush leather of Darman's passenger seat, it strikes me that his two modes match the horizons of a brilliant undergraduate. Intensely, painfully status-conscious on the one hand, grandly theoretical on the other—youth doesn't yet intuit the middle ground that will make up most of life. Darman too seems to lack any attachment to the median reality. But this is what Washington really manufactures for the multitudes outside the Beltway: taxes and Medicare and student loan policy—decisions that Americans have to live with, decisions that last longer than the hummingbird concerns of Washington's in-crowd, and which are experienced in far more immediate ways than the long-term abstractions of which Darman is so fond. When he grows up, Darman believes, he will be free to move from his near-term strivings to his far-term visions. The secret good guy knows—he just knows—that he's incorruptible enough to bide his time. And that may be the true measure of his arrogance.

—July 20, 1990

THE WIFE
(BARBARA BUSH)

Even Barbara Bush's stepmother is afraid of her. Over the course of a half-hour interview, Willa Pierce, the South Carolina painter the First Lady's widowed father married in 1952, hasn't commented on anything much more controversial than her famous stepdaughter's shoe size. But now, in a quavering voice, she is re-evaluating her decision to say anything at all. "I could get in so much trouble if I said something she didn't agree with," the elderly widow says pleadingly. "Because you know how she is: She knows how she wants to appear to the world."

Indeed: Barbara Bush is America's grandmother, casual, capable, down to-earth; she is fake pearls and real family. "I'm not a competitive person," she once said, "and I think women like me because they don't think I'm competitive, just nice." She bakes cookies, knits, does needlepoint. She is funny, but mostly at her own expense. She is a woman so modest that she writes in the voice of a dog.

At a time when George Bush has slid almost fifty points in most polls in a little more than a year, Barbara Bush stands as close to universal popularity as any figure in American life. Her approval rating is forty—even fifty—points higher than her husband's, and she gets as many as eight thousand letters a month. Aides call her "the National Treasure"—"the treasure" for short—in sly tribute to the qualities that make her an awesome asset to her husband.

The First Lady's hard work on causes ranging from AIDS to illiteracy has been justly praised, but it has also helped to obscure the void of the

Bush domestic policy with a theater of activism. She is, first and foremost, her husband's alter ego, charged with showing his compassion in the areas that an aide merrily summarizes as "poverty, pain, and degradation, basically."

"In the thirty-some years I've been around American politics, she's far and away the greatest political spouse I've seen," says political strategist Edward J. Rollins, one of the managers of Ross Perot's presidential campaign. Her help has never been more important than at the current moment, when political advisers to Bush have taken to joking that every one of the president's speeches should include the phrase "Barbara and I . . ."

It is an extra stroke of luck for the president that the Democrats' answer to Barbara Bush is Hillary Clinton. "I'll take a matchup between George and Barbara Bush and Bill and Hillary Clinton any day," says a senior Bush adviser. "People like Barbara Bush. And people don't like Hillary Clinton." Even if Ross Perot, not Bill Clinton, proves to be the greater threat to Bush's re-election, Margot Perot seems unlikely to divert much attention from the symbolic face-off between her more famous counterparts. Republican strategists will be working overtime to remind us that the Arkansas governor's controversial wife is the perfect foil for the First Lady's image as the embodiment of all cardinal virtues.

It is an image that has been perfectly honed through almost four years at the White House. "Short of ax murder," says former Bush spokeswoman Sheila Tate, "I think she could get away with anything. She's so benign."

Then why are people so scared of her?

Current and former associates inevitably set anonymity as the price of any statement at variance with the myth. "People always said Nancy Reagan would kill you if you said bad stuff about her," says one staff aide who worked closely with the Bushes during his vice presidency.

But I always thought Mrs. Bush was the one who would kill you. . . . No one sat around and gossiped about Mrs. Bush. I don't think it was that people loved her; I think everyone was scared of her. It was just like when your mother said, "I have eyes in the back of my head."

People who have worked with the Bushes use words and phrases like "difficult"; "tough as nails"; "demanding"; "autocratic." A 1988 campaign staffer recalls that "when she frowned it had the capacity to send shudders through a lot of people." One longtime associate explained his refusal to talk—even to describe his most positive feelings about Mrs. Bush—by saying, straight-faced, "I don't want to be dead. . . . I really like her, but I don't go anywhere near her."

Some of the fear she inspires is a function of her position: No one wants to piss off a president by crossing his wife. But the widespread apprehension that Barbara Bush creates is also a fear of the woman herself.

The same reporters who spin misty reports of Barbara Bush toiling in soup kitchens discuss a different reality among themselves: the flinty stare she fixes on the source of a question she doesn't like; the humorous dig; the chilly put-down. For behind her rampart of pearls, the nation's most self-effacing celebrity is in fact a combative politician. Always there, not far below the surface, is the Barbara Bush who briefly emerged in 1984 to denounce Geraldine Ferraro as "that $4 million—I can't say it, but it rhymes with 'rich.'" This Barbara Bush has a brilliant grasp of image, and has always understood a chief source of her appeal: that she is—as folks in Washington never tire of pointing out—Not Nancy.

During inaugural week in 1989, she made unmistakable digs at her predecessor, especially by spoofing her own new clothes: "Please notice— hairdo, makeup, designer dress," she said at one event. "Look at me good this week, because it's the only week." Washington lapped it up—despite the fact that Barbara Bush had been wearing makeup, designer dresses, and "hairdos" for years. True, her earlier instincts had run to shirtwaists and circle pins. But by the time George Bush became president, his wife was a faithful customer of Arnold Scaasi and Bill Blass. Similarly, she has commissioned interior designer Mark Hampton to work on every house in which the Bushes have lived since 1981, both private and official.

Yet, today, she has successfully established her image as one too down-to-earth for fashion. "Personally, I think she's tougher than Nancy, but in a much more sophisticated way. . . . She's a pretty slick lady," says one sharp-eyed former Reagan aide, who counts such details as the $1,245 Judith Leiber bag that was a gift from the designer.

While she has excelled by poking fun at herself—her hair, her age, her waistline—aides have learned that they cannot count on this self-abasement: The First Lady is not amused when someone else tries to inject this note into a speech written for her. Barbara Bush controls her press more tightly than Nancy Reagan ever dreamed of doing. She uses publicity to good effect when she sees an opportunity to deliver a useful message. In one of her first public events as First Lady, for example, she arranged to be photographed holding an AIDS baby, to convey the message that the disease can't be contracted through casual contact.

But she almost never sits down alone with news reporters who cover the White House regularly. Instead, she speaks to them a few times a year over ladylike luncheons in the family quarters, where they feel constrained by her hospitality. Reporters are social creatures, too, and are far less likely to lob a hostile question over the zucchini soup. (Mrs. Bush declined to be interviewed for this article, and most of her family, including her children, followed suit.)

Privately, she is a caustic and judgmental woman, who has labored to keep her sarcasm in check—with incomplete success. And once she notes a soft spot, says a longtime associate, "she hangs on forever. She never, ever, ever, *ever* lets go. She can just get under your skin and needle you."

"I mean," elaborates a former aide, "she's a good person, she talks about AIDS and stuff. But she's not this *nice* person." One Washington regular—the second wife of a prominent man—tells of meeting the First Lady at a party. Mrs. Bush, who had a slight friendship with the man's first wife, seemed "hostile" to the couple, "her vibes, the look on her face, everything. . . . She looked at me, and if looks could kill, I'd be dead," the woman relates. Hoping at least to make the conversation smooth, the second wife mentioned a mutual acquaintance, a Bush-family friend. She had met him, she said, through political circles, and had supported him in a recent, unsuccessful bid for office. "Well," retorted the First Lady, "that is undoubtedly why he lost."

On a personal level, she can be domineering. Aides, old friends, even family members give eerily similar accounts of her offering unsolicited advice on appearance: "You've got to do something about your hair," she told one aide; to another, who had just grown a mustache, she said, "Has George seen that? Shave it off!" She is full of admonitions about smoking, now that she has given it up, and diet—*especially* diet.

Peggy Stanton, a friend from the years when Bush served in Congress, remembers being embarrassed at lunches of the congressional wives' club. "I was a pretty healthy eater, and Bar would say, 'Now, watch Peggy, she's going up for her third helping.' Which was true, but I didn't necessarily want the world to know."

"You're too fat," Barbara tells her younger brother, Scott Pierce, when he puts on weight. And when Bush was vice president, according to an aide, Barbara boiled over one day at the sight of the staffers eating junk food on Air Force Two. "She said we were all fat, we all ate too much, and from then on we would only get fruit and so on," a change that was instituted immediately.

The more people talk about Barbara Bush, the more confusing grows the disjunction between the image and the woman. Two apparently contradictory threads run through her history. The first is her rigorous fealty to the gender roles of her day. The second is the clear force of her personality—the commanding will that has been diverted and disguised, but never extinguished, by her life as the humble helpmate of George Herbert Walker Bush. The two threads of her life come together in an uneasy suspicion that she has paid a heavy price for the image she has lived.

If this is Tuesday, it must be Miami Beach. Clean white limousines are packed like Chiclets at the curb of the convention center, where a thousand loyal Republicans have gathered to salute First Lady Barbara Bush as "National Statesman of the Year." They have forked over a little more than $800,000 to their state party, in amounts ranging from $500 to $10,000, for the privilege of eating a chicken dinner in her presence.

At seven o'clock they are herded into a curtained-off area of the huge exhibition space, its concrete floor and cavernous ceiling wanly cheered by a few potted ferns draped in Christmas lights. Like all political dinners, this one is interminable, with a dozen separate speeches, an invocation, the Pledge of Allegiance, a twelve-piece band, and a rendering of "God Bless America" by a choir of overmiked children.

The First Lady has been up since 5:30 in the morning, and has already flown to San Antonio (for a lunch-hour fund-raiser) and then back East to Miami. But to judge by her facial expressions, greatly magnified on a huge video monitor suspended over the crowd, she would rather be spending this night with a thousand rich Florida strangers in an echoing exhibition hall than spend it anywhere else on earth. She rewards every speaker's peroration with emphatic nods of agreement; she traverses even the dullest bits with her attentive, First Lady–listening expression firmly in place.

And these men do talk. The hour is ticking past 9:30 when Barbara Bush finally rises to speak.

She is *overwhelmed* by this whole evening, she tells the crowd.

She thanks the priest for his *bee-ooo-ti-ful* prayer.

She comments on the *won-der-ful* music.

She does so in a rich, cultured, carefully modulated voice that is still soaked, after forty-five years of Texas and politics, in the affluent air of her childhood. A slight shock attends anything she says: for all the familiarity of her image, you suddenly realize that you have almost no memory of hearing her voice. It is one of the chief requirements of her job that she say as few genuinely memorable things as possible.

"I've known for years that I was the luckiest woman in the world," she says. "I do have the most *marvelous* husband, children, and grandchildren. We live in the greatest country in the world. And tonight you have honored me with such a great honor," she says. "I don't deserve it. Of course I'm going to accept it, but I don't deserve it."

To some degree, Barbara Bush's persona is a simple function of beautiful manners. I have watched her over and over in these First Lady tableaux: at a White House tea, cuddling a child who has a brain tumor; in New Hampshire, choking down yet another chicken breast at a Keene senior citizens' center; at the home of a grandmother in DC's drug corridor, where she escorted the Queen of England—and where she actually made good enough small talk to bridge the gap between the hostess and her royal visitor.

Her exigent private manner is balanced, in public, by a universal graciousness. The only way to reconcile these two facets of Barbara Bush is to understand her as a woman of her class: the American social stratum that has always raised its children to assume their own superiority—and also to mask that assumption at all times.

Her roots are in Rye, New York, the kind of town that imparts an unconscious confidence: not quite so rich as Greenwich, Connecticut, just up the way, where George Bush was raised, but secure and WASPY and well-to-do.

The Pierces lived on Onondaga Street, in a five-bedroom brick house almost at the border of the Apawamis golf club. They didn't have a fortune, but they had a large social inheritance: Pauline Pierce was the daughter of an Ohio Supreme Court justice, and Marvin, a member of a once wealthy Pennsylvania iron clan, was a distant relative of President Franklin Pierce.

"We weren't rich" compared with some of the neighbors, says Scott Pierce, who still lives in Rye. "But we were certainly upper-middle-class."

Barbara, the third of four children, had a caustic tongue even as a child. June Biedler, who was one of Barbara's best friends, remembers her as "very articulate, very witty," and as "kind of a gang leader." When the girls boarded the school bus in the morning,

> Barbara would have decided "Let's not speak to June today." Or Barbara would decide "Let's not speak to Posy today," and so the rest of us would obediently follow along and give that person a miserable time. And I don't remember that there was ever a "Let's not speak to Barbara today" arrangement.

Biedler stresses today that she loves and admires Barbara Bush, and believes that her friend grew up to be a kind and generous woman. But as a teenager, she recalls, "I thought Barbara was really mean and sarcastic." Among other things, she teased Biedler about her painful childhood stammer.

This cruelty, Biedler suggests, may have been the result of having "a mother that was a little mean to her." Pauline Pierce was a beautiful woman, but an exacting observer of social status. She was rather humorless, "austere," according to Biedler; "formal," in Scott Pierce's memory. She was particularly critical of Barbara, according to Donnie Radcliffe's biography, *Simply Barbara Bush*. In several of the stories Barbara tells of her childhood, one makes out Pauline's unpleasant concern that her younger daughter—a big girl, who by the age of twelve was five feet eight inches and weighed 148 pounds—might not cut it in the marriage market.

For her junior year in high school, Barbara followed her sister, Martha, to Ashley Hall, a genteel ladies' prep school in Charleston, South Carolina, the kind of place where a chaperon accompanied the girls to dances at the Citadel. As photos attest, she had by then developed into a slim and pretty teenager, with pale skin and large, dark eyes. She was "at her prettiest," muses Biedler, "probably in her early twenties or in her late teens," but even then "she always had somebody who was prettier, like her sister." Martha, five years older, was devastating competition, a knockout who during college appeared on the cover of *Vogue*. Rosanne M. (Posy) Clarke, one of Barbara's friends, remembers that Martha "was gorgeous—tall and skinny and beautiful. Barbara . . . was pretty, but Martha was *glamour*."

Barbara was far closer to her father, a well-liked, genial man, than to her mother. From these parents, she learned her earliest lessons in gender politics, a model of how moms rule the roost but dads win the popularity contests. "Mother was kind of the glue of the family," says Scott Pierce, "although my dad was the one everybody admired."

By 1941, the year Barbara turned sixteen, Marvin Pierce was nearing the top of McCall Corp., publisher of *McCall's* and *Redbook*, among other magazines. The company's flagship magazine, which his younger daughter read avidly in her dorm room, had by then developed the blueprint of her life. Amid cautionary tales about women who were not humble or kind or careful enough to land and keep a man, ads advised that the goal of life was to tie the knot (*"She's engaged! She's lovely! She uses Pond's!"*).

Within weeks of Pearl Harbor, while home from school on Christmas break, Barbara met her destiny. It was at a dance at the Round Hill Club in Greenwich, the kind of tame affair designed so that boys home from Taft and Andover and Deerfield could practice their mating calls on suitable girls home from Miss Porter's and Saint Tim's. Barbara Pierce and George Bush, only sixteen and seventeen years old, locked onto each other with a striking seriousness, an intense mixture of teenage crush and wartime gravity that is almost unimaginable today. Three years would go by before the wedding day arrived, but the outcome was never seriously in doubt.

Most of their friends are at a loss when asked what so quickly cemented this couple. The answer often boils down to social class—that they were, as George's redoubtable mother put it, "sensible and well suited to each other." On her side, there was the glamour of his enlistment, his string-bean handsomeness, his reputation as a big man on the Andover campus. "He was a real catch," emphasizes Posy Clarke. "He was terribly attractive—this young naval officer—and the Bush family was certainly prestigious." On his side, the most intriguing account comes from his brother Jonathan, who once said, "She was wild about him. And for George, if anyone wants to be wild about him, it's fine with him."

Barbara went—again in Martha's footsteps—to Smith, but even while she attended classes she seemed hardly there at all. "She was different from the rest of us in that her destiny was already fixed," says Margaret Barrett, a roommate. "Her whole life was bound up in [George]." She made plans to return sophomore year but canceled at the last minute, in August, dropping out for good. "I was just interested in George," Barbara has said.

They married, with all the trimmings, while he was home on leave in

January 1945. Their plan was that after the war he would take up his education at Yale, and she would take up the life of his young bride. They honeymooned on Sea Island, GA, where George dashed off a magisterial bulletin to his sister, Nancy: "Married life exceeds all expectations. Barbara is a fine wife!"

"It was a real storybook romance," says Posy Clarke in wry summary. "They married and went to New Haven, and she worked her tail off the rest of her life."

Meet Mr. and Mrs. Bush, the WASP patriarch and wife: He is lanky and spare, with sharp bones and a youthful hardness to his jaw, graying but still handsome. She, though, is lined and bowed, snow-topped, spreading at the middle. So unfair, what nature can do to men and women, and what society makes of the results. By the time George and Barbara Bush reached their early forties, she was conscious of the disparity in their looks. Over time she tried different strategies for dealing with this painful contract—including, for a while, unsuccessfully dyeing her hair—until finally she settled on a rollicking self-satire that firmly beat observers to the punch.

These days, no one admits to being among the advisers and hangers-on who once carped about her looks (*Can't we do something about Barbara?*). Each and every one of her courtiers understood all along how fabulously refreshing she was. The White House had the power to turn her hair from gray to "silver," and her style from matronly to "natural."

And still, the contrast between her and her husband remains, insistently pointing to another possibility: that she is his picture of Dorian Gray, the one who wears the life they have lived together. "She's tougher than he is," runs the standard refrain of friends and aides of George and Barbara Bush. For decades, going back almost to the start of their marriage, Barbara bore the hardest parts of this couple's lot.

The division of the burdens was subtle initially, not untypical of family life in the late 1940s and early '50s. In almost every account of their first years together in Texas, George Bush is out doing and being—starting his own company, raising money back East, enjoying what he would always describe nostalgically as a great adventure. And Barbara is living a parallel life of grinding hard work.

In the first six years of their marriage they moved at least eleven times, first in the service, then to New Haven, and then out West, into the oil business: from Odessa, TX, to Huntington Park, CA, Bakersfield to Whittier to Ventura to Compton, then back to Texas, where they settled in Midland. Over fourteen years, Barbara bore six children: George, Robin, Jeb, Neil, Marvin, and Dorothy.

For long periods Barbara managed the family alone, while George traveled. "I remember Mom saying she spent so many lonely, lonely hours with us kids," the Bushes' daughter Doro told Ann Grimes, author of the book *Running Mates*. "I can understand how she felt. She did it all. She brought us up."

"The kids were much more afraid of their mother than their father, I think," says Susan Morrison, who got to know the family well as a press secretary during the 1980 campaign. "If she said it, it went. And if he said it, maybe there was a way around it." His natural aversion to conflict, his great eagerness to be liked, made him the quintessential good cop; her basic toughness, her acid wit and strong will, made her the perfect disciplinarian. As with Barbara's parents, Mother was the glue, and Dad was the fun. To this day, says one who knows the family well, "he uses her to throw some bombs, while he sits back and calms the waters."

The greatest burden of Barbara's young life, though, was the death of her second child, Robin, at the age of three. Here, too, one can see the Bushes dividing roles in a way that assigned Barbara the more painful tasks.

In the spring of 1953, Robin, then the Bushes' only daughter, was diagnosed as having leukemia. "You should take her home, make life as easy as possible for her, and in three weeks' time, she'll be gone," the doctor told the Bushes. But this was not their style. Instead they flew Robin to New York, where George's uncle was a big wheel at Memorial Hospital, and where doctors from the Sloan-Kettering Institute agreed to treat her aggressively. They managed to gain seven months of life.

At almost exactly the time of Robin's diagnosis George had begun a new business partnership, hugely increasing his business stakes, and the demands of his work presented a welcome escape. It was Barbara who sat with Robin every day in the hospital, she who was a daily witness to her daughter's pain, the torment of treatment with drugs and needles. She laid down the law: no crying in front of the girl, who was not to know how sick she was. Thomas "Lud" Ashley, a Yale friend of George Bush's, was then living in New York and saw a lot of Barbara during the ordeal. "It was the most remarkable performance of that kind I've ever seen," he says. "It took its toll. She was very human later, after the death. But not until then."

Only twenty-eight years old, she was alone when she made the final decision of her daughter's life: While the prognosis was hopeless, the doctors offered a chance to arrest the internal bleeding caused by all the drugs Robin had been given. It was a risky operation, but might buy more time. George, who was on his way to New York, couldn't be reached. George's uncle advised against the surgery, but Barbara decided to go ahead. Thirty-six years later, she cried when talking to a reporter about this lonely decision. Robin never came out of the operation, though George reached the hospital before she died.

In defining herself solely as a wife and mother, Barbara Bush was like millions of other women of her generation, sold on a romantic vision of domesticity. Even so, she seems to have pursued the whole package more emphatically than most, working at homemaking like the strong-willed woman she is. "Bar was the leader of the pack," says Marion Chambers, a friend from Barbara's Midland years. "She set the example for us." Her children had the best, most elaborate birthday parties in the neighborhood, as well as the most carefully name-tagged clothes. Her house was spotless; others felt, in contrast, like slackers. She ground her teeth at night and smoked Newports by the pack.

Every year, a week before Christmas, she made an elaborate gift of cookies to her friends' children—a decorative packet for each child, containing a differently shaped cookie for each day before Christmas; the idea was to tie it onto the tree so the child could work his or her way toward the big day. She also threw herself into charity work, the hospital, the local women's league.

Above all, her rule was to accommodate her husband. "The one thing she made sure of was that George Bush was comfortable—she's been very clear about that," says Susan Morrison. At first glance this, too, seems an unremarkable policy for a woman of Barbara Bush's generation. But women who have known her in different stages of their married life say that she went even further to cater to her husband than most of her peers did in their marriages. "She was very thoughtful of him in every way," says Peggy Stanton, who befriended Barbara in the congressional wives' club after Bush was elected to Congress in 1966. "Probably more so than most of us. . . . I just remember that she wouldn't impose on him in any way."

George Bush is famously frenetic, "desperate to be in constant motion," in the words of one of his oldest friends, FitzGerald Bemiss. His omnivorous sociability has meant constant hard work for his wife. Peter Teeley, a longtime adviser, says,

> Look, he is very boyish in the sense that he would say, "Let's have fifty people over this weekend, we'll serve 'em so-and-so and so-and-so," and then not worry about how the food is going to be purchased, and who's going to get it there, and who's going to cook it, and so on. He'd say, "Well, I've got to go golfing." Or "play tennis."

Barbara would sometimes grumble about this, but she never seemed to say no. By 1974, when other women were discovering the wounded, angry sister who had so often shadowed the bouncing figure in the women's magazines, Barbara could still send this description of her activities to the *Smith Alumnae Quarterly*: "I play tennis, do vol. work and admire George Bush!"

From the very beginning, George Bush's political career was simply a larger canvas on which to paint her domestic destiny. All that discipline she had; why, sacrifice was her middle name—*of course* she was happy to visit all 189 precincts in Harris County, TX, in 1962, to help him win the post of Republican Party county chairman in his first race ever. By the time he ran for Congress, of course she would listen to the same speech, over and over and over and over, while madly needlepointing red, white, and blue patches bearing his name for the good ladies of Houston to sport on their purses.

Her iron manners, too, made her a champion political wife. Admiral Dan Murphy, who was Bush's first vice-presidential chief of staff, remembers sitting next to Barbara at an official dinner somewhere in Africa.

> We had been warned by the doctors not to eat any salads, anything that hadn't been cooked. So I didn't, but she was going along eating the salad. I said, "Mrs. Bush, the doctors told us we shouldn't eat things like that." And she said, "This is their country, and they're serving salad, so *I'm going to eat it.*"

She soldiered her way through a losing Senate race, two terms in Congress, and a painful second Senate loss. She smiled at George Bush's side through his stints as Richard Nixon's ambassador to the UN and then as chairman of the Republican Party—though she had strongly counseled him to avoid the GOP post, which was offered him in the midst of the Watergate cover-up. They spent fourteen months in Beijing, where he was special envoy to the People's Republic of China.

And suddenly, after their return to the United States in late 1975, she fell into a black depression—the only time that Barbara's will openly rebelled against Barbara's life.

"I would feel like crying a lot and I really, painfully hurt," she later told *U.S. News & World Report*. "And I would think bad thoughts, I will tell you. It was not nice."

In some interviews, she has attributed her depression to "a small chemical imbalance." In some, she laid it at the door of the women's movement, saying, "Suddenly women's lib had made me feel my life had been wasted." But in others she has hinted that it was the classic mid-life crisis of the woman who had been raised to gain all her identity through the service of others, whose lives had now left the cozy orbit of her care. Not only was 1976 the year her youngest child, Doro, turned seventeen, but it also marked a devastating shift in her relationship with her husband.

She had suddenly gone from feast to famine. In Beijing, with the younger children off in boarding school, the Bushes were alone for the first time since their marriage, exploring their strange new world together. "I loved it there," she has said over and over. "I had George all to myself." When he was called back to Washington to become director of the CIA, he was all at once in a job whose very nature reinforced the old divide in the Bushes' daily lives: this time, he *couldn't* talk about his job at night.

But even if 1976 was the year Barbara's frustration reached a crisis, it was not the only time that she expressed it. The Bushes' history is full of poignant references to her unrequited desire for his company. Even if his work didn't draw him away from home, his frenzied social life did. "His attitude is 'If you want to see me, great, get your clubs.' I think she's constantly trying to make the marriage work that way," says a former aide. "Do you think they ever sit alone and have dinner? I think she'd like that, but she knows it's never going to happen."

Barbara Bush took up golf last year, she told reporters, in the hope of spending more time with the president. But he declined to play with her—just as he had stopped playing tennis doubles with her years before, because he didn't think she was a good enough player. In what one person on the scene described as a "pathetic" tableau, Barbara and her friend Betsy Heminway went "tagging after him" while he and three buddies played Kennebunkport's Cape Arundel Golf Club. As Maureen Dowd of the *New York Times* reported then, the president gleefully announced to the press that his wife's game "stunk."

"When the president, pressed by journalists, finally agreed to play with his wife, the disillusioned First Lady shot back, 'When? Just like he's going to garden with me one day.'" "The joking wasn't pleasant," reports one person who saw the scene. "It wasn't fun, Nick-and-Nora repartee."

Even at times when the Bushes' lives meshed more closely, there was an undercurrent of insecurity in Barbara. "She was very aware that he was so young-looking," says a friend from the late '60s. By then, Barbara was already hardening her defenses, beginning to make jokes that lanced the wound before someone else could press on it. "I noticed that years back, that she would joke about her appearance," says Peggy Stanton.

Bush often seems to treat Barbara more like a buddy than a wife. In public they present their relationship as a partnership that had transcended sex, entering the realm of teasing friendship. Last summer, on Barbara Bush's sixty-sixth birthday, the millionaire president gave her twenty pairs of Keds as a gift. When he was vice president, says a former aide, his advance teams would joke about having to remind him to open doors for her.

With other women, however—the dozens of attractive young women he meets in his work—George Bush is famously flirtatious. "A *biiiiiiig* flirt," says a female former aide. Rumors have circulated since 1980 that Bush has had extramarital affairs. But they are unlikely to be proved unless a party involved chooses to talk about it. All we can intuit, through outward signs, is Barbara Bush's long, more subtle struggle to remain as important a part of her husband's life as he has been of hers.

In this regard, his sporting relationships with his male buddies, his manic insistence on constant motion, and the presence of crowds seem as great a challenge as the other women do. During the Thanksgiving weekend after his election, the Bushes invited the reporters covering them in Kennebunkport to come to the house for wine and cheese. When *USA Today* reporter Jessica Lee burbled her thanks to Barbara, the future First Lady responded grimly, "Don't thank me. Thank George Bush. *He* invited you." (In these moments of exasperation or pain she often refers to him by both his first and last names.)

"I think there's an essence of sadness about her, way deep down," says someone who has worked with Barbara Bush in politics. "Maybe a lot of who she is developed in reaction to sadness."

When her depression hit, she was not the type to deal with it introspectively. Her husband urged her to talk to someone about it, but her style was to tough it out. She was helped, paradoxically, by Bush's growing political ambitions. His entry into presidential politics opened up a new world, and a more expansive role for her beyond the threshold of their house. The higher George Bush rose, the more he needed Barbara in his political life.

In pictures taken of the early planning meetings for the '88 campaign, there are seven or eight advisers lounging around the pretty green living room of the Bushes' Kennebunkport home. In the background, intent on a jigsaw puzzle or a knitting project, hardly paying any attention at all, is Barbara Bush. She is doing what she once did as a young bride at Yale, sitting for long hours behind home plate while George played ball—keeping score.

This is the first of her two roles in his career: the watchful monitor of internal politics who judges each man and woman by the standard of his or her devotion to George Bush. This role is mysterious to almost everyone who works with Bush, for she is infinitely careful. Yet no one around them doubts that she has great power to influence her husband, especially in his views of people. Some go as far as to suggest that she is his number-one political adviser, "first among equals."

But, at almost all times, she maintains the ultra-traditional façade of the old-style political wife, who is there only to see to her husband's comfort. Aides and associates from every period of his political career hasten to explain that Barbara Bush is not Nancy Reagan. She does not carry her own agenda, or choose political goals for her husband; she doesn't muck around with policy or sit in on Cabinet meetings. Aides to Sam Skinner and John Sununu say that neither chief of staff, even in the most troubled passages of his tenure, heard often from the First Lady.

But every successful politician has a quasi-official "family" around him, an inner circle in which personality has a great impact on politics and policy. It is in this realm that Barbara Bush is influential. Here, staffers learn that Barbara is always "just within earshot, just out of sight," in the words of one campaign staffer. Courtiers tread very, very carefully in this domain, knowing, in the words of media adviser Roger Ailes, that "she wants what's best for her husband, and boy, she's strong."

Her second role in George Bush's career is a version of the role she played in their family life—the disciplinarian. Bush is skilled at surrounding himself with others who will draw the heat away from him. Ed Rollins says, "George Bush is a man who wants to be loved. As opposed to respected. It's very important to him that everybody like him." Thus Bush works harder than most at delegating the more unpleasant parts of his job.

In 1988, for example, Bush assigned the role of bad cop to his campaign manager, Lee Atwater; for the first three years of his presidency, Bush's chief of staff, John Sununu, played the heavy. (The effectiveness of having such a tool has become clearer than ever since December, when Sununu left. Lacking this essential foil, Bush has assigned the role piecemeal to various aides, as when spokesman Marlin Fitzwater was sent out to blame the Los Angeles riots on the programs of the Great Society. But because the men who now fill the White House seem too bland to personify evil, responsibility seems to be laid at Bush's door faster than it used to be.)

On a subtler level, Bush has always cast family members in similar roles. Today his son George W. Bush plays the role of enforcer or executioner when a tough call must be made: It was the younger Bush, for example, who told Sununu that his time had run out. And many suggest that, especially during a political race, Barbara plays a more light-handed version of the same role. "She definitely is the institutional memory of slights," says one former political staffer. "She is one distinct other level of the Praetorian Guard."

"I think George Bush has gotten a whole lot of mileage out of letting Bar be thought of as the heavy," says a former political associate. For example, several reporters have been casually told by the president, during one-on-one interviews, that Barbara was angry over something he or she wrote about him. "Look out, the Silver Fox is really mad at you . . ." he'll say, effectively delivering the warning that the reporter's copy has offended, without having to risk any personal conflict himself with the reporter.

Whether Barbara's role is conscious and deliberate, or something that evolved wordlessly out of a long marriage, only the Bushes know. Some believe that it is more conscious on her part than on his. "She knows this man very, very well, and his strengths and weaknesses, and I think she probably compensates for his weaknesses," says Rollins. "She's probably a better judge of character than he is."

"I think she's much more judgmental about people than he is," says another longtime associate. "I think she really takes a bead on someone, and for good or for bad, you're in that box; she's got you pigeonholed." It is widely believed in Washington that Barbara Bush got fed up with John Sununu earlier than her husband did. But "she's wily in that regard," says a former staffer. "She knows how things work, and if she doesn't want to read about what she did, she won't do it in that way."

Sometimes, however, her intercession is in a staffer's favor. When Transportation Secretary Sam Skinner took over from Sununu, one of his first instincts—clearly communicated, through the grapevine of leaks, to the newspapers—was to replace David Demarest as communications director. But Demarest kept his job—reportedly because Barbara defended him. "Word around the White House was she liked him a lot," says one senior White House aide. It was an important bureaucratic defeat for Skinner, contributing to an early perception that he couldn't follow up on his own intentions.

Typically, Barbara works at the margins, letting staffers know obliquely—but unmistakably—when they are coming up short. In one legendary story, Barbara clipped the wings of Craig Fuller, chief of staff in Bush's second term as vice president. Word got back to her from friends and supporters around the country that Fuller was out of touch, hard to reach. So one day, on Air Force Two, seeing him leaf through an inches-high stack of phone messages, she told him—in a voice carefully modulated to reach her husband—"Keep looking . . . you'll find a couple from me."

She uses humor, too, to keep staffers on their toes. In '88, she closely monitored the negative campaign tactics of Atwater and Ailes, because she was concerned they would bring too much criticism down on Bush. When Ailes entered a room in which she was present, she would sometimes greet him jovially, "Here's my bad boy." Coming from Barbara, it's hard to read that as anything but a reminder: *I'm watching*.

If George Bush walks a fine line in his political tactics, Barbara is the line referee—making sure that he doesn't cut things too close. Aides expect her to have a large role in monitoring the propriety of the Bush campaign this fall. While she has not yet shown a strong influence on campaign strategy, she has expressed concern over how tight—and negative—a race is shaping up. Campaign operatives have been warned that the First Lady will not tolerate tactics so inflammatory that they will provoke retaliatory attacks on the Bush family—especially on her sons.

In talking about Barbara Bush's great influence, however, almost everyone agrees that its boundary is clear. All of her vigilance is directed solely to the greater glory of George Bush. Aides who have tried to draw her into the open on substantive matters have been firmly turned down. Deborah Steelman, Bush's adviser on domestic affairs in the '88 campaign, tried to draft Barbara Bush as an ally on issues like child care, health care, and early education and "just was rebuffed, officially, at every turn," Steelman recalls. "You only had to do that to her a couple of times to realize that was off bounds."

To the extent that Barbara weighs in on policy, it is in the dimension of taste—as a protector of her husband's reputation. She is said to disagree with the president's stated opinions in several areas; White House aides are especially eager to suggest that she differs from him on abortion and gun control, fanning some faint hope among Republican moderates that she is fighting a good fight over morning coffee every day. But it seems unlikely that Barbara Bush actually works to change her husband's mind on such issues: His positions in those areas are dictated by politics, and she is as shrewd a politician as anyone around him.

Her role in placating moderates may be more important this year than ever before. In a three-way race that includes Perot, the two major-party candidates will likely be forced to defend their traditional bases, which means they will have to appease the most extreme elements in their coalitions. For Bush, this means waging a fall campaign that offers lots of red meat to social-issue conservatives. Barbara Bush's help will be crucial in telegraphing a contradictory message to more liberal Republicans, especially women angry at Bush over his appointment of Clarence Thomas to the Supreme Court and over the issue of abortion.

Up to now, Barbara Bush has been able to have it both ways. She has offered herself as evidence of her husband's good intentions, while going out of her way to disclaim any power at all to shape the policies that affect the lives—the squalid schools, the threadbare health care, the marginal services—of the unfortunates who people her photo ops.

When Bush decided, in the late '70s, to run for president, Barbara pondered what her major "issue" should be and came up with literacy, a canny choice. On the one hand, as she often explains, it touches on every problem in society, ranging from crime to childhood poverty; on the other hand, it doesn't invite any controversy.

As the vice president's wife, she joined the board of the child-oriented Reading Is Fundamental, and as First Lady she founded the Barbara Bush

Foundation for Family Literacy, to which she has donated all the profits from *Millie's Book*. It gives away half a million dollars in grants every year to programs that address illiteracy as a self-perpetuating problem passed from parents to children.

But if her signature issue was chosen with calculation, there has been nothing artificial about her good works. Even before Bush's political career began, she was a dedicated volunteer in hospitals; over the years, she has quietly worked at such places as the Washington Home for Incurables, and has served on boards ranging from that of the Ronald McDonald House to that of the predominantly black Morehouse School of Medicine.

Today, you can easily see that she has a greater capacity than her husband has to look death and pain in the face. To cancer wards and AIDS clinics, she brings not only helpful publicity but a full self, a capacity to let in the suffering around her and give it its due, which is one of the few gifts any stranger can confer. The president, on the other hand, is famous for squirming through visits to hospitals. When he visited the bed of a Los Angeles fire fighter shot during the riots, the only consolation he could think to offer was for himself: "I'm sorry Barbara's not here," he said miserably.

Every afternoon, the First Lady has her staff send up to her office in the family quarters a clip file of stories related to poverty, education, literacy, child care—her issues; and sometimes she reacts quickly to what she reads. In 1989, for example, she was angered by reports that the Salvation Army had been barred from making Christmas collections at some of the snootier local shopping malls. She made a trip to a mall that did permit the solicitations and took along a press pool to capture her dropping some change into the bucket, which successfully shamed most of the Scrooge-ish merchants into line.

This is as good a use of celebrity as exists in America. It is, by the accounts of Democrats and Republicans, blacks and whites, all of those who have fallen in love with the grandmotherly image of the First Lady, the very best of Barbara Bush. But even in the uprightness of this image lies a certain moral complexity. For the past three-and-a-half years, the First Lady had almost single-handedly symbolized her husband's good intentions in the realm of domestic affairs. Extended to a society's breadth, the Bush model implies a return to an era in which women relieved their powerful men—relieved government—of responsibility for the disadvantaged. It is the old Victorian contract, in which life was divided into two spheres, male and female; while men ran the world, their women ran the soup kitchens.

Bush advisers have worked hard over the years to suggest that Barbara's compassion will one day rub off on her husband, to imply that she can (and should) be relied on to police his interest in social services. "Every time he says 'Head Start,' that's Bar," spokeswoman Sheila Tate told reporters at the dawn of his administration. And for some time the country seemed to accept the idea that Barbara was a facet of George—a reliable indicator of his goals. At the time of Bush's inauguration, columnists raved about how Barbara would be "the conscience of the White House."

But without Barbara, Americans might have noticed sooner that the self-styled "education president" had offered nothing meaningful in the way of education reform. Without Barbara, voters might have noticed from the start how disengaged Bush seemed from domestic concerns. Barbara Bush successfully silenced the logical question that called out for response: Isn't the *president* supposed to be the conscience of the White House?

As George Bush campaigns for a second term, a lot rides on Barbara Bush's careful balancing act. She is the answer to a frightened campaign's prayers, a surrogate campaigner who can command almost as much press and hoopla as the president can—while incurring comparatively little risk. As early as last winter one could trace the dawning importance of her role. She was sent to New Hampshire to file the papers for Bush's candidacy, "because nobody would dare to boo Barbara," in the words of a strategist. She spent more time campaigning in the state than the president did.

When Bush officially announced his candidacy, it was Barbara Bush who introduced him. In a classic reversal of roles, the candidate quoted his wife, referring to "my favorite political philosopher, Barbara Bush."

All through the spring, once the threat of Pat Buchanan's primary campaign had faded, Barbara traveled far more than her husband did, headlining as many as thirty major fund-raisers around the country.

Republican strategists go as far as to say that they believe voters who are ambivalent about George Bush may think twice about voting his wife out of the White House. It's an extraordinary exception to the normal wisdom, which suggests that the best most spouses can do is adhere to the Hippocratic oath of politics: Just do no harm.

Opinions differ about how badly Barbara Bush wants to stay in the White House. She is said to blame the presidency for the problems of her son Neil, implicated in the Silverado Banking, Savings and Loan Association debacle. Friends also surmise that she has had a more difficult time than she lets on dealing with Graves' disease, the thyroid condition that has tired her and painfully distended her eyes.

But by most accounts, she has reveled in her time as First Lady. Even as the president floundered through the spring and early summer, his polls in free-fall, Barbara Bush lived in a charmed circle within her control. She has reached the apotheosis of the life she read about in her daddy's magazines, a victory she presents as grand affirmation of the ultra-traditional plan she has lived by. "My mail tells me that a lot of fat, white-haired, wrinkled ladies are tickled pink," she said on the eve of Bush's inauguration. "I mean, look at me—if I can be a success, so can they."

But only one person gets to be married to the president of the United States. It is a rare full-time homemaker and college dropout who receives an honorary degree from Smith, who is asked to speak to the graduating class at Wellesley, who appears on the covers of *Time* and *Life*.

George Bush's political ascent allowed her to enact her role of helpmate on a vast, symbolic scale—one that offered more ego gratification than the same role performed as an anonymous daily sacrament. This was how she staved off the fated collision between her cramped idea of women's role and her great strength of personality. It is also how she tamed the most turbulent themes of her own life.

Toward the end of the Republicans' May dinner in Miami Beach, two videos about Barbara Bush were shown on the giant screen that hung above the diners. Together they suggested just how far she has traveled.

The first was a brief, condescending biography prepared by the state party. It showed more events from George Bush's life than from his wife's, and included all the same photos that appear in standard Bush biographies—showing handsome young politician George Bush surrounded by his happy brood of children and, standing at the back of the picture, his stocky, weathered wife with her oddly dyed hair and uncertain smile.

But then, with the second videotape, a spectral George Bush appeared on the screen to salute his popular spouse.

"Remember her Wellesley commencement speech?" he asked rhetorically. "Some students protested, saying she's just a woman who followed her husband. Well, they got it wrong. In countless ways, I've followed Barbara."

"I think it's appropriate," he continued, "that Barbara would be honored at the Statesman's Dinner. Someone once said that a politician thinks of the next election, but a statesman thinks of the next generation. Well, that's Barbara Bush, in so many ways."

It seemed an unconsciously honest moment, alluding not only to the reasons America loves her but also to the reasons America now scorns him. Suddenly, it was strangely poignant to watch his video-blurred face, to hear his canned voice, as he talked about the famous, widely loved woman being celebrated in the flesh.

The moment seemed to summarize the ironic reversal being played out before the nation: Now he is the burdened one, she is the butterfly. He can no longer maintain the buoyancy that has been the hallmark of his life, while for her, public goodwill remains at flood tide, affirming her life's choices.

How impossibly sweet it must feel to her. Today she helps her husband most by embodying the levity that was always, until this hour, his to claim.

—August 1992

THE RAINMAKER
(VERNON JORDAN)

Once upon a time, this man brought the vote to the most frightened and most oppressed black citizens of the Deep South. He braved the jeers of a mob for the sake of integrating southern education; he marched in solidarity across Selma's Edmund Pettus Bridge. As head of the United Negro College Fund and the National Urban League he raised millions of dollars to help blacks gain college educations and job training and decent housing.

Now he cocks a perfect wingtip against a drawer of his desk, pressing his long frame back into the smoky-blue leather of his chair. His suit is an immaculate charcoal; his shirt, London's best, is a subtle stripe of white and yellow and gray. The yellow fabric of his necktie, spotted with more gray, is echoed in the handkerchief that winks from his breast pocket. He wears chunky gold cuff links, a gold watch thin as a stick of gum.

"It's not extremes," he is saying of the great, great distance he has traveled. "It's *breadth*." He is describing, in part, the journey of the self-made man, a drama doubly moving when told by one who has overcome all the hurdles assigned in this country to those born with black skin. The grandson of a sharecropper, the son of a caterer and a mail clerk, Vernon Eulion Jordan Jr. is, at fifty-seven, a close confidant of the president of the United States. He is richly educated and widely known, a wealthy man and a happy one.

But Jordan is also acknowledging his transformation from $35-a-week civil-rights lawyer and NAACP field director to seven-figure corporate hired gun, a journey whose moral resonance is much less clear. Today, he is everything that America loves to hate about Washington: a lawyer-lobbyist, a rainmaker, an influence peddler. He sits on eleven corporate boards—including the board of a tobacco company that once tried to market a cigarette explicitly targeted at blacks. He is a managing partner in one of the most politically aggressive law and lobbying firms in Washington, Akin, Gump, Strauss, Hauer & Feld. He makes between $1 million and $2 million a year.

When Bill Clinton appointed him to chair the presidential transition in partnership with Warren Christopher, another well-heeled corporate lawyer, it sparked doubts about how seriously the new president intended to follow up his campaign rhetoric on taming Washington's special interests. On a more personal level, it threw into a sudden spotlight the quiet contradictions that rule Vernon Jordan's life.

Naturally, Jordan quarrels with the premise that his former life and his current life are hard to reconcile. "It's a continuum," he says. "If you have some notion that sitting on X, Y, or Z board makes me forget how I got there . . . or the people I met along the way, then you have totally miscalculated me."

But consider his left lapel, where he sports the crimson ribbon that signifies empathy with sufferers of AIDS. In Vernon Jordan's version, the ribbon takes the form of a tiny pin, less than an inch high. Against the rich austerity of his clothes, it is but a small, pleasing dash of vivid color: the perfect totem for a man who values his liberal politics, but rarely lets them clash with his overall design.

Among the various good-government Democrats who have waited twelve long years for the election of a soul mate, Jordan's appointment to head the transition was greeted with mild shock. But when reporters groped to explain precisely why, they were plagued by the standard journalistic necessity to find the smoking gun, the single fishy deal or seamy alliance that constitutes an official conflict of interest. The one they came up with the most often was Jordan's service on the board of RJR Nabisco, Inc., the nation's second-largest tobacco company. Didn't his $50,000 annual fee from RJR create a conflict for a man who might help choose the next secretary of health and human services, the next surgeon general?

It probably did. But the real discomfort created by the appointment wasn't susceptible to that kind of analysis. It sprang from nothing illegal, nothing that could be called unethical by the technical definitions that rule the city. It wasn't any one specific business connection that made Jordan's appointment surprising; it was his very identity in Washington.

Vernon Jordan's friends and connections constitute a gallery of power, money, and fame, ranging from Democratic grande dame Pamela Harriman to Federal Reserve Board chairman Alan Greenspan, from financier Theodore Forstmann to NBC anchorman Tom Brokaw, from former Housing and Urban Development secretary Jack Kemp to former Secretary of State Cyrus Vance. His board work makes him a colleague of Henry Kissinger, Nancy Reagan, and more than two dozen current and former CEOs of major U.S. companies. He relates on a first-name basis to former president George Bush, who invited him to White House parties, lunched with him privately, and sometimes sought his advice. (Indeed, he found himself last year in the curious position of advising *both* President Bush and candidate Clinton on how they should respond to the Los Angeles riots.)

Every summer he rents a house on Martha's Vineyard, not in the traditionally black section of Oak Bluffs, but in the predominantly white community of Chilmark. "Kay Graham," he notes offhandedly, "runs the best kitchen on the Vineyard."

He lives well. Since the mid-1970s, he has ordered his shirts from London, custom-made by Turnbull & Asser or Charvet to his 17H–37 measurements. He and his wife, Ann, live in a generous brick house, purchased in 1986 for $550,000, that sits on a hill overlooking Georgetown. They both drive Cadillacs, his a red Allanté convertible. He has a passion for fine cigars, and requires that a single flower in a bud vase grace his desk every day.

He is a trustee of the Brookings Institution and the Ford Foundation, and he belongs to all the right clubs: in New York, the Century Association, the University Club, and the Council on Foreign Relations; in Washington, the Metropolitan Club, the Alfalfa Club, the Kenwood Golf & Country Club, and the Robert Trent Jones Golf Club in nearby Gainesville, VA. He is a member of both the Trilateral Commission and the Bilderberg Meetings, the high-status European policy confab. When Bill Clinton got his first invitation to the meetings in 1991, it was as a guest of Vernon Jordan.

His corporate success makes him a source of complex feelings among African Americans. There are those who "see Vernon as someone who takes care of himself—who only looks out for Vernon," in the words of one black Washingtonian long involved in civil rights. But for others it is a source of great pride to see an African American so successfully join the white elite in its own game.

Within that elite, the moral dignity of Vernon Jordan's first journey, up from poverty and past the obstacles of race, has tended to obscure who he really is and what he's really after. His long history of service to the civil-rights movement is a form of camouflage.

The week after Jordan's appointment, for instance, the *New York Times* editorial page tied itself in knots trying to find the correct tone with which to treat Jordan. First it soundly damned his tobacco connection, in a tough unsigned editorial written by black staff member Brent Staples and titled "Vernon Jordan's Ethics." The next day—apparently without any pressure from Jordan or anyone else outside the paper—the *Times* issued a convulsive clarification, couched, on the orders of publisher Arthur Sulzberger Jr., as an entirely new editorial, titled "Vernon Jordan's Integrity." Jack Rosenthal, who then ran the editorial page, explains that he "just felt a little sheepish" about how harsh a headline had accompanied Staples's editorial, and that he and Sulzberger "both agreed that it needed some redress." The second editorial, he points out, said very much the same thing as the first. But, in fact, its tone was so much more tentative, more ingratiating, that it amounted to a striking act of insecurity from the newspaper of record.

"I'm convinced," says one well-known liberal on the *Times* staff, "that if we'd written that about the standard Washington white guy, we would never have backed off it."

Similarly, Jordan has always benefited from the fiction that he is a breed apart from the *real* lobbyists who crowd Washington law firms, including his own. Amid the controversy following Jordan's appointment, *The Wall Street Journal* (whose parent company, Dow Jones, numbers him among its board members) reassured its readers that, while Jordan's law firm "does engage in high-powered lobbying and represents foreign interests," Jordan himself "is primarily a corporate lawyer."

But of course he's a lobbyist—though at a level so exalted that he is able to present himself as transcending the petty pleadings of his brethren. And now, after just eleven weeks' work in Clinton's transition, he is poised to become the lobbyist in chief, his profile hugely increased by the universal knowledge that he is a Clinton-administration insider.

* * *

After my first interview with Jordan—a short, somewhat wary meeting on a Friday afternoon in December—I am expecting to hear from his secretary, or from a Clinton-transition spokesman, about scheduling a second interview. But when the call comes, it is his own beautiful voice that flows from the phone: deep, southern, musical. "Marjorie," it wheedles without preamble, as to an old friend. "You're not done with me yet?"

Charm is a difficult thing to describe, but charm is Vernon Jordan's essence. Says his old friend Eleanor Holmes Norton, the District of Columbia's delegate to Congress, "It's a combination of a personality that seduces men and women differently, but nevertheless seduces."

There is the touch—the lingering handshake that greets you, and the hand that on parting squeezes your shoulder, salutes the small of your back. There is the instant mastery and constant use of your first name. There is the steady gaze—full on, never wavering from your face. Above all there is the smile, a sweetly gorgeous thing he flashes like the asset it is, like a wad of cash.

Finally, there is the way he tells a story. In 1988, Jordan says, he offered some minor advice now and then to the Dukakis campaign. Michael Dukakis "was going to speak to the National Baptist Convention," Jordan recalls.

> And they sent me this talk and said, "Please read it and get back to us." And so I get it and I read it and I call them back and they say, "What do you think?"
> And I say, "You all ever heard of *Jesus?*"
> They say, "What do you mean?"
> I say, "You all ever heard of *Mo*-ses? Sojourner Truth? Harriet Tubman? Booker T. Washington? W. E. B. Du Bois?"
> They say, "Yeah, what are you talking about?"

Jordan's voice is wreathed in sarcasm. "I said, 'This speech quotes John Winthrop *fi-i-ive* times. John Winthrop doesn't mean *anything* to 40,000 black Baptists.'"

Jordan himself is a famously compelling speaker. He once reportedly instructed DC mayor Sharon Pratt Kelly, a woman of somewhat icy mien, that she had to emote more in her speeches. "Giving a speech is like sex," he told her. "You're supposed to be exhausted when you're done."

There is something marvelous about watching Jordan deploy his charms, the swagger with which he uses his difference from every white lawyer in Washington.

"He's not a charming carbon of a white man," notes Norton. "That charm is unmistakably black. Nobody who listens to Vernon can doubt that it all comes from the blackest of roots." She has put her finger on something important: Jordan is not someone who succeeds by "passing." In talking about him, blacks often observe that he is remarkable for having succeeded in spite of the fact that he is very dark-skinned. Says Julian Bond, who was a founder of the Student Nonviolent Coordinating Committee and later became a Georgia state legislator, "There used to be a joke in Atlanta, in the early 1960s, that the way you could prove a restaurant was integrated was that they would serve Vernon Jordan. . . . Because he's so tall, he's so dark. He's so *him.*"

It's safe to say that none of the other high-powered lawyer-lobbyists in Washington quote Scripture the way Jordan does, as many as four times in the course of a single breakfast. (He even wields the Bible when I press him on why a man with his history as a black leader would lend his symbolic weight to the board of a tobacco company, given the grim imbalances in the rates at which African Americans smoke and die of smoking-related diseases. "I made that decision in 1980, when I was asked, and I'm not ready to back away from it," he says. "There's an old, old biblical inscription which says, 'Woe be unto him who puts his hand upon the plough and turns back.'")

Another part of his currency is gossip: He is a joyous purveyor of news and speculation about his huge circle of acquaintance. "Dead men's talk," he will say invitingly, leaning across the lunch table to dish. "This is dead men's talk, now."

With men, his style is a towel-snapping, slightly ribald wit. He's a great teller of dirty jokes, according to one old friend, who says, "He never does not have a new story to tell."

With women, he is universally flirtatious and has long had a reputation as a ladies' man. Howard Moore Jr., a former colleague from Jordan's earliest civil-rights days, recalls that "when he was still in the South, women would break out in a sweat talking about Vernon in his tennis shorts."

Watching him greet the women who cross his path during his workday—his fond attention to every waitress on the breakfast shift; a chance encounter with Tipper Gore in the hall outside his transition office ("Now, you must do Vernon justice," she purrs. "He's just the *best.*"); the passing affection he lavishes on women colleagues at Akin, Gump while waiting for the elevator—one imagines him fine-tuning a sophisticated weapon, turning up the dial until it is set on "Stun."

"He flirts outrageously," notes one of a chorus of women friends. "Holding hands, long looks in the eyes. . . . It goes a little over the edge, maybe, sometimes, but nothing that makes you feel harassed. Vernon's not *slimy.*"

Another woman, however, remembers having him to a large, formal dinner in the mid-1980s, before he married his second wife. Midway through their dinner badinage ("He was pretty hard to talk to, because it was *all* innuendo"), Jordan suddenly observed, "You look like a woman who likes to fuck."

"I was speechless," says the woman, who could think of no riposte until later in the meal, when Jordan had turned his attentions to a friend who was seated nearby. Dinner? He was pressing her. Tennis?

Hearing the second woman tentatively agree to a tennis date, the hostess leaned across the table and warned, "If you play tennis with him, you better wear your diaphragm at net."

To understand how Jordan has reached the top, it helps to think of his life as the tale of two cities, yesterday's Atlanta and today's Washington. For his youth in the first of these segregated cities prepared him especially well for his eminence in the second.

Jordan was born in 1935, the middle of three sons. He was named for his father, a mail clerk at a local military base. But the key to Vernon Jordan, clearly, is the force of nature who gave birth to him, a small but powerful woman named Mary Griggs Jordan.

The daughter of a sharecropper from Talbot County, GA, she started a catering business in the Depression and labored seven days a week to boost her family into the middle class. Although the Jordans were poor, "Vernon was less poor than most of us," recalls Lyndon Wade, president of the Atlanta Urban League.

Mary had a posh clientele on the city's north side, in the highest reaches of Atlanta society, for weddings, teas, cocktail parties, dinners. In the office from which her youngest son, Windsor, continues to run the business, two photo albums show the daily backdrop of the Jordans' lives, page after page of white: the white of fine linen, of deviled eggs, of thickly iced wedding cakes, of brides' dresses, of Mary Jordan's uniform, of her clients' faces.

From their earliest days, Vernon and Windsor Jordan were in and out of those clients' houses. They passed hors d'oeuvres, washed up, poured the punch; in the summer, they stood sentry by the buffet and shooed flies away with giant fans made from newspaper. From pre-adolescence, Vernon learned to serve as a bartender, pouring for revelers after Georgia Tech-Vanderbilt football games, mixing drinks at Georgia Tech fraternity parties—places he would never, under any other conditions, have been invited to go.

Everyone who knows Vernon Jordan thinks these experiences were formative. Says Lyndon Wade, "It takes some of the mystery out of how the other side lives. It tells you there *is* another side. . . . And I think it helped give him an idea what money and power were all about."

The main lesson absorbed from his mother, according to Windsor Jordan, was this: "It was like you knew there were two worlds, two lifestyles. And the idea was to get to that other style."

That style was also displayed at home, where Mary Jordan made her family the same fancy food she made for her clients. "We wanted to eat chitlins and collard greens and things," says Windsor, laughing. Most excruciating for the little boys, he says, were the sandwiches they found in their lunchboxes: elegant things, the crusts cut off, chicken salad or papery slices of ham. "You couldn't match it up against a good Spam sandwich."

It wasn't as though Jordan had only white models to consult. Atlanta, in the 1940s and 1950s, was a relative mecca for southern blacks. Thus, though the city was rigidly segregated, even a poor black boy had the opportunity to see people like him in the roles of doctor, university president, banker, lawyer—men like A. T. Walden, who litigated the earliest civil-rights cases. And Vernon lived near Atlanta University Center, the enclave that houses six historically black colleges, including two of America's best, Morehouse and Spelman.

Atlanta's thriving black middle class is often cited as a reason the city produced so many leaders of the civil rights movement. But "what set Jordan apart," says Julian Bond, "was that he also saw into the other world."

Every month, from the time Vernon was thirteen, Mary catered the meeting of the Lawyers Club of Atlanta—filet mignon and strawberry shortcake. Vernon was especially fascinated by these men. This was something different from admiring the handful of black lawyers he knew; it was only when the white bar gathered that he could see lawyers as the rightful rulers of their own subculture. It was the number of them, the *ease* of them, that struck him.

"I liked the way they dressed," Jordan recalls. "I didn't like the way they talked necessarily; I didn't like what they said, sometimes not stuff that I thought was right. But I liked their demeanor, their *decorum*. I was impressed by that and liked the way they wore their shirts and stuff."

Even at a young age, Jordan was attuned to matters like clothes. "Vernon was always conscious of being dressed," remembers Windsor. "Going to school, I'd always have to stop and wait for him to go back and change *again*, so he'd look, as we'd say, *sharp*."

Though *Brown v. Board of Education* was decided the year after Vernon graduated from high school, the civil-rights movement was not a chief concern of Mary Jordan's. "With my mother, it wasn't about color," stressed Windsor Jordan. "It was about money. It was about business and money. She'd say, 'If you got some money, you can do most anything you want.'"

When Vernon was ready to graduate from high school, an honor student, he took all these lessons to heart. With the encouragement of a New York service organization, he looked north to choose a college, and enrolled in Indiana's DePauw University (Dan Quayle's alma mater), where he would be the only black student in his class. "I liked it because it was different, and I liked it because it was a challenge," he says.

When it came time to pick a law school, however, he chose DC's black Howard University. By then it was clear that the most important legal work in the South was in the area of civil rights, and Howard was the chief training ground for those who were bringing legal challenges to segregation in state after state.

By 1960, Vernon was ready to go home, armed with a law degree and an ambition large enough to encompass both a revolutionary social movement and a desire to make good.

While Jordan's friends tend to romanticize his civil-rights years as two decades of self-sacrifice, detractors tend to describe him as a man of more flash than substance—a civil-rights leader whose eye was always on the corporate path. The truth is less simple than either of these formulations allows. For Jordan, as for many other participants, civil rights was legitimately a career as well as a cause. And just as his work today bears traces of his civil-rights work, his years in the civil-rights movement foreshadowed his current choices in life.

His first job was in the law firm of Donald L. Hollowell, an eminent black attorney who was handling many of the breakthrough legal cases that would desegregate colleges around the state. He was, says Julian Bond, "Georgia's Thurgood Marshall. . . . For Vernon to be associated with his firm was a real plum, and meant Vernon was a comer, and was on his way—not in terms of riches, but in terms of being in line for a lifelong, illustrious career in civil rights."

Hollowell and an Atlanta civil-rights organization had recruited two young black students, Charlayne Hunter and Hamilton Holmes, to apply to the University of Georgia, in the hope of creating a case that would force the state's compliance with the Supreme Court's ruling that public education must be desegregated.

It was Jordan who, in weeks of digging, found the final bit of evidence that countered the university's stalling tactics—identifying a white student who had been accepted in spite of a set of circumstances identical to the ones the admissions committee claimed stood in the way of Hunter's admission. In January 1961, a federal judge ordered that the students be admitted, and it was Jordan who escorted them through a surly crowd for their enrollment.

From Hollowell's office, Jordan went to work for the NAACP as the Georgia field director. It was the first of a series of jobs that would characterize him as a member of the more conservative, administrative end of the movement. In the early '60s, the venerable NAACP was criticized by members of younger, more aggressive groups such as the Student Nonviolent Coordinating Committee, and even by Martin Luther King Jr.'s more moderate Southern Christian Leadership Conference.

But it would be unfair to see Jordan only as an NAACP bureaucrat who played it safe. Says Bond,

> Part of his job involved going into these little rural towns where there was some danger being a black man in a suit, let alone a black man from the NAACP. Being seen in a suit, driving a car, in some of these little counties where everyone knows each other, was a real act of courage.

From the NAACP he moved to the Southern Regional Council, and then to the Voter Education Project, which was begun under the council's auspices. Funded by New York-based foundations, it was a Kennedy-inspired program started in 1962 to channel the civil-rights movement's efforts in a way that would keep racial strife off the front pages of the newspapers and, as a happy by-product, produce hundreds of thousands of new Democratic voters. Jordan's term as director of the project, from 1965 to 1970, may constitute his most lasting legacy to the civil-rights movement.

Taylor Branch, author of *Parting the Waters: America in the King Years 1954–63*, was hired by Jordan as a graduate student to work for the project. He observes,

> It was unglamorous scut work—registering voters in the South—at a time when everyone else had turned into a revolutionary or a business executive. There was a terrible irony: that the Voting Rights Act had finally been passed [in 1965], and all the people who had sacrificed and risked so much were running off to join the Black Panthers. There was no one to follow through. Vernon was one of the few leaders who stuck with it. . . . When he worked for the Voter Education Project, which is when I knew him up close, he didn't really fit the image you hear a lot of people knock him with.

If it was laborious work, it was also the beginning of Jordan's exposure to the world of foundations and corporations. Having revealed his gifts as a fund-raiser, Jordan was lured north in 1970 to be executive director of the United Negro College Fund. But he had served less than two years when Whitney Young, the longtime leader of the National Urban League, drowned during a trip to Nigeria. Jordan, only thirty-five, was asked to succeed him.

Jordan became a national figure there—and an accomplished corporate politician. The Urban League had always been the black organization most closely allied with business, reaching back to the days of its founding, before World War I; its original mission was to alleviate the poor living conditions of urban blacks, with special emphasis on job training and placement. And after the racial violence of the late '60s, corporations and the federal government were more ready than ever to strike alliances with a moderate group that could speak their language.

Jordan was brilliant at exploiting this. He was so good at raising money that the group's operating budget doubled in the ten years he was director. And he became well known among corporate CEOs at precisely the time that they were beginning to understand that they would have to integrate their boards of directors. In his decade at the Urban League, Jordan was invited to join the boards of R.J. Reynolds, Xerox, American Express, Celanese, J.C. Penney, and Bankers Trust.

* * *

Increasingly, Jordan's social circle and his aspirations lay with this corporate world. He lived in New York, in a co-op on Fifth Avenue overlooking Central Park. His approach—while outwardly more political, more aggressive in advancing a civil-rights agenda, than the League had been in the past—was sometimes criticized for being too attuned to the concerns of the black middle class, at the expense of the poor. But the grumbling was kept in check by Jordan's undoubted dynamism. He had developed a high visibility for himself and for the League at a time when the news media were looking for a way to explain the fractured civil-rights movement; Jordan—handsome, well connected, with a large and respectable organization as his platform—was a media darling.

During his time at the League, Jordan faced two personal ordeals. The first was the decline of his wife, Shirley, who had been diagnosed with multiple sclerosis in 1965, only seven years after the couple married and when their daughter, Vickee, was only five. By the late 1970s, Shirley could no longer get around without a wheelchair. "She held on to the end," recalls Commerce Secretary Ron Brown, who worked with Jordan at the Urban League. "She resisted, *resisted* going in a wheelchair. She wanted to do as much for herself as she could. . . . . [But] in the end she became very dependant on him." She fought the disease until 1985, when she died at the age of forty-eight.

"That's very personal," Jordan says, when asked to discuss it.

That was a major trauma for our little girl, for me, and for her. But you do what you have to do in this life, and so you make all the necessary adjustments, sacrifices, to see to it that she could live as normal a life as possible—and she did that.

The second crisis of his forties was as sudden as a sniper's bullet. On May 29, 1980, at two o'clock in the morning, Jordan was shot in the parking lot of a Marriott hotel in Fort Wayne, IN. It was an astonishing crime, for racial hatreds had cooled somewhat from their peak in the previous two decades, and, in any case, Jordan was not the sort of leader who had ever really incited those passions.

At first, the police suspected that the shooter's motive had been personal: At the time of the attack, Jordan was getting out of the car of a white woman, an attractive, four-times-divorced local Urban League volunteer named Martha C. Coleman. He had had cocktails with Coleman after giving the speech that had brought him to Fort Wayne; at one o'clock in the morning, they told police, they had left in her car to have coffee at her house.

Though Jordan and Coleman told the police that they had spent less than half an hour at her house, the circumstances were such as to suggest that some disgruntled lover of hers might have tried to kill him. Ultimately, however, the local police and FBI developed strong evidence that the shooting had been a racial act committed by a stranger. The Justice Department indicted an avowed racist named Joseph Paul Franklin on charges of violating Jordan's civil rights. By the time of his trial, Franklin was serving four life sentences for the murders—committed three months after Jordan's shooting—of two black men he had seen jogging with white women in Salt Lake City. But though many of those involved in the Jordan case—including Jordan, up to the present day—felt that Franklin was indeed the shooter, he was acquitted for lack of evidence.

Jordan, who suffered a wound the size of a small fist just an inch from his spine, spent ninety-eight days in the hospital. Today, he bats away questions about the shooting. "There's only one thing to say about being shot and that is I woke up this morning and put my feet on the floor and that's it, that's history." On his doctors' advice he saw a psychiatrist for a few months. "He is convinced and I was convinced that I was not traumatized by it," Jordan says. "I don't dream about it, I don't think about it. I have no bitterness and I am not afraid."

Even before the shooting, Jordan had grown restless in his work at the Urban League. It was a staggering idea, to other black leaders, that Jordan should want to quit such a high-visibility job. He sensed, however that his power base as a civil-rights leader might be parlayed into a different kind of power on a wider stage. There were still two worlds, and the idea was still to get to that other one.

Jordan asked his friends Walter Wriston, then head of Citicorp, and C. Peter McColough, then head of Xerox, to put out feelers to law firms in New York and Washington. McColough mentioned Jordan's ambitions to Robert S. Strauss, the Washington lawyer-lobbyist and founding partner of the Texas-based firm, Akin, Gump. Strauss jumped at the chance to hire Jordan.

Akin, Gump is one of the most aggressive firms in Washington at plying the seam between the public and private sectors. It has more than two dozen partners who are registered as lobbyists, for clients ranging from

AT&T to Burger King, from the governments of Columbia and Chile to Japan's Fujitsu and Matsushita, from the Motion Picture Association of America to the National Football League.

The firm's Washington practice was built largely on the strength of Strauss' ties to political figures. A relentless self-promoter who has back-slapped his way to the status of Washington power broker, Strauss served as Democratic National Committee chairman from 1972 to 1977 and as U.S. trade representative in the Carter era. That Akin, Gump is a highly political firm is attested to by its fund-raising: For example, in the 1990 election cycle—through both individual donations and the firm's political-action committee—it gave more money to federal candidates than any other law firm in the country, according to an analysis by the Center for Responsive Politics.

From the moment Vernon Jordan arrived in Washington, he made it quite clear that he was breaking with his past. "He said, 'I ain't no civil-rights leader anymore,'" recalls Eleanor Holmes Norton. "'I'm not going on television to talk about it anymore; that's for people whose job that is.'"

Jordan told another friend in the early '80s, "When I left the Urban League, I determined that I would do nothing for the next 10 or 15 years but make money for myself." Adds this friend, dryly, "He came to the right place in Strauss' firm."

Jordan earns, according to informed speculation, legal fees of close to a million dollars a year. In addition he earns handsome board fees. To the boards on which he already sat (minus Celanese, of which he was no longer a director), he added more after joining Akin, Gump: Dow Jones, Corning, Sara Lee, Union Carbide, Ryder System, and Revlon. Assuming Jordan attends all scheduled board meetings, as well as meetings of board committees on which he serves, his fees, according to information compiled by the nonpartisan Investor Responsibility Research Center, amount to at least $504,000 a year.

Jordan's wife, Ann—a former professor of social work at the University of Chicago whom he married in 1986—is herself on five corporate boards: Capital Cities/ABC, the Hechinger Company, Johnson & Johnson, National Health Laboratories, and Primerica. Her board fees add a potential $202,600 to the family's annual income.

When he retires, Jordan's boards will pay him at least $160,000 annually for the following fifteen years. And he controls stock worth more than $1.5 million in all the companies he serves. A final benefit of Jordan's board service is in the legal work he scares up for Akin, Gump. Of the eleven companies he is associated with, six are clients of the firm.

But what exactly does Jordan do for his law firm? His major clients include American Airlines and Mazda; his major areas of concern are variously described as mergers and acquisitions and, in the words of a partner, "counseling clients who have problems in which Washington plays a substantial role." He has also, on at least one occasion, put his civil-rights background to use for a client: when the Pharmaceutical Manufacturers Association went to war against a proposed law that would have cut Medicaid costs by mandating the substitution of generic drugs for more expensive name brands. As part of Akin, Gump's lobbying campaign against the proposal, orchestrated largely by Jordan, groups representing minorities argued that the proposal would consign those minorities to inferior medical care.

But Jordan is registered as a lobbyist on only one account, American Airlines. Typically, men like Bob Strauss and Vernon Jordan easily slip through the porous lobbying-disclosure laws. While lobbyists for foreign interests are required to register with the Justice Department, and those who lobby senators or House members must register with an office in Congress, no one need register in order to lobby for a domestic client before any agency of the federal government. And even in areas requiring registration, someone at Jordan's level isn't necessarily reflected in the records. "Guys like him, they don't like doing legislative work much," says a former colleague. "So they'll outline the strategy and then some associate will go up and do the work."

"The tricky thing about rainmakers is you never can really tell what they do," says Charles Lewis, executive director of the Center for Public Integrity. "They don't have to register anywhere; all they do is meet with people."

The presumed expertise of men like Strauss and Jordan is not in any legal skill but in their supposed great knowledge of Washington, their "judgment" on corporate affairs. "Vernon does not do a lot of heavy lifting, to put it mildly," says one person close to the firm.

"If you have some notion that I spend a lot of time in the library," says Jordan, "that is not the highest and best use of my time. . . . I don't need to do that—there are people who do that for me." Echoes Strauss, "Vernon and I are never going to be great lawyers. Vernon sure wasn't brought in here because we wanted him to read the fine print of the law."

Still, a rainmaker has to deliver. And in his early years at the firm, Jordan was something of a disappointment, according to a 1986 article in *The American Lawyer.* "He was not quite as big a star as he was expected to be," says one former colleague. But, over time, his reputation improved. Firm members learned that he was a gifted stroker of clients and a talented contributor to the internal politics of the firm, and they elected him to the management committee in 1991.

Jordan's association with Bill Clinton clinched his importance. "Of course, now they're thrilled with him," says one source about Jordan's partners. "Now they all think he's the greatest thing since sliced bread."

He may be especially crucial in light of Strauss' recent miscalculations. Once known as "Mr. Democrat," Strauss dealt with twelve years of Republican rule by assiduously courting Reagan and then Bush. When, in 1991, Strauss accepted Bush's appointment as ambassador to the Soviet Union, it looked like a canny move: The 1992 election was shaping up as a debacle for Democrats, and a role as senior diplomat would be a good alibi for his absence. When Bush bombed and Clinton unexpectedly succeeded, Strauss returned to Washington eager to drop the phrase "my law partner Vernon Jordan."

If it is hard to pin down the precise nature of Vernon Jordan's law practice, that fact is itself a key to understanding him. The role of any lawyer-lobbyist is amorphous, based at least half on perception; in addition to selling his clients' wishes to the federal government, he is also selling his client on the idea of his own omnipotence within Washington.

And Vernon Jordan has an especially rich lode of symbolic weight to offer. So rich that in many parts of his life it is enough for him simply to *be* Vernon Jordan, going the places he goes and seeing the people he sees. Knowing Jordan, being associated with Jordan, is a commodity with a particular value in each of the spheres he occupies—social, corporate, and political.

In September 1990, Jordan was a guest at a surprise forty-fifth-birthday party for Michael Boskin, the chairman of Bush's Council of Economic Advisers. Held by former "Wonder Woman" Lynda Carter and her husband, attorney Robert Altman, it drew a predominantly Republican crowd: a few Republican senators, a smattering of media, and a handful of Bush Cabinet members, such as Jack Kemp.

Kemp stood to give a toast, which led him to talk of his eye-opening experiences as HUD secretary. In the last year, he remarked, he had probably been to more public housing projects than Vernon Jordan.

"And Vernon," recalls one observer, "with that great booming voice, yelled from the back of the room, 'And I don't intend to go!'"

It is a story that illustrates something of Jordan's special function in the world of Washington society. For Washington is two cities, the federal city and the local one. The federal city, and the ingrown social life that revolves around it, is overwhelmingly white, but the city onto which it is grafted is mostly black, with a government that is almost universally black. "Washington is an extremely segregated city," notes Peggy Cooper Cafritz, a black civic activist married to a prominent white real-estate developer. Most social events in white Washington, she says, include only "somewhere between 1 and 10" African Americans.

Most of those who move in white government circles exhibit a sort of anxious resignation about this. Their culture is fundamentally a liberal one, and they have a nervous feeling that they *should* do better. Thus they speak about Jordan with an enormous relief, even gratitude. He is their exception, their touchstone.

He is their black friend.

"It's very hard to have good black friends in this town," says a very prominent Washingtonian. "It damn well is. . . . I mean *real* friends: people you see, where you go to their house. And Vernon is that to a great many people."

Says a well-known woman,

> There was a period in the '60s when everyone socialized with blacks to show how hip they were. They invited all the blacks they knew to parties, and made sure to kiss them and touch them. And it was all artificial. . . . So then in the '70s and early '80s, everybody pulled away from that. Like, "O.K., we've proved we're liberal—let's just do what we're comfortable with."

The result was a return to the all-white dinner party. "And then along came Vernon. And it was clear he knew how to speak the language—not just the white language, but the Washington social language. He'd say, 'I was talking to Liz and Felix [Rohatyn] last week. . . . '" Ann Jordan, she adds, "can talk about Porthault linens and buying a little Chanel bag."

In other words, the Jordans are seen as the *class* equals of anyone in

Washington. "People feel grateful, because they feel that they're not racist but that it *really is* hard," continues the woman. "There's a wall of glass between blacks and whites socially. And with the Jordans, you feel that you're their peer, a social equal—there's no barrier there."

Vernon Jordan would not be nearly so valuable in this role were he not a certified civil-rights hero. Some of his Washington friends were a little shocked when Jordan's transition service caused newspapers to write about the full extent of his board work: They treasure the idea of Vernon Jordan as a man still fundamentally devoted to good causes, and the knowledge that he served not on four or seven but on eleven boards suddenly colored his life a bit differently. It is precisely because his image touches such extremes—the civil-rights movement and the company of Liz and Felix— that he is in a position to bring comfort to the guilty members of the liberal elite.

Jordan's role in corporate boardrooms, where he is the only African American on all but one of the boards he serves, is similar. According to a recent study by the Connecticut newsletter *Directorship*, blacks hold 222 seats on boards of the Fortune 1,000 companies, out of a total 9,592; Jordan occupies a staggering 5 percent of those seats. Some of Jordan's detractors complain that his board service is merely a form of tokenism. It is a fact that, in the words of compensation expert Graef Crystal, the typical CEO looks to stock his board with "10 friends of management, a woman, and a black." But Jordan's achievement, for better or worse, is that on those boards where he sits, he is not only the single black but also one of the club—a friend of the CEO.

Only a member of the club would find himself a guest at California's exclusive all-male Bohemian Grove gathering. In July 1991, he gave the annual lakeside talk, choosing civil rights as his topic. "Business does not come to the debate with clean hands," he said. "I sit on enough corporate boards and enjoy the friendship of enough corporate executives to know that there isn't a company in the nation that can be satisfied with its hiring and promotions record."

Or, as he paraphrased the speech to a white friend back in Washington, "just because you invite some nigger to this place, that doesn't let you off the hook."

But it's not clear whether, for the corporate chieftains who thronged around the lake, this constituted anything more than a ritual shriving.

Leslie Dunbar, who was once Jordan's boss at the Southern Regional Council, says, "I think somehow or another they know they can take their medicine from Vernon, and then afterwards they can share a drink with him."

In *Barbarians at the Gate,* an account of the leveraged buyout of RJR Nabisco, authors Bryan Burrough and John Helyar paint an unflattering portrait of Jordan as a board member concerned more with his own benefits than with the long-term interests of the company.

Jordan raises this before I do. "There was a suggestion in *Barbarians* that I was a patsy for CEOs. Well, that's just bullshit," he says. "I've never been a patsy for anything or anybody. . . . They don't know what the fuck they're talking about."

On six of his boards, he sits on the public-responsibility committee or its equivalent, which puts him in a position to ride herd on the companies' equal-employment policies. Harry Freeman, formerly a top executive at American Express, says Jordan was very aggressive. "It wasn't lip service. He would say, 'How are we doing on minorities? What are the latest statistics on minority recruiting, and how do they match the statistics on minority population?' He would say, 'Have you tried X, Y, or Z college?'"

These efforts are in keeping with other efforts Jordan makes in the context of his legal work. He is chairman of the National Academy Foundation, a private group that promotes corporate involvement in urban high schools. He is said to be a generous counselor of young black professionals. He chairs a forum created by the D.C. Bar to promote the advancement of minorities in the city's law firms. And in 1990 and 1991 he logged long hours trying to broker cooperation between corporate America and the civil-rights community in supporting a new civil-rights act.

To his fans, he seems to have struck the ideal balance between doing well and doing good: "Don't misunderstand me," says Dunbar. "Vernon is quite prepared to benefit personally. But I don't believe there is any position he's ever held that he has not tried, usually successfully, to make his situation in that job of benefit to other blacks."

But others point out that those efforts tend to go toward helping blacks who already have a surfeit of opportunity. "The only people he helps now are the ones already on the ladder. The talented 10th," says Cathy Hughes, the controversialist host of a black-oriented DC radio talk show. "It's the 90 percent who are not the exception that the Vernon Jordans of the world don't reach back and touch."

Jordan sees himself as holding "emeritus status" in the civil-rights movement. "I'm not a general, but I'm still in the army. And you can't leave the army, in a sense. . . . I am not so assimilated that I have lost my sensitivities to the basic inequities confronting minority people in this country."

But, finally, aren't there bound to be conflicts in the heart of a man like Vernon Jordan? I tell him that I am mystified by the apparent lack of tension in his life, the contradictions that show no ripple in the surface, if they are experienced as contradictions at all. He shrugs, steeples his hands on his spotless desk, and smiles his most radiant smile. "Well," he says finally, "I can't help you with the *mysss-ter-y*."

The answer to the riddle may be more interesting than a simple hypocrisy. To a young black boy growing up in Atlanta, working for white people while living and fixing his aspirations among black people, it was a fact of life that different standards applied in the two worlds he inhabited. It wasn't wrong to bow to this knowledge; there was, ultimately, a kind of authority in playing your role in the white community well.

The facility for filling separate, even contradictory, roles is not something Vernon Jordan learned recently. But he has put it to great advantage in his career. And in choosing to go to Washington, and, more recently, into Democratic politics, he may have found its highest use.

Vernon Jordan met Bill and Hillary Clinton some twenty years ago. His friendship with Hillary was cemented by their joint work on the board of the Children's Defense Fund, while he and the future president kept in touch the way ambitious politicians will do.

Perhaps they recognized that they are somewhat similar: Like Jordan, Clinton is the product of a matriarchal home that propelled him up from the lower middle class. Like Jordan, he is a man skilled at, perhaps addicted to, the seduction of everyone he meets. And like Jordan, he is a real liberal, except when he's not—a complicated mix of personal ambition and purer motives.

When Clinton decided to run for president, Jordan was an early and fervent supporter. He developed an informal advisory role in the campaign, which led to his appointment as transition chairman.

Once again, he was not the man hired for the heavy lifting. As the transition unfolded, the most important work was done in Little Rock, under director Warren Christopher's efficient managerial eye. What Jordan did do, back in Washington, was serve as Bill Clinton's ambassador-at-large to the strange new country Clinton had conquered: charming the television cameras, stroking the reporters—infinitely reassuring, no matter what kind of reassurance you were looking for. When women's groups became upset at the way the Cabinet was taking shape, Vernon was the man to soothe them. When certain congressional leaders needed assurances that Clinton would not muck with this or that prerogative, Vernon was the man to pass the message. "He's the show horse and [Christopher] is the workhorse," said one sharp-eyed Democrat during the transition. "He's like the expensive greeter at the restaurant."

And there was a larger message being sent, on a grander scale than the day-to-day stroking of interest groups and egos. Clinton's campaign had brilliantly balanced the tensions that have pulled at the Democratic Party since the late '70s—between its low-income constituents and its high-income donor base, between its populist, liberal character outside the Beltway and its wealthy, business-oriented power structure within Washington. Now that the campaign was over, Vernon Jordan was the wink and the nod—the sign, from the new president to the Old Guard, that he understood their culture and would not combat it.

This was precisely what distressed reformists observant enough to understand the appointment's meaning. "I'm not saying Vernon Jordan is the worst guy who ever walked," says Charles Lewis of the Center for Public Integrity. "I'm just saying it was disappointing. . . . My objection to Jordan is that he is part of politics as usual."

While there were dozens of men (and they *are* all men) who might have provided the same kind of reassurance Jordan gave to the barons of Washington, there were none who carried the same aura of liberal probity. Jordan, with his elastic persona, his sure touch for the extremes of American society, was the perfect symbol for the new president. For Clinton ran on the proposition that a party could embrace extremes as great as those Vernon Jordan has lived out, and he hopes to govern by the same assumption.

As the transition went on, Clinton's disinclination to disturb the mores of Washington became even more obvious. Among his permanent appointments were several people with lobbying portfolios far more controversial than Jordan's, notably Ron Brown as commerce secretary (with former clients including the government of Haiti under Jean-Claude Duvalier and a host of Japanese corporations) and Mickey Kantor in the role of U.S. trade representative (with former clients ranging from Philip Morris to Lockheed, Martin Marietta, and Occidental Petroleum).

Why was Vernon Jordan not among Clinton's Cabinet picks? For some weeks he was widely thought to lead Clinton's shortlist for attorney general. Was entering the administration ever a serious possibility? "Sure, it was in question," Jordan replies. "I spent some time being titillated by the governor. Then I went down to Little Rock . . . and had a great conversation with Bill and Hillary and we worked it out. That's all I'm going to say." It's the practiced answer of a pro: just enough to convince the listener that he was a serious contender; not enough to be pinned on if in fact he was never offered the job.

Washington speculated that Jordan didn't want the hassle and potential embarrassment of a confirmation hearing, didn't want to take the cut in pay, and—most plausibly—didn't want to cut himself off from the corporate world in which he has such a singular role.

But all of this speculation somewhat missed the point. Jordan can continue to be an advisor to Clinton, a message bearer to and from the White House, a member of that famous club of men who earn, to their own tremendous profit, the Washington sobriquet of "wise man." The point is: Vernon Jordan already has a job in the new administration.

—March 1993

THE HACK
(TONY COELHO)

"This is a man who, in my view, is extremely bright, is extremely dedicated, is extremely political," says Tony Coelho, discussing Bill Clinton with the slightly contemptuous generosity most political handlers bring to describing the boss. "He has all the tools it takes to be extremely successful. But I think it's a question of understanding what the public wants. He came in understanding that he was running against Washington, that Washington was the problem. And what's happened is that he got trapped in Washington."

It is not the substance of this observation that startles, but the source. Speaking within days of the Democrats' stunning losses in the November election,* the senior political adviser and former congressman is mouthing what has already become the conventional wisdom about why American voters so summarily rejected the president's party at the polls. But there is high irony in hearing this line of analysis from Tony Coelho. For he is the very embodiment of the Washington culture that voters so resoundingly rejected. And nowhere was Clinton's imprisonment in the snares of the capital more apparent than in his reliance on Tony Coelho.

Coelho was appointed in August 1994 to be a temporary "senior advis-

---

* It would be difficult to overstate what a fiasco the 1994 midterm elections were for the Democrats. For the first time in more than forty years, Republicans won a majority in the House of Representatives. They've held onto it ever since. The GOP also won a Senate majority, and, excepting a two-year interruption from 2001 to 2003, they've held on to that, too.

er" to the Democratic National Committee, a high-profile post that made him, in effect, the party's chief. The fifty-two-year-old former Democratic whip was in the enviable position of having a direct line to the White House, an unpaid post that allowed him to continue his lucrative new career as an investment banker, and a public status that marked him as one of the party's most highly valued strategists. Most important of all, the quasi-formal role offered official redemption to the once-disgraced Coelho, who had quit the House five years earlier in response to a personal financial scandal.

Come November 8th, Coelho partisans were quick to point out that no political operative, appointed just a few months before a midterm election, is in a position to determine the outcome of hundreds of congressional races. But if he was not accountable for the Democrats' losses in the immediate terms by which political hacks keep score, he was, on a deeper level, an architect of the disaster—perhaps the one man, besides Bill Clinton, on whom the party's failure is most justly pinned. For, not only did he incarnate Clinton's hapless attachment to the idea that Washington insiders hold special wisdom and deserve special tribute; he also was, in a very real sense, the man who had built the self-serving Democratic House of Representatives that was swept from power on Election Day. Pundits and historians may wrangle for years about the final meaning of the 1994 election. Yet, already, it is clear that it represented the fall of the House of Coelho—the end of an era in the life of the Democratic Party.

But not, ironically, the end of Tony Coelho, for whom the '94 campaign represented something of a resurgence. Indeed, Coelho may be the only Democrat in America who got what he wanted out of the midterm elections. While his party suffered its epic defeat, Coelho passed through the final cycle of the process by which the Washington culture launders the reputations of its disgraced children. *Los Angeles Times* White House correspondent David Lauter describes it as a four-step ritual. "In the first stage, you're a pariah," he muses.

And in the second stage, you're a former pariah who's sort of allowed back into society but has this large scarlet letter stitched to your chest. Then you get into this third stage, where you can take the letter off, but you can't go into a position that requires Senate confirmation. And then if you're really good at it, you get to the fourth stage, where you're deemed to have been purified.

This may explain why Tony Coelho, even in the wake of cataclysmic defeat, wears an air of boundless optimism. I have hardly finished asking him how he feels about the Democrats' loss when—"GREAT!" he says. "Basically, we've been freed, and let's get out there and stand up for what we believe in, and we'll show what the difference is, and come back in '96."

He turns to a parable often cited by his fellow Californian, Ronald Reagan. "You've got to keep looking for that pony when you see a lot of straw," he exhorts. "People accuse me all the time of having my glass half full," he adds. "Well, maybe that's why I'm a success."

Washington is commonly said to be an unforgiving city, bent on the destruction of any man or woman who slips up in the course of public service. And it's true that the capital has a gleeful obsession with small mistakes: the gaffe, the blunder, the ethical lapse; the spousal freebie, the doubled-billed expense, the personal use of a public plane. But the big errors, the mortal sins, the ones that actually leave a lasting mark—these often don't count. The big mistakes, if they are massive enough, and if they unfold slowly enough, and if they are accomplished by people who can boast of short-term achievements, may pass unnoticed in a culture that has no capacity for long-term memory. Tony Coelho is, among other things, just one more piece of evidence that in Washington you can be a "player," a "winner," even a "wise man," despite a history of destructively poor choices.

Coelho spent twenty-five years in the House—thirteen years as an aide to his hometown congressman from California's Central Valley, and twelve as the congressman's successor. He occupied his highest rank, as Democratic whip, during his final term in the House. But it was his service, from 1981 through 1986, as chairman of the Democratic Congressional Campaign Committee (DCCC) that made him, for a time, the most influential young congressman of his generation. Ronald Reagan's first landslide had just snatched the White House and the Senate from Democratic control; it was a political commonplace, at the time, that the House would be the next to fall in this overwhelming realignment. The chairman of the DCCC had been one of the losers in the 1980 election; the barons of the House saw little to lose in assigning the job to the green but gung-ho Coelho.

"The D-triple-C" was a sleepy little shop that held one fund-raising dinner every year and automatically sent small contributions to incumbent members. But Coelho shrewdly understood its potential. In his first four years, he more than quintupled its fund-raising and made it an aggressive instrument to solidify Democratic control of the House. For the first time the committee had its own field staff, its own opposition research and polling; for the first time, Coelho withheld money from safe incumbents to give it to challengers who had plausible shots at taking down Republican members. In the process, Coelho modernized the party's understanding of how to combat Reagan's telegenic appeal, and gave his fellow Democrats a new faith that the GOP juggernaut wasn't unbeatable. "If you go back to '81, '82," recalls Democratic pollster Peter Hart, "everything seemed to flow from Tony."

The positive way of summarizing what Coelho accomplished is to say that he placed a limit on the GOP realignment, preserving the House as a seat of Democratic resistance to Reagan's realignment all through the '80s. Less generous accounts conclude that Coelho sold the party's soul in the process, by vastly expanding the contributions of business political action committees—and the expectations those contributors felt in return. By 1985, Robert Kuttner described him in the *New Republic* as "the Democrats' Dr. Faustus" and "the Milo Minderbinder of the Democratic Party, with something to sell to just about everybody." The crux of Coelho's appeal to businessmen was the unsubtle reminder that Democrats already controlled the House. He went to business and said, in effect, "You might not like us, but we've got our hands on the levers right now; you *have* to give to us." Former DCCC staffer Thomas R. Nides, who joined the Clinton administration as chief of staff to U.S. Trade Representative Mickey Kantor, summarizes Coelho's attitude with a perhaps unconscious candor, saying Coelho felt that "if a member deserved business support, that there's no reason just because they happen to be a Democrat that they shouldn't receive it."

"He was the mastermind of the candidates' appeal . . . to the corporate world, through their business PACs," says Ellen Miller, executive director of the Center for Responsive Politics, a political reform group. "What that has meant, pretty clearly, is a kind of stifling of what had been the predictable Democratic response on a whole host of issues."

Under Coelho, the DCCC for the first time began accepting "soft money," donations that are raised and used in ways that get around federal giving limits. Basically, these "party-building" funds—used for everything from voter-turnout programs to office overhead—are a back-door means of getting contributions from wealthy interests that are willing to spend more than what they are allowed under federal ceilings; it's also the only way that corporations can make direct political donations. He also started the "Speaker's Club," which offered business PACs, for a contribution of $15,000, the chance to "serve as trusted, informal advisers to the Democratic Members of Congress."

This was, in short, access-peddling. Republicans had pioneered many of these tactics, but for them, cozying up to business posed no conflict with the party's ideology; for Democrats, on the other hand, reliance on business money challenged the party's basic identity. For the first time, Coelho had explicitly severed the connection between the party's goals and the sources of its funding.

In Washington, a conversation about political money is conducted in cliches. It is a conversation dominated by pragmatists like Coelho, who say that political contributions are just a means to an end; that you have to play by the rules that are on the ground, whether you like them or not; that you can't unilaterally disarm while your opponent is socking away PAC money. All these claims have a limited truth. What changed during the '80s, however, was that the House Democrats—with Coelho leading their charge—upset the delicate balance between means and ends: Incumbency became not only the means of furthering Democrats' favored policy goals, but an end in itself.

So proud was Coelho of his achievements that he allowed Brooks Jackson, then a *Wall Street Journal* reporter, to follow him around for the entire election cycle of 1986. It was, observes a Democratic lobbyist, "the dumbest thing Tony ever did." For the result was the book *Honest Graft: Big Money and the American Political Process*, a guided tour of a modern political machine at work.

In the book, we see Coelho shaking down recalcitrant PACs with thinly veiled threats about how their "good relationships" with House Democrats might be "damaged" if they didn't come through for a particular candidate he was backing. We see him fighting the 1986 tax reform bill on behalf of some of the wealthy people and industries who benefited from the most egregious loopholes that the reform bill was meant to close: dealers in real estate tax shelters, independent oil and gas drillers, and the wealthy Gallo wine family (family members were constituents in his district as well as heavy contributors to the DCCC; he helped them avoid inheritance tax on $104 million of their fortune). We see him taking in $95,000 in soft money in one election cycle from Jackie Presser's Teamsters Union, then trying to help Presser, under indictment for embezzling from the union, avoid an anti-racketeering suit brought by the Reagan Justice Department. We see him wrapping his colleagues even further in the contributors' embrace by steering financially strapped members to industry and labor groups that offered them speaking fees and free vacations. We see him helping to kill a campaign finance reform measure that would have limited PAC spending and required full disclosure of soft money.

Most damningly, Jackson and other reporters exposed Coelho as he leapt blindly into bed with the savings and loan industry. He appointed as the DCCC finance cochairman one Dallas multimillionaire, Thomas Gaubert, who was eventually convicted of S&L fraud and barred from the Texas thrift business by federal regulators. Another major DCCC donor was Donald Dixon, later convicted of looting Texas's Vernon Savings & Loan, which ultimately cost U.S. taxpayers $1.3 billion. Coelho was given the use of Vernon corporate aircraft and a luxury yacht, the *High Spirits*, for travel and party fund-raising; when this was reported, he was forced to reimburse almost $50,000—more than half of it from his personal campaign committee—to Vernon, which was by then run by federally appointed conservators. Speaker of the House Jim Wright tried to intercede with federal regulators on behalf of both Gaubert and Dixon—in the latter case, at Coelho's direct urging. In 1987, Coelho also helped S&L owners by scaling back a bill authorizing funds that bank regulators desperately needed to stay on top of the exploding crisis.

The S&L bailout, which ultimately cost taxpayers more than $200 billion, was a spectacular failure of public policy in which both political parties and several government agencies were complicit. Among Democrats, the better part of the blame rests with the leaders of the House of Representatives in the 1980s—and Coelho is entitled to a large portion of that.

This reckoning was still years away when Coelho was elected, in December 1986, to the number-three slot in the House leadership, as Democratic whip. It was the first time that whip was an elective rather than an appointive position, and Coelho called in the many chits he had earned in showering money on his colleagues. Coelho had risen so far and so fast almost exclusively on his affinity for politics. He was a stickler for constituent service, and worked hard for the big agriculture interests in his district; his colleagues also valued him as a sharp legislative tactician. But, beyond a commitment to expanding the rights of the disabled and a generally liberal outlook on social programs, Coelho wasn't widely identified with a policy agenda. "Tony wasn't really interested in the substance of issues," says former Oklahoma congressman Mike Synar. "He was good at 'em, but that wasn't his forte, that's not where he wanted to make his mark."

Coelho is a small man, and slight, but he carries himself like a big guy—the effect, perhaps, of having spent a quarter-century of his professional life in the orbit of men like Dan Rostenkowski and Tip O'Neill. He is a man of great and sunny energy, who gets only a few hours of sleep each night and jokes about the daily doses of phenobarbital he takes to manage the epilepsy he has had since he was a teenager. "My staff," he told me brightly, "always comments, what would I be like if I weren't taking downers every day?" He was the first in his family to go to college, powered by an ambition that carried him far from the failed dairy farm of his parents, second-generation immigrants from the Azores. Yet, he is not one of those public men in whom you imagine a hidden richness that belongs to the private man alone. With Coelho, it all goes into his work, into a life of driving effort and shiny surfaces.

His political method is an incessant networking: getting others to like him, or better yet, to need him. He has a vast, seamless web of "friends"—political connections, financial associates, former staffers, family acquaintances, charitable contacts. Today he maintains a computer Rolodex of 4,361 names; he holds a reunion, every other year, for former members of his staff, right down to people who once worked for him as interns and pages. One advantage of his method is the armor it provides: "I don't know anybody who really despises Tony Coelho, on a personal level. I don't know anyone who thinks this is an evil man," says Brooks Jackson, who is now a reporter for CNN.

There are liberals who think he's sold his party's soul; there are conservatives who are upset because he beat them all the time. But, on a personal level, he always kind of reminded me of Hubert Humphrey: that he's a likable guy. That was kind of Coelho's stock in trade—that he was a world-class guy at making people like him.

Another function of Coelho's method—knowing people, putting them together, obligating them to him—is that it stands in place of his having to believe anything in particular. After just five terms in Congress, he was near the top of the hierarchy; it was often said that Coelho would be speaker one day—if he could muster the patience to wait out those ahead of him in line. But in 1989, as the House was traumatized by a series of ethics investigations that eventually unhorsed Speaker Wright, Coelho too came under scrutiny. And, in keeping with Washington's strange hierarchy of sin, he was called to account not for the web of corruption he had cast over his colleagues, but for smaller, more technical transgressions.

Three years earlier, Coelho had accepted a $50,000 loan from Thomas Spiegel, the head of California's high-flying Columbia Savings & Loan Association, to help Coelho buy a $100,000 junk bond sold through Michael Milken's Drexel Burnham Lambert. (Milken too was a major Coelho backer.) Not only had Coelho failed to report the loan on his disclosure forms, but Spiegel had held the bond until Coelho could arrange the rest of the financing, and so Coelho had ultimately paid only the face value of the bond, pocketing for free the $4,000 or so it had appreciated while Spiegel had held it. Coelho explained most of the problem as a failure on his accountant's part but, given the gathering public awareness of the S&L scandal, his connection to Spiegel couldn't be shrugged off. Furthermore, the bond purchase itself, first reported by the *Washington Post*'s Charles R. Babcock, had the air of a sweetheart deal, for it was part of a hot offering that wasn't normally available to individual investors; some of Milken's most powerful customers were unable to get in on the action.

For Coelho, it was part of a larger pattern of risk, of playing a bit too close to the outer edge of the rules. He was also criticized by Republicans for his investment, in the mid-'80s, in a California firm that marketed computer software for dairy farmers. As chairman of a House subcommittee that dealt in dairy programs—including elements of a huge 1985 farm bill—Coelho was at least theoretically in a position to benefit his own business. (Had Coelho stayed in Congress, he also would have faced a major political problem three years later, after the House Bank scandal* erupted. Coelho was revealed, in 1992, to be on a House ethics committee list of twenty-two "top abusers" of the bank. He had been a member

* The bank in question was a cooperative run by and for House members.

for only twelve of the thirty-nine months that the committee studied, and in every one of those months he overdrew his account—by 316 checks totaling $292,603—effectively giving himself interest-free loans at his colleagues' expense.)

At the time, House Speaker Wright, beset by financial scandals of his own, was clinging to his office by his fingernails. Coelho understood perfectly how his torment would unfold: the long, drawn-out investigation by the House ethics committee that would ensue; the drip, drip, drip of leaks from the inquiry opened by the Justice Department. And, according to Terence McAuliffe, formerly Coelho's finance director at the DCCC,* he was concerned that broader investigations would ensue: "With the tide turned, getting as ugly as it was—were they going to go back and look at every donor who had ever given to the Democratic Congressional Campaign Committee?"

"Tony is a winner above all," says Rochelle Dornatt, who was one of his floor assistants. "And when he got to the point where the cards were stacked against him, and he knew he couldn't win, he changed the game." So Coelho jumped without being pushed, earning the undying gratitude of his shell-shocked fellow Democrats, and admiring reviews from many of the reporters who had covered his career.

But his impact on the House would continue, for the party Tony Coelho had built was a mirror of Tony Coelho. Modern and energetic, infinitely accommodating, and superficially state of the art, it was, in a deep sense, a party without moorings. Coelho had seen to it that the Democrats held on to the House as their one bulwark in Washington. For the next decade, the Democratic House became the party's center of gravity; and from behind the ramparts built with Coelho's money, the House Democrats were able to avoid the painful reckoning that Reagan's vast popularity should have wrung from the opposition party. They retained those parts of their base that couldn't possibly join the Republicans—African Americans, the poor, the determinedly liberal—and broadened their appeal, through Coelho's machine, to a pragmatic business class. For a long time, they would be able to paper over the fact that they hadn't a clue about how to address the realities in between—especially the economic issues that galvanize the traditionally Democratic middle class, whose silent disaffection would only increase as the 1980s became the 1990s.

* Subsequently, he was chairman of the Democratic National Committee.

Coelho was way too smart to hang around Washington, hat in hand, lobbying his former colleagues. The only way to cleanse himself was to change venue entirely for a time, so he turned his sights to Wall Street. He joined Wertheim Schroder & Co., a mid-sized, very Republican investment banking firm, where he became head of the asset management division—the department that invests large pools of money for such clients as unions, state governments, and private pension funds; it's the sort of banking for which you need about $2 million just to get in the door. Many in the firm, where his hiring was not immediately popular, were amazed at how quickly he caught on. But as Representative Steny Hoyer (D-MD) points out, "He chose, obviously, his strength, which is raising capital." His new associates are all quick to say that Coelho is valued for his management skills as well; but his connections were clearly paramount. Wertheim hired Coelho "for his brains and his drive," says president and CEO Steven Kotler. "And, of course, the relationships he made over two decades in politics."

In 1989, the asset management division was in desperate trouble. Despite the bull market of the '80s, its investments had done poorly; its assets under management had fallen by about two-thirds, down to $700 million. By the end of 1994, however, at Coelho's five-year anniversary, assets had topped $4 billion; at least half of the gain, a colleague says, was attributable to Coelho. What his presence did, explains William Smethurst, chairman of Coelho's division, was enable the bank to shorten its recovery.

> When you've been through a bad patch, large clients—especially in the large pension fund area—they want to watch you for three or four years to make sure the improvement can be sustained. . . . But with Tony, as long as we could demonstrate that we were credible, he was able to compress the time frame.

Wertheim's new investors included many of Coelho's old contacts in labor, and several of his longtime allies in business (E&J Gallo Winery, for example) entrusted $19 million to Wertheim's care. While Coelho didn't work as a lobbyist, his Washington connections made him a formidable door opener for Wertheim and its friends. For example, Wertheim decided to try for new business by cosponsoring, with *Variety*, an annual "Business of Entertainment" conference. "It's very difficult to start up something like this," notes Davia B. Temin, Wertheim's marketing director; it was much easier to draw participants to the first conference after Coelho got House Majority Leader Richard Gephardt to speak. Coelho also serves on the boards of five companies, including cable giant TCI, the Nevada casino company Circus Circus Enterprises and Service Corporation International, a huge chain of funeral homes and cemeteries.

Still, for all Coelho's success in New York, it was clear to anyone who knew him well that he was eager for at least an important part-time role in Washington. If you are an insider who has wandered outside and wishes to go back inside, here is what you do:

You keep in touch, dropping in on former colleagues' fund-raisers while in town—not so much that you look hungry, just enough to keep your name on people's lips, create a few chits. You talk a lot to your old allies in the House, then make yourself available to reporters who still value you as a source in finding out what's happening on Capitol Hill.

You dispense advice, which is now held to be tempered by the "perspective" you have gained from leaving Washington. You encourage old colleagues in the House to think of you as someone to whom they can turn for advice on how to deal with the political consequences of a tough vote, or how to structure their fund-raising, or how to earn millions when they, too, leave Congress. You direct your advice to both sides of the aisle; it's especially helpful if a champion schmoozer like George Bush occupies the White House. "Bush and I were always good friends," Coelho says, explaining that Bush's first chief of staff, former New Hampshire governor John Sununu, often sought his advice. "After he got in, he would call me and say, 'Look, I don't know this town. . . . What do you think?'"

You partake of respectable, vaguely bipartisan public-policy causes, as when Coelho signed on to the Committee for Peace and Security in the Gulf, a volunteer committee founded in 1990 to support Bush policy in the Persian Gulf.

You say things like, "I have a sense of obligation to the process."

You rush to the defense of the president's wife (a trail blazed in the era of Reagan, when Nancy Reagan, with her designer-dress scandals and expensive dishes, was constantly offering occasions for opportunistic chivalry). Coelho's chance came early last year, when the story of Hillary Clinton's commodities trading broke. "If a man would have done that, we'd be saying he's smart," Coelho told the *Washington Times*. "Hillary is a symbol, and symbols are the ones that get beat up the most." He publicly advised a group of Hillary defenders, calling themselves the Back-to-

Business Committee, on such matters as placing supportive ads in the *New York Times*.

You work your former staff, the cadre of loyal young men and women who now have attained positions of some importance. When Clinton got elected, these seedlings Coelho had planted over the years bloomed in the persons of former spokesman David Dreyer, who became an influential aide in the White House communications office; Rahm Emanuel, deputy director of communications; Marcia Hale, who was first Clinton's scheduler and then the director of intergovernmental affairs; and Tom Nides, who began the administration as chief of staff to U.S. Trade Representative Mickey Kantor. Coelho also had a good relationship with senior adviser George Stephanopoulos, dating back to the younger man's days as a Capitol Hill staffer. "I think a number of us were pushing, pushing," says Emanuel. "First it started with a number of us calling him. Second, we would say, 'Tony suggested this'—in a meeting, or whatever. It just blossomed."

You send a check to the president's legal defense fund and, for good measure, volunteer ostentatiously to raise money for it if anyone asks you. (In the end, Coelho says, "I was never asked"—perhaps because the trust administering the fund has learned that legally it cannot solicit funds. But last July, he was telling *Legal Times* that "I'm willing to be a major player.")

You see to it that your name is floated for jobs, as Coelho's was, beginning as early as the spring of 1993, for everything from White House deputy chief of staff to Democratic National Committee chairman. David Lauter notes that this "serves both the function of gauging how much resistance there is, and also the function of—it's like desensitization shots that people take for allergies. After repeated exposure, you no longer sneeze when you see the name."

And you make sure, through intermediaries, that all of this is being registered in the public eye. In particular, savvy Coelho-watchers noted a raft of stories about a year into Clinton's presidency that described Coelho as an adviser of rising importance to the White House—and that noted, in passing, that Coelho had received a letter from the Justice Department announcing the close of an investigation that most newspaper readers hadn't even realized was going on. "That sent a signal to the people who *did* know that the whole junk bond deal was not going to result in any charges," says Brooks Jackson. "You don't go around telling people 'I'm not going to be indicted' if you don't have some pretty strong ambitions."

Gradually, through all these means, Coelho became one of a core of "outsiders" to whom the Clinton White House turned for advice. (When White House staffers speak of seeking advice from outsiders, they really mean they're talking to insiders who just happen to work outside of the building.) Beginning with the passage of Clinton's first budget, and continuing with the tough congressional battle over the North American Free Trade Agreement, Coelho was a quiet counselor to his former staff members, and then, through them, to more senior officials. Chief of Staff Thomas F. "Mack" McClarty, as a newcomer to Washington, was an especially receptive target for his expertise. When Leon Panetta became chief of staff, Coelho's influence was clinched: Panetta had also been a congressman from the Central Valley, and the two men had been close political friends for years. Soon Panetta moved to formalize Coelho's role, naming him "senior adviser" to the Democratic National Committee through the fall campaign. In reality, it was a White House political appointment: Coelho got through the entire campaign without setting foot in DNC headquarters on Capitol Hill. His chief roles were to come to Washington at the end of the week and, in Thursday evening and Friday meetings, consult with the president's political staff on matters of "message" and strategy; and to serve as a party spokesman on television, projecting a more mature and combative persona than Clinton's youthful staff had been able to achieve.

The appointment was, in addition, a way to test Coelho's passage through the Four Stages of Redemption; in Steny Hoyer's words, "to see what residuals there were from the '89 resignation." By giving him an official title, the White House would find out how much fire Coelho was likely to draw; but by making it a DNC appointment, Panetta ensured that any squawking over ethics couldn't harm the president too much. But, in any case, Coelho drew very little fire; only a few critics in the liberal advocacy community complained about his new title. As Chuck Lewis, executive director of the Center for Public Integrity, observed with a sigh, "No one seems to mind, except a few of us yammering naysayers." It was a powerful illustration of Washington's unspoken statute of limitations, the promise of amnesia that Coelho won by slipping out of Congress so gracefully when his troubles came. But in order for the Clinton administration to take Coelho in, it had to sign on to a series of fictions.

The first was that he had nothing to gain by being anointed a White House insider. "Obviously, Tony really didn't have any agenda beyond being helpful," says Coelho acolyte Tom Nides. "It wasn't like he was looking for a government job; it wasn't like he was doing business in this town."

Republican congressman Frank Wolf tried to pierce this fiction in a letter to Panetta, charging that "Mr. Coelho's financial, legal and business ties to unions, corporations, pension funds and the like, make his access to the White House and involvement in personnel and policy matters . . . an area ripe with potential conflicts"—especially given the fact that he wasn't required to disclose any of his private clients.

New York Times reporter Stephen Engelberg, in one of the few skeptical newspaper stories about Coelho's new life, documented one of the ways that Coelho had offered his influence as an informal adviser to benefit friends in business. In 1993, the chemical giant Monsanto sought Coelho's help in persuading the Agriculture Department and the Office of Management and Budget to duck a congressional request for a study that might slow down approval of a new genetically engineered hormone to increase milk production in cows. Coelho called a former aide who had gone to work for then-Secretary of Agriculture Mike Espy—a former congressman in whose career Coelho had been very influential. Coelho had helped elect him to Congress in 1986, had talked him up for the Cabinet post in 1992, and then had helped him choose his senior staff. Ultimately, with the OMB's blessing, Congress approved production of the hormone. Gaining an official title could only serve to increase Coelho's influence within the government. Yet he and the White House maintained the merry fiction that, because Coelho wasn't on the federal payroll, he couldn't benefit from having a close, well-advertised association with the president of the United States.

The second fiction was that Coelho had been fully exonerated after his departure from Congress in 1989. "I think the sense was that it had been fully investigated and disposed of," says George Stephanopoulos. Chuck Lewis counters, "He wasn't exonerated; he just wasn't prosecuted. It's a big difference. There's this great Meese-ian notion of ethics, that if you're not indicted, you're an Eagle Scout." In fact, the Justice Department's 1992 letter informed Coelho simply that it had "closed its investigation" of the bond deal; and the House ethics committee never fully aired the matter, because it dropped its investigation when Coelho quit Congress.

Finally, the Clinton administration sold itself on the fiction—more precisely, the legalism—that Coelho's fall from grace was an isolated incident.

In fact, Coelho's fall had everything to do with the manner of his rise. And even though the specifics of his foray into junk bonds did not result in criminal sanctions, they might reasonably have caused Clinton to take a second look at the circumstances of that rise, bearing in mind journalist Michael Kinsley's maxim: that, in Washington, the real scandal lies not in the illegal acts people commit, but in what they can do legally. But Clinton had long since embraced Washington's view that "ethics" is a legal term, and that the only things that matter are the short term, the narrow event. The story of Coelho's rehabilitation is, finally, the tale of how a new young president, on confronting the ancient rites of the capital, went native.

Clinton had, of course, run for president against exactly the politics-as-usual tradition that Coelho exemplified. In his 1992 speech accepting the Democratic nomination, he railed that government had been "hijacked by privileged, private interests" and promised to "break the stranglehold the special interests have on our elections and the lobbyists have on our government." Yet, from the start, Clinton showed a perfect willingness to do business with the existing power structure. By using men like Washington lawyer Vernon Jordan on his transition team, he signaled that he would not challenge the prerogatives of those who had arrived in Washington before him.

And once Clinton was in office, his signals were self-contradictory: Even as he talked of changing the way the Capitol did business, he sought out men like Lloyd Bentsen and Warren Christopher to bring Washington-style respectability to his Cabinet. To chair the DNC, he appointed campaign director David Wilhelm, who once worked for the reformist lobbying group Citizens for Tax Justice, and who promised to return the party's fund-raising base to the small donor; at the same time, Clinton raced to exploit the new advantage that gaining the White House gave the Democrats in raising soft money. In the eighteen months after his election, the DNC raised almost $27 million in soft money, twice what it had raised in a like period during the Bush administration; more than half the money was from business. As time went on, Clinton staffers solicited a close relationship with the lawyers and lobbyists of K Street, bringing them in for regular meetings, making them a part of his legislative strategy in hard-fought battles on the Hill.

Despite these overtures, whenever the president made a political error, he was subject to a constant chorus of criticism that he didn't understand how Washington worked; that his administration lacked "serious players." Clinton seemed weirdly willing to accept the idea that there was some transcendent quality of Washington savvy that his operation lacked. He responded by hiring as temporary advisers a series of men who knew the secret handshake, propitiation to the Gods of Insider Wisdom. First came the appointment of Republican David Gergen, in May 1993, as counsel to the president. Then came the hiring of superlawyer Lloyd Cutler as counsel, in an effort to salve Clinton's Whitewater wounds. Coelho was just one more in the series, brought in to stifle congressional Democrats' crisis of confidence in the White House political operation. House Democrats reacted predictably. Massachusetts Representative Barney Frank says, "My reaction to Tony being there was, 'Hey, great, the adults are back.'"

Up to a point, one can understand Clinton's inclination to play along with the conventions of a theater that he did not invent. For the press corps tends to promote this game, treating appointments like these as substantive signs of presidential sagacity. As one of Clinton's more centrist, "New Democrat" advisers comments, "Sometimes things get to the point where the only way you can quiet Washington insiders is to give them something to get them off your backs, even if it isn't something real." Moreover, some practical lessons can be learned from insiders about how not to ruffle feathers unnecessarily—lessons that Jimmy Carter, for example, ignored at great cost. But Clinton characteristically aspires to ruffle no feathers at all, and in trying so hard not to make Carter's mistake, he ended up fighting the last war.

From the start, the Clinton administration faced a choice between playing the careful coalition politics of the congressional leadership, especially the House leadership, or the more daring politics that the president had articulated during the 1992 campaign, by which he would try to take directly to the people a series of appeals to common interests that might cut across traditional political lines. From the start, in almost every instance, Clinton chose to play the game as the congressional leadership wanted it played. The truth was, the administration was packed with young (in many cases, Coelho-trained) staffers suckled on the congressional creed of gradualism and "realism" and inflexible interest-group politics.

In its effort to "put some points on the board," as a White House official puts it, the White House bowed to the fact that the Democrats' center of gravity still lay with the House leadership. Instead of trying to shift that center, or create a new one, it relegated initiatives like campaign finance reform—anathema to House Democrats, in particular—and welfare reform to the end of the line. This strategy enabled Clinton to pass a good deal of legislation, for which he probably got insufficient credit. But it also identified him, in the public mind, with the most loathed body in American politics. "We would be better off—even if we hadn't passed some of those reforms—if we had pushed really hard for them," says a White House aide. "Congress is the most unpopular institution in America, and we ended up tied to them." Of course, House Democrats will tell you that it is Clinton who dragged *them* down; but the truth is more complicated. Locked in their desperate embrace, Clinton and the Congress had a sort of mutually amplifying effect, like a poorly matched married couple—spouses who, whenever they go out in public, bring out the very worst in each other.

Coelho was a good enough politician to understand some of what Clinton was up against in November; and he was willing, from his new perch, to give advice that ran against the wishes of his old colleagues in the House. According to several White House sources, for example, he was among those who urged in late summer—unsuccessfully, and probably too late—that the president push hard on some sort of reform legislation to create a centerpiece in the fall campaign.

But when it came to the final weeks of campaign strategy, Coelho was among those who favored some of the creakiest, most familiar weapons in the Democratic arsenal. He scoffed at Newt Gingrich's canny "Contract With America,"* rejoicing that Gingrich had handed the Democrats a weapon—not because he saw it as a chance for Clinton to articulate an alternative vision, but because it offered a target in making narrow appeals to various Democratic interest groups. Use it with senior citizens, he urged Clinton, to charge that Republicans had a secret plan to gut Social Security; use it in Iowa, to buy off farmers by assuring them that farm subsidies were safer in Democratic than in Republican hands. It was far too late for any such tactics to make a difference. Really, even if Tony Coelho's advice had been pure genius, and even if he had had a larger role for longer

* A Republican manifesto crafted for the 1994 election that promised less regulation, lower taxes, and various restrictions on Congress itself, including limits on the number of terms members could serve in Congress. This last fell by the wayside as the newly Republican Congress consolidated its power.

than three months, he couldn't have bailed his party out: He did far too good a job, a decade earlier, creating the Maginot Line that he and his colleagues in the Clinton White House were now desperately trying to hold, even as the more imaginative enemy swarmed around it.

When he talks of his life, his past, and his future plans, Tony Coelho exudes the salesman's total conviction. Now, a scant week after the election, he is selling a new set of goods. "I didn't have really any input until recently," Coelho says, explaining his total lack of involvement in the Clinton administration's many errors. "I did not know the president. People have a hard time understanding that I did not know these people; I did not. The more I've gotten to know them, the more I like and respect them, but my first lengthy conversation with the president was in, I think, December" of 1993.

Listen to Coelho, who pauses only to shoot his army's wounded on his way off the field: This is the unsentimental insider at work, in one of those moments when reality shifts and a new reality must be accommodated. It's not Tony Coelho who will pay for his party's mistakes.

True, he may have to revise what was, until November, his clear ambition to run President Clinton's reelection campaign. A loss like the midterm election is precisely the sort of measurable event that Washington does keep track of, and for which it does mete out punishment; so Coelho has been assigned a certain amount of short-term blame for the defeat. And without his old comrades at the helm in the House, he's not quite the valuable political commodity he seemed just a few months ago.

But then again, it may be the better part of shrewdness to duck a high-profile role in Clinton's next campaign, which is shaping up as a torturous undertaking. Coelho still has a powerful ally in Leon Panetta; and he has entirely escaped the sort of long-term reassessment that might identify his true culpability in the fortunes of his party. He can simply remain, for the time being, one of the White House's outside insiders, and if he plays his cards right, he'll be holding a good hand two and six and ten years from now. After all, your true insider is a bipartisan sort of fellow. "I love Bob Dole!" Coelho tells me. "I have great friends on the Republican side . . . [GOP lobbyist] Jim Lake and I are as close as brothers!" As for the new House speaker, well, it seems Tony Coelho was the guy who arranged an introduction between Newt Gingrich and Frank Luntz, the young pollster who helped Gingrich assemble the elements of his Contract With America. Tony Coelho is in this for the long, long haul. Some day, when he's ready to go to pasture, he'd like to seize the final prize that awaits any insider of good repute: the ambassadorship to the country of choice—in Coelho's case, to Portugal.* And he's made a giant step toward that goal.

The Democratic Party may have a terminal disease, but you'll notice that when Tony Coelho's name comes up, no one even sneezes.

—*January 8, 1995*

* Coelho would, in fact, be named by Clinton to be U.S. commissioner general of the 1998 World Exposition in Lisbon, a post that bestowed the title "ambassador." Some questions about Coelho's handling of government funds were later raised by the State Department's inspector general, and were widely assumed to play some role in Coelho's giving up, in June 2000, a higher-profile position as chairman of Al Gore's presidential campaign. But Coelho said, at the time, that he gave up the job for health reasons; he'd been hospitalized with a severe case of diverticulitis.

THE SIBLING
(JEB BUSH)

George is placed in front of the stars; Jeb is farther to the right, in front of the stripes on the giant flag that dominates the stage at this meeting of Florida's Veterans of Foreign Wars. Otherwise the brothers Bush are outfitted as virtual twins: grayish suits, deep blue shirts, red ties.

Jeb Bush, Florida's forty-seven-year-old governor, warms up the crowd for George W. Bush, the Republican candidate for president. "You're going to hear from my older, smarter, and wiser brother," he says, "who I hope and pray will be the next president of the United States."

When George rises he offers reciprocal praise. "I particularly want to say something about the governor of Florida—my big little brother," he tells the 900 or so veterans and women's auxiliary members who are assembled in the ballroom of the Hyatt in Orlando. "We're all proud of him and we know you are as well. . . . And both of us are successful because we've listened to our mother."

The crowd is eating them up. This group, men in crisp white shirts and women in bright-blue skirted uniforms, is of an age to find a display of filial pride adorable, to see Jeb and George as Fine Young Men. Yet the graceful "After you, Alphonse" particulars of this brother act don't conceal the essential strangeness of watching the two eldest sons of former president George Bush on stage together. For one thing, the famous parents are uncannily present in the faces of their sons: George bears his father's coloring, brindled light brown hair, and squinting eyes, while Jeb, with his brown eyes and thick, dark hair, looks eerily like old pictures of Barbara Bush before she went gray. As Jeb sits to the right of George, applauding warmly, his face is tilted upward in precisely the same posture of admiring attention his mother used to bring to her husband's every performance.

But there is another odd thing about watching the brothers together: The man on the left, with his bunched, ruddy face, is the habitual C-student who barks out his bullets of verbiage with a striking vehemence, as if trying to fill a space that is a little too big. You can't help noticing all the reasons that the man on the right—smarter, deeper, and in many ways more admirable—was supposed to be this generation's political star.

"He was always seen, in the '80s and early '90s, as the political comer in the family," says James Pinkerton, who served in their father's administration as domestic policy adviser. "The most intense, the most ideological, the most handsome."

Jeb, six and a half years younger and five inches taller than George, was elected governor of Florida in 1998, after running and losing in 1994—the same year that George won his first term in the Texas statehouse. Jeb had been widely expected to win; George, in a race against the popular Democrat Ann Richards, had been expected to lose. When both predictions proved wrong, it was George who became the big-state governor and had a full term under his belt by the time the Republicans began casting around for a plausible presidential candidate; almost ever since, Jeb's political life has been conducted in the shadow of George's anticipated run for the White House.

"Everyone who knew the family was astonished when George won and Jeb lost in '94," says another old Bush hand. When the family celebrated George's first victory, at the Bush presidential library in Texas, Barbara Bush joked to friends, "Can you believe this?"

Here in Orlando the veterans greet the brothers genially, as if they were a single two-headed phenomenon. But many Republicans in Washington quietly deliver the opinion that it would have been better for the party had political fate made Jeb the Bush son with the standing to run this year. "Let me put it this way," says former Republican Party chairman Rich Bond. "I hope George W. Bush is president some day. I know Jeb will be."

"Jeb will always seem more thoughtful," a somewhat plaintive George told the *Miami Herald* in 1994. Because, above all, Jeb Bush has the genuine interest in ideas and the mastery of the details of social policy that his father and his brother conspicuously lack.

Jeb, in turn, made no secret of his annoyance when his older brother decided to run for governor in 1994, beginning his campaign months after Jeb had begun his own. "It turns it into a *People* magazine story," he told Maureen Dowd of the *New York Times*. And George wasn't above stealing some of Jeb's best lines: "I am running for governor not because I am George and Barbara Bush's son; I am running because I am George P. and Noelle and Jeb's father," Jeb said on the stump. "I am not running for governor because I am George Bush's son. I am running because I am Jenna and Barbara's father," came the echo from the Lone Star State.

Family and friends counsel against jumping to the obvious conclusions about the brothers' relationship, dismissing the idea of either a desperate rivalry or a Jack-and-Bobby closeness. The age difference between the two men means that their relationship today is not informed by either the great bond or the primal rivalry that closely spaced siblings can carry into their adult lives. If there is a race between them, it seems a settled, manageable fact of life. "Whatever it is, it's been there since they were young, and they've worked it out," says Elsie Walker, one of Jeb's cousins. "Competition in that family is sort of brought out in the open."

"They kind of tease each other about good news that comes out," says their uncle William Bush. "George will call up and say, 'Just got my education reports back, how are you doing?' Knowing full well that it's less good. They kind of needle each other, but it's kind of fun and friendly and brotherly."

Jeb Bush's staff hates questions about The Brother Thing. "The press corps thinks our office calls the Austin office every day and says, 'What are we going to say today?'" says Jeb's chief of staff, Sally Bradshaw. "And the truth is, these are two different men who have two separate states and separate lives."

Not so separate, though, that Jeb isn't an essential part of George's White House strategy. Jeb has one job on November 7, and that is to deliver the state of Florida. Analysts agree that Florida, with twenty-five electoral votes, is most likely to go to Bush. But Clinton won the state in '96, and Gore might conceivably threaten Bush—especially, polls suggest, if he were to tap Florida's popular U.S. Senator Bob Graham as his running mate. So Jeb's network may be crucial to turning out the vote for his brother.

In the meantime, everything Jeb does and says is seen through the prism of the presidential race. The worst controversy of the younger Bush's tenure so far—his plan to replace Florida's affirmative action laws with a group of measures he called "One Florida"—reached political crisis largely because of suspicions that it was developed to help his brother win the state in November.

The sense that everything must bend to George's campaign applies to the extended Bush clan. "Right now we all want to get George elected," says uncle Jonathan Bush, in declining to give an interview. "The problem is, if it's real positive about Jeb, people might say, 'George isn't as good.' I can't win."

It is, then, impossible to see Jeb Bush apart from the twin contexts that have ruled his career: the family background that propelled his father into the White House and the ambition of his brother to follow the same path. The most interesting thing about Jeb is the way he has chosen to define himself against that legacy.

He is surely the only member of the extended Bush-Walker clan to have chosen a bride—which he did at the age of seventeen—from a city in central Mexico (leading to the indelible moment, at the 1988 GOP convention, when nominee George Bush pointed out his three Florida grandchildren as "the little brown ones"). His early decision to make his career in an entirely new place—the teeming souk where business and politics intersect in Miami—and his conversion, five years ago, to Catholicism mark him as a man who has tried both to embrace the gifts of his background and also claim some other ballast.

The brothers, who preside over two of the four largest states in the land, appear to favor nearly identical programs of "compassionate conservatism," balancing such mainstream Republican fare as tax cuts, the death penalty, and school vouchers with a warm rhetorical concern for the dispossessed. But beneath the surface similarities lies a world of difference. "Jeb is someone who's really curious," says one observer who has dealt with both brothers. "He knows what he doesn't know, and he's interested in finding out about it. Where I think George W. just doesn't care—he isn't interested in what he doesn't know."

The difference is perhaps best summarized by the books the two have published to burnish their political personae. George's ghosted autobiography, *A Charge to Keep* (1999), was pasted by critics as a vapid campaign pamphlet. Jeb published a policy-heavy tome called *Profiles in Character* (1995). A meditation on civic character and Aristotelian virtue, the book—coauthored by an aide but supervised closely by Bush—quotes Edmund Burke, Edward Gibbon, Ralph Waldo Emerson, and Elihu Root.

As Jeb follows George to the podium at another joint event in mid-June, it is easy to see that Jeb is the family's natural politician. George has just given his standard stump speech, including all the compassionate tropes around which he has built his campaign: *No child left behind. . . . The American dream should touch every willing heart.* But when Jeb stands to tell the rich audience at this $2 million fund-raiser for the state GOP what he has done for Florida, his speech has a felt quality that is absent from his brother's.

He talks first about prosperity and tax cuts, of course. But then he begins to talk about education and his passion for ensuring "that every child in this state gains a year's worth of knowledge in a year's time." His voice drops to a conversational level: "Imagine what it would be like if 2.2 million students, starting in August and ending sometime in June, gained a year's worth of knowledge in a year's time. Starting in kindergarten, ending in twelfth grade." His delivery is so well modulated, so reasonable in tone, that he can get away with concluding, "Close your eyes and dream of a state that could accomplish that."

Jeb Bush has launched a more ambitious agenda in Florida than his brother has in Texas, passing during his first year tort reform, an education reform bill that included school vouchers, and a $1 billion tax cut. "I call him 'the Bush brother with balls,'" Republican strategist Mike Murphy once said. ("It caused Jeb big heartburn with his brother," Murphy says today, somewhat sheepishly declining to expand on the comment.) Jeb has also made more enemies than his brother ever has. Although he curbed the more hard-edged parts of his creed after his 1994 loss, he can seem dictatorial, stubborn, even self-righteous—a quality that one critic summarizes as "almost this moral smugness."

He also works around the clock. On days when he can't get out to exercise, he runs up and down the stairwells of the twenty-two-story Capitol building. His chief of staff admits to reminding him to go home at night. "We throw him out, at 6:30, 7 o'clock," says Lieutenant Governor Frank Brogan. "But along with him goes his laptop. You can count on getting stacks of mail, email, phone calls from him before the next morning," including email fired off at 3:30 AM.

Part of this discipline, surely, comes from a continuous effort to exorcise the silver spoon that some Floridians have always envisioned in his mouth. But there is also a faintly missionary streak that runs through Jeb's life. He once bragged to a journalist (who hadn't asked) that he had never slept with any woman but his wife. In contrast with his rakish brother, Jeb put his nose to the grindstone at age seventeen or eighteen and hasn't looked up since.

Yet even beyond that drive there is an indefinable intensity, a sense that Jeb Bush prizes self-discipline in an almost monkish sense. He works not in the ornate ceremonial office of the governor but in a small, spare office attached to it. "He just never felt comfortable in this big, formal office," says Bradshaw.

Jeb's old friends, associates, and family all grope to put a finger on this quality, settling without satisfaction on words and phrases like *gravity* and *sense of purpose*. "He does have a kind of smoldering quality to him," says Pinkerton. "Has anyone ever seen Jeb smirk?"

He "runs quite deep," says his cousin Elsie Walker. "I think life is a very serious thing to him."

John Ellis Bush is the second child of Barbara and George Bush. But even so simple a sentence may hold one of the keys to what set Jeb apart. Begin again: John Ellis Bush, born February 11, 1953, was the third child of George and Barbara Bush. Only weeks after his birth, his older sister Robin, then three years old, was diagnosed with the leukemia that would kill her. During the next seven months, newborn Jeb hardly saw his mother, who was in New York most of the time with her dying daughter.

Who knows what sadness becomes, as it leaches into an infant mind? All we can be certain of, by the testimony of many people who knew Jeb along the way, is that in the big, boisterous mix that the Bush family became, Jebbie was different. He had a sense of fun, like the rest of them, but "he was always pretty serious, even as a kid," says his brother Marvin, the sibling to whom he is closest. "Sometimes you'd sort of want to say, 'Come on, take it easy, be a kid.'"

It has long been said that Jeb is his formidable mother's favorite. Most family and friends bat the question of favoritism aside, but Elsie Walker concedes that "[Barbara's] relationship with George, it's this great sort of hijinks and fun. . . . With Jebbie there's a real sweetness and love. When Barbara is talking about Jeb, there's a more sort of maternal, loving quality."

Because Jeb is almost seven years younger than George, he was essentially the oldest sibling in a cluster that included Neil, Marvin, and Dorothy, all born within six years of his birth. Whereas George was the child of the family's years in the wide open oil fields of west Texas, Jeb spent most of his childhood in the more sedate enclaves of upper-class Houston, where the family moved when he was six.

But the central fact of life in the Bush family was, of course, the size and weight of the family history: Jeb grew up with visits from U.S. Senator Prescott Bush, his grandfather; and long summer trips to Walker's Point in Maine, the domain of his indomitable paternal grandmother. He watched his father rise to the top of Houston's civic elite, always enunciating the ethic of noblesse oblige, and then watched him launch his own political career.

But it fell first to George W., the namesake, to wrestle with the size of the family's legacy; Jeb got a chance to watch from the sidelines as his brother dutifully followed his father into the old school, into Yale, into the oil business. In tenth grade Jeb, too, followed the patrilineal path to Andover. But in his senior year he settled on the most dramatic possible way of defining himself away from the family. In a class called "Man in Society" he signed on for a work-study trip to Mexico, where he and his classmates were to help build a school in the central highland state of Guanajuato.

There, in the city of León, he met Columba Garnica Gallo, who stood a dainty five feet tall. She was a sheltered, middle-class girl strictly raised in Catholic schools. Yet something in her spoke to him, and each of them spoke enough of the other's language to get by. When he returned to Andover it was with the certainty that he had met "The One."

"We were all surprised at the time, and he was very sure," says Walker. "He was so *vehement*." I ask her if this passionate plunge into difference was a sign of some eagerness to leave the family shadow. "It's just sort of the way people position themselves in a family," she replies. "Young George has a very broad, big personality. . . . George took up a lot of space, so Jeb went off in another direction."

But Columba, whose father had abandoned the family when she was three, also answered some ardency in young Jeb. "He had more social empathy, I guess you'd say, at that age than most boys," says Baine Kerr, an old family friend. "His marriage, I guess you'd say, was an example." The Bushes, in keeping with what old friends describe as a genuine tolerance, were basically accepting. "I was always amazed, and proud of the Bushes," says a family ally. "Some of the old farts in the extended family probably had some things to say about it, but the immediate family was great."

Jeb blazed through the University of Texas in two and a half years, bent on marrying as early as possible. He majored in Latin American Studies and graduated Phi Beta Kappa. Then he and Columba—"Colu" to the family—struck out for new territory. First Jeb got a job with what was then Texas Commerce Bank; the bank made him a vice president and sent him to Caracas, Venezuela. In 1979 the couple moved back to Houston, but it didn't suit them.

Columba had a bumpy entry into American life. "I think it took her a long time to get her sea legs in this big family, and in the U.S., and to develop confidence," says Walker. So in 1981 the couple, with two children in tow, moved to Miami, where Columba's mother and sister lived.

It is striking how quickly and wholly Jeb became acclimated. "He belonged here the day he showed up," says Armando Codina, the Cuban-born real estate developer who took him on as an agent peddling office leases. After a few years Jeb became a full partner. At the same time he wove his way into the city's civic elite, becoming a power broker of sorts in the nexus of business and politics, especially within Miami's burgeoning Cuban exile community.

It is a sign of Jeb's confidence in his Miami roots that he managed to make himself nearly invisible this year while Little Havana was melting down over Elián González.* True, the Elián affair offered no obvious cause for state—as opposed to local or federal—intervention. Nonetheless, someone with Bush's close ties to the community might easily have blundered into this briar patch, as officials from Vice President Gore to Miami-Dade County Mayor Alex Penelas managed to do. The governor clearly made a shrewd calculation: He could not afford to oppose his core support in Little Havana, but he also had nothing to gain from pouring gasoline on that fire. So he confined himself to a few early assertions that the matter ought to be settled in family court, and then largely vanished from view.

* A five-year-old Cuban boy rescued by fishermen in 1999 after the others in a small boat headed for Florida, including Elián's mother, had drowned. A custody dispute ensued between Elián's relatives in Miami and his father in Cuba, and the matter became a huge ideological *cause celebre*. Elián eventually was returned to Cuba.

Cuban-American activists were sympathetic to his dilemma. "I think probably to the extent anyone was able to deal with this at a state level—since this was a federal case, and a foreign policy case—he did," says Ramon Saul Sanchez, president of the Democracy Movement, which was heavily involved in the Elián affair. "Maybe the Elián González case, being more complex than some other issues of concern to us, required him to have a more conservative participation in it, and that we understand."

Jeb Bush is secure in the deep bond that has developed between the Cuban exile community and the state GOP, the ascendant power in Florida politics. He got in on the ground floor of that growth, chairing the Dade County party in the mid-'80s and serving for two years in Tallahassee as secretary of commerce. Because his father was vice president and then president, Jeb became a local symbol for the national party, as well as a man who could get your phone call returned by the federal bureaucracy if you had a nasty regulatory problem.

This has caused him problems along the way, and Democrats have ascribed a form of profiteering to Jeb's career. In 1985, for example, he phoned an official at the Department of Health and Human Services on behalf of a client who ran a giant Florida health maintenance organization and who wanted a waiver to enroll more than the allowed number of Medicare patients. Later, the man was discovered to be bilking Medicare. (Bush says he was only calling to help his client get a "fair hearing." The client fled the country before he could be charged with Medicare fraud, but was convicted in absentia on labor racketeering and wire-tapping charges.)

The *Wall Street Journal* also raised questions about whether Jeb had played a role in arranging for Nigeria to sign a $74 million contract for agricultural pumps made by a company run by a business associate, a deal that was supported by loans from the U.S. government's Export-Import Bank. But Jeb's controversial dealings, which have been extensively scrutinized, seem to fall into the borderline category of opportunistic but legal.

Jeb made a fortune of just over $2 million in Miami. However, it was no secret to his friends that his real ambition lay in politics. According to Jeb's brother Marvin, their father's 1980 presidential campaign set Jeb irrevocably on that path. Within weeks of George Bush's 1992 reelection loss, Jeb's gubernatorial campaign was ready to go. It stirred up immediate animosity: Was Jeb an arrogant, underqualified rich kid reaching for what he saw as his birthright? His Democratic opponent, the incumbent governor Lawton Chiles, was only too happy to say so.

Jeb played into Chiles's hands by pushing an abrasive, hard-charging conservatism that stressed anticrime initiatives (teenage criminals needed "more boot camps and fewer basket-weaving classes"), greasing administration of the death penalty, and making all tax increases subject to public referendum. He spoke of "clubbing the government into submission." He lost by fewer than 75,000 votes. But he made the best possible use of the loss, studying its lessons intently for the next four years. He founded a think tank, which kept his staff together, and pondered the issues that had tripped him up in '94. At the same time, he joined with the local Urban League to found a charter school in Liberty City, one of Miami's bleakest areas.

He also undertook what friends describe as a personal reckoning. After the '94 campaign he had come home to find a family he hardly knew: One of his children had a drug problem, and his marriage, he said, was unraveling. He described the situation as "devastating." The family entered therapy, and Jeb finally committed to Catholicism; he had long attended the church with his family, but he had never formally converted to the religion.

When he ran again, he seemed like a different man. Now he spoke of the state's responsibility to "the weak, the sick, and the poor," and he didn't go out of his way to emphasize the more confrontational parts of his creed. One measure of this change: In 1994, Jeb had promised to abolish the state's department of education. In 1998, he asked the state's education commissioner to be his running mate.

Voters liked the tale of humiliation and redemption he now offered, and he won easily. "Probably the best thing that happened to Jeb was to be defeated in his first race for governor," says Tom Slade, former Republican Party state chairman. "After four years of basically being a policy wonk, he emerged from that process in full control of his advocacies."

It is ironic that a man who has been as critical of government as Jeb Bush now presides over a place so entirely a creature of the government as Tallahassee, a town of 125,000 in northwest Florida that seems largely cut off from the vitality of the state's other centers of power. In the ten blocks between the capitol and the governor's mansion, even the gracious old houses you pass are inhabited by trade associations and lobbyists. To get a measure of how artificial the city can feel you need only duck around to the back of the block that holds the forty-three-year-old governor's mansion. Across the street an entire city block is for sale, zoned for development; at present it is a forest.

But if you take the nickel tour of the mansion's public rooms, one detail compels your attention. In the foyer is a picture of the governor's family: Jeb, Columba, George P., Noelle, and "Jebbie." In this picture Columba has flowing light-auburn hair that spills lushly down over one shoulder. But by the time you reach the formal living room, she has become a buttoned-down political wife, with darker, short-cropped hair and a smile of cool, unknowable friendliness.

"She changed considerably," says Columba's brother-in-law John Schmitz. "Very gradually, over a long period of time; I guess it sort of paralleled the growth in Jeb's political career." Yet she seems, still, something of a mystery, hesitantly described by Bush's friends and political associates with antiseptic words like nice. Private. Sweet. Fashion-conscious. Even those close to the Bushes seem to have little sense of how the marriage works, especially with all three children essentially gone from the nest. Their older son, George, is living in California, campaigning for his uncle and preparing to enter law school. Their daughter, Noelle, just graduated from community college. And the youngest, Jeb, attends a boarding school in Jacksonville.

"I think if it was up to Columba they wouldn't be in such public life," says Jeb's former partner Armando Codina. Columba's hesitancy was only compounded by her one disastrous appearance as a national news story, during Jeb's first year in office: On returning from a trip to Paris, Columba failed to declare $19,000 in clothing and jewelry purchases to customs, bringing down upon herself a $4,100 fine and a world of bad publicity.

Jeb told reporters that her motive had been to conceal from him how much she had spent in Paris. Skeptics, especially in the Florida media, derided this moment of marital nakedness as a lame attempt to cover up for what they saw as a parable of greed.

But those who know the Bushes find the more human version both more credible and more discomfiting. Since then, Columba has begun again tentatively, doing tame first-lady appearances around the state, reconciling herself to the career path of the man she met at sixteen.

When Jeb Bush moved into Florida's governor's mansion, he was the first Republican Southern governor since the Reconstruction to preside over a legislature entirely controlled by his own party. In addition, he came in at a time of surplus; and he pressed these advantages for a smooth first year, easily passing a $1 billion tax cut, a crime bill setting tough sentences for offenders who used guns, a bill that streamlined the death penalty appeals process, and an education bill that included a voucher program for failing schools. Although it was more modest than the plan he had espoused earlier, that bill made Florida the first state in the union to pass a statewide voucher program. (Both the voucher bill and the death penalty measure were struck down by Florida courts; Bush's administration is appealing both rulings.)

Overall, Jeb has probably remained a more hard-edged conservative than George, and he seems to armor himself with a moral self-assurance that flows from the systematic way he has thought through his beliefs. "Jeb likes to wear a halo," says a Democrat who has observed him closely. "He's got a notion that he doesn't do the political thing."

His critics in Tallahassee complain that he is autocratic. "King Jeb," reporters began to call him, for his efforts to gather more and more forms of control within the governor's office. Others complain of a kind of bullying, or pettiness, in the way Bush's office doles out punishment and reward. "I think this administration tends to take things personally," says Buddy Dyer, leader of the Democratic minority in the Florida senate. "As in, 'If you're against my policy, you're against me.'"

These flaws were all on conspicuous display earlier this year, when Jeb confronted his biggest challenge so far: the reaction to his executive order, known as One Florida, abolishing the state's affirmative action rules in college admissions and state contracting. The plan ended traditional preferences, replacing them with what Bush calls "a race-conscious but race-neutral" approach to promoting diversity: The top 20 percent of graduating students in every high school would now be guaranteed admission to one of Florida's ten public universities, and in the departments overseen by the governor state contracting officers would be evaluated according to a vaguely defined ability to "internalize our commitment to diversity."

The move was widely seen as an effort to head off a ballot initiative in Florida by California businessman Ward Connerly, who had succeeded in passing measures in California and Washington state banning gender and race preferences. Bush, his critics reasoned, had panicked, fearing that Democratic (especially black) voters would turn out in droves to vote against a Connerly initiative—and vote against George W. Bush for president while they were at it.

The legislature's black caucus firmly opposed One Florida. The controversy boiled over in January, when two members walked into the governor's office to demand a meeting. Upon being refused, they improvised a sit-in in the office of the lieutenant governor. Bush reacted intemperately: A camera caught him telling a staff member vehemently to "kick their asses out."

"He can be high-handed," says Richard R. de Villiers, who interned for Jeb's public policy foundation in the mid-1990s. "When I saw that I said, 'Oh, man, I knew this was going to happen sooner or later.'" Bush claimed that he had been speaking of members of the media who had crowded into the suite to record the drama. But the damage was done.

Bush soon found himself anathematized as "Jeb Crow" and "Pharaoh Bush." He seemed personally stung to be so heavily criticized by African Americans, after his transformation into the New, Improved, Sensitive Jeb. But he had stepped into a classic political bind: He'd alienated a segment of the public that was happy to demonize him, without satisfying the conservatives who had nudged him into action in the first place. "Never have I seen anyone take so much abuse for doing so little," says Ward Connerly.

The controversy has subsided somewhat, but it probably invigorated Bush's opposition. "The Democratic Party, which had been near death's door in Florida—if he hasn't revived it, he's put it on life support," says one Tallahassee Democrat.

Which is worse: to have your older, more lighthearted brother constantly planted on the rung of the ladder just above you? Or to spend your whole life hearing how much smarter, handsomer, more profound your younger brother seems to be?

Whether or not one of them ever makes it to the White House, by the simple fact of their parallel careers the brothers Bush present a rare experiment in political personality—a chance to examine, in their strengths and flaws, what we really value in our pols: Jeb's serious attention to policy, his intense, straight-arrow certainty about his own intentions and beliefs, or George W.'s ease and likability—the sense that he is not so deeply invested in any idea or plan that he couldn't put it aside if a better objective presented itself.

Whichever qualities seem most appealing, the final fact is that George

W.'s successful march to the nomination this year puts Jeb firmly in the back of the line for national office. In any other year, for example, a Florida governor with Jeb's record and appeal would have to be on his party's short list for vice president. This year, he is the last man the nominee could consider. And George's political fate—whether he goes down in history as the vital new hybrid who has run a charmed campaign, the callow amateur he seemed during the hardest days of the primaries, a loser, a one-term president, or a two-term leader—will cast a permanent shadow over Jeb's. If Jeb Bush really hungers for a national political role, he will have to climb out from under the family name for the second time in one young life.

"As Cain and Abel discovered, sometimes the town isn't big enough for both of them," says James Pinkerton, the former policy aide to President Bush. "Jeb is going to have to wait his turn, and it looks like it's going to be a while."

—September 2000

SCENES FROM A MARRIAGE
(BILL CLINTON AND AL GORE)

January 6 may have been the worst day of Al Gore's life. He spent the early afternoon in the chamber of the House of Representatives, presiding with fortitude over the joint session of Congress that certified the presidential victory of his opponent, George W. Bush. After almost two hours of that, he patiently signed his autograph on tally sheets and admission tickets for a stream of pages, spectators, and even senators, former colleagues who stood in line to collect evidence that they had been present when, for the first time in forty years, a vice president had to ratify the election of his opponent. Then he went back to the White House, to a party in a vast white tent on the South Lawn that gathered staffers from all eight years of the Clinton-Gore administration for one last hurrah. The Clintons arrived at the party on the famous bus that had borne the Clintons and the Gores on their triumphal cross-country campaign trip of 1992; Al and Tipper Gore arrived later.

Gore got a rousing ovation when he came in, but it was hard not to notice something strange about the long, elaborate program the White House staff had organized. It had testimonials from men and women who had served in every part of Clinton's presidency—his personal assistants, his political consultants, even Hillary Clinton's chiefs of staff. The tributes went on and on, interspersed with video clips enumerating Clinton's many trips abroad, his major legislative achievements, his political victories. The only thing the program did not include was much mention of Al Gore. "You had to work at not having Gore included in that," says a former

White House aide. "They obviously did." It was a fitting obituary for what had once been the successful partnership of Bill Clinton and Al Gore. The president and vice president were barely on speaking terms by then, after a campaign that had pitted the two men and their staffs—in many cases, old friends and comrades-in-arms—against each other in a battle of wills.

The pair had faced each other down in a bitter White House meeting, a few days after Gore conceded the election, that matched grievance for grievance. The sit-down, which took place at Gore's request, aired the fury the vice president had been carrying for months, even years. In response, Clinton vented his anger that Gore had refused to run on the record of their administration. Their fight has been mirrored ever since in acrimonious postmortems among Democrats all over Washington. The Gore side argues that Clinton's affair with Monica Lewinsky cost Gore the election, and that Clinton compounded his sins with obstructive complaints about the competence of Gore's campaign. The Clinton side argues that Gore bungled a simple campaign he should have won—and, in sidelining Clinton for the duration, showed wretched disloyalty in the bargain.

Clinton has told a confidant that "[Hillary] was able to figure out how to deal with her relationship with me and win by 10 points. *He* should have been able to as well." This source adds, "It was clear [Clinton] was just in total disbelief that Gore had run the kind of campaign he had." And Gore has complained to associates about Clinton's "trashing his campaign," in the words of one man who has discussed it with Gore. "I think Gore thinks that if it weren't for all the mistakes the president made in the second term he'd be president now."

The break appears complete. As of mid-May, the two men had not spoken since the day of Bush's inauguration. "They're both leading very separate and very busy lives," says Clinton spokeswoman Julia Payne, with the matter-of-fact brightness that Hollywood publicists bring to discussing celebrity divorce.

For eight years, we watched the marriage of Bill and Hillary Clinton, marveling at the glue that kept it together, wondering if Bill's misdeeds would finally blow it apart, certain that if the end came it would make for a spectacular explosion. And all that time, it turns out, we were watching the wrong marriage. The split between Clinton and Gore presents itself as everything from a personal spat to an ideological divide, from a battle between pollsters and consultants with a huge stake in the question of why Gore lost to a shell-shocked lack of consensus over who will now have the standing to lead the party. But most accounts of the schism, which assign all of the blame for the break to Gore's repulsion and fury over Clinton's affair with Monica Lewinsky, are somewhat off the mark. "The idea that this relationship just went off the skids when Monica came along, and Gore said, 'Oh, shocking. As a husband and a father, I just can't stomach this,' is wrong," says a former White House official. "It was all there, in a deep and profound way, long before Monica Lewinsky ever showed up." Months after the campaign's end, the bitterness of the Clinton-Gore split is vividly present in the language of former aides and associates on both sides, who sound like the children of a bad divorce. "I'm telling you, these are Zantac moments," says Gore's campaign manager, Donna Brazile, summarizing what it was like to run interference between the Gore campaign and the Clinton White House. "It tore me up. It was personally excruciating."

It is hard to say which side is more withering in its view of the other. Former Gore consultant Bob Boorstin says, "Did we make mistakes? Yes. Would I say that Clinton was the only reason we lost? No. Would I say with absolutely zero doubt in my mind that we would have won the election if Clinton hadn't put his penis in her mouth? Yes. I guarantee it. The guy blew it!" From the Clinton side: "It's about incompetence," says a close former staffer. "It's unbelievable how [Gore] fucked the Clinton relationship up as it related to his own campaign."

The truth, of course, is that all their complaints have some justice. Here on the far side of the separation, interviews about it have the quality of psychotherapy: time and again, I sat down with a witness to the relationship who, once invited to talk, could scarcely seem to stop. Almost no one would agree to speak for the record, but it is appropriate, in a way, that the story should be narrated by a Greek chorus of former aides and officials. For like many bonds that are described in Washington as warm friendships, this was a relationship heavily mediated—glued together, maintained, and eventually undermined—by staff.

On Clinton's side, this is the story of his generosity to a smart, relentless, ungainly successor—a man who, in exchange for his loyal service, got a political opportunity he could never have had if Clinton hadn't chosen him for vice president and then given him unprecedented authority. On Gore's side, it is the story of his uneasy alliance with a much greater political talent and much more unruly, undisciplined man than himself. Gore's struggle to serve the two masters of Clinton's need and his own career recapitulated some of the most painful themes of his dutiful, self-dimming life, investing the final disillusionment with an explosive power. "If people are shocked now by the way the relationship hit the skids, they shouldn't be," says a former White House official. "There was an almost unnatural suppression and denial in the first six years."

Ultimately, it is this side of the story that is harder—and more important—to understand. Bill Clinton, as the alpha dog, controlled the terms of the relationship at its founding. But it was Al Gore who insisted on its destruction.

A few scenes from the earliest days of the partnership:

In 1992, the Clinton campaign conducted its vice-presidential search under a cloak of darkest secrecy, smuggling potential candidates through a service entrance of Washington's Capitol Hilton. When campaign staffer Mark Gearan called Gore's scheduler to set up a meeting, he recalls, "I can remember telling [her], 'We'll be by to pick up the senator at 11.' She said, 'a.m.?' I said, 'No, p.m.' She said, 'p.m.?' I said, 'Yeah.' From the start, it was an interesting little window into the respective body clocks and approaches of the two men." Al Gore, the most ordered, most analytical politician you could hope to meet, was stepping onto the ride of his life.

When Bill and Hillary and Al and Tipper embarked on the famous bus ride across America, the media covered "the boys on the bus" as instant friends and boon companions, the foursome as two fun couples on a marvelous double date. But the friendship was always oversold. "The whole bus tour, the foursome thing, the press really wanted to believe that," says a former White House official. "The press went with it, and there was no reason for the president or the vice president to shoot it down."

Already, Al Gore was learning the special discipline of a partnership with Clinton. Not far into the trip, he had a knockdown fight with Clinton scheduler Susan Thomases, who drew her clout from a close friendship with Hillary, over extending the bus tour. Gore had talked Clinton (or so he thought) into a longer trip than originally planned; Thomases disagreed, and "Clinton crumbled," says a close Gore associate. This was Gore's first clue that, in dealing with Clinton, you couldn't always trust what you heard. "Invariably, you're going to come away thinking he said yes," says the Gore associate. "It doesn't mean that at all; it just means

Clinton isn't going to look you in the eye and say no. . . . It took a while to kind of refine the language, dealing with Clinton, to get a good understanding that you've got to pin Clinton down, and then you've got to get someone else in the room, to memorialize it."

It's one thing to learn that you're going to need a witness every time the president makes you a promise. But there was something more: Gore's ability to plunge headlong into the role of helper, guide, stalwart sidekick. It took him no time at all to fall into the newlywed's cardinal error of trying to fix his partner—beginning with Clinton's atrocious junk-food diet. "I can remember him getting to an advance person to have only fruit on the buses, for Clinton's weight," says someone who spent time on the bus. "So he was both big brother and little brother, trying to make sure he was eating an apple instead of a Milky Way bar." Clinton, of course, continued to ask for his Milky Ways. "And, of course, someone would deliver him a Milky Way," continues this source. "But at least it would delay him a stop: at least you'd get to Terre Haute before he had a Milky Way."

Of all the thankless jobs a vice president could be called on to perform, serving as Bill Clinton's superego has to be one of history's most challenging. But that was Gore, loyal son of an outsized southern senator who had methodically raised his namesake to follow in his own footsteps. Gore had spent the first forty-four years of his life, with only a few diversions along the way, dutifully fitting himself to the role that had been laid out for him at birth. Al Gore was the reliable boy, the sensible man, the one who steadied the more mercurial souls around him. He brought these lifelong habits to the task of making himself indispensable to Bill Clinton.

"Gore was absolutely determined to make it work. . . . He knew the ability to get anything done depended directly on the president's goodwill," says Roy Neel, who worked for both men in the White House. "In the early days, there were a hundred reasons to keep that relationship working well." Almost everyone agrees that "work" is the operative word. "Gore worked his way into a relationship with Clinton," says a former Clinton staffer, "but Gore always worked to have a relationship." Still, this achievement can't be underrated. The historic relationships among presidents, vice presidents, and their staffs offer an endless chronicle of mutual suspicion, contempt, alienation, and backbiting. Clinton and Gore did a remarkable job of containing the tensions inherent in the deal, and of wringing the best from their association.

On the president's side, you have to credit his intellectual security:

Clinton knew that Gore knew things he didn't, and Clinton was happy to delegate specific areas of responsibility—technology, the environment, government reform, and several foreign-policy subjects—and to give great weight to Gore's advice across the board. When you put aside the uncertainties that make it so difficult for Gore to present a coherent political persona, the truest, most reliable parts of the man reside in his grasp of the substance of government. At his best, Gore can be formidably decisive, straightforward, and tough. He offered a desperately needed steadiness to the storm-tossed White House of Clinton's first term, and Clinton was smart enough to accept it. Additionally, Clinton trusted Gore as a smart, bureaucratically savvy peer. "At the end of the day, a lot of being president is, you're in a meeting, and two smart guys say something, and three smart guys say something else, and it's really hard to decide," says a former Clinton adviser. "Gore was a huge player in this."

The relationship "didn't stretch beyond the kind of day-to-day business that they had to confront," says former Clinton chief of staff Leon Panetta. But even Clinton partisans who are now dumping on Gore's campaign grant him warm praise for his contributions to the administration's successes. When Clinton worked himself into a temper, only Gore could step in with his dry, ironic humor to lance the boil; press secretaries learned never to schedule a press conference when Gore wouldn't be in town for the "pre-brief."

"He had a really light touch with Clinton," recalls former press secretary Dee Dee Myers, describing the scene at a typical press-conference rehearsal. "Clinton would say, 'You sons of bitches don't care about the future of the country.' And Gore would go, 'I think that's exactly the right tone.'"

From the start, however, it was possible to see where the alliance began and ended. There was, for one thing, the past to consider: Clinton had declined to endorse Gore when he ran for president in 1988, and Gore had returned the favor during the early 1992 primaries. Some of those around Clinton were acutely aware that Gore had never been a particular help to them until he was tapped for vice president. And it must have been complicated for Gore to watch Clinton prosecute, successfully, the game plan Gore felt he'd pioneered in the 1988 campaign, running as a southern moderate "New Democrat." But it was a plus that the two men had never run against each other—indeed, while each had long eyed the other as a potential rival, Gore's 1988 endorsement request was the most substantive encounter they'd ever had before Clinton chose his running mate.

Gore came into the White House determined to hold the Clinton staff to every part of the bargain the two men had struck, which gave Gore unusual bureaucratic power: an inviolable weekly lunch alone with the president, a staff presence in all important West Wing meetings, and a say in all major appointments. Gore aides studied Clinton's schedule intently so that the vice president could be at any important meeting. "He had people there all day long telling him what was going on," says a former Clinton staffer. Under the rule that face time is all, Gore would cancel meetings of his own to be able to shadow the president, accommodating himself to Clinton's unpredictable rhythms—even if it meant sprinting down the hall to make it to a meeting he had learned about at the last minute.

Gore especially policed the sanctity of his weekly lunch with the president, the one place he could sit down alone with Clinton to take up his own agenda. And, as one might expect, Gore came to these meetings armed with a multi-item memo and plenty of backup material. One Clinton aide remembers, "Clinton would come in, 'What's for lunch?' Gore would come in with a stack of work under his arm." On one Friday in January of 1996, Clinton aides cleared a room in a Nashville restaurant so that the president and vice president could have a belated meal after a day of joint political appearances. Gore insisted on it despite the fact that Air Force One was standing by to take the president to visit U.S. troops in Bosnia. Aides eyed their watches incredulously as Gore marched through his agenda, not at all daunted by the knowledge that Clinton faced a nine-hour flight into a tense situation.

"He wouldn't let Clinton skip one of those lunches if the fucking missiles were coming in from Russia," says a former White House official. No one on Clinton's side of the house blamed Gore for his insistence on these prerogatives, exactly: He was only doing the smart thing. But they did laugh at him a bit, and constantly pushed back for bureaucratic reasons of their own. For Gore, there was also the Milky Way problem to contend with—the gargantuan indiscipline of the president's work habits, his ability to talk a thing to death, the experience of thinking you'd talked him around only to discover the next morning that he'd sought five more opinions in the middle of the night. "Clinton drove Gore nuts," says a former Gore aide. "Gore's much more disciplined in terms of how he makes decisions and the way he demands things to happen. There's nothing more irritating as vice president than to be waiting around for a Clinton meeting that starts forty-five minutes late."

The two men were, at bottom, as different as could be: Clinton had a thousand friends; Gore, former associates believe, had either few or none. Clinton's famous temper blew hard at anyone in his path, but then passed like a summer storm, whereas Gore did everything with a profound correctness, confiding in almost no one outside of his family, controlled by an inner thermostat that held his manner at a constant room temperature. "He was always very measured and disciplined about what he said around people he didn't trust, which was virtually everybody," says a former White House staffer. Aides learned to read Gore's feelings by small signs. He "was careful about what he said [about Clinton], but didn't hide his feelings that much," says a former Clinton aide who remembers Gore's "winks, nods, facial expressions, sort of the rolling of the eyes. . . . The thing about him always leaching Clinton's anger out—that was true. But underneath that was a very real dismay about Clinton's weaknesses."

One of Gore's roles, from the outset, was to bring the president to closure. A famous episode chronicled in Bob Woodward's *The Agenda*, an account of Clinton's first year in office, had Gore admonishing the president to "get with the goddamn program!" White House staffers learned that this was one of the vice president's great uses. "It would be common to say, 'O.K., it's time to go see Gore,' and get him to tell the president to do something," says a former White House official who has ties to both men. "And it made a lot of sense at the time. 'This works well for everyone' was the feeling. But inside each man's head, it stops being cute after a while." This source believes that

> the abiding bathtub ring it left with Gore was "Omigod, the guy is undisciplined, and now they're going to send me in there again." And if you're Clinton, to read in every account that Gore always had to come in at every crucial moment and tell you what to do, that is going to create some real resentment.

Some associates also saw in Gore an occasional wistful awareness that, while Clinton trusted him, they weren't exactly friends. One official from the first term remembers Gore looking at a schedule that included one of the Clintons' movie nights at the White House, and saying, "You know, I've never been invited." This former senior aide continues, "There were so many emblems of uncertainty. . . . He felt Clinton genuinely cared about his success. But I think it was also really important to him that he feel needed, valued, and respected. And sometimes when your older brother doesn't show you need, value, and love, you yearn for it." And there was, too, the question of Tipper Gore's role in the administration. Given Hillary Clinton's high profile, "Al was always trying to make sure Tipper had standing," says a former aide. "There was always a perception that Al was trying to give her standing that in Clinton's mind she didn't have."

While Tipper and Hillary had done a great job during the campaign of playing up their bond, the truth was that their relationship contained all the tensions that this era can create between women who have chosen radically different paths in life. "Hillary thinks that Tipper is an unintellectual, nice lady who doesn't have a brain in her head," says one source who watched them closely. "And Tipper thinks Hillary's an ambitious, rather uncoordinated, grasping, difficult woman." During the first term, says a former White House official, "there were little reminders that [Tipper] was not an equal, and they rankled. It would come up in discussions with Gore and the First Lady's staff about who was getting what plane to go somewhere."

It all added up to a delicate collaboration. In his every action, Gore reconciled himself to the hard truth that the best way for him to succeed was to help Clinton succeed. But "the fact that they managed to form an effective team professionally never really cured these tensions," says a former White House official who knows both men, adding

> . . . in some ways, Gore's approach to the job exacerbated them. The more Gore was rigidly disciplined, and rigidly played his part, the more his resentment grew. . . . This is a guy who, instead of blowing up sometimes and venting at all of the natural tensions in the vice-presidential role, is letting it accumulate and accumulate, and build and build. . . . There was just a lot of shit being built up inside.

Gore's frustrations had their pale mirror image on Clinton's side of the house. Most sources I questioned insist that Clinton's grudges were shorter-lived than Gore's; Clinton is a more elastic, more forgiving soul than Gore. "His favorite saying," a Clinton supporter reminds me, "is 'He can't help it, he was born that way'"—and, significantly, he held the upper hand through the first six years in the White House. But there were limits on his side, too. Sometimes he chafed under the relentlessness of Gore's help. "I never saw resentment on Clinton's part," says a key former staffer.

"What I saw more was 'When is this guy just going to leave me alone? Give me a break!'"

In its best hours, the Gore staff was adept at mediating the relationship. "I always viewed my job as 80 percent prosecuting Gore's agenda with the Clinton team," says one former Gore aide. "But the other 20 percent was the hardest part: going into Gore's office and saying, 'Stop—don't ask for more. Enough, you need to back off.'" It is also worth remembering that the Clintons never successfully made peace with the Washington establishment—the same elite in which the Gores were utterly at home. And Gore got glowing press throughout Clinton's first term, while Clinton got hammered—for his administration's lack of discipline, for Hillary's health-care debacle, for the dreadful congressional losses of 1994, for Whitewater and Travelgate and Troopergate.* "Clinton felt he gave a lot to Gore, and did a lot for Gore, and tolerated a lot from Gore," recalls a well-placed observer. "And what he's reading in the paper are stories about how Gore did a lot for him."

"I think they had a good relationship early on," says a staffer from the first term. "And I think it was pretty good for quite a while. But I think the more stupid shit Clinton did, the more disapproving Gore got. And Clinton's attitude was 'Yeah, buddy, and when you can do what I do, then you can stand in judgment of me.'"

"They did a pretty good job of holding it together" throughout the first term, says a Clinton supporter. But then came the first serious tear in the fabric—the 1996 campaign-finance scandals.

Reports of Gore's fund-raising phone calls from his office, and of his visit to what turned out to be an illegal fund-raiser at a Buddhist temple in California, made him the emblem for the party's omnivorous attempts to evade campaign-finance laws. Up to that point, Gore had been miraculously free of any taint from the scandals that followed Bill and Hillary Clinton like Pigpen's dirt cloud. Now, suddenly, Establishment Washington was arching its collective brow at the formerly golden vice president. When you lie down with dogs, you get up with fleas, they said—and Gore

---

* Three heavily-publicized scandals of the Clinton White House. The first involved a land deal made back when Clinton had been Arkansas governor; the second involved personnel changes at the White House travel office; and the third involved a state trooper who maintained that, as governor, Clinton had used him to procure mistresses. (This last accusation has since been renounced by David Brock, the conservative-turned-liberal reporter who brought it to light.)

was receptive to this construction of his problem. In truth, he had been an enthusiastic participant in both devising and carrying out the campaign's plan to raise huge amounts of "soft" money—large donations made to the party instead of the candidate —and then spend it on ads that would circumvent federal limits on the campaign's spending. But from the moment Gore read a March 2, 1997, Bob Woodward story in the *Washington Post* that termed him the "solicitor-in-chief," he seems to have begun to question whether he could survive his close association with Clinton. "The Woodward story really affected Gore's head a lot," says a former senior official. "It was the first time he'd gotten slapped down by the old guard inside the Beltway."

By September of that year, Gore's favorability rating was more than twenty points lower than Clinton's. And "he was envious that Clinton had gotten off scot-free," says another close associate. Most infuriating was the fact that Gore was in trouble because he had done what he'd said he'd do—dialing at least forty-five donors from his desk—while Clinton had ducked the phone calls assigned to him. "It's the whole nature of his being—of Gore's, and Clinton's—writ large," says a former White House staffer.

'Cause Clinton's out there not doing what he's supposed to be doing, and somehow that protects him? Wait a minute—is that in the rule book? We all know people like that. We went to college with them. They never came to class, then they'd write a brilliant thesis and get an A. . . . You always think, Oh, it's going to catch up with guys like that. And somehow it never does.

The scandal unnerved Gore in a way that he never quite seemed to recover from, and it was amid this crisis of confidence that the Monica Lewinsky affair detonated.

We can't know exactly what Bill Clinton said to Al Gore, in the early days of the Lewinsky scandal, about what he had or hadn't done with the comely intern. The great likelihood, most observers feel, is that Clinton lied to him only indirectly, in the sense of including him in the great, finger-wagging lie he told the entire country. Gore knew his boss well by then, and sophisticated students of the relationship doubt that Gore would have sought a direct yes-or-no answer. "I know that Gore deliberately never put Clinton in the position of having to lie to him," says a Gore confidant. "It was 'I'm not asking anything you don't want to tell me, but if I were you and I had anything to say, I would say it."' When Clinton persisted in his cover-up strategy, this source says, Gore was "flabbergasted that Clinton would handle it in a way that was so contrary to logic. I know Gore thinks that if Clinton had just fessed up, apologized, said he'd made a mistake and moved on, it would have been a lot better for everybody."

Even with his closest staffers, Gore had enormous discipline: no gossip, no words of anger, above all no speculation about whether Clinton might resign. Staffers, however, did see hints of his feelings—above all, incredulity. ("I think he can barely even comprehend why Clinton would behave the way he behaved," says a friend.) But, as always, Gore sucked it up and did what he had to do, which in this case was to express his full support.

And here is the fascinating thing about Gore's support for Clinton over the next difficult year—the tendency that explains almost everything about the bitterness with which Gore eventually turned on his patron: At every step in the Lewinsky saga, Gore went even further than he had to in his statements of support. Faced with any repugnant task that he perceives as his duty, Al Gore will do it to the extreme. As a young man, he had enlisted to go to Vietnam. As a politician, he had prodded himself into being one of the best fund-raisers on Capitol Hill. This gritting of teeth is, in one way, an admirable trait. But it is also what drives him to the opposite extreme after the fact, when emotion has had a chance to catch up to duty and intellect.

The week after the scandal broke, Clinton and Gore traveled together to the Midwest. The trip had originally been planned as a way to shore up Gore politically, to let him share in the lift that Clinton's State of the Union addresses always brought. Instead, it turned out to be yet another chance for Gore to help his boss. At the University of Illinois, he delivered a full-throated defense of Clinton, writing the closing lines of the speech himself: "He is the president of the country," Gore told a roaring crowd in Champaign. "He is also my friend. And I want to ask you now, every single one of you, to join me in supporting him and standing by his side." That August, when Clinton finally testified before a grand jury and admitted to his affair with Lewinsky, the Gores were on vacation in Hawaii, a trip that had been planned months before. When Gore's office wrote a statement of support, several aides questioned the wisdom of the words "I am proud of him," but Gore insisted on leaving them in. And on the afternoon of December 19, when the House voted to impeach the president, Gore stood with him on the South Lawn and made his famous assertion that Clinton would be "regarded in the history books as one of our greatest presidents." That line was extemporized, despite the advice of anxious staffers that he not go too far.

But from Clinton's perspective, says another observer, it only made sense that Gore should be giving him cover. "Gore was simply helping him out in a way that seemed natural, given everything he'd done for Gore," says a former White House official. "Clinton just kind of felt like Gore was doing his job."

Al Gore may be slow to act on his feelings, but that makes them all the more forceful when he finally does. From the time he began seriously pressing his own campaign, in late 1998 and early 1999, Gore brooded about how Clinton's behavior might hurt him. The conventional wisdom at the time said it would not: Democrats had done very well in the 1998 midterm elections. The economy was flying high, and Clinton's job-approval ratings along with it. And many of Gore's advisers assumed that the vice president's straight-arrow personal life would insulate him from any association with the one part of Clinton that dismayed voters. But Gore's poll numbers were stubbornly low. And one easy explanation was that the problem wasn't him. Sources say his family—both Tipper and the couple's oldest daughter, Karenna—felt strongly that Clinton was at fault. Smart observers suggest that there was more at work here than simple personal outrage at Clinton's behavior. Both of the Gores, after all, had gone into their partnership with the Clintons knowing of his "zipper problem," and both had spent decades in politics, where womanizing (if not on the presidential scale) was common—frowned upon, to be sure, but common. As much as anything, sources say, Tipper's antipathy to Clinton was a means of loyally seeking a palatable explanation for why her husband left voters so cold. "What the Clinton people underestimated," says a former White House official, "was how much influence Gore's family had, and how much shit he was getting at home."

In any case, Gore had few outlets for his gathering concern: He and Clinton had done too good a job of knitting together their staffs—placing Gore people in the White House and Clinton people in Gore's campaign, and essentially merging their political operations. Gore's pollster, Mark Penn, and media adviser, Bob Squier, both worked for Clinton too; his campaign manager, Craig Smith, was a Clinton loyalist whose ties dated back to Arkansas.

Enter Naomi Wolf, the feminist writer whose role in the campaign would eventually make Gore a laughingstock. In late '99, political reporters discovered that Wolf had been handsomely paid to advise Gore that he needed to shed his "beta male" image and adopt warm earth tones for his wardrobe. But this caricature of her advice greatly understated her true significance, which was her role in persuading Gore that his anguish over Clinton was well founded. Having started a full year earlier, she played "an absolutely critical role in the unraveling of this relationship," says someone who observed Gore closely in this period. "She is the Lady Macbeth of this drama." It was Karenna who drew Wolf into Gore's orbit, and his early consultations with her took place outside the campaign's staff structure. Aides sensed that she revved him up: "Her biggest danger was that too often she told him what he wanted to hear," says a former Gore associate. "When he was pissed off, she'd tell him he was right to be pissed off."

"She becomes a tremendously powerful force in taking those dynamics and playing them up," says another insider. "It all resonated with Gore's sense that for six years he's been the guy cleaning up after Clinton."

In addition to hardening Gore's growing fury, Wolf had another important effect. Up to that time, success within GoreWorld, as it had come to be known by the White House, was defined by how well you could work with (and work) ClintonWorld. Wolf's example taught people coming into the Gore campaign that the fastest path to the candidate's heart was now anti-Clintonism. And within the White House, presidential staffers watched the shift in sentiment around Gore with growing alarm.

Throughout the summer and early fall of 1999, Gore jettisoned advisers who had ties to Clinton, including Penn, Squier, and Smith. Many in the replacement cast had their own difficult history with Clinton, having either worked for candidates who had run against him or been cast out of the Clinton circle at some point. (One pollster, Harrison Hickman, while working for Senator Bob Kerrey's presidential-primary campaign in 1992, had urged reporters to dig into the story of Clinton's draft-dodging; another, Stan Greenberg, had been pushed aside by Clinton after the disastrous midterm elections of 1994.) And the new boss of the campaign, former congressman Tony Coelho, consolidated his own power by pushing out of Gore's circle many of the people—including his vice-presidential chief of staff, Ron Klain—who had the strongest working ties to

ClintonWorld. At the same time, Gore pretty much vanished from the White House. "People would joke, 'Gore? I haven't seen him around here in decades,'" says a former Clinton staffer. "Gore really made a decision to get out of the White House in 1999—to stop being vice president. And Clinton thought he was kicking away another of his assets." And so the relationship crumbled.

'You've got to look at it as a series of little, small breaks," says Donna Brazile. But the first break that was irreparable came with Gore's announcement speech on June 16, 1999. The same day he opened his campaign on the steps of the courthouse in his hometown of Carthage, TN, ABC aired an interview with Diane Sawyer in which Gore said three times that the president's behavior had been "inexcusable."

"From then on, the antipathy was much more public," says someone with ties to both camps. "It was a match on the huge pool of gasoline that had been accumulated." The White House, which had received no warning, felt blindsided by the attack, and assumed it had been orchestrated. "We couldn't figure it out," says a Clinton partisan. "Why launch your candidacy that way? We were pissed because of how he was treating Clinton, and we were pissed because we thought it was stupid politically."

In truth, according to senior campaign officials, there was no grand strategy to make separation the theme of Gore's announcement. The choice of language, and its vehemence, seems to have come from Gore alone. This episode was the template for all that would follow in the campaign: Gore, by insisting on his independence from Clinton, seemed at every turn to tangle himself more fully in the drama of his difficult relationship with the president, all the while asserting that this was just the routine separation that every vice president goes through when it's his turn to run. It was at this stage that the Clinton factor became a self-fulfilling prophecy. "It seems that this was something that really paralyzed the campaign internally," says someone who had a ringside seat. "They got further and further behind on that, and it got away from them, fundamentally."

The confusion over Clinton went way beyond the question—heavily picked over in the press—of whether the president should have campaigned for Gore. Even many people on the Clinton side understood the risk of having Clinton out in public, given the importance, in several battleground states, of independent voters who had very negative feelings about the president. The bigger problem was the campaign's resolve to steer clear of Clinton's record. "I would have done whatever was necessary to elect Al Gore," says pollster Stan Greenberg. "I would have had Bill Clinton carry Al Gore around on his back if I thought it would get Al Gore elected president." But, he insists, "what our research showed . . . was that when Al Gore went out running on that record, he performed more weakly." It made a crude kind of sense, on paper: All the data said that talking about the past—even to brag about the unparalleled prosperity of the '90s—led voters to unwelcome thoughts of Bill Clinton.

The only thing this calculus omits is common sense, for it left Gore without a strong rationale for his run, making him a candidate who seemed less than the sum of his parts. "If Gore were to find in the polling data that having worked with Clinton was a negative, it doesn't mean that pretending not to have was a positive," says Bill Curry, a Connecticut politician and former Clinton aide. "He was so connected to Clinton that it was impossible to separate himself from Clinton. . . . And in his anxiousness to separate himself from Clinton, he separated himself from himself."

What Gore presented instead, starting with his convention speech, was a sort of diffuse neopopulism. It even worked for a time, producing spikes in the tracking polls. But it wasn't enough to counteract voters' larger impression that Al Gore wasn't a coherent figure whose real substance was available for examination. "With Gore, [voters] see this lurching back and forth, indecision, uncertainty about his relationship with Clinton," says a longtime Gore ally. "They see a guy who is, bottom line, in some ways unsteady." Perhaps Gore would have faced this bedrock problem without the drama of the Clinton factor. But his anxiety over Clinton magnified it, making it the very backdrop of his entire campaign. He ended up wrapping himself in the most dangerous parts of the Clinton legacy—voters' doubts about values and trustworthiness—while getting no credit for the parts that had sustained Clinton's approval ratings throughout the impeachment process. Curry says flatly, "[The Gore campaign] skewed all their own data out of pique. . . . Someone had to misread the data horribly to choose that strategy. It was so much about people's grievances and wounds."

"The psychodrama overpowers everything," says someone who knows Gore well. "I think the guy just so much wanted for this to be *his* victory, and not Clinton's. He didn't want to wear the older sibling's jeans."

This, finally, is the other explanation for why Gore seemed so unnerved by his Clinton problem. As the son of a forceful father who had bragged of raising him for the presidency, Gore had struggled all his life with the assumption that he was wearing borrowed clothes. Even under the best of circumstances, it might have been harder for him than for others to manage with grace the eternal vice-presidential conundrum of how to stop looking like a second fiddle when his turn finally came. On some level, in addition to the real difficulties he posed, Bill Clinton was a very persuasive foil for Gore's drama of filial rebellion.

But try telling that to the squire of Chappaqua, who spent the entire campaign yearning—burning—to be part of the action. "Clinton is going nuts," says someone who spoke to him in the late stages of the campaign. "He's going, 'Don't use me, O.K. But, God knows, use my presidency. Use my record!'" Clinton's frustration, says one observer, "ran infinitely deeper than just 'He isn't running on my record.' He felt he had spent eight years basically knocking obstacles out of Gore's way."

Staffers on both sides learned to manage a volatile, high-test battle of wills between Clinton and Gore, trying to satisfy Clinton's great hunger for information and a role in the campaign while also tiptoeing around Gore's great determination to exclude him. "This dynamic developed," says a Clinton partisan, "where the Clinton guys thought the Gore guys were stupid, and the Gore guys thought the Clinton guys were assholes, that we weren't giving them enough room."

A constant struggle was being waged in which the White House pressed for a bigger role, and the Gore campaign labored to contain the 800-pound gorilla. Campaign chairman Bill Daley, who had served in the Clinton Cabinet as commerce secretary, fielded phone calls from the president as often as three times a week. Brazile recalls being buttonholed by the president at a White House social event: How were the polls? In Arkansas? In Pennsylvania? What about Michigan? The Gore campaign sent occasional delegations to brief the president on the campaign's progress. On one occasion, Daley and strategist Tad Devine were primed to tell Clinton, in no uncertain terms, the limited number of appearances they wanted from him. Just before the meeting, Devine said to Daley, "You're the chairman, you're going to do it, right?" And Daley replied, "Oh, no, Tad, you're going to do it. The guy put me in the Cabinet."

Then there were the back channels. Even when the White House appeared to bow to the campaign's wishes, it was trying other angles of attack: Gore aides received constant phone calls saying that Congressman So-and-so was begging the president to come to his district, that Senate candidate Thus-and-such had demanded an appearance. "I believe Clinton used practically everyone he could get his hands on to send messages to Al Gore," says Donna Brazile. Direct conversations between the president and the vice president had slowed to a trickle by the late summer of 2000, according to aides. On the few occasions when they did talk—and the even rarer occasions when they met in person—Gore aides tied themselves in knots to conceal the contact from a press corps that had fixated on the story of the tension between the two men. "Sometimes they would just talk, without our scheduling it," says a former Clinton adviser. "Clinton would say, 'I need to talk to him,' and pick up the phone. And then [the Gore side] would get all in a lather about whether to tell anyone about it."

Tensions may have reached their apogee on October 20, when the Clintons and the Gores both attended the funeral of Missouri governor Mel Carnahan, who had died in a plane crash. That very morning, the *New York Times* had published a yeasty, highly detailed story about the disaffection between the two families. "So everyone had to go through the motions of being friendly," recalls a former Clinton aide. "It was a brutal article—it had everyone but the pets in the families at war with each other. It picked over every scab there was." Yet there they all were, sharing a motorcade together. "It was all very awkward and very weird," recalls the aide. "They didn't erupt or anything . . . but it had a feel like, your family gets together over someone who died, and people haven't talked for a while, and they sort of have to go through the motions."

Gore's behavior seemed to those in the White House to ignore the plain fact that, had it not been for Clinton, it is unlikely Gore would have reached the nomination. "Clinton just felt, 'Suck it up, man!'" says a close associate. But Gore's sense of grievance ran far deeper than Clinton's, for the obvious reason that he had much more at stake. "Look. He kept his end of the bargain," says Marla Romash, a former Gore press secretary.

The deal was: I will do everything I can to make your presidency successful, and you'll try to help me get elected. . . . He stood by every decision, even the ones he didn't agree with, bless him. He carried Clinton's water politically, substantively, every way. And Clinton broke the deal in the one way that could undermine everything Gore had worked for.

In the wake of Gore's loss, recriminations flew almost immediately. On Gore's side, because he won the popular vote (and, many Democrats argued, the electoral vote too), there was a certain zany insistence that the operation had been a success if you could only overlook the fact that the patient had died. Of course our strategy was sensible, this argument ran; we won the campaign, didn't we? To the extent that we failed to actually get our guy inaugurated—well, that was Clinton's fault.

Gore strategist Carter Eskew published a *Washington Post* op-ed piece suggesting that Clinton had been "the elephant in the living room" during the campaign—the one insuperable obstacle. Eskew says Gore did not read the piece in advance, but he was told about it—and tacitly approved by not protesting Eskew's plans to publish it. Clinton partisans responded to the piece and to other anti-Clinton analyses with contemptuous statements of their own. "[Gore's] failure in this last campaign is indicative of the fact that he can't carry himself," rails a Clinton supporter. "He didn't have the juice." They pointed out, too, that Gore's loss involved blunders—including his performance in the debates with Bush and his failure to carry his home state of Tennessee—that had little or nothing to do with Clinton.

Clinton himself considered—but then dropped—the idea of authorizing some response to the Eskew piece. Wrapped up in the drama of his own farewell to the White House, he didn't have nearly the level of rage that Gore did. "His feelings are hurt, he thinks he should have been used, he doesn't really understand why Gore didn't ask him to help, and he doesn't think Gore is a great politician," says a friend. "But under all that, he feels badly about what happened."

Moderate Democrats gathered in earnest confab to debate whether Gore lost because he turned away from the supple centrism of Clinton to a more "old Democratic" populism. And the pollsters who had worked for the party's two principals during the campaign—each of whom had at one time in his career been dumped by the other side—published contending polls supporting the wisdom of their own camp's view.

But this was really just the same Clinton-Gore divorce dressed up in ideological clothing. "It's a big intellectual debate that is being driven by the big personal stakes of the guys around them," says a former Clinton adviser. "As a party, if we want to spend the next decade the way we spent the '80s, we couldn't make a better start than creating a lot of false choices about why we lost the election."

And this, ultimately, is one of the reasons why the sour end to their relationship poses a larger problem for their party. Gore's campaign turned out to be the field on which Democrats in some sense thrashed out their ambivalence over what Clinton had cost them, and the ongoing bitterness of the debate about why Gore lost continues to obscure the party's path out of the Clinton years and into the next stage of its life.

A few days after Gore conceded the election, he and Clinton finally had it out themselves in their tense White House meeting. Clinton aides had the sense that Gore—who instigated the meeting—came in loaded for bear, with years' worth of anger to get off his chest. Both men laid out the nature of their grievances, including, on Gore's side, his fury that Clinton had spent the weeks after the election deriding the competence of Gore's campaign. But it was far too late for the meeting to do anything more than anatomize why the partnership lay in ruins. Both men had some truth on their side. "It's not fair for Gore's people to say he lost because of Clinton," says one judicious soul. "And it's not fair for Clinton's people to say that Gore's loss had nothing to do with Clinton." But it is fair to say that, to the extent that candidates' fears and feelings shape their campaigns, Al Gore's history with Bill Clinton cost him the 2000 election.

On the day of Bush's inauguration, Clinton and Gore walked together through the labyrinthine halls of the Capitol to take their places on the stage. Television cameras caught them in a last characteristic tableau of their partnership—Clinton glad-handing every guard along the route, waving and smiling, while at his side Gore gazed stoically ahead.

With that, the two men seem to have walked out of each other's life. In mid-February, guests at a dinner thrown by UN secretary-general Kofi Annan for Richard Holbrooke, Clinton's ambassador to the UN, watched in fascination as the former president talked with Gore's daughter Karenna. "It was so weird," says one person who was there.

> They didn't really speak to each other. And then, at the very end, Karenna went over to say good-bye to him, and it was very cordial, but there was sort of this weird tension you were aware of. He's saying, "How's your dad doing, and how often does he get up to New York?," and stuff like that. And you're just noticing how strange it is that he has to ask the guy's daughter, in passing.

The following month, Clinton asked another man who has dealings with Gore how the former vice president was doing, making it clear that the two hadn't spoken. "I don't think that relationship has gotten any better," says this source with some amazement. By the same token, Gore apparently sent Clinton no word during the winter and spring, when the former president was enduring his own mud bath of controversy.

Some Gore associates chuckle over the strange irony by which Gore's shunning of Clinton can now be seen as prescient. Clinton's gigantic shadow and his dominance of the Democratic Party have been violently dissipated by the Marc Rich pardon* and all the other Milky Way bars the president consumed on his way out of office. "Oddly enough, distancing himself turned out to be a lucky stroke," says a friend—at least in the lower-stakes game of hindsight. "Every story about the bad blood between them sort of disconnects them more." Through Clinton's acts, Gore may finally be getting the separation he wanted.

But, characteristically, it is Gore who has nearly dropped from sight. Clinton—underemployed, alone in the big, under-furnished Chappaqua house that was bought to launch his wife's new career in another city— makes incessant calls to friends, acquaintances, former associates. "Clinton talks to everybody—he's very lonely," says a political associate of both men. "Everywhere I go, I've run into people who have talked to Clinton in the last three or four weeks. And I have trouble thinking of anyone who has heard from Gore, other than sort of a perfunctory call." Friends say that Gore has thrown himself into the several teaching jobs he accepted in the wake of his defeat, and, with Tipper, into the writing of a book about families. He has gained something like thirty pounds, and has resisted all attempts to draw him into comment on the early acts of the Bush administration. "He's O.K. I wouldn't say he's great," says a friend. "I think about 70 percent of the time he's fine. And the other 30 percent of the time he realizes he's supposed to be president now."

In May, I asked Clinton's spokeswoman, Julia Payne, if the boys on the bus had had any kind of contact with each other. "I know [Clinton] tried to call him on his birthday, but I don't think they connected, and that was back in March," she said. "We weren't too sure where he was staying," she added. The only connection they've made, it appears, is a birthday note Clinton dropped in the mail. As Payne observed, "You never forget someone's birthday."

—July 2001

* Marc Rich, who fled to Switzerland after being indicted for tax fraud, received the pardon after his ex-wife contributed an estimated $1 million to Democratic candidates, including New York Senator Hillary Clinton, and to Clinton's presidential library.

PART 2

ESSAYS

MAKEUP AND *MS.*

I can deal with the existence of a hit movie starring Susan Sarandon as a grown woman who supposedly wears stockings and a garter belt around the house even when she doesn't know that Kevin Costner is about to drop by and have sex with her.* I manage, by turning the page fast, to get past the new Continental Airlines ad campaign featuring the waxen George Burns surrounded by Young Things in bathing suits and high-heeled pumps, over the caption "With all these attractive low MaxSavers, I just can't make up my mind." I know that, if I keep working at it, I'll be able to ignore *Esquire*'s emetic new "Women We Love" issue, with its praise for "pulchritudinous limbs and sculpturesque lips, and talent, yes, and brains, and flesh."

I do know what decade I'm living in—really, I do: It's 1988, and there's a woman on the Supreme Court, and last year a woman almost ran for president, and women are working as rocket scientists and jockeys and television producers.

I was doing fine until I got the press release. "*MS.* LAUNCHES FIRST BEAUTY ADVERTORIAL," it is headlined. "'Time Out for Beauty' will contain cosmetic and beauty advice for women on the go," it advises advertisers interested in participating. For those who have not yet noticed the recent explosion in this cynical craft, advertorials are those multipage sections in which advertising is surrounded by—and incorpo-

* *Bull Durham* (1988).

rated into—"articles" and other text that resembles editorial matter. Editors are touchy on the subject, for advertising executives admit freely that the point is to blur the distinction between ads and magazine articles. *Ms.* Editor in Chief Anne Summers notes that the beauty advertorial will not be produced by *Ms.* staff, and swears that "it's going to be clearly demarcated from the rest of the magazine." But it is intended, she acknowledges, to provide "a quasi-editorial environment" for beauty advertisers.

Was it a feminist who pointed out that it's impossible to be a little bit pregnant?

The new *Ms.* offering was conceived, according to the release, after an industry survey showed that a greater proportion of *Ms.* readers than of any other women's magazine's audience buy certain cosmetics and toiletries. "We are not surprised," said national advertising sales director Linda Lucht in the release. "There has been a general misconception about the *Ms.* Reader. Now the facts speak for themselves." You know which misconception she means: that *Ms.* readers are h-u-m-o-r-l-e-s-s f-e-m-i-n-i-s-t-s in Earth Shoes, leg hairs growing wild beneath baggy fatigues. In fact, says Lucht reassuringly, *Ms.* readers are rated first among "heavy users" of lipstick and lip gloss, second among "heavy users" of eye shadow.

When it is suggested to Summers that a cosmetics advertorial might tend to blur the magazine's traditional message, she points to the "heavy user" data. "Our readers have already made that choice," she says. "They're already buying the stuff." Which is exactly what the drug dealers with the bags over their heads tell Geraldo Rivera.

Summers is commendably frank about what *Ms.* is up to. "Obviously, we want the ad pages and we need the revenue." She and *Ms.* publisher Sandra Yates just finished buying the magazine from their erstwhile employer, John Fairfax Ltd., the Australian conglomerate that had bought it last fall from the nonprofit Ms. Foundation. The two-step change in ownership, Summers acknowledges, made advertisers skittish; despite positive early reactions to a handsome redesign, advertisers were staying away in droves by the time the August issue closed.

To give the new team its due, the women have brought a renewed flair and seriousness to the magazine's coverage of issues. Freed from the tax-exempt status that hampered *Ms.* under its previous ownership, Summers has hired a Washington editor and expanded political coverage. But the new owners have also shown a markedly greater penchant for the frivolous: two standing features on clothes; a guest column in which a woman writes each month about the cultivation (literally) of her garden; most notably, a surrender to the truism that celebrity sells. The cover of the July issue presented "The Case for Cher," and August features Cyndi Lauper in fishnet stockings, lingerie, and lace-up black leather boots, with this hard-hitting query perched above her exposed right thigh: "Is she still having fun?"

It's not that the lessons of the women's movement were so wrong, *Ms.* seems to be saying; gosh no, it's just that they're obsolete. Times have changed, and these days, it seems, we're all having fun. "People today work within the systems that exist to bring about change," Linda Lucht explains patiently. "Years ago, in the work force especially, women were not treated with respect for their decision-making ability." Good to know we cleared that up. "To ask for equal opportunities to maximize women's potential was radical," Lucht continues. Back in those olden days, "some of the people quit wearing makeup. . . . To make a statement, women did things that were outside the normal realm."

Okay, so it's 1988: sixteen years after the founding of *Ms.*, twenty years after feminists demonstrated against the Miss America pageant in Atlantic City, twenty-five years after Betty Friedan published *The Feminine Mystique.* But when, exactly, did the women's movement become a quaint collection of "things that were outside the normal realm"? Time was when feminists questioned whether there could or should be such a thing as the normal realm, and spent a lot of time wondering who defined it. The question of definitions was crucial. (Do we really need to go over this ground again?) The most tired axiom, once the most radical one, redefined the personal as political. Before women could hold equal power, it said, they had to learn that their personal lives, habits, perceptions, and language were at once products and enforcers of their powerlessness. They had to fight sexism not only in their offices, and in their kitchens and their classrooms and their beds, but above all in their own minds.

In the area of appearance, said this critique, there was too great a chasm between the woman designed by biology and the woman admired by society; "femininity," it said, was the web of artifice designed to conceal that gap, and if women were not its inventors, they nonetheless spun it tirelessly. Cosmetics were only one strand of the web, but they had a special symbolic power for the women's movement.

Susan Brownmiller wrote in *Femininity* of the "appalling" contradiction inherent in makeup. "If women's faces are supposed to benefit from cosmetics, the underside of the equation is that the wearer of makeup dislikes her face without it." Or, as novelist Lois Gould wrote, "Make up. Meaning invent. Make up something more acceptable, because that face you have on right there will not do."

At its most ponderous, this kind of feminist critique pitted women against each other, and turned them away. "More women supported the Equal Rights Amendment and legal abortion than could walk out of the house without their eye shadow," Brownmiller wrote. "Did they bitterly resent the righteous pressure put on them to look, in their terms, less attractive? Yes they did. . . . Of all the movement rifts I have witnessed, this one remains for me the most poignant and the most difficult to resolve." Substitute curlers, or pricey lingerie, or electrolysis—any other furbelow that consumes time or effort or money: They all divided women among and against themselves in those years.

But, at its best and most profound, the feminist critique persuaded women to believe that their unadorned selves did not merit contempt. Even among those who took it to heart, most sooner or later shrugged inwardly and concluded that it was too exacting to observe fully in a world of men and women. "It was probably inevitable that the anti-makeup forces should lose," wrote Brownmiller. "We were bucking too much of history." We went back to our makeup (or similar vice: my own difficulties, for the record, arise over politically incorrect shoes), a decision made with no little difficulty, and no little relief. But surely, even in 1988, the part of that decision with which we must live most gladly is our ambivalence. Instead, we seem in danger of forgetting that the critique ever existed.

Already, *Ms.* denies one of the movement's clearest early perceptions: that advertising holds a terrible power to determine self-image, to question self-worth, to induce self-loathing. When Summers says, "I think that feminists and the women's movement ought to be mature enough after twenty years to know that [using makeup] ought to be a woman's individual choice," she is correct, but she also ignores the truth that advertising executives are paid hundreds of thousands of dollars a year to discourage the practice of rugged individualism.

To be a magazine editor is always, perforce, to enter a world of pragmatism: Magazines are funded largely by advertising. And *Ms.* has always solicited advertising from the makers of beauty products. But, until now, it has sold only space in its pages. An advertorial is different because it sells a piece of the charter—sells it, in the case of *Ms.*, because nothing else will work on Madison Avenue. For advertisers, in their wisdom, are reluctant to buy space in a magazine that has traditionally stood for a habit of mind inimical to their message. It makes me nervous when the advertisers are the ones telling the truth.

The ultimate risk, of course, lies in boosting the creation of a new "normal realm," in which women must measure up to old standards and new. As Lucht tells advertisers, "the *Ms.* reader, she's beautiful and she's smart." If anyone should be alert to that risk, *Ms.* magazine should be. If anyone should be holding on to tenable pieces of the feminist critique—measuring them against a changed world, letting them out or trimming them to fit—*Ms.* magazine should be. It is tough to see how a purportedly feminist magazine can skirt this job; it is tough to see how a magazine that skirts it can advance a feminist agenda.

Acts, said the women's movement, have meaning. Symbols, it said, have power. And women, it said, had for too long practiced denial of how much they changed themselves to win accommodations in a world run by men. For *Ms.* to deny the meanings of its acts makes nonsense of these ideas.

Lucht says that the reaction among advertisers so far has been encouraging. "We've been able to get into doors that we haven't been able to get in for a while. . . . The beauty advertisers have loved the last two covers. They think Cher and Cyndi Lauper are upbeat, they wear makeup, they have an attractive image."

In the words of one of the first people on Madison Avenue to perceive that the women's movement could be induced to eat its young: You've come a long way, baby.

—August 3, 1988

READER, I MARRIED

You, he said. *You think of getting married like you start out with a certain amount of capital, and that's all you're ever going to get, and you start to spend it the day you get married.* By which he meant emotional capital, of course, and he was right: It was exactly what I believed. My parents had divorced after thirty-five years together. I must not get married, I thought, until I found myself in a relationship so manifestly rich that thirty-five, forty years, a lifetime could not spend it. It was a new idea to me that marriage could be a source of capital, instead of the thief of my hard-won store. It was the concept that changed everything.

I've been to a wedding on a farm, in 1969, where the bride wore a diaphanous white dress and no shoes and the groom wore a mismatching suit and no shoes and a funny Daniel Boone hat, and the service took place in a cornfield. The couple were friends of my best friend Julie's parents, and after the ceremony the groom took me and then Julie on motorcycle rides. I was eleven, and the day's novelties—seeing what I took to be actual hippies, and being alone with the groom, holding loosely as I dared to the warmth of his back, and riding a motorcycle, which would surely have horrified my mother—still carry a wild romance for me.

I've been to a wedding on a golf course newly carved out of a bluff overlooking the San Diego Freeway, with golf carts still whirring toward the clubhouse as the bride and groom came down the aisle, and a stiff Santa Ana worrying the chuppah. Later, inside the clubhouse, the groom's mother gave a toast, holding microphone and cigarette in the same manicured hand.

I've been to the wedding of my former high-school boyfriend, who got married a year out of college on the bank of a lake in Upstate New York. Everyone, including me, seemed to think it made fine sense for me to be his best man: The bride and I had become friends by then, too, and he was something like family. Hours after the ceremony I found myself sitting alone on the damp grass, drunk, under a whirling sky. I carefully timed my retreat to bed so I wouldn't have to talk to anyone on the way.

I've been to the wedding of close, close friends radiant with the rightness of their marriage. The wedding of my college roommate, who married her boyfriend of seven or eight years with her usual air of having known since she was six exactly what she was destined for. The wedding of my sister, thirteen years ago; of my father, only two years back; of near-strangers who assumed an immediate definition for me through the intimacy of their celebration. But a lifetime of going to weddings, I am learning, is scant preparation for having one. Doing one? Throwing one? There is not even a verb that relates the bride and groom to their wedding, except for planning, a correct but wildly incomplete description.

As I write this, our wedding is five months off. We allowed ten, from the time we got engaged: Tim and I have lived together for two years—there was no rush, and we had a shared instinct that we would need the time. To assemble all those details without having to drop the other threads of our lives, for one thing. But also to enjoy the planning, to meet each piece of it consciously and with care.*

We learned, quickly, that there is a genial conspiracy in the world toward nuptial hysteria. *Not until October?* people asked. *That hardly counts as engaged.* There was something—*plodding*, it was implied—about allowing time to experience this promise we were making. *You should do what we did*, they said, *and*:

> *Elope.*
> *Get married next week at a friend's house.*
> *Run away and get married in a cave in Hawaii.*
> *Decide not to get married.*

For some couples, the decision to strip their wedding to essentials may be their own way of preserving or heightening its meaning. But the advice

---

* The bride was too discreet to mention a less ethereal consideration: The groom, a free-lance magazine writer, was flat broke when she accepted his proposal. About three months before this essay was published, he (that is, I) found gainful employment as a reporter in the Washington bureau of the *Wall Street Journal*.

comes through as a call to urgency. Hurry up, hurry past; the covert message is that marriage is just too frightening an undertaking to enter into deliberately. Paradoxically, these scoffers-at-ceremony have a lot in common with the camp that favors drowning a wedding in oceans of ritual and formality: They share the urge to avert their eyes from the occasion's meaning.

All weddings, I think, are ruled by the tension between ritual and meaning. Rituals hold meanings, of course: You cut the cake, you dance the first dance, in the South you send guests home with a boxed piece of groom's cake, to slip under their pillows for dreams; you say the vows, you break the glass, you toss the flowers. All of these practices are containers of meaning, but every person who gets married has a choice: to use the ritual to keep the meaning contained, or to pour out the meaning, and taste it.

For a man, the invitation to evade his wedding's meaning comes wrapped in the generic packaging of stereotype: the near-universal suggestion that men's lives aren't supposed to be all that rich in emotional meaning. Tim is routinely told by friends (especially married ones) that he should resign himself to being a pawn at his own wedding. For a woman, the invitation to distraction is more lavishly seductive. There is the tradition that brides should fret, making up in a surfeit of nervous feeling for the groom's supposed stoicism; there is all the pressing hokum of the bridal magazines: I am urged to "start working on" my choice of bouquet three months in advance.

I still can't make up my mind about the bridal magazines. I've bought them, to be sure, skulking compulsively into magazine stores, approaching the cash register with the studied nonchalance of the porn store habitue. And they are a kind of pornography, promoting as they do the whole aspect of weddings that objectifies *the happy pair* on *the most important day of your life*; that especially objectifies the bride, her beauty (brides are always beautiful) and her body. On the other hand, you can find between all those ads, as you find it few other places, the earnest message that something important is afoot.

But of course, I buy them for the ads. For a woman in her thirties, marrying more than ten years after she first read *The Second Sex*, wedding porn has a certain added charm—the one-time-only offer of legitimacy for the abandoned, forbidden sweets of girl-dom. *Peau de soie*, I find myself saying, the words hilarious but tasty on my tongue. And *tulle*, and *stephanotis*. Will I buy little white shoes swathed in satin? How preposterous. With little covered buttons, maybe? What fun.

At the bridal salon, mothers and daughters contend over dresses in the international language of mother-daughter aggravation. Over necklines, to be specific, the daughters yanking the bodices down to the cleavage, the mothers turning to the saleswomen, those masters of diplomacy, to suggest that the lines of the dress are lovely, but perhaps a little veiling . . . here, above the bodice—and up to the neck—like so. Sit there long enough, waiting your turn to be conducted into one of the dressing rooms and back to another century, and these exchanges take on an uncanny sameness. A daughter tries on confection after confection, all of them designed to make her look gorgeous, until finally she is unlucky enough to hit on one that does nothing for her. Nine times out of ten, this is the one that brings the mother out of her chair in admiration.

Standing in front of a long mirror, surrounded by other brides-to-be, I can usually remember that this part is simply the costume. At other times, it seems to me the ultimate act of self-definition: As I marry this person, who am I? I know I am not ruffles, not beads; I know I am exposed shoulders, a bit of swagger. This one is definitely too fussy, this one perhaps too severe. Goldilocks in the dressing room—I seek the one that is just right.

My oldest sister, like my mother, got married at twenty-three. My sharpest memory is of knocking over a Coke bottle while helping her with her hair, nearly splashing it down the front of her dress. She jumped out of range in the nick of time, but when I think of it, more than a decade later, my heart can still beat faster with fear. Such is the terrible weight of weddings. I've watched perfectly level-headed friends unravel under the pressure; I've watched as the smallest things began to take on otherworldly significance for them. (CAN YOU BELIEVE MY SISTER-IN-LAW WANTS TO BUY BRIDESMAIDS' SHOES WITH A LOWER HEEL?) I never understood until now that it is because there is no easily found seam between the two meanings of marrying, the day's events and the life's commitment. Hence the parade of bridal anxieties: The trivia of menu planning (and we are talking trivial here—two kinds of mustard or three, to go with the ham?) gives way to the largest issues in our relationship, now out on the table as the first work of our marriage; in the next moment, these seem less pressing than how long the musicians should play. There's only so much meaning, it seems, a person can stand.

Since I got engaged, I've learned that people—intimates, acquaintances, near-strangers, family—have large reactions to the inherent emotional power of this thing Tim and I are doing. Tides of response rush at or past us, some of it very intimate and dear to us, some of it absurdly misplaced.

It seems a function of people's own marriages or weddings, of the unknown roles in which people have cast us, as people always will. But for every sudden sting or acid comment that must be turned aside, every *Don't worry, you can always get divorced*, there is an assertion of love, a claim on my friendship or his, that cannot go unmet.

Of course, any wedding is two weddings, if you add in the social event taking place for the four or sixty or 300 guests. Weddings are one of our last great vessels of clannishness, rigorous schools of cultural education. What's more, even if the bride and groom marry by themselves, in a Vegas wedding chapel or a lean-to on the tundra, they never marry alone. Every wedding is at least a little haunted by the children they were. Whether or not they avail themselves of it, a wedding is each bride and groom's most explicit chance at our common, three-word heart's desire: *Look at me*. And the child's experience of that wish—whether it was expressed or fulfilled, whether it was answered too much or too little—is present in the decision to elope as surely as it is present in the happy exhibitionism of a couple who marry before a throng.

One friend, the radiant one, confided that she hated the idea of holding her reception in a single large room. For her, and the child she had been, there was unbearable tension in demanding that her guests focus so constantly on her and her business of the day; far better to give them choices, other rooms, other (possibly more interesting?) things to do. But she and her groom did it anyway, deliberately, making themselves the shining center of a great big room full of their pasts. And so her ghost of former years was only a very faint presence and, I thought, a grateful one.

Halfway toward October, the tide of wedding hysteria sucks ever more strongly at our ankles. With each decision we make that successfully steers away from reflex, whether over a grand or a trivial matter, we feel a surge of pleasure to find ourselves still in control, still masters of the event instead of its objects. One decision I made was to ask a very close but relatively new friend to be my only attendant. An old friend from college would have been an easier choice (I was her maid of honor four years ago), but I wanted with me someone who knows me exactly as I am today. Another, mutual, decision was that we would serve at the reception only food Tim and I both liked. (Whether the salmon constitutes an exception is a whole other story.) A third was to find a site only blocks from our house, for the sake of making our promise with feet planted in the center of our lives—not in some glade, however gorgeous, unrelated to our every day. In each decision there is a moment of stopping to will away the automatic impulse: to try to look beyond what background or family tradition or social convenience or *Checklist for a Perfect Wedding* or sex stereotypes say we should do.

Sometimes our decisions coincide with the advice of these oracles. Some wedding ritual, I have decided, may help me by remaining just that: an underpinning of custom to lift us all past the anxiety of family reunion. For part of what my wedding will mean to me is seeing my parents together, in the same room, for the first time in more than four years; a room in which my stepmother will also be a welcome guest. Everyone will behave well. But the prospect touches in me, as weddings always do, every familiar bruise. I am astonished at my hubris in marrying *as long as we both shall live*. I have to concentrate to remember my confidence that I have learned how to compound interest.

If it will ease this reunion to rely sometimes on what the rule book says, so be it. But I want to know that, in making each decision, I have at least uncorked the bottle and sniffed at the essence inside. We have not decided what vows to say, for example, but we liked the advice we got from the old friend who has agreed to marry us: Even if couples want a standard ceremony, he asks that they also, privately, write their own vows, to make sure they can articulate to themselves and each other what promise they are making. In the same way, I want to know I have teased what meaning I can from all the other rituals of the day.

When I think about my wedding, some of my wishes are things that are only partly in my control. Ways I would like people to be with me, and connections I hope to make—with my sisters, for example, or with particular friends. But my biggest wish is one whose fulfillment is entirely up to me. It is that between now and October, I cultivate in myself a generous enough appetite that I can take it, or let it, all in.

—*June 3, 1990*

PERSUASION

MEMO TO: Editor
FROM: Marjorie Williams, staff writer
RE: Story idea—"New Research: Men Listen To Bimbos"

For my next project I want to write about a new study of men, women, and language. It shows that men, while acknowledging that a woman who speaks assertively seems more competent and knowledgeable than a woman who talks tentatively, would rather respond to the advice of the mealy-mouthed one! Men are simply more willing to be influenced by women who speak with lots of tippy-toed self-deprecation: Phrases like "I'm no expert, but . . ." or "I may be wrong . . ." or "I'm not sure. . . ." Or qualifiers ("kind of," "sort of," "a little bit"). Or else statements that defer final judgment to the listener, like "It's wrong to murder pets, isn't it?" Or "This is a good idea, don't you think?"

According to Linda L. Carli, an assistant psychology prof at Holy Cross, men more or less divorce the question of whether they're being addressed by someone competent/confident/knowledgeable/smart/etc. from whether the person seems "likable." I interviewed her this morning and she said, with admirable nonacademic bluntness, "Men are apparently willing to be influenced by an incompetent woman, as long as she's likable and nice."

Women, on the other hand, form their opinions according to the perceived competence of other women. They like women who speak straightforwardly and assertively; they don't like or trust women who mouse around.

This is a great story for Washington, because Washington is such a male culture, and women have been taught for so long that the way to fit in is to assert, compete, talk knowledgeably about the Redskins. Apparently it's never going to work.

The study appeared in the November *Journal of Personality and Social Psychology*.

I say, let's do it.

Let me know ASAP.

MEMO TO: Editor
FROM: Marjorie Williams

I was disappointed you didn't like the idea right off the bat. I think I can persuade you you're mistaken.

I see why you think it's kind of a dog-bites-man story. It is true that this is what feminists have been saying for a long time—that men equate deference and weakness with femininity, and assertiveness or confidence with "pushiness." But the news here is that men will go for the less persuasive argument in spite of recognizing that the woman who speaks more assertively obviously knows more of what she's talking about.

You might need to know a little about the academic background. Basically, social scientists and psychologists have known for years that men and women tend to communicate differently, and that around men, women will speak less assertively than the men do (and less assertively than they speak to other women). But most of them have assumed this puts women at a disadvantage in mixed-sex conversations, that they don't get heard over the din.

Carli's leap was to intuit that talking tentatively "may be functional" for women. Meaning they wouldn't be talking this way if it weren't getting them somewhere. "I believe people behave in an expedient manner," Carli says. "They do what works."

Also, I think I should stress how strongly this study states its case: "It may be important for a woman not to behave too competitively or assertively when interacting with men in order for her to wield any influence, *even if she may risk appearing incompetent*" (my emphasis).

Think about all those women doing duty in the Persian Gulf. Um, I'm no expert, but I think maybe it would be better if we pointed that doohickey at their side, wouldn't it?

MEMO TO: Gene
FROM: Marjorie

I really appreciate your spending so much time on this. I mean, maybe I'm overselling it, but I still think the subject is fresh.

In answer to your first question, I'd obviously have to put in a certain amount of explanatory apparatus about how she did the study: It's actually two studies, which she performed with students who didn't know what the project was about. And in the second one she controlled for the possibility that the listeners might actually be responding to other qualities—e.g., looks, charm, clothes, etc.

In answer to the more complicated question of why: I guess no one knows. Carli thinks it has to do with what academics call "status cues": that for men, the simple fact that the speaker is a woman means that a perceived subordinate is talking. Men therefore respond most positively to the behavior they'd most appreciate in subordinates. "If there were more women in positions of power," she says, "I don't think you'd get this effect. Because gender wouldn't convey information about status."

Again, that's a bit of an oversimplification, and I'm not positive I completely understand it, but I think with your help I could get it across.

MEMO TO:
FROM:

Dear Gene,

Thanks for your note. I really appreciate the help, and I'm glad you've decided we should go ahead with the story. I sort of worry, though, about the fairness of couching this, even tongue-in-cheek, as a piece of advice to women. Carli is pretty careful about that, and it would be kind of easy to corrupt what she's saying into a handbook that counsels women to be deferential. "The solution is for women to have more positions of power, not be more indirect," she says.

I kind of think it might be unfair to imply otherwise.

Anyway, I may be wrong, but I think we should try to play it fairly straight.

What do you think?

Marji

—*January 14, 1991*

WHY CHARACTER MATTERS
IN POLITICS

Pity the politician, beset by sharks and vultures, fanatical reformers and a moralistic press. For at least a decade, it's been open season on anyone foolish enough to run for office or serve in government—an age of "mindless cannibalism," in the words of former speaker of the House and one-time entree Jim Wright.* Or so say Suzanne Garment** and Larry J. Sabato,† lending their very different voices to the chorus of analysts who have lately specialized in second thoughts about the cloud of scandal that enshrouded the Reagan administration and then drifted down Pennsylvania Avenue to engulf the House leadership‡ and the Keating Five.†† Their books both argue that the ethical, financial, political, and sexual scandals of recent years represent a kind of hysteria, and that Americans

* Wright resigned as speaker in May 1989 after a lengthy House ethics committee investigation into his personal finances. His chief accuser, Newt Gingrich, would himself become House Speaker in 1995 and receive a formal House reprimand in 1997 for providing the ethics committee with false information in connection with a separate investigation into whether Gingrich had violated tax law. Gingrich resigned as speaker the following year after the GOP made a poor showing in the midterm elections.
** In *Scandal: The Culture of Mistrust in American Politics* (1991).
† In *Feeding Frenzy: Attack Journalism and American Politics* (1991).
‡ As noted in "The Hack" (p. **99**), Tony Coelho resigned as House majority whip under an ethical cloud not long before Wright resigned as speaker.
†† In 1991, four Democratic senators (Dennis DiConcini, Arizona; Don Riegle, Michigan; John Glenn, Ohio; and Alan Cranston, California) and one Republican (Arizona's John McCain) came under fire for having pressured federal regulators to lay off Lincoln Savings and Loan, a failing thrift whose chairman, Charles H. Keating Jr., had contributed to their political campaigns. Keating would eventually go to prison for bank fraud.

in general and journalists in particular need to reevaluate how far they are willing to go in judging the human creatures elected to govern us.

But their books offer very different explanations. Sabato's, devoted almost exclusively to press coverage of political scandal, simply argues that the press has become too prosecutorial, too herd-like, and insufficiently respectful of politicians' private lives: "The press has become obsessed with gossip rather than governance; it prefers to employ titillation rather than scrutiny; as a result, its political coverage produces trivialization rather than enlightenment."

Garment makes a more sophisticated, more provocative argument that the entire political culture of America has shifted so that its components perpetually collude to produce scandals—among other things—as a distraction from having to produce intelligible policy. It's not that politicians have become more corrupt, she writes; it's that we have become a nation of goody-goodies. "Today's myriad scandals come in much larger part from the increased enthusiasm with which the political system now hunts evil in politics and the ever-growing efficiency with which our modern scandal production machine operates."

She details this apparatus at length, including the investigative and prosecutorial machinery within the government: the Office of the Independent Counsel,* the Justice Department's Public Integrity Section, the ever-swelling oversight committee staffs on Capitol Hill, and the agencies' inspectors general. Outside, the public advocacy groups have grown adept at feeding journalists leads and information; the post-Watergate rules and regulations police everything from political contributions to revolving-door employment to financial disclosure. New mores allow reporters to cover issues and events formerly off limits—or to cover familiar areas of politicians' lives with a new kind of skepticism.

The crux of Garment's argument is that each of these new inventions or developments feeds the others to create a vicious cycle of perceived corruption, voter mistrust, and ever-closer regulation:

> Out of distaste with the grubby realities of democratic politics, recent reformers managed to weaken those centers of power, like political parties, where much of the fundraising and favor-giving in politics

---

* Effectively shut down after the Clinton impeachment won congressional Democrats over to the Republican view that the law creating independent counsels ought not be renewed. Although a few extant investigations limped along toward conclusion, no new ones could be launched after the law expired on June 30, 1999.

once took place. Today, such activities must be more closely attended to by individual officeholders themselves. At the same time as this change was taking place, the same anti-political distaste brought about new rules making all the wheeling and dealing much more visible than ever before. We are now given a more detailed view of our officials doing decreasingly exalted things. The distaste thus increases, as does the pressure for more reform.

It is, of course, possible to point to reforms that boomeranged. The sorry hegemony of political action committees, which was the result of post-Watergate campaign fundraising reforms, stands as the best testament to the law of unintended consequences. And, yes, there have been examples of officials abused or mistreated in the course of ethics investigations. Garment is also on the mark in arguing that we are too quick to criminalize anything that smacks of political scandal. We don't always serve ourselves best by trying to nail a problem's creators: Once the logic and rules of criminal procedure are put in place, they can crowd out attempts to address what is more fundamentally a program flaw or a policy question.

But Garment goes far, far beyond where her evidence takes her, and into a realm where there seem to be no public misdeeds alarming enough to justify vigilance. Officials are never responsible for their acts; they are driven to them by prosecutorial do-gooders, or they are being held to preposterous new ethical standards. As an example, Garment writes that "even Clark Clifford, whose political perspicacity and survival skills were admired in Washington for some 40 years, has had the end of his career marred by a post-Watergate scandal," as if this were irrefutable proof of how absurdly picky Washington has become, rather than the fruit of Clifford's manifestly bad behavior in fronting for a shady international bank. "In fact," Garment writes, "the focus on specific prohibitory rules may make us less rather than more able to control the offending behavior." What she means is that, in the good old days, politicians controlled *themselves*; today their moral clarity has broken down under the weight of all these pettifogging rules.

Standards really have changed in Washington, in a lot of different areas. It's a mistake—which both these authors make in their dissimilar ways—to codify these shifts as a single political sea change, brought about by the sudden dominance of one faction, one public mood, or one fashion in press coverage. Sabato, a political scientist to the bone, draws up somber charts and graphs tabulating thirty-six events that exemplify the "frenzy phenomenon." They range from Watergate to Chappaquiddick, from Edmund Muskie's tears to Jimmy Carter's brush with the killer rabbit—events that really can't be meaningfully examined as a single phenomenon. Sabato writes from the trap of considering all reportage an exercise in "perception," as if the events he describes had no reality at all separate from their coverage.

Lest mine seem a knee-jerk reaction by one of the press corps jackals, I must grant Sabato some of his specifics. It is horrible to have a mob of journalists camped out in your begonias. Yes, journalists too often rely on group instinct to set their narrative direction during a scandal-in-progress. He also quite rightly criticizes the press when it prints or broadcasts unfounded rumors on the grounds that the existence of the rumor is itself news because everybody—that is, in the community of a thousand or so people who make up insider politics—is talking about it.

That said, Sabato, like Garment, leaves himself open to the supposition that he is writing in service of nostalgia—of a profound preference for the old ways that Washington did its business. Sabato betrays himself when he sighs that persecution by the press has gotten so bad that some pols are forced to consult with media heavyweights in order to gauge their liabilities. He cites the example of a prospective 1988 presidential candidate who approached Jack Nelson, *Los Angeles Times* Washington bureau chief, to ask, in Nelson's words, "how long I thought the statute of limitations was for marital infidelity. I told him I didn't know, but I didn't think the limit has been reached in his case!" Sabato advances this anecdote in sympathy for the unnamed pol, who eventually decided not to run—and passes without comment over its far more extraordinary testimony: that pols and big-wheel journalists still see themselves more as cooperative peers than as people with distinct, often competing missions.

Sabato advises journalists to

take to heart the delightful slogan of one of their most marvelous institutions, the Gridiron Club: "Singe but never burn." Since 1885 the annual Gridiron dinner has good-naturedly roasted president and press alike, relaxing the tensions that inevitably exist between reporters and politicians. A little of the Gridiron spirit of tolerance . . . could be usefully applied to coverage the year 'round.

The Gridiron dinner is, in fact, a festival of mutual stroking, dedicated to the proposition that politicians and the people who cover them are all members of the same jolly, inside-the-beltway fraternity.

My observation, in five years of Washington journalism, has been that the major media more often betray news consumers through excessive coziness, power lust, and the simple eagerness to be liked than through the will to drive hatchets into the powerful men and women they cover. In Washington reporting it isn't true, as Sabato claims, that all the laurels go to the writer who kills the king; success comes more easily to the one who befriends him.

If all the changes examined in these two books—the sunshine laws, the more expansive contemporary definition of government ethics, the press's greater efforts to delineate character—can be boiled down to any one observable theme, it is that Americans no longer trust a political elite to regulate their affairs behind closed doors. You can argue all you want about the roots and reasons: Vietnam, Watergate, feminism, the sexual revolution, the anti-authoritarian spirit of the sixties, the collapse of the political parties. But rather than see the changes as a sign of a sad diminution of trust in our institutions, one could choose to value them, as well as the increasing diversity they reflect among the people running, governing, and reporting of our affairs.

This is where Garment comes in again, brandishing an unacknowledged ideology. She has an assiduous compassion for the families of Reagan-era officials who became the "victims" of scandal, but she has only contempt for young men and women who come to Washington—usually for far less money—to agitate for good government. To suggest that the entire public advocacy corps in Washington (what she calls "the Ralph Nader conglomerate") comes here simply to delegitimize government is to turn common sense on its head: In Garment's world, the desire to strengthen government accountability is an act of radical cynicism.

To be sure, the press today has far greater discretion—which is to say power—in deciding what people should know about their leaders. And while the media do not exercise that power with perfect judgment, assigning this function to the media comes at least one step closer to letting citizens decide what they care about.

In his famous invitation to "follow me around," Gary Hart gave the media a wonderful fig leaf. Although the *Miami Herald* was already staking out his town house the day the Hart interview was published in the *New York Times Magazine*, it gave reporters a retroactive justification: Hart forced us to write about his sex life. But I do not believe we needed his invitation. As Suzannah Lessard argued persuasively in a 1979 essay about Ted Kennedy published in the *Washington Monthly* when he was preparing to run for president, a man's apparently compulsive womanizing might say something important—if not to person A, then to person B or person C—about a man's character. At any rate, everyone should have the right to decide for himself.

That's not to say that everything a journalist learns should go into the paper. To return to the example of the politician who sought Jack Nelson's advice: Unless I am mistaken about the man's identity, every political journalist in Washington is aware of him, and of the rumor that he decided against running in 1988 at least in part because of a long-standing affair. No one has printed this information, partly for the good reason that, to most of the journalists, it is only a rumor. But there are two other reasons why a journalist who had this information as a rock-solid fact probably wouldn't print it, at least not now. One, because the affair in question reportedly is or was a single relationship of long duration, not part of a pattern that might indicate compulsive behavior or habitual deceit. And two, because the man decided against running for president, and there exists an informal rule that politicians on the next-lower rung of the political ladder—senators, governors, members of the House—can expect more privacy than presidential candidates. In other words, that the surrender of privacy should be proportionate to the extent of the power a politician aspires to hold over our lives.

These are both rules of thumb. (Franklin D. Roosevelt and Lucy Mercer* would have qualified for protection under the first rule, but not the second. John F. Kennedy would have qualified under neither.) The easier case is the politician whose extramarital sex life has some illegal or dangerous aspect (Buz Lukens** or, again and always, JFK, who became involved with Mafia moll Judith Campbell Exner), or clearly bears some relation to the job. Take, for example, a member of Congress sleeping with

* Social secretary to Eleanor Roosevelt, Mercer had a love affair with FDR when he was assistant secretary of the Navy that resumed decades later when he was president. She was with him when he died in Warm Springs, GA, in 1945.
** Representative Donald "Buz" Lukens, an Ohio Republican, was convicted in May 1989 of having sex with a minor.

a staff member who is paid by the taxpayer (Wayne Hays with Elizabeth Ray*), or with a lobbyist (Tom Evans with Paula Parkinson**).

At the next-easiest level is the politician whose private behavior bespeaks a striking hypocrisy. If a gay congressman goes out of his way to give homophobic speeches, for example, he is a fair candidate for "outing" not only by gay activists but also by the mainstream press. A radical outing publication has recently been trying to interest the major media in a civilian Pentagon official who is gay. This is a far tougher case. Is his presence in the Defense Department a form of collusion in the military's medieval prohibition on gay servicemen and -women? Lacking any evidence that he has a central leadership role in extending that policy, I would vote to preserve his privacy. It does terrible violence to the ideal of a common interest to carry too far the insistence that a particular person, by virtue of gender or sexual orientation or color or any other index, has a greater responsibility than others to address a particular issue. And it would be a very bad idea to set the press up as arbiters of special-interest purity.

Alcoholism and drug use offer clearer standards than sexuality. Postwar Washington offers a sad catalog of powerful men whose alcoholism was covered up, overlooked, and denied. Former House Speaker Carl Albert, former House Armed Services Committee Chairman L. Mendel Rivers, former House Majority Leader Hale Boggs, former Senate Minority Leader Everett Dirksen, former House Ways and Means Committee Chairman Wilbur Mills, and former Senate Finance Committee Chairman Russell Long are just a few of the influential men whose alcoholism, though widely known, went unreported. (Mills and Long are both recovering alcoholics today.) Even in the most destructive hours of Senator Joseph McCarthy's career, the press never reported that he sometimes swigged from a liquor bottle during press conferences and ate butter by the stick to salve his ulcers. Although there were disturbing and unfair elements of the "character" coverage surrounding John Tower's nomination as secretary of defense, it was encouraging to see Washington at least beginning to wrestle, for the first time, with the reality of alcoholism in its midst.

* In 1976, Ray admitted that Hays, an Ohio Republican, kept her on staff to be his mistress. "I can't type, I can't file, I can't even answer the phone," she famously alerted the Washington Post.
** Evans, a Delaware Republican, admitted in 1981 that he had an affair with Parkinson, who subsequently lobbied against a crop-insurance bill that Evans voted against.

Critics of the "new moralism" fear the press corps as a pack of teetotaling, prudish character cops. But the best argument for an expansive approach to reporting on politicians' backgrounds, habits, histories, and families has very little to do with vice. At the end of Freud's century, we understand that people are infinitely complex beings who integrate a huge number of motives and passions in everything they do. Man is not easily compartmentalized, as Washington has long liked to believe; weaknesses and strengths may all be relevant. This complexity is what journalists are edging toward when they mutter their arguments about how something or other speaks to a candidate's "judgment." We have only begun to invent a journalism that can write honestly and responsibly about the subtleties of human nature in politics, but I do believe that is what we are trying to do, and that it is a laudable goal.

Finally, there are cases that do not pose themselves as familiar questions of public interest, but of which the public should unquestionably be informed. An excellent case was the *Washington Post's* publication, in the spring of 1989, of a story detailing the ordeal of a woman named Pamela Small. Sixteen years earlier, she had been senselessly attacked in a store by a clerk who lured her to a back room, pounded her skull in with a hammer, and left her to die. She survived, but her attacker served only twenty-seven months in a county jail. One reason for his lenient treatment was his relation, by marriage, to Representative Jim Wright, who interceded on his behalf and promised him a job. Over the years, the attacker, John Mack, had worked his way up to become a top aide to Wright and perhaps the most powerful staffer in the House. When Small finally decided to tell her story, the reaction in political Washington was astonishing: *Oh*, said many people on the Hill. *We knew that.* It turned out that most of the reporters covering the Hill had known about Mack's crime but had concluded that he'd paid his debt to society. The crime had taken place long ago; and, after all, he was a source. So they hadn't thought to mention it—not even, in many cases, to their editors.

The Post was widely criticized (and is criticized by both Garment and Sabato) for running the story in the midst of Wright's ethics troubles. But it was a riveting story, and it said some mighty interesting things about the culture of Capitol Hill that a man had so easily sloughed off the burden of an unfathomably vicious crime. Surely ordinary men and women, the people out there paying Mack one of the highest salaries in government, had a right to consider whether there are or should be limits to the concepts of rehabilitation and atonement. (When the story ran, they did, and apparently there were. Mack resigned under pressure a week later.)

Journalists will go on debating what should and should not be grist for their mill. Standards will continue to vary enough so that there will be no clear "statute of limitations," no bright line dividing the areas of his or her life that a politician will and won't be seeing on the evening news. The lack of consensus will be confusing and sometimes messy. But recent events suggest that the public is capable of a carefully modulated response to "scandalous" news about public figures. Think, for example, of the different reactions to the dope-smoking pasts of two Supreme Court nominees. Douglas Ginsburg was judged harshly because he had smoked marijuana in the presence of students while a professor at Harvard Law School. Clarence Thomas is judged more leniently because his drug use, as reported by the press, was less a matter of habit and further in the past. (Also, the Reagan administration, which nominated Ginsburg, may have been slightly more vulnerable to charges of hypocrisy than the Bush administration.)*

Sadly, Sabato and Garment are both persuasive in arguing that a majority of talented reporters would rather write about personalities and peccadilloes than face the difficulty of writing about government with sophistication and depth. Here Sabato has the smarter observation to offer: It's not that journalists are heavily biased in political races, he argues. They're so anxious not to seem biased, in fact, that they cling to a concept of journalism in which they are merely recorders and scorekeepers rather than analysts of what is at stake. Both authors are right in arguing, too, that scandal reporting tends to distort politics. If the latest and most lowdown gets the biggest play, it's impossible for any news organization to provide context for the work of reporters who are out there digging around in General Accounting Office and inspector general reports or analyzing program costs for a new weapons system. This, Garment argues, is the case with the Savings & Loan scandal.** If our headlines are constant banners of sleaze, how can the public be expected to grasp the mag-

---

* This essay was published shortly before Thomas was publicly accused of sexual harassment by Anita Hill, his former aide at the Equal Employment Opportunity Commission. Still, the marijuana point remains valid, and it's worth noting that the sexual-harassment charge, which Thomas denied (despite some persuasive corroboration), didn't prevent the Senate from confirming him. He remains on the Supreme Court to this day.

** By 1990, it became clear that sloppily executed legislation during the previous decade that had eased restrictions on federally insured savings & loans, combined with some spec-

nitude of a decade-long blunder costing hundreds of billions of dollars? The boy has cried wolf too often.

But both authors err in seeing scandal coverage as the source of every weakness in contemporary journalism. Sabato and Garment posit some past golden age of journalism in which gross misprision and policy blundering were easily and often exposed by reporters—when it was, they do not say. In fact, many of the restraints that both authors seem nostalgic for also restrained journalists from covering topics that the authors profess to value. Which reporters were systematically exposing the political cynicism that lay behind the Truman administration's loyalty program? Where was the outcry in the fifties, when U.S. soldiers were exposed to atomic tests in the Nevada desert? The same mourned-for respectability and forbearance that turned a blind eye to successive presidents' philandering also, all too often, deferentially overlooked affairs in which the public had an even more obvious stake.

Garment's regret that there wasn't an earlier, more intelligent monitoring of the S&L scandal thus contains an irony: She is talking about assigning the press a watchdog role she otherwise wishes to deny it. The press actually succeeded in naming some of the mess's component parts, and in running (usually on the financial pages) well-informed stories about local and regional S&L problems and the changes in regulation and enforcement that helped fuel the mess. What it did not do—and undoubtedly should have done—was present it as an urgent and coherent problem, and keep at it and at it and at it, even showing the absence of politicians' interest. (As Garment notes, the S&L scandal went unnoticed for so long in part because it implicated both Congress and the executive, both Democrats and Republicans. No simple adversarial relationship means no sources means no story.) In newsrooms, we call this "setting the agenda"—a form of press behavior that Garment abhors in every other circumstance.

Garment summarizes the problems of today's press coverage by writing that

> the aggressive, investigative, adversary style of journalism and the attitudes that go along with it have become the accepted measure of journalistic excellence. All good reporters, in this view, should mistrust official explanations, and reporters should occupy themselves by

tacularly reckless investment (and outright fraud) by S&L owners, had exposed the government to massive financial liability.

digging for things that established institutions do not want us to know. The central purpose of the journalistic craft, the argument continues, is to bring to citizens' attention the flaws in their institutions and leaders. .... Indeed, the basic reason for giving the press very broad protections and privileges in a democracy is that people need to know the bad news in order to perform their duties as citizens.

That's a failing?

—September 1991

THANK YOU, CLARENCE THOMAS

Milling around in the Senate Reception Room Tuesday afternoon, waiting to find out whether they had passed this week's grueling test of their political clout, the leaders of women's groups seemed to be experiencing a kind of vertigo. For ten, fifteen, twenty-five years they've been working at it—wearing their power suits and dignified pumps, going to law school or running for office, dealing themselves into the circle of power and earning the precious labels of belonging: Pragmatic. Effective. Reasonable.

But ever since Monday morning, they and women all over America had felt anew the astringent shock of institutionalized sexism. Whatever the fate of Clarence Thomas's nomination, there is a second dynamic at work now, created almost wholly by the initial myopia of the U.S. Senate. Through what seemed senators' casual dismissal of Anita Hill's allegations, their indignant phrumph-ing about the violation of their "process," these men achieved what scores of dispirited feminists had been unable to do these past ten years: They revived the feminist critique.

Once upon a time, women undertook a radical, comprehensive examination of all the ways in which they felt like second-class citizens: at work, at home, in society, in bed. The personal is political, they told each other. Men are subjects; women are objects. At its height, the women's movement pondered every aspect of women's lives: how much they were paid and how often they did the dishes, how they spoke to their doctors and whether they used makeup, how they regarded themselves and whether their work in and out of the home was valued. Nothing was trivial, for everything touched on women's rights to negotiate their own boundaries, and to define femininity for themselves.

But for the past ten years or so—all through the Reagan era—the rhetoric and philosophical underpinnings of the women's movement have been treated as embarrassingly out of date. "Women's lib": It took on an air of quaintness. It was Bella in her big hats, Betty with her hollowed eyes, masses of braless women yammering about whether to shave their legs. Feminism in the '80s was stripped down and streamlined. Women leaders mapped a pragmatic battle against society's structural sexism, defining "issues" that could be fought in the public policy arena: pay equity and child care, political parity, and safe, legal abortion. And women around the country—whose lives' possibilities had been infinitely enriched by the Bettys and Bellas—got on with it. They went to business school, they became steelworkers. With the help of a more supportive legal structure, some of them hit back when they were excluded or scorned. They made a few more cents on every dollar earned by a man, if not yet the 100 cents their labor was worth.

No one talked anymore about the personal side of feminism: about women's feelings of embattlement, or about whether society's images of female sexuality still seemed to describe some other species. The feminist critique of male-female relations was like a low-rent background women were a little ashamed of; women sidled away from the F-word, as from a bad smell.

And then along came Anita Hill. Now, suddenly, women find themselves using a rusty language of relationship, explaining to men they know how small a woman might be made to feel by a man who insisted on discussing pornography with her, when he had even an implied power to coerce from her even the passive act of listening. Women explain the law, if they have to: that someone needn't be touched to be harassed, what a "hostile environment" is under Title VII of the Civil Rights Act.

In talking to women about the Thomas explosion, I've noticed how quickly they segue from sexual harassment in the workplace to the ambient noise, the daily insults, of their lives. What happens when they walk past construction sites. The kind of casual sexism that comes from men who don't hold power to hire or fire, but who hold the human power to make them feel humiliated by denigrating their gender. Me, I've been remembering the time I came up too close behind a man who was donning his coat at a restaurant checkroom. Reaching his arm back suddenly to catch his sleeve, he clipped me across the nose, knocking my glasses to the floor. "Sorry," he said, laughing. "I try never to hit a woman unless I mean it."

What's this got to do with Clarence Thomas? Nothing. Everything. Because it explains the outrage that many senators aroused in American women this week. It is the baggage women bring to weighing whatever Anita Hill tells us in the hearings about what took place between her and her boss. It is baggage that, in our hardheaded campaign for political equality, we have been hiding, denying, minimizing.

If your workplace is anything like mine, it has been full this week of animated, anxious talk—the kind of conversation where people find, in the middle, that they are talking a little faster and more vehemently than they expected to. We swap stories about insults we have felt—elsewhere, and here at the *Washington Post*. We talk about how we handle it, sometimes making an issue of it, sometimes not. The decision in each case, we agree, is almost entirely political: Will I create more resentment in him than I get rid of in me? Is it worth it? Women make these calculations everywhere, every day. We just didn't talk about it anymore until this week, when we suddenly found ourselves angry, all of us, at the same insult. We are so afraid of whining, sounding like victims, of earning the bad labels that are the flip side of "reasonable" and "effective": Strident. Humorless.

If the environment is sometimes hostile, it is also, often, nurturing. Our lives are different from our mothers' and grandmothers'. And we do feel, a lot of the time, that we hold the power to run our own lives. But never doubt that the anger is down there, that the insults do happen, and that we believe the distress that sometimes mars our daily lives is intimately connected to the way the U.S. Senate almost treated Anita Hill.*

These past few years, our most explosive political scandals have seemed a matter of digesting our history. We keep adjusting, belatedly, to the social revolutions of twenty years ago, tripping the land mines laid back then by the civil rights movement, by Vietnam, by the women's movement. Did it matter that Douglas Ginsburg had smoked marijuana, like almost everyone else his age? How harshly did we want to judge Dan Quayle for skipping Vietnam, like almost everyone else of his social class?** Members of Washington's political elite, controlled by a generation that served in World War II, had never before grappled with these issues, which defined and shaped the generation succeeding them. And

* The Senate Judiciary Committee was initially reluctant to hear Hill's testimony accusing Thomas of sexual harassment; a flood of angry phone calls changed its mind.
** Like President George W. Bush, Quayle served stateside in the National Guard.

now, whatever happens in the Senate, the decade-late reckoning of Clarence Thomas and Anita Hill reminds us all of how radically we have tried to renegotiate the social contract between men and women.

It would be unjust for Clarence Thomas to have to answer for all of the rage this has stirred up. Clearly, the Senate must now exert great, belated care in weighing Hill's allegations. But whatever happens to the Thomas nomination, I can't help rejoicing in this turmoil. In the education everyone is getting about the specific subject of sexual harassment, yes. But also in seeing America roiled and perplexed by this old-fashioned dose of feminist anger.

—*October 11, 1991*

THE PRINCESS PUZZLE

Two nights after the death of Princess Diana, my four-year-old son happened to tell me, in our habitual bedtime chat, about an important difference between him and his best friend. "When Zoe grows up," he told me, "she's going to be Princess Honorine."

And what, I asked him, are you going to be?

"I'm just going to be Willie," he said, in the patient tone of one stating the obvious. And there it is, already, the essential divide that explains why men and women, in America at least, had radically different reactions to Princess Diana's death.

As women swapped confessions about crying when they heard the news, many men scratched their heads in anthropological wonderment at the convulsive grief around them. While women talked about "Di" as if she had been someone they really knew—about her genuineness, her charity work, the way she raised her boys—men seemed to fix on the chemistry of whether the driver had imbibed three times—or was it four?—the legal alcohol limit before climbing behind the wheel. The contrast was perfectly captured by Internet chat rooms, where women posted messages of devastation describing an "angel" and a "saint." The men—greatly outnumbered—seemed chiefly animated by conspiracy theories (Was it British intelligence? Or was it the palace?). In the online magazine *Salon*, a female contributor, Kate Moses, wrote an article explaining "Why part of me died with Diana." The magazine's section for reader responses had a discussion thread titled "I Don't Give a Rat's Ass About the Death of Diana." It was, of course, initiated by a man.

Royal-watching has always been more the province of women than of men. Where male Anglophiles go in for hunting prints and Winston Churchill biographies, female Anglophiles fill their homes with Windsor tea caddies and coronation plates. Not surprisingly, 89 percent of the readers of the British magazine *Majesty* are female. But Diana's entry onto the scene in 1981 launched a far more visceral phenomenon. Diana meant something to women from the first time we saw her. As the wedding approached, some women bought into Diana's nascent myth with the same uncomplicated hunger that sent them to paperback romances, while others saw it as a chance to sneak a wistful snack from the enchanting bridal pastry. Many women of Diana's own generation, schooled in feminism, wallowed a bit ruefully in the fantasy being enacted before our eyes, yet still we wallowed. A female colleague who was then in the Air Force remembers her fellow military intelligence trainees, fresh from the rigors of basic training, sitting a predawn vigil in their barracks to watch the royal wedding, their eyes glazed with yearning.

The reason wasn't hard to grasp. Diana brought to life, on the grandest scale, the archetype of the princess inscribed on every girl's heart. It is written there by fairy tale, by girls' games and jump-rope rhymes, by Uncle Walt and his insidious successors at Disney. (Even today, Disney's fall merchandise catalog includes not only a junior Cinderella costume, but an adult version, priced at $56. "You're never too old to dream of being a princess," the ad copy advises.) Every little girl has, at some age, some totem—a swirling dress, a tattered wand, a spangled tutu—that is her own claim to the throne.

Note, though, that it is the rare little girl who wants to grow up to be queen. To wish to be a princess is not simply to aspire upward, to royalty; it is also to aspire to perpetual daughter-hood, to permanent shelter. To dependency. And this is where Diana's grip on our imagination grew more complicated. For even at the start, it was easy to see the drawbacks. There was the complete loss of freedom. There were the medieval undertones to the whole deal. (How did they *know* she was a virgin? we asked our friends; and, well, who conducted the negotiations on this point, and how?) And there was that chilling suspicion that Charles was, by nature, a less than fervent suitor: When an early interviewer asked the couple if they were in love, and the dewy bride-to-be Diana replied, "Of course," Charles muttered the quintessential guy disclaimer, "Whatever love is." Any modern woman who had been around the block knew *this* routine.

Over time, Diana's awful marriage subverted the myth as fully as she had embodied it in the first place. Women only loved her more for this. Those who most deeply believed in the fairy tale felt a great sense of loss, to be sure. But these women remained fiercely attached to her in her trials, stubbornly hoping to see the dream redeemed. Women of a more feminist bent felt relief, even gratitude, at the crumbling of the Windsor marriage. With every sign of her unhappiness, we could tell ourselves that, yes, our yearnings toward dependency notwithstanding, it really was a better deal out here on the pavement. Whichever way we saw it, we had crucial things at stake in the collapse of the myth.

While her example enabled us to escape some of our illusions about life in the castle, Diana wasn't so fortunate. She never really escaped the castle itself. And she was let down, not just by her own marriage and her role, but by almost every man she seems to have loved. Beyond Charles there was Captain James Hewitt, the riding instructor who kissed and told. And there was Dodi Fayed, with his fast life and bad debts and abandoned California fiancée. There remained some women—those whose illusions had the hardiest roots—who hoped he might finally prove to be the happy ending, the One True Prince. But he was so transparently a bad bet: a man who, in another age, would have been called a bounder.

And, even if she found some well-deserved delight in his arms, he failed her in the end as badly as one person can fail another. Once the hysterics surrounding the paparazzi's deplorable behavior subside, there will be only one clear conclusion to draw from Diana's sad end in a car owned by the Fayeds and driven to its violent stop by an intoxicated Fayed functionary: that for all her fame and her thirty-six years and her accomplished motherhood and her millions, the life of a princess prepared her very poorly to look after herself.

And this is why the manner of her death, even more than her life, has a terrible power for women. It is such a stark lesson to us all, from those who still cling to their princess fantasies to those who have entirely relinquished them to the greater number of women who fall somewhere between those extremes. As long as Diana was out there, plying her glamorous, uncertain path to a full self, we could at least retain our ambivalence about the myth. We've known for a while that trying to be a princess can stifle you, but it's horrible to think it can kill you.

This is where men begin to adopt puzzled frowns. Can this old drama really be so powerful in the lives of modern women? In fact, this drama *is* girlhood and young womanhood in America: a succession of choices between the possibilities of independence and the seductions of dependence.

It is the rare woman who hasn't a story about silencing her own fears while riding shotgun, as a teenager or a young woman, in a car driven recklessly by a guy she wanted to please. I have my own humiliating memory of riding through France, as it happens, on a vacation—in a car with three other people: my boyfriend, his brother, and the brother's girlfriend. I was almost ten years younger than Diana was at the time of her death. The brother, at the wheel of our rented Renault, drove at a terrifying speed around the stony corners of the towns we passed through. It was one of the few times I've feared for my life in a car. But in the course of four or five hours, I only managed to peep a few times, in my most apologetic, placatory, good-girl tones, that I wished he would slow down. My cowardice is unthinkable to me today. Yet I still have pangs of nostalgia about being swept off to France; and there are times, I regret to say, when I miss that good girl's easy manner and pleasing ways.

This, finally, is the difference in men's and women's feelings about the life and death of Diana, Princess of Wales. The moral of the story is that whether she's riding in a gilt carriage that bears her to St. Paul's Cathedral for the wedding of the century, or in a black Mercedes that bears her to her death, a passenger—which is the most a princess can hope to be—is never in charge. It's a hard lesson for women to learn, and it's one that men knew all along.

—September 15, 1997

ENTOMOPHOBIA

Willie began to worry about bugs in the fall of last year, when he was three. Time after time, when he had reluctantly gone to bed, he would call us back up the stairs to complain that there was a bee in his room, or a fly; something that buzzed. One night he insisted hysterically, eyes wide with terror but mind still trapped in some cave of sleep, that he saw ants marching across the bedcovers. The sighting of a single wasp could end an afternoon at the playground.

I asked his preschool teacher if children were often scared of bugs at this age. She was a shy woman whose slow, light voice, pitched to the emotional receptors of three-year-olds, concealed an impressive precision of mind. At three, she said without hesitation, children begin to understand just how big the world is, and just how indifferent to their well-being. Typically they handle this awful news by grappling with one or two specific terrors.

I felt foolish when I heard this answer, which sounded an altogether graver note than I had expected. What I had sought, I realized after the fact, was something tidy, a reassuring summary of a Known Fear, or Classic Stage: *Bugs, Fear Of: Occurring predictably between forty and forty-five months; see also Bed, Monsters Under. . . .* Looking back, I marvel at my obtuseness. For I already knew what large fears could be encompassed in a horror of the tiny.

My own fear of bugs began when I got my first apartment, in New York City, and found myself in a war of attrition with the cockroaches. I was nineteen, and had only the smallest purchase on this new life; defending my territory seemed a desperate business. My tiny sixth-floor walk-up reeked of pesticide, and even before the morning I woke to find a roach under the sheet, groping its ticklish way up my bare chest, I carried a can of Raid with me everywhere in the apartment. I put on my glasses to go to the bathroom in the middle of the night.

Once I was invited to dinner by an acquaintance from work, a cheerful, round young woman who favored dresses with pouffy sleeves and lace collars. She wrote romance novels on weekends and lived in the same genteel first-job poverty I did, in a one-bedroom near Lexington Avenue, with the same castoff furniture, the same bookshelves groaning with paperbacks, the same small collection of mismatched dishes. But she inhabited the parallel universe that lay beyond surrender: Her apartment seethed with roaches. They were on every surface of her kitchen, crawling, ignored, up all four walls of any room we entered; as she chopped the final garnish for the chicken salad she had prepared, she reached into the bowl to pluck out a roach and placed it casually on the counter. It felt like being in a horror movie, in which the hostess seems normal until she offers up a platter of eyeballs at the cocktail hour. As my friend chattered on, oblivious, I moved sideways through her doorway and then perched on the edge of my chair, trying secretly to levitate away from any contact at all with her world.

I left New York, for a more expansive life in Washington. But the sudden revulsion of happening upon an insect, the twitchy, outsize fear, never left me. During cricket season, no power on earth can coax me down the basement stairs after dark. They grow to the size of small frogs down there—stupid ones, that leap blindly when you startle them and thump with an unexpected heaviness against your thigh. This year, we've had a stubborn infestation of moths in our food cabinets, and it doesn't seem to matter how many times I throw out all the flour and cereal and macaroni and graham crackers—all the foods on which they might possibly thrive; still they propagate, fluttering drunkenly forth in pairs and triplets every time a cupboard door is opened. For a time we had a cartoon-perfect wasps' nest under the eaves at the back of the house, built in just the right spot so that one or two wasps danced, on and off through the day, at the window of my second-story office, a small omen in my peripheral vision.

Having children only made the problem—the volume of the insect life, and also my fear of it—worse. My son is now four and a half, my daughter two, but during the highchair years there was always a sheen of pear syrup and peanut butter, riches beyond the wildest ant-dreams, on a sizable patch of the kitchen linoleum.

I tell myself that all parents wring their hands over the chaos of family life, but I think perhaps I fight it harder than most. I resent it, in ways that I am often ashamed of: the external chaos of living with small children and all their stuff, yes; but especially the internal chaos, the way my mind seems colonized or overrun or even, in my darkest hours, infested by motherhood. The loss of control is exquisitely incomplete, just partial enough to lure me into a constant struggle to get on top of things. I can remind myself that the will to impose order isn't only about housecleaning; that my fear of losing these modest battles is in some way a surrogate for the larger, unthinkable losses to which parenthood opens one. And still I fool myself: If I could just get this done, I am tempted to think, or this, or this, or this. . . . But always there is some little bug. Some fly in the ointment. Something slipping through a crack.

It is because of the wasps' nest that we finally call the exterminator, one of those national monoliths that now dominate the business, dispatching an army of technicians who seem to have only first names. Dennis appears late on a Friday afternoon and walks all around the house, inside and out, and finds infestations of every conceivable pest that might require monthly applications of insecticide. Pests that even I have not thought to be pestered by. He finds, besides crickets and moths, earwigs and silverfish and yellow jackets, house ants and carpenter ants. He finds termites in a rotting stump out back. He mentions brown recluse spiders.

I must look like an easy mark, like the guy who takes a taxi out to the car dealer. But I am delighted to be sold such a comprehensive solution to our bug problems. Great, I say: Bring on your cyfluthrin, your propetamphos, your Dursban Pro. I thrill to the idea that we can actually make a clean sweep. Imagine a home (I think) where I never have to jump at the sudden sight of an earwig on the threshold, the tickle of an ant scaling my leg. I look out over the living room, with its slag heap of plastic toys; over the crumb-infested kitchen, with its sticky place mats and the minefield of books and puzzles seeded across its floor. Imagine, I think, living in a house where *something* seems under control.

On the evening of the same day, I find myself on my hands and knees in the back yard, holding a green plastic magnifying glass. I am trying, with my son, to catch an ant. And when we have caught it, and put it in a plastic bucket that stands ready, *we plan to bring it into the house.* I know, even as I do it, that this is an insane activity for a woman who spent her afternoon courting Bug Armageddon. But Willie wants this bug, and so I am going to help him get it.

In hindsight, we could see with perfect clarity that Willie's bug fear set in at about the same time he slowed his dash toward everything new. At two, he had been a grinning boy who greeted strangers with a chattering faith that their pockets must be lined with gifts for him. His hair was a bright blond, just turning to caramel. But at three, his outlook clouded. He absented himself, through some process invisible to us but perfectly legible to his peers, from the tentative rites of early friendship; he preferred the company of grown-ups, or of a book, or of himself. Drawn to the intricate and the cerebral, he seemed repelled by the new loudness, the physicality of his classmates, who heaved the playground mulch at each other whenever the teacher's back was turned. Now he moved sideways toward anything new, face tense with the understanding that surprise could be bad as easily as good.

It was a difficult year. His little sister was a challenge. He wasn't chronically unhappy, by any means, but this final passage from the beaming simplicity of his toddlerhood into something more spiky and complex often seemed to flatten him. Yes, yes, I can hear myself insisting to the Brazeltonian figure who rules my parental conscience: Of course there was also richness in this new stage. Of course this passage was also about the growing strength of his mind and his wit. But the fact remains that there was loss in it. For Willie, a loss of ease. And for me, the loss of my ability to cure every woe. I could still keep his body safe, but his soul's repose was more and more up to him, and he was finding it a struggle. Sometimes, when he didn't know anyone was watching, his eyes would take on a discouraged puzzlement that made me want to shake the mulch-throwers until their teeth rattled.

So that is why Willie and I are searching, in the patchy grass of our city yard, for an ant to catch. Because Willie, having chosen his particular fear, or recognized it as a familiar, simply went about beating it, bug by bug.

His excellent preschool helped, with its "bug habitats" made from old fish tanks, and its director, a girlish genius in her fifties, who with Willie examined every leaf on the playground in a search for ladybug larvae. And so did a field trip to Washington's Discovery Creek Children's Museum, where naturalists lead children on bug-hunting expeditions through a woodsy ravine that lies just to the west of MacArthur Boulevard. There an animated young woman assembled the children in a circle and lectured them briefly, in their terms, about ants and bees and spiders. ("Can you say *com-pound eyes?*")

James and the Giant Peach also helped. Willie especially liked a scene in the book in which James, along with the foolish Centipede, seems to have fallen off the great peach transporting him and his huge bug friends across the ocean. The gentle Earthworm bursts into tears, crying, "I don't care a bit about the Centipede, but I really did love that little boy!"

"I really *did* love that little boy," Willie would mimic out of the blue, over dinner, in a kind of sobbing falsetto. And then he would laugh his old, untrammeled laugh. Soon we were having long, Manichean conversations about virtue and evil in the bug kingdom. "Mommy, are ladybugs good bugs or bad bugs?" An easy one: good bugs. "Mommy, bees are bad bugs because they sting you." Well, yes, I explained, but they also make honey, and help flowers grow. But Willie was not interested in mitigating circumstances. "Mommy, are moths good bugs or bad bugs?" Well . . . I think they're not good or bad. They don't sting you, but they don't do much for you either. "*Mommy*, all bugs are good bugs or bad bugs. So I think moths are good bugs."

Finally, by late spring, his work was complete. We were sitting on the kitchen floor one day when Willie spotted a fat ant. The week before, he would have said, "Mommy, smoosh it, quick!" This time, he said, "Mommy, catch it!" And so, in spite of myself, I did. Now he has two little plastic jars, with screw-on tops, that we use to scoop ants off blades of grass. We've used, for temporary quarters, an array of plastic tubs and buckets and paper cups with rubber bands and Saran wrap and tinfoil. With my help, he's caught several ladybugs, numerous beetles, the occasional slug, a roly-poly, a handful of daddy longlegs, a miscellany of spiders.

And to my surprise, I love our insect hours. Part of it is the familiar way that time slows and expands when you make yourself truly stop and be where your child is, doing what he is doing, trying neither to manage nor to escape it. As Willie searches, his self-consciousness falls away. I can surreptitiously inventory his newly skinny body, the arms and legs that are suddenly, shockingly long. (I did love that little boy.) I can covet the sweet spot at the back of his neck, just below his hairline, until he shoots a swift glance upward at me: "Oh Mommy, you missed it. You were supposed to look at the spider." He says this with sympathy, for my opportunity lost.

And even this gift, this sweet present, contains another from the past: the dimmest memory, lost until now, of a day when my own mother held up a caterpillar, inviting me to touch the velvety length of it, and an era when my sisters and I flitted in our white nightgowns through the bluing air, catching lightning bugs to take up to our bedrooms in old mayonnaise jars. Watching Willie's serious absorption of new information, I recall, for the first time in years, the deep childhood contentment of learning new facts: the order of the planets, the notes of the scale, the ages of man. *Thorax. Ootheca. Exoskeleton.*

But it is respect, above all, that sends me to my knees in the rough grass. Since the days of the sixth-floor walk-up and the ever-present Raid I've taken plenty of risks in my life—the standard grown-up risks of work and love and family—and have courted, along the way, the healthy fears that follow. But I can't say I've ever faced a fear as directly as my son did: simply looking at it, straight on, until he found what he could love in it.

One evening, Willie spotted a praying mantis in the flower bed near the back fence. It looked huge, and jumped when he approached it. At first I tried to avoid any part in its capture. I feigned concern for its welfare; I explained how rare and special it was; I may even have sunk so low as to suggest that it would miss its mommy. But inevitably I was lured into stalking it, in a giddy, lurching dance through the day lilies. And when we caught it, I could see that it was breathtaking, with its strange red eyes, its swiveling lozenge of a head, and the fern-like forelegs with which it felt all around the bowl that imprisoned it. Watching it, I felt both revulsion and awe—felt them fully, and sharply, and simultaneously, as Willie must feel things all the time.

Now my son and I conspire to hold both of these elements between us, forever in tension, the terror and the appreciation of what is going on under our roof. *Yuck,* I say, when I see an inch-long beetle lurking in the corner of the doorway. *No, he's beautiful,* Willie says, and of course he's right, and I'm glad to be made to see that the beetle is the color of cafe au lait, with perfectly symmetrical black spots on its shell and legs elaborately carved from ebony.

This is not insect biology alone, I finally see, but also the physics of motherhood, a lesson in the two forces that will press upon me for as long as my children are young, or longer. On the one side there is the maddening disorder, the constant, unexamined fear, the dark possibilities that live within the walls of even the best-ordered life. The knowledge that something vital may be slipping through the cracks. But on the other side, exerting a blessedly equal force, there is wonder: the way that a four-year-old can capture and hold in his hand the brightness of a firefly, and then release it still glowing to its life.

—*December 14, 1997*

THE ALCHEMIST

The last thing my mother really hungered for was a lump of cottage cheese with mayonnaise on top.

"*Mayonnaise?*" my oldest sister cried.

"You mean, on *top?*" I asked. "Really?"

We were entitled to our shock. My mother's passion for good food was the clearest thing about her, the one brilliant shade in a palette that disguised most of its colors by blending them to their duskiest forms. She was a truly gifted, self-trained cook, and when she ate, she did it slowly, seriously, like an archaeologist plucking bones from a fossil bed, teasing out only the choicest specimens. I see her now in her sunny dining room, one ankle hitched over the opposite knee, working the Acrostic puzzle in the Sunday *New York Times* while eating lunch in her deliberate, cat-like way. She could make a whole hour's work of a single sandwich of grilled Gruyere.

She loved sharp tastes, savory tidbits: olives and sardines, cornichons and blue cheeses and redolent pates. At the end of her life, when her doctors had made her give up almost everything she loved—caffeine and alcohol and fats and salt and sugar of any kind—the salt was perhaps the one she minded most. (That's putting alcohol aside for the moment; giving up liquor was what she must have minded most, of course, but by then her cirrhosis was so advanced that drinking any at all had immediately gruesome consequences.) All she had left, at the end, was her cigarettes, and by then it was almost a pleasure to bring her the ceremonial ashtray, the Bic, the pack of Carltons she had bought by the carton as far back as my memory goes. The hospice nurses looked gently shocked. Had they ever seen a family so avidly pressing carcinogens upon a dying parent? Their kind faces said not.

But our inability to comfort—ourselves, each other—through food was excruciating. And hearing her ask for cottage cheese with mayo was the rough equivalent of learning that Vladimir Horowitz's deathbed wish was to hear Elton John. It was the real thing, one more undeniable sign that my mother meant to die.

I see Beverly always in her kitchen, moving from sink to refrigerator to stove in her loose, comfy, dark-colored cottons. She moved more and more slowly as the years went by, but always with a dancer's lightness. Especially in her last years, when she wore mostly sneakers, my mother walked with soundless grace.

In cooking, she almost never took shortcuts. She insisted on buying a restaurant-quality Viking gas stove, way back in 1963, before it was a standard badge of Yuppie cultivation; the men who delivered it had to remove its legs to get it through the front door. She would happily use three pans in a recipe for which I might use one, if three would give her even an ounce of effect—braising a few tablespoons of minutely diced celery, for example, to liven up the peas. She made an art of such tedious jobs as chopping scallions. First, after washing them and trimming the ends, she would take her smallest paring knife and cut up from the end of the scallion, then she would turn it a quarter turn and bisect the first cut with another, again working the knife almost to the trimmed green tips. Only then would she lay the scallion against her weathered cutting board and chop it briskly, *cuk cuk cuk*, with her big Sabatier chopping knife. The scallion would fall neatly into tiny quarter-slices thin as postage stamps.

She put masses of butter in everything—real butter, from a covered white butter dish that lived perpetually on the counter, so the butter inside would always be pleasingly soft. Butter, and wine, and onions, the holy trinity of French cuisine. She taught herself to cook really well around the time when *Mastering the Art of French Cooking* first appeared, and French cooking was always the basic template for her efforts. Later she got interested in Italian cooking, too, in the years when my parents scratched together enough money for regular vacations in Italy. There was a brief phase when she made her own pasta, with a hand-cranked machine, hanging the long irregular strings over the ladder-back kitchen chairs until the pot was on the boil. But the real magic of her kitchen always lay in the basics of French cooking: the long, slow simmers of concoctions that smelled of Madeira and beef broth, the huge cuts of top-quality meat, the loving administration of artery-clogging creams and cheeses.

When she first learned to cook she was the mother of three small children, born in a span of four years. We lived way out in the country then, in a fieldstone house in Bucks County, Pennsylvania, from which my father commuted to New York and to which he returned late in the evening. I picture her passing long, weary afternoons at the stove, as she worked her way through the techniques that Child and Bertholle and Beck laid out for what they quaintly called "the servantless American cook." As an adult I asked her several times what she had felt, living in the country with three little girls and few near neighbors in a time when motherhood involved the laborious boiling of formula and the washing and line-drying of cloth diapers. "I do remember," she said, "the first time I managed to get you all out of the house and into the car." She said this with a faraway look in her eyes, but in a weighted voice, as if she had just told a complicated story full of passion and incident. Only after I became a mother myself could I picture her exhaustion, and the scramble of diapers and snowsuits and runny noses and tiny mittens that any such expedition would involve.

In moving to the country and becoming a wife and mother, she had given up a job she loved, in a lab at the Sloan-Kettering Institute in New York. I've always imagined that the contained intrigue of cooking spoke to the chemistry major in her: for a student, for a good girl, science and cooking share the reassuring quality of exploring the unknown within a preordained scheme. There was a scientific rigor to the way she excised every last bit of offending fat from a cut of meat, to the way she chopped vegetables: Her broccoli had the petite uniformity of Legos.

There was a time, two and three years after my birth—I am the youngest—when she turned her hand to writing about food. My father was a book editor, so there were contacts in the business; writing professionally was a plausible dream. Among her files, after her death, I found the slim records of this abortive ambition: a slick, garishly colored clip from *Ladies Home Journal*, titled "Ham: The Most Versatile Actor in the Kitchen," for which she was paid the then-handsome sum of $500. Another piece, never sold, called "Soup is the Answer." ("For anyone who cooks, be she the bride of a week or the most practiced hostess in the land, soup is the answer to all problems.") Notes toward a third, "My Ten Favorite Expensive, Calorific, Time-Consuming, Difficult, Delicious Spectacular Utter Dreamy Desserts for Feckless and Festive Occasions."

The effusiveness of these writings was not typical of her; it was only canny marketing. "The copy," my mother wrote in a note to the literary agent who was helping her place her pieces, "is patterned as closely as I could manage on the *Journal*'s kind of yummyese."

In another note to the agent, she wrote, "I'm trying to work out an arrangement which will give me one whole free day a week (!!!) at the typewriter, but before I set out to hire all that baby-sitting I really would like some professional counsel from you." What counsel was forthcoming the file doesn't say, and I don't know if she ever asserted her claim to that whole free day a week. There are a few mildly encouraging letters from others in the file—one is a carbon copy of a note that one of my father's colleagues at Little, Brown wrote to James Beard, asking his advice on the possibility that my mother might write a cookbook about "the feeding of children"; another is a note from Alfred Knopf Jr., of Atheneum Publishers, urging her to give him first crack at any cookbook she might write. ("The idea that you might have to compete with other publishers for this leaves me gasping with helpless mirth," she replied, with the graceful humility that governed all these efforts.)

At some point (I can't find a date on the manuscript, or any suggestion that she tried to sell it), she turned her hand to an account of her own self-education in food. "It was not until I gave up my job and began having babies that I really began to enjoy cooking consciously—anything to get away from pablum and strained vegetables," she wrote, with an asperity that was resolutely expunged from her spoken statements on motherhood.

> I badgered my husband for a copy of *The Gourmet Cookbook*, and spent hours over it. I discovered right away how wrong I was about salads. . . . I now learned that I must dry the lettuce, preferably in a French lettuce basket; I must tear the leaves, or if determined to cut them, I must use a silver knife; I must never, never put tomatoes in a green salad, they make it watery; I must use a wooden bowl which I must never wash; I must rub it first with a cut clove of garlic, and make the dressing in the bowl; I must add the washed, chilled greens and toss at the last possible minute.

And so she always did.

I made quiche lorraine and coq au vin; veal parmigiana and boeuf Bourguignon; I made an eight-layer dobas tort which the dog ate when my back was turned; I had to get a special French pan (iron, rustable) for crepes instead of using my Revere ware (steel, stainless); I made my own stock from scratch, and mixed my own curry powder in a mortar and pestle, and eschewed all that was frozen; and in what I now recognize as the crisis of my disease, I made a croquembouche.

As you see, my mother had a dry wit and the rhythms of a born writer. But our family narrative assigned all the verbal genius to my father and, over the years, my mother was ever less able to show this plumage. At the end of 1962 all the correspondence simply stops. Soon after that, she began working as a substitute science teacher at a private day school in Princeton. And, by 1963, when we moved to Princeton, she was a full-time administrator at the school. Ultimately she did all the scheduling there, and stayed there until her retirement in 1993, becoming one of those quietly powerful characters who stealthily run all the world's social microcosms. I believe she liked the work a lot, and I have no way of knowing whether she regretted the abandonment of her brief effort to write about her passion. But I find myself treasuring these few letters and articles, as evidence of a time when her passion for food seemed to be aligned—or do I mean allied?—with her best, most cheerful energies.

I can't put my finger on when she changed. In one compartment of my mind I see a mother of graceful shape and flashing eyes, who wore her long hair in a sleek bun, held with big tortoise shell pins. As girls, my sisters and I watched her dress for an evening out: I see a stiff red silk, heavily embroidered in gold thread; a little black dress with a plunging neckline; a flowing, cobalt caftan covered in bright flowers.

But in the next, much larger compartment is the mother I knew for most of my life, who dressed to conceal. This was the mother we teased because she never wanted to go swimming, until finally, one day, she told me that she just couldn't stand to be seen in a bathing suit. I associate the change in her with one of those nights out, when she went to New York to meet my father, and then appeared at breakfast the next day with her hair chopped bluntly to her chin. But that's just a trick of memory: It was a much slower process, cresting when my sisters and I were adolescents.

Looking back, it is as if her camouflage deepened in step with the flowering of her culinary skills. Her table became famous among her friends for its loving excellence. My parents threw frequent dinner parties, at which bittersweet chocolate mousse was served for dessert in old china demitasses, with spares made in the chipped cups for me and my sisters to eat upstairs, with tiny silver spoons. Once James Beard came to dinner, massive and pleasant; my mother made a crown roast of lamb, and always remarked on the way that none of the guests dared utter a satisfied word about the food, so cowed were they by the master's presence. By the time I was old enough to understand something of adult life, I knew that my parents were an awesome tag-team: My father's career was in its ascendance, and the guests who came to eat my mother's food were sometimes famous. I have some fine first editions with inscriptions from their authors praising my mother's food or thanking my parents for a pleasant evening. My parents' house drew the town's writers, and the writers who came through Princeton as temporary faculty learned that it was a haven where they would eat the best food in town.

My parents cannily mixed these writers with Princeton's anxious gentry. Most of their local friends had far more money than they did, bigger houses and more formal lives. But they loved to eat from my mother's old pine table, to sit on the second-hand Naugahyde sofa in the book-lined living room, and to fancy that this was Bohemia. Once my parents planned a spectacular dinner for Carlos Fuentes—how they snagged him I don't know; they hardly knew him—and invited a tableful of people who were more ornaments than friends. Afterwards, one guest—the wife of a famous Cold Warrior—wrote my mother a gushingly patronizing note, all about what a wonderful cook she was, and what a terrific outlet this must be for her creative energies.

My mother bore such condescension well; she was used to being addressed as my father's supporting cast. She seemed hardly to sit down at these parties, or at big family meals, and always occupied the chair nearest the kitchen so she could dart back and forth. Her province was the kitchen, and my father's was the living room; thinking back over my childhood, I almost reflexively place myself in the short passage between these two rooms, by the back stairs—the one spot from which you could see into both rooms and both lives. The conversation in the living room was, to a teenager and young adult, literally fascinating—the fun these grownups seemed to have, their joy in their own cleverness, the easy eminence of some of the guests, the satisfaction of everyone who was included in the circle of my father's regard. I listened hungrily for evidence of what adult life might be, and how it could be managed along lines less self-denying than the example my mother was setting in the next room.

I think my mother loved the brightness that burned around him, but she loved it silently, and at a remove, because there was always something in the other room that had to be stirred or turned or browned or basted. When things in the kitchen were briefly under control, she would steal quietly into the living room, ashtray and cigarettes in hand, and curl with her dancer's fluidity into a chair; from there she would take in the scene, seldom interjecting herself, until she finished one cigarette and the timer in her head told her that the potatoes were done or the flame should be turned down, and she would steal quietly out again.

The cooking she did for family was almost as effortful as what she turned out for company. Somehow she struggled home from her job every evening, and managed all the shopping, and turned out a real meal every night of our lives. In our early years we girls ate first, separately from the grown-ups, and even those meals were elaborate: almost always a meat and a starch and a vegetable, and often a child-friendly salad, with half a canned pear on top, perhaps, smiling from a food-coloring face applied with the tip of a toothpick.

There was a sacramental quality to all the care she took. A few days after my son was born, by a harrowing emergency C-section, she took the train to Washington. She wasn't one to gush over a grandchild, and she didn't have a lot of motherly advice to offer, but she stood in my kitchen for three days and raised a rich miasma of smells that wafted up to my bed and surrounded me in a downy blanket of home—her home, the primordial, childhood home. When a friend came by with a turkey, my mother reduced its leftovers to sub-atomic particles, leaving in the freezer the makings of four different dinners and a quart of rich turkey stock. She made filet of beef, and a potato gratin swimming in cream lushly fortified with stock; she roasted a loin of pork, and served it with wild rice and broccoli steamed just so, al dente, and dressed with lemon and pepper. I remember every meal she made for me in those three days, down to the chef's salad we ate in the den just before my husband drove her to her train. Before she left she peeled me an orange, undressing it in a single careful spiral, picking all the little white veins off each slice and then fanning them prettily on a plate.

With adulthood, I had found that food remained one of the few clear channels between me and my mother. She sent me recipes and gave me cookbooks and china and fine Le Creuset pots and Calphalon pans for Christmas; I called her in the middle of dinner parties, to ask why my Yorkshire pudding looked so peculiar. *What are you eating?* I would ask her, if we happened to talk during dinner. Or *I made that chicken from Giuliani Bugiali the other day, remember that?* Yes, she'd say, but I hope you took the skin off; he doesn't tell you to, but it's much better that way.

But this was never an unmixed pleasure, this talk. It's a truism that mothers express their love through the food they put on the table. Yet my mother seemed not so much to express her love, or sublimate it, through food, as almost to overcome it. For she was not an effusive woman or even, in our later years together, a warm one. Cooking, which others praised as her glory, seemed to me her bunker. Some time during my adolescence, the mother I loved had vanished into the faultless form of giving that ruled her orderly kitchen. You could eat at her table every night and never once taste the thing that you were really hungry for.

I know I remember a warmth emanating from her in my earliest childhood: how much I loved to lean into her, hugging the stalk of her thighs. I have tiny patches of memory about moments when we were alone together—that priceless state that to a youngest child seems rarer than anything else on earth. One cold morning my mother showed me how she could make brilliant red spiders dance above the logs in the fireplace by strumming the poker along the glowing sides of the wood; another day she held up a small blob of mercury from a broken thermometer, inviting me to wonder. As I write these memories I am struck that they draw her as mistress of the elemental.

But as we grew along, and the elements she commanded seemed so determinedly rooted in her kitchen, I learned to think of her mastery as an ordinary one, almost perversely self-limiting. While she loved good food, she seemed much less interested in consuming it than in sending it forth; her own pleasure in eating was a private, almost illicit, affair. Unlike other mad cooks I've known, she had little interest in visiting the great restaurants of the places she traveled: She did it when the chance came along, and liked it a lot, but there was never anything avid in her consumption of other people's cooking.

And that, finally, is why I am fascinated by the still life of my mother at the stove. It seems to hold the mystery of her. It certainly felt like love, a lot of the time, to be on the receiving end of all that effort; any time I doubt it, I remember the sacrament of the post-partum orange and feel embraced by the conviction that she loved me. I am bereft that I will never again sit down to a plate filled with her tender, melting gifts. Yet at the bottom of me, where the crucial certainties live, I don't really believe that my mother's lavish, exacting, whole-hearted cooking had much to do with generosity. Could anyone so self-abnegating feel truly generous, for decades at a time? I shrank, and still shrink, from thinking so. And while it's true that I'm grateful for all of what she fed into me with her food— for knowing what good food tastes like, and knowing, as much as I really want to, how to cook well myself; for having been a child whose mother took the time to paint faces on her pears with a toothpick—it's also true that I always felt wary about what I might swallow along the way.

Because here is the rest of the story: My father eventually got tired of living in a marriage divided by that passage past the back stairs. He left my mother for a woman the same age as my oldest sister; a very good woman, as luck had it, who could slap a roast or a turkey into the oven as well as any other middling-good cook. He had his own hungers, of course, and it's possible that no one could have answered them completely. I think my mother had overlooked for years his enormous need to seek the love of women elsewhere; sometimes it was sexual, and sometimes it was not, but it was always omnivorous. My father's mother had killed herself when he—the youngest, and gentlest, of her three sons—was eleven years old. It may be too simplistic to draw a straight line between that event and his unassuagable appetite for love and approval, but when you hear hoof-beats, why think zebras?

I think what I watched, over all those years, was my mother's decision to look away: to ignore and overrule her most immediate passions, the bit-ter stew of jealousy she has to have tasted all the time; has to have, I insist to myself even now, since I can know this only by the work of my intel-lect, never by what I witnessed in her outward behavior. She schooled us all to laugh at the time he spent an entire party under his host's piano, locked in flirtation with a woman he admired. She welcomed, as a friend of the family, a woman with whom he had an affair of many years' dura-tion. She scolded curiosity into silence. I think she rose above and rose above until she had reached a place where she was quite cut off—from him and also from almost everyone else, including her daughters.

It was only in secret that she was queen of her own domain. It was the land of late at night, when I would hear her downstairs, moving quietly around her kitchen, straightening a thing or two in the living room, then back to kitchen. *Clink*, went her ashtray on the counter, as she stood at the sink to start the dishwasher. *Chrhissshh*, went her Bic as she lit another Carlton. She sipped from her glass of cranberry-juice-and-soda, which might or might not also contain an illicit jolt of Vodka. It was the world of the kitchen, where she made such bounty that you never thought to wonder at the fact that it required her constant removal to a part of the house where she was alone.

My mother had been working at her death for years. She had in her bedroom all the Hemlock Society books that are available; she joked about how if she ever got sent to a nursing home, her best friend was going to come and put a pillow over her face. Once I sought to probe a little past her jokes and brisk comments, and she gave me a look that I only saw about half a dozen times in my life with her: unvarnished by good manners. "Don't you know?" she asked. "Whenever there's no one your age around, that's all people my age talk about."

And that was before she was really sick. Once her cirrhosis was advanced, she often raised the subject of her estate. "While you're home," she said each Thanksgiving, "we really should have a talk about things." We never had the talk, because when push came to shove it didn't seem she wanted to. But she continued to drop in allusions to her coming death: She'd leased a car instead of buying one, she told us more than three years before she died, because it might be cheaper from an estate-planning point of view. Once, when we came home for a holiday, my sister opened a cabinet to get a glass and saw, against the back wall, a tiny Post-it note: She had saved the box these glasses came in, she wrote, in the basement jam closet; that way it would be easy to pack them up and move them.

One January, her doctor told her that she was unlikely to live for more than another year or two. And once she was given that verdict, she more or less lay down and died. I think now that she'd been maintaining her life by the greatest silent effort, and that it was a relief to her to surrender it. My sisters and I got her into hospice care, at home, and there was a relative minimum of physical indignity. Once she needed full-time care, she pretty much lost her hold on reality, with only brief windows of lucidity; from the time a visiting nurse deployed her first adult diaper, it was less than three weeks to the end.

One of my sisters lived nearby, and the other sister and I spent most of those last weeks in Princeton. Once again, we three were the daughters of the house, greeting visitors and answering the phone and taking charge. Amid the sadness and confusion of my mother's death, it was a weirdly pleasant experience—to spend so much time with my sisters, in my mother's well-ordered universe, away from the demands of our own homes and children. Deluged by kind friends with roasted chickens and caterers' trays, we even had the illusion of reexperiencing the miraculous plenty of my mother's larder.

But the mystery of Mummy's life hung over us constantly. Something about the situation—our bafflement about what we might do for her; the strange normality of the routine that surrounded her desperate condition—mirrored our lifetimes of trying and failing to meet a need that was always obscure.

There she was, in the hospital bed that had been brought in and set up in the corner of her bedroom, comatose some of the time and the rest of the time small and frail, with an avian air of confusion. In those times when she was conscious, she had odd, urgent appetites: for things like cottage cheese slathered in mayonnaise. When she was past talking, but still conscious, she would simply open her mouth in a silent demand for drink; and one of us would stand over her with a medicine dropper, dripping milk or ginger ale or water into that gummy, dank-smelling maw. We would drip, she would swallow, drip, swallow, drip, swallow, and still her mouth would yawn open again, almost regal in demand.

That she was faintly demanding in her death we accepted, or tried to; won't we all, shouldn't we all be? So we asked ourselves and each other. We read *Howards End*, her favorite book, to her, and Yeats, her favorite poet; we got her morphine when she was in pain, and held her hand and stroked her brow. I'm glad to know that I did well by my mother. But beneath my actions, I found in myself an undercurrent of outrage. For my mother remained as self-contained, as unexpressive, as always. It seems impossible to me that when I die my last thoughts will not be of my son and daughter, my last urgent will to express myself not some wish to tell them what joy they have given me and what joy I wish for them. She had none of these words for us. On one of the last days when she was able to get out of bed, she came downstairs for a meeting with the hospice social worker, who asked her about her life story. Because of the cirrhosis, which acts on the brain chemistry, and the surreal social anxiety of the event, my mother delivered a strange, half-real version of her life. In it, her career all took place at Sloan-Kettering. She knew she had three grandchildren, but she told the hospice worker wrongly (though brightly) that she'd never met my little girl. I tried with all the force of my forty years to honor the medical origins of this mistake. And yet I couldn't push away—and still can't—feeling hurt that my little Alice, who is so large a piece of me, was one of the facts of her life that my mother mislaid.

A few days later, when she briefly came out of what the hospice nurse had confidently predicted was her final coma, she had a strangely girlish, radiant smile. But this she directed chiefly at my middle sister's boyfriend, a man who had come on the scene quite recently. That same afternoon, my mother's best friend descended from a visit to the bedroom to tell the three of us, "Your mother just told me, 'I love you.'" And the three of us cried, "She did? She *did*? Really?" My eldest sister asked, "Did she just say it, or did you say I love you to her first, or ask her if she loved you or something?" Later we laughed off our rivalrous reaction, but our first response was the true one.

It may just be a child's solipsism to wish for anything at all from a woman who is dying. My mother always said, with a matter-of-factness that made one feel all the more guilty, that love runs downhill. Surely it is permissible for a dying woman to stop, finally, the selfless outpourings that imagery suggested. But then why did it feel so familiar to crouch there, looking up longingly at the sere hillside?

One of my feelings, I see now, was a dread that her sudden appetites—such basic, nursery appetites—might confirm what I had always believed about her life. That her self-possession was in fact isolation. That her apparent kindness was the grudging fruit of her wounds. Here at last were her wants, and they seemed, to a daughter, at once tiny and bottomless.

It is not, I should make it clear, that my mother was friendless. She had a troupe of women friends, who tended her perfectly in her death, tiptoeing in at all hours to bring her a trio of daffodils in a little jar, or a sheaf of pussy willows. They stood by her bed and stroked her hair and clucked over the flower arrangements that my sisters and I had failed to clear away as they withered. They were wonderful. But I couldn't help feeling that everyone who crossed the threshold, everyone but my sisters, romanticized the woman who thrashed in the mechanical bed. So kind. So generous. Always so ready to give beauty and bounty to everyone who came to her door.

That woman was real, but that woman also drank herself to death at the age of seventy. And all my life I have wondered: If that is the definition of being a loving person, how am I to live? I never knew which would be worse: to be right or wrong in my hunch that her life was an unhappy one. I suppose I will always wonder if it is self-justification that makes me see tragedy in the perfection of her kitchen. I only know that, frozen in the passage between my mother's moon and my father's sun, I made my choice many years ago. But, although I always craved the gaudy satisfactions of my father's sun, it is my mother's life that fascinates me now. And it is my love for her that both comforts and pains me more. In life, I shrank from what I took (rightly, I still think) to be her judgments of me, her anger at my repudiation of the bargains she made. Now, I dream about her often, and usually I wake from them with delight—at a sense of their somehow sustaining me, and at the fact that they are usually woven around food. In one, I went to bite into a pastry she had made, and found instead that it was a copy of *Howards End*. In another, my mother made gorgeous individual pizzas for me and my sisters, and I spent the dream wrestling with the age-old temptation to keep one of my sisters' pizzas for myself, to tuck it away in the freezer against a rainy day.

Mostly, it seems right that I will never have my mother's equanimity about seeing my efforts devoured by others. These days, I don't often make the laborious gravy to go along with the chickens I roast for my family. I usually throw out the chicken carcass, buying my stock ready-made from the supermarket. Sometimes I ask my husband to get take-out on the way home from work.

Yet still there are moments when it stops me in my tracks to realize that I will never peel an orange the way my mother once did for me. And sometimes those moments are almost too much to bear.

—1998 (approximate)

IN CONVERSATION

Editor's Note: Marjorie was a frequent contributor to the online magazine *Slate.* She had a knack for writing *Slate*'s epistolary features, which paired writers to exchange lively emails about new books ("Book Club"), stories in that morning's newspapers ("The Breakfast Table"), matters of public policy, or cultural controversies ("Dialogue"). What follows are a few memorable excerpts from Marjorie's half of these discussions.

From a "Breakfast Table" exchange with her husband, Timothy Noah, July 16, 1998.

Dear Tim,

Let's not hurt each other. If you know what I mean. Nice little marriage you got there; shame if something happened to it.

That out of the way, it's exciting to be launching into this breakfast-table chat with you. Talk around our real breakfast table, as any parents of two small children could attest, concern the merits of Lucky Charms vs. Frosted Flakes, and whether Tiny Alice can be taught not to wipe her hands on my bathrobe, and where Willie's [expletive] sandals are, lest the Efficient Mother we share carpool with turns up to find him once again unshod. At these times, your game tries at discussing the news of the day tend to come at me as simply another layer of the morning din. I've had entire months in which it seems like you're trying to tell me, every morning, that Red Skelton just died. . . .

I'm really interested in your last point, about whether it's acceptable for non-members of some social group to make observations—even simple ones—that members of that group would readily make about themselves. (The common example, of course, being the way some blacks feel comfortable with certain uses of the N-word, but reasonably report being enraged to hear whites saying it.) This question, I think, marks one of the most fluid areas in our otherwise ice-locked conversation about race.

It makes me think of my father, who died two months ago. I happened to ride along in the ambulance when he left the hospital to go home to die. Here we are, bumping along the Manhattan potholes in the back with a young, black, female Emergency Medical Technician. My father is bundled and strapped to a gurney like Hannibal Lecter. Although he has only a few days to live (two, as it turns out), the EMT's stupid rules say that she has to take a medical history during the ride, and check to make sure he's really okay to be released; if she doesn't think he's good to go, she'll route him right back to NYU Hospital. Imagine his anxiety: If he doesn't pass this test, he will lose his chance to die at home. So finally she gets to the point on her checklist where she asks questions to test his alertness: what day is it, who's the president, and so on. "What," she asks him, "was the first thing you noticed about me?"

I see panic on his face—the face of a life-long liberal who thinks the best things went out of politics with Adlai Stevenson. The obvious answer is her very dark skin. Yet he rouses himself, and says in his most sort of humbly gallant manner, "That you're so . . . *trim.*"

Later we all sat around his bed, drinking strawberry daiquiris (him too) and laughing until we wept at this crystallization of his himness. But to this day I'm awed by the scene, its evidence that the social taboos around acknowledging racial difference—the suspicion that terrible bruises can bloom from the simplest truth—could be so important that we would carry them, literally, to the end.

I was raised in that liberal tradition of respecting racial difference, the kind of respect that says it's too electric even to mention. It's obviously better to try to muddle into the mess, giving offense here but making a connection there; sure is scary, though.

From the same "Breakfast Table", July 21, 1998.

Please read, in this week's *New Yorker*, John Bayley's "Elegy for Iris," his account of wife Iris Murdoch's descent into Alzheimer's. It's agonizing, gorgeous, full of the cold-blooded detail that a born writer can't leave out, down to the "grubby white label" on the back of her trousers that tells him which way to put them on her in the morning. I'm torn about this piece. On the one hand it's very accepting, madly admiring of the woman she was, full of the comforts of an old marriage. Yet I had to beat back, constantly, the feeling that it was faithless for him to publish such an intimate thing while she's alive.

In general, I'm of the firm opinion that any writer's story belongs only to him or her, and that moral judgments about the propriety of airing one's own life are beside the point. (The anti-memoir backlash, which peaked with Kathryn Harrison's *The Kiss*,* seems only crabbed and tedious to me. So don't read it if you don't like it!) But in this case, I found it creepy that Murdoch is neither dead, on the one hand, and past all claim to privacy, nor really alive in the sense of being able to know what has been written about her. (Usually, the living at least have the privilege of reacting to a writer's decision to expose them.) Murdoch doesn't even know, as Bayley points out, "that she has written twenty-six remarkable novels." And although this isn't his only tone, at times he writes about her with a kind of terrifying dispassion: about how she "sometimes twitters away incomprehensibly," about the way his ritual jokes will bring on "a sudden beaming smile that must resemble those moments in the past between explorers and savages, when some sort of clowning pantomime on the part of the former seems to have evoked instant comprehension and amusement on the part of the latter."

. . . I suspect that what sent my needle into the red zone was the Avedon photo that leads the piece, in which Murdoch stares into the camera while Bayley scrutinizes her from the right side of the frame. Her expression is unreadable, but after you've made your way through the piece, the one thing you're sure of is that she didn't know she was being captured in her old snowflake sweater by Richard Avedon for the consumption of hundreds of thousands of Americans.

* An incest memoir.

From a "Breakfast Table" exchange with Atul Gawande, March 15, 1999.

I never noticed, until I went to work for a newspaper (the *Washington Post*, in the late '80s), how conveniently devoid of news the Monday paper tends to be. It was a new and alarming idea to me: that except for actual events—a plane crash, an earthquake—whose coverage couldn't be ducked, all other news was essentially voluntary. And Sundays were seen, in the newsroom, to be days agreeably free of developments that required the presence of more than a skeleton staff. This means that Monday papers are huge news holes into which management pours long, theoretically worthy stories that can't make it into the tight weekday news budgets. Half the time these stories are stinkers, and half the time they're so much richer than all the obligatory coverage that they make you wonder why you bother to read the real news all the other days of the week. I love the anarchy of Mondays.

Today's stinker is the *New York Times'* Page One story, "One Precinct, 2 Very Different Murder Cases," which ponders the public treatment of two recent murders in Brooklyn's 77th Precinct. One, the unsolved stabbing of white graduate student Amy Watkins, got big play in the *Times* and all the other New York media; the other, the stabbing of Jamaican immigrant Marvin Watson, got no notice at all. Here at my actual breakfast table in majority-black DC, when we see the *Post* showing the same egregious double standard the Watkins/Watson story addresses, we sing out, When Bad Things Happen to White People! But the *Post* is at least free of the *Times'* disingenuous self-consciousness. The *Times* story, by Jim Yardley and Garry Pierre-Pierre, does note that Watson's death went unreported by the tabloids and the *New York Times*. But it presents this as just one of those unfortunate realities, folks—like the alignment of the planets; not as a failure the *Times* should perhaps be re-examining. Did this silence from the paper of record have anything to do with the fact that the city's finest assigned two dozen detectives to the first case, while handling the second as a routine homicide? *The Times* doesn't speculate. And the story re-commits the moral error it is supposedly exposing, noting, for example, that the white Kansan had an ex-boyfriend who now attends Harvard Law School. (Who cares?) Worst of all, it closes with a quote from the girlfriend of the dead man, in which the *Times* somehow gets her to ratify its original, brutal news judgment: There are a lot of killings in New York, and I don't think all of them could be covered, she says. That's a relief. Whatever twinge of doubt caused some editor at the *Times* to assign this story is now assuaged.

From a "Breakfast Table" exchange with Joel Achenbach, April 12, 2000.

My favorite story today is historian Deborah E. Lipstadt's total victory, in a British court, over Hitler apologist David Irving. Although she is American, Irving, who is a Brit, sued her there because England's libel laws are so much more favorable to the plaintiff than ours. He claimed that she erred in calling him a "Holocaust denier," which is what he plainly is; the judge wasn't buying it. This is a real victory for plain truth.

Earlier in Irving's career, his archival research in Germany earned him some genuine regard as a military historian. My father was his editor at the Viking Press (I teased him to his dying day about having written, in the flap copy for *Hitler's War*, that it would "stand athwart the annals" of somethingorother), and always claimed that if you told David Irving that you had just been shot and were bleeding to death, he would reply, "Hmmm, yes, well, as I was saying, Himmler then said to Goebbels . . ." Every year, when my parents went to London, they had to endure the dread ritual of Dinner at the Irvings: "We are girding loins for dinner with David Irving," my father wrote home in November '76. "Do hope he doesn't bring out X-rays of Hitler's skull until dessert." It was always hot in the Irvings' flat, where they were served (this is my mother now) "the same horrible thing—German champagne well-laced with Campari." And while Irving was bending my father's ear, Mrs. Irving would lead my mother to the kitchen for unsought confidences about the Irving connubial life. "David is as strange as ever," my mother wrote. "All he is really interested in is his Book(s), so that he looks at Alan as a kind of extension of his Hitler book, and just puts him under glass and gazes at him fondly. I do believe Alan could spit in his face and he would just say, 'Oh, yes, jolly good,' and go on gazing."

Even then, when Irving was regarded as respectable and had not yet flatly denied the reality of the Final Solution, my father always sounded a little defensive about publishing him. Ron Rosenbaum has a great op-ed in today's *Wall Street Journal* about the fallacy of fellow historians who praise Irving's fact-gathering while disowning his conclusions. Research and conclusion are ultimately inseparable, Rosenbaum argues, "Can one praise a fact gatherer who somehow has failed to find the facts of mass murder behind Hitler's pattern of denial?"

From a "Book Club" exchange with Christopher Caldwell, July 26, 1999.

Your allusion to Earl Browder* fell wide of the polemical mark with me, because I actually lived next door to Earl Browder as a child. His son Bill was a professor in the Princeton math department, and his granddaughter Julie was my best friend. So I knew Browder as a somewhat gloomy but kind old gent who took a daily constitutional up the block to Nassau Street, where he would buy me and Julie a package of Hostess cupcakes—the orange-flavored ones, with icing squiggles on top.

From a "Breakfast Table" exchange with Tucker Carlson, October 30, 2000.

I'm convinced that there is a genuine Mars/Venus gap that rules the behavior of men and women on game shows. Have you ever noticed how, on the "Final Jeopardy" question on Jeopardy, men are apt to bet the whole farm whereas women contestants are more likely to offer up just a third or a half of what they've already earned—even if it means that they will certainly lose the game? I always despair for my sex when I watch *Jeopardy*.

From the same "Breakfast Table" exchange, November 2, 2000.

I couldn't afford to drink very much during my brief stay in college. I can even remember going to the bank and standing in line (this being before the days of the cash machine) to withdraw exactly $5. Don't I sound like I went to school in 1936? Anyway, two years was definitely enough to convince me that college is wasted on the young.

Instead I went to work in book publishing, a pursuit that involved far more boozing than college had—I actually had lunch with people

---

* Browder ran for United States president on the Communist Party ticket in 1936 and 1940. He died in 1973.

who drank the proverbial three martinis, and it took me about four years to figure out that I couldn't get all the way through one without seeing double for most of the afternoon. Dropping out of college was certainly the right thing for me to do at the time, but I can't say that reading the slush pile and typing letters for an editor (an impossibly old fellow of 30) was more ennobling than two more years of school would have been.

From a "Book Club" exchange with Sarah Lyall, December 19, 2000.

You convinced me that I should try the butternut squash soup from the Portale.* The word "caramelized" in a recipe always earns my optimism. I love butternut squash soup, and the only one I make follows the traditional bake-it-first pattern. I've been asking myself, in light of your generous experiments with him, why I took against his cookbook so completely. It's partly that it gives off a whiff of Martha—the rigid, managerial scheme of arranging food into 12 "seasons," or chapters, and then into menus; all that shimmering bad prose about the seasons and the feelings they bring and blah blah blah, when really you know that he's dying to get on with the Nurse Ratched parts. ("This book, then, is a chef's-eye view of the relationship between human beings and animals, fruits, and vegetables as the Earth revolves around the sun, taking all of us through our intertwined annual cycle.") He always uses a 10-dollar word where a nickel would do, and it all seemed annoyingly pretentious. I don't want to measure the "vulnerability" of my vegetables, or ponder the "poignant" effect of my side dishes.

And I don't think this is just a tic or a distraction. I thought the food was pretentious too. I might not feel this way if I had a chance to pay a lot for it in a restaurant. But why would I want to make "Bosc Pear Carpaccio with Microgreens, Pecorino Romano, and 25-Year-Old Balsamico Tradizionale" in my own kitchen, when I could just throw together a nice salad made with good lettuce and ripe pears and a fine vinegar and a little cheese? (How would I let my guests know it was supposed to be carpaccio, when even in his version it looks very much like thinly sliced pears? How could I subtly work into the conversation the age of the vinegar? *What if my guests*

* Alfred Portale with Andrew Friedman, *12 Seasons Cookbook* (2000).

didn't notice how very tiny the greens were?) If you can't make something ambrosial out of these ingredients minus the puffery, then you definitely don't have the chops to make most of what's in this book.

Even the easy recipes seem labor-intensive. Take "September: Recipes for Busy Times" (What a Martha chapter title!), which is "devoted to relatively simple and quick dishes for those taxing weeks." Orecchiette with Chicken, Swiss Chard, and Parmigiano-Reggiano, which looks wonderfully like comfort food, involves soaking white beans overnight, browning a chicken, then simmering it in stock (which you have made yourself), taking the chicken apart to cut up the meat, reducing the stock you've cooked it in, cooking the white beans, boiling the pasta separately, and of course washing the chard. It involves washing at least five vessels, by my count, and that's if you soak and cook the beans in the same container, which he doesn't, and don't count the cheese-grater. This is the kind of dish about which chefs like to write brightly (as Portale does) that it's perfectly fine to make it 24 hours ahead of time. I have been falling for this gambit for years now—it has sucked me into untold numbers of complicated cooking projects—and only just figured out that it doesn't help: I never have more time 24 hours earlier. Anyway, I get what I imagine to be a similar comfort and taste amperage out of winging a similar orecchiette dish that a friend made for me once: It uses sausage (you only have to sauté it) and broccoli rabe, though any bitter green would probably do, and Pecorino Romano along with the Parmesan. No beans.

The more I think about it, the more Portale strikes me as the epitome of what I don't like about celebrity chefbooks. In the end I don't really care if his recipes are wonderful, or even unprecedented. The world is full of amazing recipes already; what I'm always looking for is a companion who will tell me how, and who won't make it more complicated than he has to, and who will give me good reasons for what I'm doing (reasons better than because I said so!), so that I learn something, too, that I can apply to the rest of my cooking.

From a "Book Club" exchange with Katha Pollitt, March 6, 2001.

It really is an act of genius to render family life so perfectly, with its private economy and all its cross-alliances and helpless repetitions—above all, with a grasp (or memory?) of the way the world really looks to a child. The same people who like to consign women writers to the doily-lined shelves at the back of the shop conceive of anything related to family as "domestic" fiction, a dainty realm in which nice linear relations between family members have nice simple effects. Domestic fiction is usually thought of as a small canvas, in which even seething and betrayal are accomplished quietly.

But *The Man Who Loved Children* is big and noisy and smelly and messy, like a war novel, or the saga of a civilization (which is in fact what it is). [The author, Christina] Stead often reminds us, through her imagery, of how the family encloses and seals off its members. ("Just as Louie had got to the last three steps and had stopped to stare out at the wan, withered, and flourishing world, seen through the blue, yellow and green panes of the pointed hall window, and at the fire-bellied newts in the aquarium, Henny's raucous shout came from the kitchen.") I think it's that combination, of insularity and explosion, that makes it such a powerful book.

And what a place to be sealed into! Sam, that "vague, eclectic socialist," is a monster through and through. I can't do better than Randall Jarrell, of course, in describing Sam's narcissism: "Sam asks for everything and with the same breath asks to be admired for never having asked for anything. . . . He is so idealistically, hypocritically, transcendentally masculine that a male reader worries, 'Ought I to be a man?'" Jarrell writes of Henny that "your heart goes out to her, because she is miserably what life has made her, and makes her misery her only real claim on existence. Her husband wants to be given credit for everything, even his mistakes—especially his mistakes, which are always well-meaning, right-minded ones that in a better world would be unmistaken. Henny is an honest liar; even Sam's truths are ways to get his own way."

But the experience of reading the novel allows you none of Jarrell's comic distance. These days we would say that Sam has boundary issues. . . . But that hardly prepares you for what it's like to read the breakfast scene in which Sam ("your poor little Sam," as he often calls himself, when addressing his brood) amuses himself by chewing his food and then forcing it into his children's lips with his own:

> Mottled with contained laughter, he stretched his mouth to hers, trying to force the banana into her mouth with his tongue, but she broke away, scattering the food on the floor and down the front of her much spotted smock, while everyone clamored

and laughed. Sam himself let out a bellow of laughter, but managed to say,

Get a floor cloth, Looloo-girl: you ought to do what I say!

You're right: If this were Jane Smiley, Sam would be sneaking into the girls' beds at night. I'm so accustomed to this element in contemporary fiction that in a couple of passages I actually thought this was where Stead was heading. But she's so good that she shows up our contemporary focus on the incest plot as a sort of cartoon representation of the kind of intimate harm the Sams of the world inflict.

From a "Book Club" exchange with Sarah Lyall, April 4, 2001.

I need to tell you at the outset that I'm a huge Stephen King fan. I can remember the very weekend I started reading him, in 1979, when I curled up with *The Shining* and never looked back. My taste for him has waxed and waned over the years, but there's no one like King for nailing your attention to the page. He's the least cynical of popular writers; where other filthy rich writers with a fat franchise repeat themselves over and over (hell, even the dead ones, reincarnated by their publishers with the help of hungry ghostwriters), King is always trying something harder and more interesting than what he's done before. *Pet Sematary* is one of the most frightening things I've ever read, and I thought *Hearts in Atlantis*, of two years ago—a book of contiguous novellas, if that's the right description—was marvelous.

I tell you all this because I found *Dreamcatcher* pretty disappointing. Bluntly, I think it has more of the author's vices (excess, especially) and fewer of his virtues than almost all of his work of the last six or seven years. The typical pattern of a Stephen King novel is that it starts out subtly: The life dilemmas of an Everyman—mourning for a loved one, dealing badly with age, being haunted by a past misdeed—blossom into something stranger and wilder. The premise almost always gets a little (or a lot) over the top by the end—how he does love to pile effect on effect—but usually he has built toward this stage so effectively that you just shrug and take it all in stride. *Dreamcatcher* follows almost the opposite pattern: It starts out with big, repulsive doses of premise and continues at that pitch almost all the way through; you have to dig down for the most gratifying thread.

A personal digression, in partial response to your last question of yesterday (concerning the needless words you'll find in *Dreamcatcher*). I happen to know for a fact that Stephen King sits still for editing because my father was his editor for a time, first at Viking and then at Putnam—from *Firestarter*, I think, through *The Tommyknockers*. My Pa was really crazy about King, partly because he was tickled pink to be midwifing honest-to-God blockbusters (he usually ran more toward high lit, the more British the better), but also because he thought he was fun. It didn't hurt that King, who was in a wilder phase of his life, took my Pa to great parties and introduced him to rock stars. My father died a few years ago, and it is thanks to King that I have a sweet memory of him coming home and announcing, somewhere in his early '60s, that Blondie (he meant Debbie Harry) seemed like a very nice young woman. My theory is that they got along swimmingly because King fed my father's curiosity about things popular while my father wrote him editorial notes that Arthur Haley probably never got from an editor, such as: "p. 50. It's Horatius, not Horatio . . . p. 130 et seq. The *deus ex machina* comes originally from Greek drama, not medieval times."

Anyway, here's a strange thing: I have a copy of a letter my father wrote to King, *actually asking him to put in something about defecation*. The letter was about *Misery* (which he didn't edit but read in manuscript)—the story, you'll remember, of an injured writer imprisoned by a crazy nurse. My father wrote, "I do think there ought to be just a bit more bedpan mechanics, maybe just a detail or two early on. I hope you won't color me coprophilic, but I do think that in a story so real in its pain and dilemma many readers are going to wonder how he copes."

My father, for the record, was a guy. Loved your theory, by the way, that men obsess about their digestive tracts because they don't have fallopian tubes to amuse them.

BILL CLINTON, FEMINIST

Okay, class, let's review: The man in question has been sued for sexual harassment over an episode that allegedly included dropping his trousers to waggle his erect penis at a woman who held a $6.35-an-hour clerical job in the state government over which he presided. Another woman has charged that when she asked him for a job he invited her into his private office, fondled her breasts, and placed her hand on his crotch. A third woman confided to friends that when she was a twenty-one-year-old intern she began an affair with the man—much older, married, and the head of the organization whose lowliest employee she was. Actually, it was less an affair than a service contract, in which she allegedly dashed into his office, when summoned, to perform oral sex on him. After their liaison was revealed, he denied everything, leaving her to be portrayed as a tramp and a liar. Or, in his own words, "*that woman.*"

Let us not even mention the former lover who was steered to a state job; or the law-enforcement officers who say the man used them to solicit sexual partners for him; or his routine use of staff members, lawyers, and private investigators to tar the reputation of any woman who tries to call him to account for his actions.

Can you find the problems with his behavior? Take your time: These problems are apparently of an order so subtle as to escape the notice of many of the smartest women in America—the writers, lawyers, activists, officeholders, and academics who call themselves feminists.

When news broke that Independent Counsel Kenneth Starr was investigating whether President Clinton had lied under oath about his relationship with White House intern Monica Lewinsky, or encouraged others to lie, the cacophony that ensued was notable for the absence of one set of voices: the sisterly chorus that backed up Anita Hill seven years ago when her charges of sexual harassment nearly stopped Clarence Thomas's confirmation to the Supreme Court.

With very few exceptions, feminists were either silent or dismissive this time. "If anything, it sounds like she put the moves on *him*," said Susan Faludi, author of *Backlash*. Betty Friedan weighed in, but only to huff her outrage that Clinton's "enemies are attempting to bring him down through allegations about some dalliance with an intern. . . . Whether it's a fantasy, a set-up or true, I simply don't care."

It was not until former White House volunteer Kathleen Willey appeared on *60 Minutes* in mid-March to make public the allegation she had formerly made in a deposition—that Clinton had manhandled her during a private meeting in which she sought a paying job—that some feminists began to make reluctant noises of dismay. The National Organization for Women (NOW), which until then had found itself "unable to comment responsibly," averred that "Kathleen Willey's sworn testimony moves the question from whether the president is a 'womanizer' to whether he is a sexual predator."

But NOW's change of heart was by no means typical of feminist activists. Many others hung tough. Anita Perez Ferguson, president of the National Women's Political Caucus—the premier group promoting female participation in American politics—described Willey's charges as "quantity rather than quality, in terms of my feelings." She continued, "There's no question that it's disturbing. . . . But to come to any judgment now is definitely not something that I think is timely."

With the exception of a few Republicans, women in Congress—including several swept to power by female outrage over the Senate's treatment of Anita Hill—have shown an equal agility of mind. Their excuses range from the procedural stonewall ("What is important for the American people to know is that there is a process in place to deal with these allegations," in the words of Senator Barbara Boxer), to the creative inversion (what about Ken Starr's "humiliation" of the women he dragged before the grand jury? fumed Representative Nancy Pelosi), to the truly fanciful twist on gender politics ("Not so many years ago, a woman couldn't *be* a White House intern," said a straight-faced Senator Carol Moseley-Braun on *Meet the Press*).

My own sampling of feminist opinion found women offering an astonishing array of strategies for avoiding the elephant in the living room:

See no evil . . . "It will be a great pity if the Democratic Party is damaged by this," the feminist writer Anne Roiphe told me. "That's been my response from the very beginning—I just wanted to close my eyes, and wished it would go away."

Hear no evil . . . "We do not know what happened in the Lewinsky case," said Kathy Rodgers, executive director of the NOW Legal Defense and Education Fund. "The only thing that is clear is that the facts are not clear."

Speak no evil . . . "We're trying to think of the bigger picture, think about what's best for women," said Eleanor Smeal, president of the Feminist Majority Foundation.

If the hypocrisy and the powers of denial are impressive, one must consider that these women have had a lot of practice. Feminists have all along muffled, disguised, excused, and denied the worst aspects of the president's behavior with women—especially in their reactions to Paula Jones, whose sexual-harassment suit they have greeted with attitudes ranging from tepid boilerplate support to outright hostility.

In the Lewinsky case, it has fallen to their enemies to state the obvious. "The C.E.O. of a corporation wouldn't have had time to pack up his briefcase before he was fired for this," says Barbara Ledeen, executive director for policy at the Independent Women's Forum, the Washington-based group that has achieved a certain cachet for its condemnations of traditional feminism.

"The president should be setting some sort of example in the workplace," says the outrageous libertarian writer Camille Paglia, who has gained prominence in part for denouncing liberal feminists. "That's all I'm talking about. *In. The. Workplace.* . . . Since when did the president use the interns as a dessert cart? '*Mmmmm*, she looks good!' When did that become okay?"

The chief reason for feminists' continued support of Clinton is clear: Clinton is their guy. Clarence Thomas was their enemy. Bob Packwood, a liberal Republican who was the next habitual boor to walk the plank, was a harder case for feminists, but in the end they tied the blindfold. Clinton, though, is the hardest case, because he is the most reliably supportive president they've ever had.

But if political opportunism is the main cause of their current blindness, it's not the only one. And it's worth examining all the reasons in detail. For you can find in them a road map to everything that ails liberal feminism today: political self-dealing, class bias, and dedication to a bleak vision of sexual "liberation" that has deprived them of what was once the moral force of their beliefs.

Feminists are quick to say that any charges of hypocrisy lodged against them are the work of the anti-Clinton right. "It's a twofer for them," says Smeal. "If they can get the president, great. And if they can get feminism, even greater."

So it seems appropriate to say here that I am a feminist and a registered Democrat. Many of the feminist activists in Washington are women I've known for years as sources; I feel an open sympathy for much of the work they do. Yet I also feel something close to fury over their failure to call Clinton to account for his actions. My anger may be bred, in part, by my own past willingness to "put in perspective" Clinton's questionable behavior with women—enough, at least, to vote for him twice. I can't defend my own past complicity, but I can say that what follows is not the brief of a practiced Clinton hater.

To be sure, it is *possible* to find a reason, consistent with at least some brand of feminism, to dismiss every allegation that has been made against President Clinton. Monica Lewinsky was apparently an eager partner. Paula Jones has allied herself with right-wingers who never before gave the first damn about the victims of sexual harassment, and as a legal matter her case is, at best, borderline: Even if the facts are exactly as she states them, it's a stretch to interpret them as violations of the laws under which she is suing. In the case of Kathleen Willey, there are the usual ambiguities surrounding any episode that comes down to she says–he says, and evidence—mitigating, in some people's eyes—that she continued to seek favors from him after the episode she describes. The White House, in fact, broke its otherwise stony silence to besiege reporters with detailed catalogues of the many friendly notes Willey had written to the president since 1993.

In each woman's case, there is enough that we don't know to support a respectable claim of ignorance. The individual pieces of the Clinton saga are complex, snaky things with their own tawdry confusions. But these are precisely the complications that Clinton has capitalized on. The truth is that, while a lot of the facts are murky, enough of them are clear.

We have good evidence, for example, that Clinton, as governor of Arkansas, had a state trooper escort Paula Jones to his suite at Little

Rock's Excelsior Hotel during her work hours, and we know that she gave contemporaneous accounts of the meeting to several witnesses which closely track the allegations in her lawsuit. We know that there is extensive evidence of a relationship between Clinton and Lewinsky that has not been challenged by the administration. We know that Arkansas state troopers have said under oath that Clinton used them to enable his sexual escapades in Little Rock. And we know that Clinton has lied about his past behavior—including the sizable lie that underlay the supposedly informed decision of the American people that they didn't care about his womanizing: his elaborately careful 1992 denials of his affair with Gennifer Flowers.

Where America's women leaders have failed is in their unwillingness to draw even the most commonsensical conclusions from the evidence of Clinton's recklessness. Instead, they have taken refuge in legalisms. In the words of an "alert" posted on the feminist Women Leaders Online Web site, "Men acting like pigs is not against the law; if it were, many women in America could be zillionaires."

But since when did feminists see their mission as defining and denouncing only that which is illegal? Didn't the phrase "men acting like pigs" once describe a fair portion of what feminists were trying to change? *Clearly* the Monica Lewinsky scandal is not a case of illegal sexual harassment. But if Clinton had the relationship with her that the available evidence suggests he had, it flew in the face of the law's spirit and reasoning: among other things, by potentially penalizing all the interns with whom he did not have affairs.

In their sudden and exclusive reverence for the law, feminists have jeopardized some of their greatest achievements. And what their elaborate excuses ignore is that they could play an important role in securing the facts they find so lamentably scarce: Women are a crucial constituency for the Clinton administration, and if feminists were to demand answers from Clinton as vociferously as they demanded a Senate hearing for Anita Hill, we might all be closer to penetrating the White House's wall of silence.

It's plain enough why feminists want to keep Clinton in office. He is pro-choice; he signed into law the Family and Medical Leave Act, which had been vetoed twice by a Republican president; he favors affirmative action, which benefits women more than any ethnic group in the country; he has made child care a policy priority this year. According to the Center for the American Woman and Politics, Clinton has appointed ten of the twenty-one women who have served in Cabinet-level positions, including the first woman ever to be secretary of state or attorney general. He also appointed Ruth Bader Ginsburg to the Supreme Court.

While most of the Washington-based women's organizations that lobby and promote women's participation in electoral politics maintain a veneer of bipartisanship, a web of relationships links them to the Clinton administration. White House Communications director Ann Lewis, who has been one of Clinton's fiercest defenders on television, was once the chair of the Democratic Task Force of the National Women's Political Caucus. Anita Perez Ferguson, who is now president of the caucus, formerly worked in the Clinton administration, as a White House liaison for the Transportation Department, and at the Democratic National Committee.

And then there's friendship: Hillary Rodham Clinton's friendships, in particular, may have neutralized some of the women who might otherwise be criticizing Clinton. When I called Marjorie Margolies-Mezvinsky, who chairs the (theoretically bipartisan) Women's Campaign Fund, her assistant cheerfully told me, "I know that Marjorie has not made any comments about recent"—here he stopped and groped for a word—"*events?* Just because she is friends with Hillary." When women activists were charging up the hill to oppose the nominations of Thomas and other conservative Reagan-Bush appointees, one of their comrades-in-arms was Melanne Verveer, then the chief lobbyist for the liberal organization People for the American Way, now the First Lady's chief of staff.

It's interesting to note that feminist investment in Clinton has grown over time, even as the allegations about his sexual behavior have increased. During Clinton's first campaign, women activists were suspicious of the "New Democratic" elements of his agenda. To this day, they remain angry at him for signing into law the radical welfare revisions of 1996, which overwhelmingly affect poor women.

But, with that exception, there has been a sea change in their attitudes toward him. For one thing, after the congressional elections of 1994, they saw him as all they had standing between them and Newt Gingrich. For another, the 1996 election marked the first time the gender gap exceeded a president's margin of victory, and suddenly feminists had, in Clinton, a poster boy for the theory on which they had long based their claims to power. (Never mind that a scant minority of the women voters in question were voting on "feminist" issues; most were moderates who liked what

Clinton had to say on education, jobs, and crime.) At last, feminists felt that they had some real leverage with the White House, and they're loath to give it up now.

Only a decade ago, a single liaison with a woman to whom he had no professional connection squashed Gary Hart's career like a bug. Yet, today Clinton is accused of traducing every boundary we have uneasily set around sex in the workplace, and Americans—especially American women—reply with a yawn. "Men are legitimately perplexed," says Katie Roiphe, the twenty-nine-year-old feminist writer who has made a specialty of critiquing feminist alarmism about date rape and sexual harassment. "They're thinking, 'Wait a minute—we weren't even supposed to compliment someone on her hairstyle two years ago or we'd get thrown out of office. And Bill Clinton is allowed to have this 21-year-old [intern] servicing him, with blow jobs or whatever, and women support him overwhelmingly?'"

The support of Clinton, she believes, shows "a reaction against the kind of sexual correctness of the early '90s. And in some sense Bill Clinton is fulfilling a sort of secret fantasy of a lot of American women, of this kind of old-fashioned, virile man."

She may be overstating the case among women voters, who at this point give Clinton "favorable" ratings only about 6 percent higher than his ratings among men. It is still possible that women will turn against Clinton. (Memo to pollsters: Keep your eye on soccer moms, who may eventually tire of trying to explain oral sex to their nine-year-olds.)

But Roiphe is onto *something*—a shift in elite opinion about both Clinton and sexual mores. Exhibit A was a bizarre January 30 gathering hosted by the *New York Observer* at the restaurant Le Bernardin, where ten Manhattan "supergals"—including writers Katie Roiphe, Erica Jong, Nancy Friday, and Francine Prose, designer Nicole Miller, former *Saturday Night Live* contributor Patricia Marx, and "retired dominatrix and writer" Susan Shellogg—were invited to drink wine and analyze the scandal.

The resulting exchange, published by the *Observer* in the February 9 issue, was galactically strange. The women agreed that they liked Clinton better for having had a titillating affair; after all, he's kind of a hunk. Jong, for one, wants a president who is "alive from the waist down," and Marx declared him "cute and getting cuter all the time." They pronounced Kenneth Starr (in Friday's words) "a big sissy," and speculated about whether

Lewinsky had swallowed the president's semen. "Oh," squealed Jong, "imagine swallowing the presidential come."

It was the most embarrassing thing I had read in a long time. But then I opened the next week's *New Yorker*, which contained a swooning "Fax from Washington" written by Tina Brown herself, describing the February 5 White House dinner for British prime minister Tony Blair. The subtext was that the Clinton scandal had marvelously improved the president's aura: It made him seem so . . . *hot.*

> Now see your President, tall and absurdly debonair, as he dances with a radiant blonde, his wife. . . . Amid the clichés about his charm, his glamour is undersung. . . . Forget the dog-in-the-manger, down-in-the-mouth neo-puritanism of the op-ed tumbrel drivers, and see him instead as his guests do: a man in a dinner jacket with more heat than any star in the room.

This is precisely the sort of retro whipped cream that feminists are supposed to be able to see through; once upon a time, they construed it as their job to help the rest of us do the same. But these days, feminists—the famous feminists, that is; the mainstream feminists; the ones who are called up by newspaper reporters and TV stations—are an established part of the country's elite: the media elite in New York, the political elite in Washington. And this is one of the major reasons they have failed to hold Clinton's feet to the fire.

As has been noted elsewhere, class dynamics, almost as much as politics, drove the differing reactions to Anita Hill and Paula Jones. Hill was a well-spoken, Yale-educated lawyer; Jones was of the lower middle class. Women's groups were probably not as apt to dismiss her out of simple class bias as was the press: Many, if not most, of the sexual-harassment victims that feminists support *are* of working-class background. But when they decided, for other reasons, to keep their distance from Jones, her Ozark roots made her an easy woman to ignore.

Kathleen Willey's emergence has further clarified the class dynamics of Clinton's feminist support. Other factors may have made her more credible than Paula Jones—her reluctance to come forward, for example. But it was surely not a coincidence that some feminists saw the light only when confronted with a gorgeous, mature woman whose voice, clothes, makeup, and manner all gave off the vibes of the upper-middle-class suburbanite. (Lewinsky, as a child of Beverly Hills, belongs to an economic class closer to Willey's than Jones's. But in status terms—the terms that matter in the East Coast elites—she is unsalvageably tacky, a creature from an Aaron Spelling show.)

The elitism inherent in the Clintons' own feminism was apparent from the very first weeks of the administration, when yuppie lawyer Zoe Baird saw her nomination for attorney general derailed over the issue of her having both employed two illegal nannies and failed to pay the requisite Social Security taxes. All the brilliant attorneys involved in preparing Baird for her confirmation had overlooked the fact that this might be an enraging issue to the chumps who couldn't afford nannies of any nationality, yet paid all the personal and business taxes they owed.

"They think only bluestockings are worth paying attention to," says the conservative writer Lisa Schiffren, a former speechwriter for Dan Quayle, about Clintonian feminism. "You know, important women with important careers and day-care needs. . . . Clearly this is a bunch of Wellesley girls saying that Wellesley girls and Yale graduates are worth fighting for, and high-school grads and hairdressers and lounge singers can be destroyed."

In easing past the contradictions of the feminist class system, Hillary Clinton is the crucial figure. It's common knowledge that she has been her husband's most important protector. "The fact that Hillary doesn't seem bothered by it gives women an excuse, in a way, to be tolerant of his behavior," says Radcliffe Public Policy Institute fellow Wendy Kaminer.

But less appreciated is a second, more subtle way in which Hillary has shielded her husband. She is, in effect, his feminist beard: the symbolic guarantor of his political bona fides. *He may hit on women like Gennifer Flowers and Paula Jones,* her presence says, *but when it came to sharing a home (and a presidency), he chose a woman like me.* Again and again, feminists cite the Hillary factor as mitigating evidence. Gloria Steinem told me, "He's married to a woman who's at least his equal, whom he clearly likes and respects." This apparently makes it okay that when he chooses a sex partner he's looking—in the words of a former Clinton staffer—"for a dopey girl who's not going to make him send flowers."

In some ways, it's baffling that feminists can still argue seriously that one Hillary trumps a multitude of Monicas. Even leaving aside Clinton's repeated public humiliations of his wife, she's always been a dubious feminist heroine: After all, she married her power, and in the White House she has wielded it without accountability. In truth, there's an awful affront to women in the apparently sharp distinctions that Clinton draws between the kind of woman you marry and the kind of woman you seek out for pleasure. We were supposed to be doing away with the Madonna and the whore—or at least trying to integrate them.

In for a penny, in for a pound: Having decided to renew Clinton's grant of immunity once the Lewinsky scandal broke, feminists weren't in any position to fire so much as a warning shot across the bow when the White House began gingerly trashing her reputation. Not when a key congressional ally, Charles Rangel, questioned whether she "played with a full deck." Not even when Clinton himself ran one of the oldest plays in the old-boy playbook, pounding the table and declaring, "I did not have sexual relations with that woman, Miss Lewinsky." *That woman. You know,* his tone said, *that crazy woman, that fantasist, that lying home wrecker.*

Far from protesting, many feminists have piled on. "Does anyone really care if young Monica found an interesting new position at the White House?" wrote Judy Mann, *The Washington Post's* feminist columnist. She chided the press for not giving sufficient weight to the possibility that Lewinsky was embellishing her relationship with a celebrity just for attention—"a standard device for dingbats of all ages." (This is the same Judy Mann who earlier wrote, about Gennifer Flowers, "I'm getting tired of these women crawling out from under rocks, claiming they've had affairs with politicians.")

Susan Faludi describes Lewinsky derisively as "sleeping her way to the bottom of the Revlon empire."

Law professor Susan Estrich wrote in her America Online column, "Lewinsky at least appears to have flirted her way to a job at Revlon and, when that disappeared, a $2 million modeling offer and the status of the most-sought after woman in the world. Not bad, some might say, for someone who can't type."

They aren't all sexist comments, but they're nasty ones, empty of even a fleeting compassion. At the end of the *Observer* gathering, Erica Jong congratulated herself and her companions on their sisterly solidarity. "I think it's a tribute to how far we've come that we're not trashing Monica Lewinsky," she remarked. A touching thought—but only if you had missed Jong's earlier contribution to the discussion: "My dental hygienist pointed out that [Lewinsky] had third-stage gum disease."

If feminists had stopped to think of Lewinsky as a real person, it might have slowed them down. "Look," says Paglia, everyone could see what kind of girl she was: she was not in control of herself. It's so obvious, that she was this California girl who was dressing provocatively and was using her sex and so on. So what should be the response of the person in moral authority? It should have been "Well, this is very tempting, but it's wrong for me to take advantage of my position here."

But feminists have an important stake in seeing Lewinsky as a competent young sexual adventuress: a portrait in avid consent. If there was consent, there was no victim; no victim, no problem.

"We're not against sex; we're against the use of sex to cajole, humiliate, coerce," says Gloria Steinem. "But, according to what Lewinsky says, this was not the case with her. . . . We need to trust the women here. If we say a 21- to 24-year-old has no sexual will, we're going against the whole struggle for self-determination and taking responsibility for our own lives."

Anne Roiphe, the feminist writer and mother of Katie Roiphe, says, "I think that if this had not come to light, [Lewinsky] would treasure this for the rest of her life as a special thing that had happened to her in her early 20s."

This is the most grotesque aspect of the feminist lapse here: this determination to depict Lewinsky's end of the alleged affair as liberated, autonomous female sexuality in action, instead of as the pathetic picture it was, of a young woman seeking a dubious affirmation in all the wrong places. To be sure, the May-December romance is always a complex, two-way transaction. But what little we know of the Clinton-Lewinsky relationship suggests that in all of the specifics that matter—when he called, when and where they met, what they actually did with each other, and even when she was allowed to speak to him—the relationship was controlled (*duh!*) by the powerful, married, fifty-ish man, not by the twenty-something woman on the lowest rung of the status ladder.

Why do feminists find it so hard to acknowledge the ugliness of this arrangement? One reason is that Lewinsky's age is a very touchy point: If you have argued for years against parental-consent laws for teenagers seeking abortions, you may feel hard-pressed to admit that many women in their early twenties are a few years shy of emotional maturity.

Another reason may be that Lewinsky is a potentially frightening mirror for her mother's generation. Her eagerness to jump into the alleged affair and her apparent concept of herself as someone who could get power and self-esteem by having sexual affairs that she talked about widely, mark her as a clueless child of the sexual revolution. Feminism's insistence that abolishing the sexual double standard was more important than anything else has led, at its worst, to a brittle, pitiless vision of sexual autonomy, in which anything goes and everyone can look after herself. "But that's how you grow up," says Wendy Kaminer. "You have a sexual relationship, and maybe you get a little used, and then you feel bad about yourself for a while, and then you grow up."

At least Kaminer believes this argument. Among other feminists, the Lewinsky matter is strangely scrambling the trench warfare that has taken place for years between libertarian feminists such as Camille Paglia and Katie Roiphe and those they accuse of being "victim feminists," prone to infantilizing women by insisting on special protections against the depredations of mean old men. Paglia, for one, finds it hilarious that her views have so many new converts. "All of a sudden these people on the other side stampede to *my* side," she says. "'[S]he should be allowed to do whatever she wants.' They're all libertarians all of a sudden!"

Among the most honest women I interviewed for this piece was Marie C. Wilson, president of the Ms. Foundation for Women, who related her experiences, from early in her career, as a lobbyist for liberal causes in the Iowa legislature. "I knew how to talk about the kinds of emissions standards I wanted for Iowa companies, and what kind of child-care standards I wanted for the children of Iowa, and *Would you please move your hand?* And most times I didn't get the emissions standards or the child care."

"Now," she says of Clinton's presidency, "I've gotten emissions standards, and I've got better child care, and I've still got the hand. But that's better than the other way."

A very few women were willing to make this argument directly: That feminists could find some honor in making a dispassionate, tough-minded decision that Clinton's value in office outweighs the sordidness of his personal life. But making this argument is something different from simply sweeping his behavior under the rug; it's the pretense, above all, that does the damage.

And this is why the feminist failure matters. By wishing the problem away, feminists call into question one of their most important victories of the past decades: the hard-won consensus that men should not use social and economic power to recruit sex partners in the workplace, and that it's fair for both sexes to expect limits on how much sexual relations are allowed to distort the system of rewards. I'm talking, here, not about feminist legislative achievements, but about a shift in the extralegal realm of mores, the shift that followed and ratified the actual laws against specific forms of sexual harassment.

Much social abrasion and anxiety went along with this shift, and much derisive complaining about the overreactions that uncertainty bred. But, by and large, it was a very healthy thing: a new social compact suggesting that behavior of the kind Clarence Thomas was said to have exhibited might or might not be a violation of Title VII of the 1964 Civil Rights Act, but that in either case it is outside the bounds of acceptable behavior.

A helpful analogy might be the 1992 episode in which candidate Clinton played golf at a club that admitted only whites. The news was greeted with immediate outrage, not because it might have led to the repeal of the Voting Rights Act, but because the candidate's choice of greens did an obvious violence to the social consensus forged by the civil-rights movement, that all Americans are entitled to at least the presumption that their countrymen will treat them as equals. Everyone recognized that violence instantly, and Clinton, with the belated sensitivity of self-preservation, apologized.

This is why even those feminists who were converted to indignation by Kathleen Willey are offering too little, too late. By acting as though Willey's allegations are of an entirely different order from all the others that have dogged Clinton in the past, these feminists define those others as none of our business. When the dust of Clinton's presidency settles, the laws against sexual harassment will still be on the books. But the social sanctions against the behavior will be irretrievably damaged.

If you doubt this, look around. In the weeks that followed the Lewinsky scandal, those who had been most affronted by the awkward new social arrangements lately demanded of them shambled out of their caves to beat their chests. Conservative columnist John Leo, for example, crowed in *U.S. News & World Report* that the scandal was "probably the decade's high-water mark of euphoria around the water cooler . . . a chance to break free from the office sex police."

It's all very well to protest that we shouldn't look to our politicians as role models: The saga of Clinton's sex life is being played out on too large a screen to ignore. You can say until you're blue in the face that public men are entitled to a realm of privacy; that certain kinds of bad private behavior do not necessarily conflict with political competence, or even genius;

and that adultery is not in itself of feminist concern. These are all irrelevancies. This mess is on our hands, and we do not have the luxury of arguing with its existence; the best we can do is call it what it is.

Finally, feminists have a special responsibility to loathe the lies, implicit and explicit, with which Clinton has consistently tried to cover his tracks. Feminism, at its core, is about helping women to respect what is true over what is convenient. It's bad enough that Clinton has hidden behind an endless chain of women to protect him from the consequences of his actions: from Betsey Wright, the longtime aide who contained "bimbo eruptions" for him in 1992, to Hillary and Chelsea—whistled home from Stanford, while classes were in session, to take part in a tender father-daughter photo op nine days after the scandal broke—to Betty Currie, the loyal secretary who will leave the Clinton White House with a mountain of legal bills. Must he hide behind the rest of us too?

When I look back over my life, I expect to remember Clinton's two terms in the White House as the Gaslight Presidency. The 1944 version of *Gaslight* stars Charles Boyer as the sinister new husband of an innocent young woman played by Ingrid Bergman and named, as luck would have it, Paula. Boyer, who plans to do away with his wife, first plots to drive her crazy—or at least to convince her and the rest of the world that she has lost her mind. He does this by stealing little objects and then convincing her that she has lost them; by dimming the gas-fueled lamps and then telling her that she is imagining the waning of the light; by insisting, in sum, that she cannot trust the evidence of her own senses. "*Paauula*," he is constantly crooning, with smarmy Latin concern. "You should lie down and rest for a little, *Paauula*."

Because the movie was made half a century ago, it's no surprise that Ingrid Bergman's character is something of a doormat, sadly complicit in the manipulation of her own mind. But we have no such excuse.

Denial is insidious; it always claims more than you think you have ceded to it. "We would not be doing our job if we didn't take into account that this president and his policies are crucial to the lives and welfare of the majority of women in this country," Gloria Steinem assures me. "That's not bending over backwards: that's being sensible. Having said that, if Clinton had raped women, beaten up Hillary—real private sins would not be forgiven, no matter what the value of the public behavior."

There it is, fellas, in case you're still confused: It seems we just lowered the bar.

—May 1998

WHY PARENTS STILL MATTER

What a chump I've been. All those nights of dragging myself down the hallway to answer the cries of a lonely or frightened child. All those baby-sitters I've interviewed to be sure I'm leaving my kids with a nice one. All those moments in which I've bitten back a temporary fury, forcing myself to speak patiently to my intransigent son or daughter. According to Judith Rich Harris, author of *The Nurture Assumption*, none of these actions, or my failure to take them in the future, is going to have any lasting effect on my children at all.

The Nurture Assumption, which was born to a glowing profile in the *New Yorker* and a *Newsweek* cover story, is commonly referred to as the Parents-Don't-Matter book. Bluntly, it is Harris's thesis that the only lasting influences on one's personality are genes and peers—the peer groups of childhood and adolescence. Our common belief that what parents say and do to children will have a crucial effect on their lives is simply a mass delusion, nothing more than "a cherished cultural myth."

Harris has an interesting history. Thrown out of Harvard's graduate program in psychology as a non-conformist, and bedridden for much of her adulthood by an autoimmune disease, she became a writer of college psychology textbooks—work she could do from home. That work enrolled her in a running seminar on the latest research in developmental psychology, while her isolation encouraged her to see all that work with an outsider's skepticism. Now a sixty-year-old grandmother, she had a Road-to-Damascus experience one day ("It was January 20, 1994") while reading a study of why adolescents so often break the law. It was, the researcher suggested, a bid for "mature status, with its consequent power and privilege." Wait, thought Harris; that can't be right. Teenagers aren't trying to be good grown-ups ("If teenagers wanted to be like adults they wouldn't be shoplifting nail polish from drug-stores or hanging off overpasses to spray I LOVE YOU LISA on the arch. They would be doing boring adult things like sorting the laundry and figuring out their income taxes"); no, they're trying to be successful teenagers.

In this beginning, Harris found the germ of a theory that enabled her to explain away all the anomalies that had troubled her in the literature on parenting styles and child development: essentially, the fact that all the developmental psychology research in the world had failed to nail down any significant, predictable correlations between how parents treat their kids and how those kids turn out—any that could not instead be laid at the door of their genetic link, that is.

Harris believes, in keeping with the research of behavioral geneticists, that about 50 percent of any person's fate is written by his or her genetic endowments. (And the way she lays out and explains this research is among the best services of her book.) But the other 50 percent, she now claims, is purely a function of the child's education at the hands of peers. "The world that children share with their peers is what shapes their behavior and modifies the characteristics they were born with, and hence determines the sort of people they will be when they grow up." In other words, Harris writes, the Battle of Waterloo really was won on the playing fields of Eton: the one place the boys of England's upper classes socialized only with their peers.

This is a fascinating, wildly entertaining, and in many ways persuasive book. Harris is a wonderful writer, who doesn't stop at drawing research from fields as varied as behavioral psychology, ethnology, evolution, and sociology; she also draws cultural allusion from sources as disparate as *Little House on the Prairie,* Darwin, and Dave Barry. She leads the reader with a sort of motherly asperity, and lards her theories with nice, dry observations. In writing, for example, about the influence of Jean-Jacques Rousseau, she notes that this great preacher of the inherent goodness of the newborn "had no children of his own—that is, he *reared* none of his own. The babies born to his long-time mistress were deposited one by one, with his full knowledge, at the door of a foundling home. They may have been born good but they were not born lucky."

THE WOMAN AT THE WASHINGTON ZOO 235

But an author this clever is certainly canny enough to overstate her case for dramatic effect, and this is what I believe Harris has done. There is a great deal of value in her book (some of the most valuable material, in fact, has been the least noticed in much coverage of Harris's work). You can't help feeling the justice of her observation that parents of my generation have come to see childhood as the story of parenthood—a drama about *us*, and *our* nifty insights into what our children want and need. Harris's contempt for modern parents' conviction that our readings of *Goodnight Moon* are all-important is, for the most part, a healthy corrective. And she has a true compassion for the parents on the opposite side of that coin: the parents of difficult children, men and women who have done the world's hardest job and been blamed for bad results that really aren't any fault of theirs.

In support of her thesis, she does an impressive job of knocking down the studies that have simply assumed that home life is the primary, and formative, element in the child's environment. Once she has led you through the available research, you'll believe that divorce doesn't cause children lasting harm—at least, not once you've taken into account the important ways that divorce affects children's peer relationships, by impoverishing parents and often forcing them to move. You'll grant a far greater latitude to the influence of genes on personality. You may have learned some respect for the inherent toughness and creativity of children amid their peers—not to mention some humility about your powers (and your gifts) as a parent. And you might even have come to believe that child-rearing, like real estate, is about one important thing: location, location, location. For the one key way in which Harris thinks parents can affect their children's lives is by choosing neighborhoods and schools in which their peers are more likely to value books, learning, and society's good opinion.

But there are three important ways in which she's overstated her case.

The first concerns the slippery subject of genes. In pointing up the huge extent to which genes determine personality, she also writes off as unaffected by parental behavior a large number of *indirect* genetic effects. It's true, she grants, that nice, socially competent, peaceable parents tend to treat their children well and to produce nice, socially competent, peaceable children. But, to a large extent, that may be because nice, etc. parents tend to have children who are nice, etc. to begin with, by virtue of their genes. So far so good. However, she goes too far in her next step: If there are some correlations between the way nice people treat their children and the way those children turn out, she says, it may also be because likable (nice, socially competent, peaceable) children have the "child-to-parent" effect of being easy to love. In other words, their parents will have "good" child-rearing styles because their children aren't terribly challenging to raise. This is undoubtedly true. But Harris scores this, too, as a genetic effect—albeit an indirect one—and therefore discards the entire family as having nothing to tell us about the effects of family environment on children.

But in doing this, she's throwing out a huge part of the relevant sample. Just because science can't tease apart the difference between nature and nurture in such cases doesn't mean that they're not both in there; it only means that science, in its current state, can't tell us everything we need to know.

Which is also the lesson of her rhetorical over-reach. What she really succeeds in showing is, as she writes at one point, that "parents have no predictable effects on their children." Regard the loophole closely. It suggests that parents may have *unpredictable* effects on their children. In an example she gives, it is possible that if two siblings have dour, undemonstrative parents, one could imagine them reacting in opposite ways: one might become dour and undemonstrative, and the other might become lively and effervescent in compensation for her gloomy home. Harris is so gleeful at having proven that the scientists can't predict which way a child will go that she glides right past what she's just conceded: that whichever way the children react, the parents have had an effect.

When Harris speaks of children who become "competent" and "successful" adults, one has to credit her conclusion that there is no correlation between the subject's competence and success—none, anyway, that can't be attributed to genes—and the way their parents raised them. But I know competent and successful adults—people who function, people who excel, even people who are nice—whose lives I wouldn't wish on a dog because of the way they are trammeled by old griefs and unseen legacies; in short, by neurosis. Don't we all?

This is where Harris's book is least satisfactory. *You only think* that your mother's emotional parsimony made you needy, *You only believe* that trying to measure up to the exacting standards of your distant father made you anxious and ambitious. *We only assume* that Bill Clinton has made a mess of his presidency for reasons that reach back, in part, to his father's death and his mother's ways of coping and his stepfather's alcoholism.

Harris seems never to consider the possibility that much of the marginal but rich human drama that occupies a huge portion of our emotional and intellectual energy might simply elude the tools with which scientists regard human life. I found suspect her very curt explanation of why we come out of childhood believing in the weight of our parents' influence: The part of the brain that processes relationships, she asserts, is accessible to our conscious mind, while the part that is socialized by peers works largely by unconscious means. Really? Who says so?

Finally, Harris fails to notice an important contradiction in her own work. Parents can't make their children love books by reading aloud to them every night; they can only throw them in the way of peer groups in which reading is valued, or at least not derided. But where do you find such peer groups? Why, in communities of other like-minded parents who read aloud to their children every night. Harris grants that children's cultures will adapt a good deal from their parents' cultures, absent some compelling kid-reason not to, but she won't admit that those parental cultures can be reduced, at some point, to lots of individual parents making those supposedly useless individual choices in their homes.

That said, Harris offers a wealth of information about peers' influence on children that should be read by every parent—and perhaps by every policy maker. The crux of her argument about how peers' behavior shapes a child relies on the evolution of group behavior: Primates, she writes, have for millennia built social groups which define themselves in opposition to other groups. Group A shares certain characteristics, group B another set; and, in order to understand themselves and create group loyalty, the two groups then exaggerate the characteristics that first defined them.

Harris believes that this explains everything from the way little boys and girls choose their toys to the reasons academic achievement is seen as "acting white" by African Americans in many city schools. (If this point seems obvious, I am doing violence to the breadth of Harris's review of these theories, including her wonderful summary of the experiments sociologists have done showing how easily student-subjects can be induced, by the power of suggestion, to identify with a wholly invented group.) If girls do less well at math, it is not because boys shout them down and sexist teachers don't call on them; it is because "group contrast effects" have worked away, since preschool, on their self-concepts.

If Harris is right about all this, her work challenges some important orthodoxies in education. The liberal emphasis in today's schools on diversity, for example, may underscore rather than combat children's sense of belonging to their own ethnic "group." And the more homogeneous the classroom, Harris writes, the less likely children are to splinter into groups that assign the characteristic of academic achievement to only one or two of the groups; if true, this would suggest that racial integration in the classroom is an even more impossible dream than we already knew. Curiously, not much research has been done into such questions as how these classroom splits can be prevented, and whether the norms of children's groups can be deliberately influenced from the outside.

No one reading the passion with which Harris tackles these issues could come away from her book with the message that has, unfairly, been attributed to her—that it doesn't matter how you treat your children. Of course it does, Harris writes, for the same reason it matters how you treat your spouse: because they are human, and because the way you behave certainly will affect your relationships with those people. The paragraph with which I opened this review was, in fact, mostly facetious. Go to your child in the middle of the night, Harris would say, and comfort her; not because it will make her emotionally secure twenty years from now, or because she is forming a template for every relationship she will ever have, but because she is frightened and she is small, and it is in your power to make her feel better.

And when you really think about it, this is a more humane reason to treat your child well than the grandiose assumption that your every action will have some power over her future. The "nurture assumption" that Harris attacks is almost by definition a narcissistic one—even if it's narcissism with a bit of masochism thrown in. In closing, Harris writes that "The nurture assumption has turned children into objects of anxiety. . . . Not only have [parents] become servants to their children: They have been declared unsatisfactory servants, because the standards set by the promulgators of the nurture assumption are so high that no one can meet them." So take Harris's book as an eye-opening chance to deepen your appreciation of your children's complexity—and to leaven, a little bit, your load. Mix it with the evidence of your senses. And as my mother used to say, while wending her trackless way through my childhood: Eat what you like and leave the rest.

—November 1998

FLYING TO L.A.

Sunday, January 17, 1999

Tonight I am Cinderella, back at her daily grind the morning after the ball. My husband and I spent last night at the Four Seasons hotel, a few miles away in Georgetown, while our kind friends Paul and Marie down the street took care of our two kids. There's nothing like a night of pampering (dual massages, a wonderful dinner a few blocks from the hotel, a vast marble bathroom that brought out everything Leona in my character) to throw into high relief the drudgery of a feed-the-kids, go-to-the-Safeway, pick-up-the-living-room, make-the-dinner Sunday afternoon and evening. Just now I am listening pitilessly as my husband and my three-year-old daughter duke it out in the hallway, on the other side of a locked door, over the Bath Question.

The reason for the getaway was our birthday. No, that's not the royal "we"; my husband and I actually have the same birthday—same year, even. Any time we tell someone this, they say, *Awwwww. . . .* But I actually (and petulantly) hate it, and not only because of the amount of time I spend explaining to banks and insurance companies that we have not made a mistake in filling out their forms. (*Awwwww,* they say, when I explain it to them.) Think about it: Who buys the cake? Who feels like saying, "Dearest, it's your birthday—you sleep late while I get the kids ready for school"? Buying each other birthday presents has the sick excitement of Mutual Assured Destruction.

Tim, on the other hand, claims that he likes sharing a birthday with me. Aside from his generally sunnier disposition, I attribute this to gender.

Until he met me, he had manly, deprived birthdays, where he'd go to work and never mention to anyone what day it was. Until I met him, I had girly, princess birthdays, on which I felt entitled to small attentions from everyone I met. When we got together, we averaged our birthdays, which was not a transaction in my favor. This is the serious part of my annual whining about the birthday: Every partnership has elements of competition—for resources, attention, and especially (if you have kids, anyway) time. In the course of things, if you're both fair-minded people, equality takes care of itself; it doesn't do to keep score closely from day to day. But somehow the joint birthday strips away everything *but* the competition and makes it more vivid than it should be. Almost every year, we have a stupid fight on our birthday.

By now you're glad *you* don't share a birthday with me. To leaven the complaint (and also because, well, it was my turn) I took a break just now to put Willie and Alice to bed. Tonight was one of the really nice ones. W and A chose a Babar story for their bedtime book. I love Babar books partly for their strangely random story lines but mostly for the archaic translation, which makes all the elephants sound like Adolphe Menjou. "The war is over!" the elephants exult, after routing some angry rhinos. "How perfectly splendid!" Then we turned out the lights and sat in a small circle on Alice's bed, where she carefully spread one of her baby blankets on our three laps, and they told me all the best parts of *The Brave Little Toaster Goes to Mars* while I breathed in their bath smell. Willie, who's almost six, said, "Mommy, I wish I had bunk beds and you would sleep on the top bunk and I would sleep on the bottom." Me: "And where would Daddy sleep?" Willie: "In his room."

Monday, January 18, 1999

I don't think we've given enough thought to root canal as a possible penalty for Clinton's behavior. I had a root canal this afternoon: my eighth, I think. (As a counterweight to whatever blessings I was born with, my genetic code included the diagrams for Job's own teeth.) It reminded me that the last time I had one, I overheard a nurse telling someone that Clarence Thomas was in the next room, having some kind of root canal emergency. I must admit that it gave me a small compensatory thrill to imagine him next door, his own jaw creaking, the same unthinkable tiny tortures at work on one of his molars.

(This sort of quotidian near-encounter with the famous is one of the puny rewards of living in Washington—the equivalent of running into Sandra Bullock, on a bad hair day, at Nate 'n Al's, in Beverly Hills. Once my husband and I were waiting for the shuttle to New York, with our son, then about a year old, at National Airport. Also waiting there, in one of the chairs, was Al Haig. Small thrill, you might point out, but Willie made a beeline crawl for him, like the most practiced White House clutch, and favored him with one of his beaming dolphin smiles. Haig returned the smile, with an avuncular twinkle, then raised a hand, finger and thumb arranged in boyish imitation of a handgun; this he pointed at Willie's nose and then made a loud, deadly shooting noise. I'd like to think Sandra Bullock would be a little more pacific, even on a bad hair day.)

But today's root canal was very entertaining, as root canals go. My endodontist got off on a long riff, addressed half to me and half to his assistant, about his cousins the cocaine dealers. (Did you know there were Jewish cocaine dealers?) I'll call them G and S; G, he said, was sort of a dummy—"so dumb he brought the stuff in from Miami by Amtrak." What's more, he took terrible care of his teeth. The cover story for his many travels was that he was supposedly booking bands to play in Miami. When G and S, who was more like the brains of the operation, got sentenced to thirty years in prison, my dentist's mother refused to believe in their guilt: Their dealing was a one-time thing, maybe, or their conviction the result of a prosecutor's vendetta.

"And I said, Ma, I said, he was traveling to Colombia. How many good bands you think there are in Colombia?"

The cousins' story brought me back to thinking about Clinton, and my own pet theory about Americans' miraculous refusal to want to hear about his misdeeds. I suspect that an astonishing number of people, more than we'd ever surmise, have lives that are bordered by the secret or the unspoken. It's not that our own love affairs have suddenly made us a wildly tolerant country, averse to throwing stones; it's that most of us go through life avoiding conscious knowledge of the impacted family secrets and compromises and half-truths that our lives just manage to grow up around, like hardy weeds around stones. My father made it to the age of twenty-five before anyone mentioned to him that his mother's death, when he was eleven, was a suicide; and he never discussed it with his brothers until they were all in their fifties. *His* father used to take one of his sons for a regular Sunday walk, as a pretext for leaving the house, and then made the boy sit for two hours on the front porch of his mistress's house (in Duluth!—in wintertime!) while he "visited" with her. My mother had a half-brother whose existence she never knew of until she was eight, who had the same name her full brother had. And these are just the *obviously* red-hot secrets, in just one generation.

Somehow, I think, Clinton is a challenge to the settled stories we all carry about our lives. When we first met him, we extended our selective vision to him; now, when his extravagant dishonesty is so plain, he threatens to clear our sight. And once you start calling things by their real names, who knows what else might tumble into the light? Most people would rather think of him as another Cousin G: a black sheep, maybe, but one hard at work finding Colombia's answer to the Beatles.

Anyway, the root canal version of censure-plus would leave future generations in no doubt about the seriousness of Clinton's misdeeds. We'd pick a lower molar, way at the back, and we could make Sam and Cokie watch.

Tuesday, January 19, 1999, at 8:00 PM PT

This, being day three, is when you may start to notice that I'm not doing much actual *work* this week. When I am actually working on an assignment for *Vanity Fair*, I work full time, biting my nails over the fact that I have to quit for the day at six, when the baby sitter turns into a pumpkin, and when Important Sources in Washington are just starting to return phone calls. I'm never their first call-back, since I don't work for one of the daily papers or networks that incite their most Pavlovian responses; but they do call back fairly promptly (could this have anything to do with their wanting to bring their wives to *Vanity Fair*'s annual party after the White House Correspondents' dinner?)—as long as I lie to their assistants and say my deadline is three days away. Usually my deadline is four weeks away, but if you tell them this, you go into an oubliette so deep that it will take three more calls just to get their assistants to take the caps off their pens when you try to leave a message.

But in between assignments, which is where I am right now, I have a blissful freedom to see to all the tedious household chores: returning a package to eToys, which was supposed to be Aunt Patsy's Christmas present for Willie (inside was a cheerful box with a card that read, "Merry Christmas, Jasmine and Jandria"). Collecting the forgotten bedspread from the dry cleaner. Forgetting to return videos. Buying small bribes with which to purchase silence when we take the kids on a five-hour plane trip Thursday. (A nosegay to the person who invented stick-on earrings for little girls.) Normally I feel sheepish that I haven't instead used my freedom to write the great American novel or something (my problem: I love situation and character, can't fathom plot), or at least write back to all the friends who sent me Christmas cards. But I'm setting the bar very low, just now, because without lifting a finger I'm performing what will be the most important feat of my year: not smoking.

I started smoking again last spring, after more than a decade of abstinence, while my mother was dying. It was an artifact of grief, I knew, a misbegotten effort to hang on to her. Among my most vivid pictures of Beverly is her at the high wheel of one of the big cars she favored (she was into SUVs way before they were cool), posture perfect, with a cigarette aloft in her left hand; my mother smoked a Carlton the way others take high tea. So I inherited, among other things, her car and her habit. But I knew I'd have to give it up again, and so I quit on New Year's Day. Which puts me, now, at almost three weeks of abstinence.

I'm using the patch—a miracle drug. The real miracle, though, is the way the world has changed since 1987, the last time I gave up smoking. I smoked for ten years under the old dispensation (when you could light up almost anywhere) and ten months under the new one (when you could light up almost nowhere). And it's an amazing difference. For one thing, I just couldn't smoke as much this time as I did last time; there weren't enough places to do it. For another, it's hard not to notice you're doing something stupid when none of your friends will let you do it in their living rooms. It's a testament to the curative powers of social opprobrium. The anti-smoking movement's success is so complete that, looking back, it's almost impossible to believe that smokers felt as entitled as we did. Can it really be true that we smoked on airplanes? In hospitals? I remember with dismay how, when I went to work on the National Desk of the *Washington Post* in 1986, a coworker and I merrily befouled the air around the seven or eight other editors who practically sat in our laps (they don't call it a Desk for nothing). One of them was even allergic, and the grand concession we two smokers made was to move our overflowing ashtrays to the sides of our terminals farthest away from her.

Wherever you are, Alison, my apologies.

It's almost midnight, and I spent the evening out at a parents' meeting at the cooperative nursery school my daughter goes to, debating a forlorn plan to raise money by selling raffle tickets. At least we know, this year, exactly how little money we have; in past years, the treasurers weren't even able to discern that much from the school's old shoe boxes full of records. (Finally—*duh!*—they got a woman to take the treasurer's job, and she whipped everything into shape in no time.) At least this time we didn't have the Toilet Debate. "Cooperative" means that parents run the whole school, except for the actual teaching, which fortunately we leave to the professionals; among the jobs we all have to do is cleaning the school on weekends. Every year the cleaning issue is debated, and every year the parents continue to clean the toilets. In my little family pod, the way we divide the labor is that Tim does the assigned cleanings, and I go to the meetings. He maintains that he has by far the better deal.

When I got home, I still faced the marathon packing involved in moving the four of us to Los Angeles to visit my in-laws for four days. Four days is no easier than nine days, really, since most of the labor is in the fine details—the little socks and underpants and tights to match the dresses and the agonized selection of only a few Beanie Babies and especially the bag of tricks devised to get Willie and Alice through that long plane ride. (Mustn't forget the box of Band-Aids, a tip from a pediatrician friend, who correctly predicted that Alice would spend hours putting them on. Who cares if she gets off the plane looking as if she walked through a plate glass window?) I admire the airborne parents who take the attitude that other passengers are lucky to be flying with their small darlings, even if they're screaming, but I don't have the aplomb for it myself.

My father-in-law tells a story about flying on MGM Grand, the all first-class airline that flew the New York-L.A. route for a while. He looked up from his seat to see a woman making her way, with a small wiggling boy, to two seats opposite a pair of central-casting, young male Industry types in Armani. They made no effort to hide their horror at the prospect of sharing their swank conveyance with a *child*. But the mother simply smiled at them and said sweetly, "Gentlemen, your worst nightmare is about to come true." In my next life I want to come back as her.

I love my father-in-law for the way he savors this story; he is definitely on her side. I am very lucky in my in-laws, though not quite so lucky as my children are in their grandparents. (Once, when we arrived in mid-summer, Willie was showered with so many gifts that the next morning he said, "Do you know what, Mommy? Yesterday it was Christmas.") But their house is not the place to go if you want to avoid the food binges that lure the quitting smoker. It's full of food, great glass jars full of Oreos and buttery cheddar crackers and cunning little butterscotch cookies, an army of breads and cheeses. My plans for Y2K are to retreat to my in-laws' garage, where Marian keeps understudies to be whisked into the house as soon as anyone makes the tiniest dent in the indoor food supply. The occasion for this trip is her birthday. Is it OK to tell a national audience how old your mother-in-law is? Best to be on the safe side. Let's just say it's an important one.

Thursday, January 21, 1999

Los Angeles always makes me feel like a little brown wren, a sobersides, a woman from an especially poky Anita Brookner novel. All those pretty people, including the men. All those mysterious status signifiers. All those fashion statements that are indecipherable to the Right-Coast eye but that are by definition cooler than anything I might put on. We came out here for a visit when I was about six months pregnant with Alice and, what with prenatal dementia and all, I had managed to persuade myself that even in my maternity overall shorts I was a pretty happening matron. I even had a pedicure, on the advice of a friend who used to live here, involving *more than one nail color*. (Using my friend's name as a talisman, I was able to get an appointment with her desirable foot artiste in under a month.) Then one night my husband took me out to dinner at a little *trattoria* in Beverly Hills, and the waitress came over to us, cocked her head, and in the nicest possible way said six words more devastating than any I could have imagined: "You're not from here, are you?" I burst into tears—not because I really meant to pass as a local, but because it was brutally clear that my not-from-here-ness was so vivid as to incite comment from strangers. Later I forced my husband to go skinny-dipping with me in my in-laws' pool, just to show myself that I still had a lively impulse or two.

In Washington, on the other hand, I've always felt right at home. There, I have the pleasure of falling toward the raffish end of the fashion spectrum. (Trust me, it isn't hard.) It's an easy city—small, leafy, navigable; a place where you can have a green backyard just a ten- or fifteen-minute drive from downtown. Of course it's a hive of conformity and caution, but that's part of what I like about it—about covering it, anyway. The mixture of that brittle, conservative set of social conventions and all the messy human stuff that goes on inside and among the people who try to climb to the top of the heap makes for such rich material. A lot of my stories (chiefly, my work is writing long, intensive profiles of people in government and politics) are really about what Washington admires, and why, and what it says about the political culture. Why Washington needed to believe that Clark Clifford—a canny old fixer who wove his own legend out of vanity and a sonorous voice—was the personification of Cold War statesmanship. Why pols and reporters promoted the idea that James Baker—the chilliest deal maker to come along in years—was also a visionary and a wonderful human being. I love working this seam between the accepted narrative, usually hammered out between the Washington press corps and its sources, and the grubby human nature stuff that is nearly always as plain as the nose on your face. Washington's status codes are charmingly straightforward: An assistant secretary is better than a deputy assistant secretary, but sitting next to a deputy assistant secretary is better than sitting next to a Cabinet member's wife. As in a Jane Austen novel, it is this very hierarchical, preordained quality that throws the city's strivings into high relief; no one gets distracted by wondering if they got the right pedicure.

I wonder if one of the byproducts of Clinton's presidency will be an end to the predictable rhythm of Washington's social rituals and hypocrisies. If so, I may need to find a new parsonage.

A SECOND THOUGHT
ON ASSISTED SUICIDE

In its recent vote to overrule Oregon's first-in-the-nation law permitting physician-assisted suicide, the Republican House of Representatives showed its usual heavy hand in dealing with delicate social issues. There was major hypocrisy, to say the least, in conservatives' sudden discovery that some issues are too important to be decided at the state level. But it's hard for me to shake an increasing sympathy for the ethical imperative on which the House was acting.

My mother was a great advocate of the dignified exit. As she neared seventy, she polished her living will and joked about having a friend dispatch her with a pillow if she ever languished in a nursing home. But it was her death, from liver failure, that overturned my settled assumptions about assisted suicide. As far as I am able to say, my mother's was an "easy" death. She wasn't in terrible pain. She was at home, in the house she had loved for more than thirty-five years, in a place of comfort and grace; she was surrounded by her three daughters and a group of women friends who tiptoed in each day with small offerings of the spring flowers that bloomed just in time. She had all the comforts and care it is possible to buy and, in her hospice nurse, the good fortune that has no price. The period from the time she entered hospice care to the morning of her death was a little under three weeks.

Yet even this short, kind end was excruciating to be a part of. She looked, at the very least, miserably uncomfortable. On the days when she unexpectedly drifted back to us, out of her semi-coma, she seemed to want something nameless, out of our power to deliver or even guess. Her dying seemed, during those weeks, an endless state, a slow, inconsistent progress that made each day open before us with dreary mystery. The nurses would tell us what we might expect, from the clinical (the cooling of the extremities that would signal the slowing of circulation) to the superstitious (pets, one nurse told us, sometimes come to lie down with an owner when death is imminent). The childlike intensity with which we, three women in our forties, watched for these signs—Look! The cat is on the bed! No, Annie brought him up and put him there earlier—told us how painful it was to drift through a crucial passage that was so entirely beyond our control.

Later I found things in that time to value: the privilege of caring well for her, the tenderness of the bond I shared with my sisters. But as we lived it, we felt most clearly our powerlessness. It was so big, that feeling, that I began to wonder if human beings can really be trusted with the suggestion that there are ways to make the process manageable, to combat the losses of autonomy and control that are the essence of death. You bear the unbearable, in the orbit of a loved one's death, because you have to. If we come to believe that we and our families can sometimes be spared that, how many of us will be willing to endure it at all, under any circumstances?

This concern is somewhat borne out by the Oregon Health Division's report on the first year after passage of the state's suicide act. Of the twenty-one persons who secured lethal prescriptions from their doctors in 1998, fifteen of whom went through with their suicides, only one cited the fear of intractable pain. More than anything, these patients cited concerns about "autonomy and personal control." Advocates of Oregon's system point out that it includes an elaborate series of safety mechanisms, of waiting periods and second opinions and witnesses not related to the dying person, to ensure against family pressure and medical cost-cutting and all the other obviously sinister temptations that are said to lurk at the bottom of the slippery slope.

But I wonder now if it is that very structure—the sensible, humane, *normalizing* particulars by which suicide is enshrined in social policy— that constitutes the threat, because it offers such reassuring authority to anyone who might be tempted to manage death away. In other words, to us all. I can easily imagine circumstances far worse than my mother's. I wouldn't dream of judging anyone—physician, patient, or family—who privately chose to end or help end the unendurable. But officially, publicly, in the open realm where our norms develop, I hope we continue to honor the assumption that death is the one matter that is out of our hands.

—November 14, 1999

THE CAT RACE

It's a dreadful story. In Japan last week a thirty-five-year-old mother of two, a former nurse, strangled the two-year-old daughter of a neighbor, enraged that the little girl had gained a place in the school she coveted for her own two-year-old. Superficially, this is a cautionary tale about the wages of academic competitiveness. More than that, the Japanese press concluded, it's a symptom of the way mothers there are encouraged to sublimate their ambitions through their children.

While it's true that Japanese women remain far more bound by traditional roles than women in most industrial democracies, we should be wary of assuming that our own fascination with Mitsuko Yamada's story lies in how unlike us the Japanese are. The story stirs us up mostly because we have such an intimate understanding of that mother's feelings, at least in their germinal stages.

Stripped to its essentials, it's just another story of the Cat Race. This is the name devised by the British writer Celia Fremlin, whose lively mysteries—now mostly out of print—were brilliant disguises for her true passion, which was the covert exploration of domestic life, especially the lives of mothers and children. "The Cat Race," Fremlin wrote in her 1969 novel *Possession,*

> begins with our babies' births and goes on—as far as I can see—forever. The biggest birth-weight—the rosiest cheeks—the largest circle of playmates—the highest marks. . . . We would be hard put to it,

most of us, to say exactly what the race is about, whither it is directed, and what the prize. But we all know, instantly and without any
doubt, who is winning at any given moment, and we know how the
points are allotted. When someone's children go off youth-hostelling
at an earlier age than the rest; when they put on a play all by themselves; when they read old-fashioned children's books, or come tops
in Math, or play games that cover them in mud and tear their jeans—
all these are point-scoring phenomena for the mother concerned,
though it would be hard indeed to say on what scale these very
diverse activities can possibly be measured.

My mother tried to tell me about the Cat Race, but I felt the standard
scorn of the feminist daughter. How invidious; how sexist; how not the
way I planned to run my life, which would be marked by open striving for
the direct rewards that really mattered. Then I had children of my own.

Now I know that the Cat Race is one of the mightiest forces in human
affairs, even if some of the details have changed. Now we do small-motor
skills. Most flexible diet ("Have you thought of trying kelp? My boys just
love kelp."). Least likely to be called to the principal's office. One chapter
of my education stands out with particular clarity: When my son was
about eighteen months old, I took him to a birthday party, where another
little boy (I'll call him Eustace. Meow) was sporting a spectacular black
eye. In an effort to be kind (and possibly to conceal some satisfaction at
this advertisement of his mother's negligence?) I made commiserating
comments about the way children his age collect injuries; my son, I said,
fell constantly. Instead of accepting my offering, the other mother gave me
a sadistically sympathetic look and said, "Huh. Interesting. I find that
Eustace is really very graceful."

The Cat Race isn't confined to mothers, of course. Fathers, who have
always stalked the sidelines of Little League with the intensity of giant
stags, are increasingly apt to compete in events like Early Reading, Shunning Nickelodeon ("Oh, Basil only watches documentaries on tropical
ecosystems") and even Sleeping Through the Night. Dads who act as primary caretaker may be the most competitive of all. This insight came to
me when one such man, having established the superiority of his family's
schooling plans, went on to initiate a conversation on the merits of different breast pumps.

Perhaps it's sexist, then, to persist in speaking of the Cat Race. But peel away the female connotations and the phrase still fits for its summoning of the universally cat-like: the soft-footed cunning; the implacability.

Few of us, of course, have lethal feelings toward each other's kids. The Cat Race is aimed not at other children, really, or even other parents; it is aimed at ourselves, and the places in us where we store the knowledge that we are hopelessly small to be trusted with the raising of people even smaller. The first, most insidious thing we learn when we have children is that we're supposed to be able to control their lives. Sanity comes with the understanding that this is impossible, but we never entirely unburden ourselves of this anxious charge.

Even under different circumstances—a society that places an extraordinary premium on control; a woman with few other ways to reassure herself of her adequacy—it seems more than a quantum leap from the self-soothing rivalries of our playgrounds to the mad case of Mitsuko Yamada. Yet to think that our little battles are cousins to murder—distant cousins, but family still—seems less far-fetched to me than I wish it did.

—December 4, 1999

GRANDPARENTS' RIGHTS

She pulls a stool to the counter and bends low, hands on her knees. "Alice," she whispers. "Would you like to make a cake?" More than a year later, my daughter still recites the sweet particulars of this event: standing on that stool in her Nanny's kitchen, creaming the butter and scattering flour over the countertop, licking chocolate off the spoon.

At its best, a child's relationship with a grandparent is idyllic, a deep familial bond that is free of the sometimes wounding intensity that flashes between parents and children. It is this ideal, the seniors' lobby would have you believe, that quivers in the balance in the case of *Troxel v. Granville*, the so-called "grandparents' rights" case argued Wednesday before the Supreme Court. More than a dozen organizations have filed briefs on behalf of one side or the other, scattering much overwrought language about the future of the American family along the way. Those weighing in on the grandparents' side warn that the Court could undermine statutes in all fifty states that permit grandparents to petition for visitation with their grandchildren. But I can't respond as anything but a parent, and for a parent, what's at stake in the case is this:

Imagine that a judge, with no finding that you are neglectful or abusive, decides that once or twice a month you have to send your children away overnight. It might be to the home of someone with whom you have a bad history, or whom you suspect of being a little too old and frail to handle your rambunctious six-year-old, or who actively dislikes you. You do not have a choice, even if your child's grandparent is Livia Soprano. And it makes no difference that your four-year-old daughter is having night terrors, or is going through a phase where she needs her Barbie night-light *and* her Squirtle sippy cup *and* the mangy doll she drew hair onto with her blue magic marker, and even then won't go to sleep unless you sing the dopey song you made up when she was two, that time she had chicken pox and itched all night. Good luck communicating the warp and weft of that routine to a couple with whom you just spent a few years in family court hell. Oh, and it cost you $30,000 in lawyers' fees to get here.

This is very close to what happened to Tommie Granville Wynn after the father of her two little girls killed himself, in 1993. The father's parents, Gary and Jennifer Troxel, sued for visitation of the girls, then one and four, and won a court order—including one overnight visit a month and a week every summer. The mother objected, not to their having a relationship with the children but to the extent of the visitation, especially the overnights. (And perhaps, the subtext of the case suggests, to the intensity of feeling the bereaved grandparents brought to the cultivation of their granddaughters.) Her appeal was upheld by the Supreme Court of Washington state, which overturned the entire statute in question, saying that parents have a constitutional right to decide with whom their children should associate, unless it is shown that they are doing the children some actual harm. The Troxels are asking the justices to revive the statute, saying it should be enough for grandparents to meet its vaguer standard of showing that their continued relationship with a grandchild is in the child's "best interest."

Judging by their questions at oral argument, the justices are unlikely to oblige. They seemed especially offended by the breadth of the statute, which said that "any person" could seek visitation with a child at any time. They may do little more than affirm the state court on this one aspect of its decision, writing a narrow ruling that would have scant impact on states with more tightly drafted visitation laws.* This would be a pity. In a perfect world, the justices would seize this chance to make clear that partisans are debating more than one issue here and exploiting the useful confusion that results. It is quite legitimate for a state to empower grandparents in cases of parental negligence or abuse or absence. Several states already recognize distinct rights, in both custody and visitation, for grandparents (and others) who have served as de facto parents.

* That's more or less what the Supreme Court did later that year.

But the subtler cases, in which good-enough parents fall out with grandparents, can find no help in the law. Something has gone seriously awry when a parent rejects the open-handed offering of a grandparent's love. How many people, after all, have the patience to help your three-year-old bake a cake from scratch? But the state has no magic tweezers that can pry the appropriate parental caution apart from the jealous act of family spite. Love and loss and pettiness and narcissism are wounds for which there is no legal cure—or only cures that tamper with the essence of good parenthood, which is to feel an investment in a child's well-being that no one else on the planet can match.

—January 14, 2000

THE PARENT RAP

We parents, it seems, are living in paradise. Just ask Elinor Burkett, the author of a new book titled *The Baby Boon: How Family-Friendly America Cheats the Childless*. We get all the best shifts and assignments on the job; we get wildly generous tax preferences so that we can all take European vacations and buy granite countertops for our kitchens; and employers are apparently tripping over themselves to provide more high-quality day care than we know what to do with.

The childless, on the other hand, are to be pitied. Our country, Burkett writes, is "demeaning its childless citizens" by "creating one set of rules for those who breed and a different set for those who do not." They don't get our tax breaks, or the groveling concern we inspire in our pols and our bosses. They have to cover for us every time we waltz out of the office because Janie has a sniffle. They can't persuade society to fund their expensive pleasures the way we have tricked it into subsidizing our pricey hobby of child-rearing. And they have to take all the business trips to Abilene and Cleveland so that we parents can pop our children into bed and then enjoy our long, leisurely evenings before the television. It says so right on Page 39.

I'd like to tell you that I have unfairly caricatured Burkett's argument, for there are genuine matters of equity to debate here. Certainly, there is conflict over the issue in the workplace. And some of her arguments are compelling. I share some of her skepticism about the way the left has learned to dress up its feminism as Family Values. And there's a lot of justice in her charge that our tax system sends to affluent parents some benefits that could be better spent on poor children. There's no reason why a couple making $200,000 a year should get the same $960 tax credit for child care expenses that goes to a single mother earning $30,000.

Yet, if this argument about social justice were her real concern, Burkett would have written a book about why the mortgage interest deduction, which dwarfs all these parents' benefits, is unfair to the poor. Her true beef, as one who has chosen not to have kids, is with the social privileging of parenthood. Boomer parents, she writes, are a whining lot, convinced that "the stress of their lives is society's fault for not adjusting its every nook and cranny to facilitate their desire to have the kinds of families they want, have full-bodied and lucrative careers, and still to have enough money left over to retire on the near side of sixty." She sees not overburdened middle-class parents but sulking yuppies laboring under "the difficulties created by their own choices."

But who, if not other people's children, will pay for Burkett's Social Security when she gets old? David Blankenhorn, president of the Institute for American Values, a family-policy-oriented think tank, notes that all citizens derive the benefits of the child-rearing done by some.

> Almost all the economic benefits of raising children are generalized. If they're good people, they contribute to society, they sit on juries and fight in the wars and tote that barge and lift that bale; the economic benefit doesn't accrue to the parents who raise them. In the modern welfare state, there's a huge imbalance: We are collectivizing the cost of growing old, but leaving private the cost of raising children.

Burkett asks one mother just what it is that childless people are supposed to get out of the deal, but seems not to understand her reply. "You get in return that you don't have children," the woman tells her, with admirable candor. You get a good night's sleep. You probably don't have peanut butter smeared on your best coat. You get to keep the nearly $17,000 annually that is the bare minimum a middle-income family spends to raise just a first child to the age of seventeen. You still have the brain cells that parents burn up answering pop quizzes over breakfast about whether a Charizard could beat a Hitmonchan in a Pokemon battle. You have *time*.

I'll grant you that parents can be annoying: our air of jolly martyrdom, our smug certainty about the value of what we're doing in this one aspect of our lives. These are the petty compensations we take in exchange for nudging the species along—the hardest work that most of us will ever do. I don't need Elinor Burkett to agree with me that it can also be one of life's greatest pleasures. But the fact that I enjoy it doesn't make it a mere "lifestyle choice." And it doesn't release her from any obligation under the social contract to which we all subscribe.

—February 18, 2000

THE ART OF THE FAKE APOLOGY

When Al Gore acknowledged last weekend that he "made a mistake in pressing the limits" in his 1996 campaign fund-raising,* he was offering up a fine new specimen of the Useful Apology. He now brings "the passion that comes from personal experience to the battle for campaign finance reform," he told the *New York Times*, a passion "fueled in part because of the pain of those mistakes." This supposed confession—dutiful, limited, and as persuasive as all regrets spoken by miscreants who are sorry they got caught—contains a lot of what drives normal people nuts about politics.

The Useful Apology is some revelation of personal weakness that is carefully calibrated to address a political vulnerability without making any concession that could attract further harm. It must be phrased in such a way that it can be justified or nullified or hurled at one's opponent in the very next sentence. Although Gore is a master of the strategic admission, he is hardly alone. George W. Bush offered us the recent example of his apology to the Catholic voters of America, couched as a letter to Cardinal O'Connor regretting ("deeply") that he missed the opportunity to decry Bob Jones University's official anti-Catholicism when he spoke there during the South Carolina primary. His letter went on for much greater length about how unfairly he had been criticized than it did about how sorry he was for what he did.

* Most famously, Gore attended a campaign fund-raiser at a Buddhist temple where illegal campaign contributions were collected.

On a more personal level, Bush likes to wear the mantle of special achievement that justly belongs to anyone who has successfully battled an addiction—so long as you understand that his drinking problem was never an addiction. "Just like you, I'm on a walk," he told a group of recovering drug addicts at a January campaign appearance, "and it's a never-ending walk as far as I'm concerned." But in other settings he has maintained that "I don't think I was clinically an alcoholic. I didn't have the genuine addiction." Giving up drinking when he turned forty was a "turning point," he writes in his memoir—but not such an important one that he couldn't accomplish it overnight, without help, Gary Cooper-style.

The master of the art of the mea-not-really-culpa is, of course, Bill Clinton. President Clinton spent most of the second half of 1998 not really apologizing for his relationship with Monica Lewinsky, and especially not really apologizing for not quite lying in his deposition in the Paula Jones case. Democrats in Congress actually embroiled themselves in endless hairsplitting discussions about whether the president had apologized enough or whether apologizing more apologetically might stave off impeachment.

But there are ample precedents in both parties. Republican presidents have made artful use of the passive voice, which is every Useful Apologizer's best friend: "Mistakes were made," Ronald Reagan told the nation when he was absolutely forced to make a statement about how Iran-Contra happened on his watch. This is the self-rescinding apology, which may be the most useful kind of all.

Yet this election year seems to be the high-water mark of the pseudo-admission. Both Gore and Bush are masters at donning the polyester hairshirt to make amends that, in the same breath, deny any need for atonement. It is hard to say why they seem so evenly, depressingly matched in this. It could have something to do with a shared sense of entitlement (Could I really be wrong if I'm George W. Bush/Albert A. Gore Jr.?). I tend to think that Bush has a genuine, if blustering, inability to see himself as a bad guy *(my own brother is a Catholic!)*, while Gore, who is more capable of self-scrutiny, has a heightened sense of shame that forbids much real admission of fault.

Bush's form of the false apology makes him look shallow; Gore's makes him look phony. Neither man is doing himself much good. The reason John McCain's reform message so galvanized primary voters, including Democrats, was not that they were panting to see this issue solved. It was the impression that his experiences—especially in being tarred as one of the Keating Five—had touched some treasured sense of himself that he had nearly sold. This quality sometimes verged on the histrionic—he never looked so happy as when he was kicking himself—but even then it seemed real. You could debate whether McCain would ever be able to convert this sense of mission into some effective reform; you could even debate whether the issue was as important as he said it was. But you never thought it was only useful to him.

We all know, in our own lives, how hard it is to make a real apology. The real thing, in the moment before we cough it up, is a dire hair ball of stubbornness and pride. A real apology is useless, in the sense that it isn't offered for the giver's gain. Otherwise it isn't a real apology. We don't expect every politician to be as self-scolding as John McCain. It may not even be a very good qualification for the presidency. All we ask of all the others is that they spare us the theater of sham regrets.

—*March 17, 2000*

REAL COMPLICATED

Real Simple, the fattest new magazine ever launched by Time Inc., hits the stands on Monday, billing itself as a "magazine for a simpler life/home/body/soul." Stressed-out women of America, the secret can now be told: The key to a simple life is to have invisible children. Even though *Real Simple* expects that about 70 percent of its thirty-something target audience will be mothers, its debut issue pictures not a single child, except in its advertisements.

If you're going to peddle a fantasy, why not go all the way? No sticky fingers, no sweaters dropped on the floor, no cracker crumbs ground into the sofa. Presto: serenity. "It was definitely our intention to do a magazine that speaks directly to the woman, and not to her roles," editor Susan Wyland says. The first issue of the magazine tells "today's over-extended, over-committed, over-scheduled woman" how to clean her medicine cabinet every month. ("Then, as you replace the toiletries, dust them." As if!) It tells her about skin-care products that "multitask now, just like the rest of us." It even tells her "how to create special moments in your day for reflecting and recharging." But it doesn't tell her what she really needs to know about simplifying her life: black trash bags. A mother's lot is the constant beating-back of a tide of things. And if you use white trash bags during your periodic sweeps of the house, your children complain about the cruelty of throwing away their old tangled Slinkies and toys from ancient Happy Meals, that fossilized lollipop from last December. You must strike at night, and use opaque black bags.

Simplifying your own life is easy; it's this living with other people, especially small ones, that's complicated. What stands between me and the spare beauty shown on *Real Simple*'s pages is a sea of late library books and stray Barbie shoes and miscellaneous rocks, which my daughter picks up on her walks and presents to me as trophies. To accept these as the gifts they are, without developing rock deposits in every corner of the house: This is not simple, whatever else it is. *Real Simple* doesn't warn a woman that she is going to have to develop a ruthless system by which to discard nine-tenths of the artwork her children bring home from school. Guerrillas of the Shining Path can't hold a candle to the cold-eyed efficiency of a mom clearing the dining-room table, according to a judicious system that rapidly tabulates beauty, effort, and the likelihood that the artist might ask after it a month from now. ("Oh, the paper-plate mermaid diorama with the blue Saran-Wrap water? Darn, honey, I don't know where that's gotten to.")

A lot of *Real Simple*'s advice amounts to: Don't forget to buy more milk before the old milk runs out. ("Of course, running out of coffee is minor compared to not having enough money to send the kids to college, but the weight of stress is cumulative, and it's often those few additional ounces of pressure that get us down," writes Francine Prose in an article reminding us to re-stock whenever we've used three-quarters of anything. Yes, that would be the same Francine Prose who recently wrote a furious polemic in the *New York Times Magazine* about the "second-rate, second-string" popular culture being offered to women today.)

But where is guidance on how to corral all the homework papers that collect in front of the toaster, sopping up a fine sheen of butter and a dusting of crumbs? Where is the method for reminding yourself to call the pediatrician for a check-up appointment a good three months in advance, to schedule it after the school year is finished but before the deadline for submitting the inoculation record to summer camp? Where is the treatise on car-pool politics, starting with the appropriate penalty for a male spouse who always hands over the phone, shrugging helplessly, when another parent (surprise—a mother!) calls with a question about car pools or play dates?

Of course the canny editors of Time Inc. are not alone in lulling harried mothers with a vision of child-free simplicity. The people who appear in home magazines, for example, almost never have children; they have collections of antique white pudding molds or English garden trugs or, if they have a nurturing streak, Orpington chickens. The ads have children in them because ad executives have always known that mothers like to look with guilty envy at these tastefully treated windows, which bear no fingerprints. But they are Ralph Lauren children, who are even less trouble than Orpington chickens.

Real Simple starts its life under a heavy burden of oxymoron, since there are probably limits to the definition of "simple" that can lure advertisers at $28,000 a page. Perhaps it was wise of the editors to avoid taking on the even larger tension between the real and the fantasy lives of their target audience. A lot of family life is an endless series of repetitive tasks that can't be simplified away, and doing those tasks with patience is the simplest rigor of our life/home/body/soul.

—March 24, 2000

DYING FOR DOLLARS

In his book *Den of Thieves*, James B. Stewart summed up the essence of the money culture of the 1980s by showing corporate raider Ivan Boesky at a business dinner, casually ordering a waiter to bring him every entree on the menu so that he could taste them all before deciding which he wanted. We've been waiting patiently for our parallel symbol, the ultimate expression of our own gilded age; the ending to the sentence, "You know the money culture is out of hand when. . . ."

The candidates are almost too numerous to name. Is it the ad campaign for the online jewelry firm, Zales.com, that pushes engagement rings with the tag line, "Isn't it nice to be passionate about something other than making money?" Is it the cottage industry that has sprung up to ponder the problem of Sudden Wealth Syndrome and to minister to the poor newborn billionaires who suffer from it? Is it the parents who buy $400 cashmere Sonia Rykiel coats and drivable, battery-powered Jaguar XK8s for their children? The Palo Alto middle school that assigned sixth-graders to prepare model business plans as their back-to-school-night projects? The advent of $39 raw-tuna-and-wasabi pizza?

No. These nominees all are plenty decadent, but they lack the full-bore depravity required to reach totemic status. We still are waiting for the crushing detail that will nail once and for all the way the very scale of getting and spending has changed in our new economy. Like Ivan Boesky, we have simply faced too many rich choices. Until now.

On Wednesday, the Treasury Department finally identified, in the dry language of a proposed regulatory change, the single most unembarrassed new manifestation of the avarice that coats the dark side of our wonderful economic boom. The winner of the Savonarola Award, at last, is an estate-planning loophole that tax advisers sometimes refer to as the "vulture trust."

A vulture trust is a variation on something called the charitable lead trust, which allows you to maximize what you pass on to heirs by designating a charity to receive income during the term of the trust; your heirs then get the balance. In its normal form, the trust allows the donor to take a charitable deduction at the time it is established, based on the anticipated amount the charity will receive over time, and also to shelter some of the assets' later appreciation from estate tax.

The new twist is that this tax dodge is far, far more valuable if you can base the term of the trust on the lifetime of a young person who is dying, because the taxes are all calculated up-front, based on the probable life span of the named person. The longer the actuarial tables say that person is likely to live, the larger the tax deduction. So the ideal person to name in a trust is one whose youth will afford you a big deduction on the front end, but who will then conveniently die, allowing your beneficiaries to get the principal before too many years have passed. You don't need to know the young person in question. In fact, it's a great deal nicer for you if you don't. All that has been required is that you find "an individual who is seriously ill but not 'terminally ill' within the meaning of the section 7520 regulations," as the Treasury's proposal to close the loophole puts it. In other words, someone not so close to death's actual door that the IRS would call you on it—just someone who can be counted on to die with reasonable dispatch once her or his usefulness is at an end.

Heck, they're dying anyway, right? Attorneys and financial planners have begun recruiting dying people and marketing their grim fates to others, paying them nothing but a flat fee—perhaps $5,000—for access to their medical records and consent to use them as a "measuring life." The dying stranger gets no further benefit from the trust. If this doesn't already seem grotesque enough to qualify for the prize, consider this: The Treasury writes that some middlemen have basically lied to their marks, suggesting to the dying that "a charitable organization interested in the individual's particular illness will receive some benefit from the transaction."

Little is known about how many taxpayers have taken advantage of vulture trusts, or how many advisers are peddling them to their clients. But the dodge has been used at least often enough in the past two years to motivate Treasury officials to end it. The new rule proposed this week* would force donors to tie these trusts to their own lives or the lives of direct relatives.

The breadth and depth of our economic boom, and its happy information-age gloss of spreading knowledge while raising prosperity, have lately given the pursuit of big money a moral neutrality it lacked in the age of Gordon Gekko. So treasure the vulture trust as a priceless reminder: If we can't be passionate about anything but making money, we can at least agree that some things make us a little queasy.

* It has since become a formal regulation.

—*April 7, 2000*

DO PARENTS SUFFER
DISCRIMINATION?

At first blush, it seems the soul of good sense: *Of course* parents shouldn't be denied jobs or promotions simply because they have kids. When President Clinton on Tuesday announced an executive order barring discrimination against parents in the federal workplace, to match legislation he proposed last year covering private-sector employees, he was asserting an apparently apple-pie principle.

But on closer examination, this is a mischievous bit of grandstanding. For one thing, we should always be wary when our leaders make a great show of redressing an evil that has not been shown to exist. As Republicans in Congress have pointed out, in letting Clinton's private-sector version of this initiative languish, the White House has never shown (nor made much effort to show) that parents are routinely discriminated against in any way clear enough to be susceptible to legal redress.

For another thing, to the extent that this problem exists, there are already some good laws on the books to address it. It is already illegal to discriminate against a pregnant woman; and thanks in part to Clinton, workers are already by law entitled to return to the same or an equivalent job after thirteen weeks of unpaid leave following childbirth or family crisis.

But the real mischief in Clinton's executive order is that it perpetuates the myth that most confounds all our debates about work-family conflict, which is the fairy-tale belief that if only there were no mean employers harboring brute prejudices against children, there would be no work-family conflict. There should be "no glass ceiling for parents," Clinton declaimed, in signing the order. But of course parenthood itself, properly pursued, is its own glass ceiling.

Being a parent almost inevitably, for a while, cuts into the professional intensity that younger, more single-focused workers bring to the job, including the willingness to work long hours on short notice. Parents often bring compensatory skills to their work: the efficiencies of experience; the clarity of purpose that parenthood, at its best, can promote; the insight that some of what they have let go is Dilbertian wheel-spinning to begin with.

But the fact is that work and family are often in competition, and good parents sacrifice work to their families more often than they sacrifice their families to their work. We hate to utter this blunt judgment, but the truth is that all the employer flexibility in the world cannot entirely banish the conflict. Our leaders do us no favors when they suggest that the onus is entirely on others—politicians, bosses, coworkers—to make this conflict seem less sharp.

In the long run, it makes us crazy to look at the world around us and be confronted every day with the suggestion that we act and feel exactly as we did before our lives changed. For women, this myth all too often leaves us wondering, "What's wrong with me?" It sets back working parents' efforts to persuade employers to see them as different but valuable: as people for whom allowances must sometimes be made when a child is sick or when a school conference calls but who return enough value—both on the job and as contributors to the social order—to be worth it. You can't simultaneously urge employers to give parents some breaks and also hector them for not regarding parents in exactly the same light as non-parents.

Clinton's ploy also encourages employers to believe that it's fair to expect everyone, without variation, to want to work all the time. Most professional women and men know that the real sanctions against their family lives in the workplace aren't the gross injuries of being fired or denied promotion; they're the insidious suggestions that if you were really dedicated, you would work work work fourteen hours a day. Ask yourself whether Clinton's executive order helps or hurts parents' efforts—in the workplace and in their own convictions—to challenge that definition of dedication.

There are always two overlapping debates going on in our discussion of work–family issues. One is the debate over personal choices that is the luxury of middle- and upper-middle-class families. (Should I work? How much? How do I balance what I gain from working against what my kids want or need?) For this debate, Clinton's pandering in the direction of "parents' rights" only obscures what's at stake.

And of course it makes no contribution at all to the second debate, which is the one our public policy should concern itself with: the question of what we can do for the millions of women who work long hours for low pay and, as things stand, have almost no chance of seeing their children adequately cared for during their work hours.

All the "rights" in the world do nothing to help when you have to get your toddler on a bus at 5:30 AM so you can get her to her substandard day care in time to get to your own job cleaning hotels by 7:30. But, of course, addressing that problem would cost a lot of money. It's much easier to stand up for our comfortable, middle-class denial of the moral weight our choices carry.

—*May 5, 2000*

THE POLITICAL WIFE, RIP

Now *that's* a low blow. The estranged wife of Rep. Albert Wynn has gone to work for the campaign of his opponent, Paul Kimble, targeting her former love with inflammatory recorded calls to thousands of voters in Maryland's heavily black Fourth District. "Albert Wynn does not respect black women," says her message. "He left me for a white woman."

Kimble, who is white, may be kindly described as an eccentric who won the Republican nomination by virtue of being the only Republican foolish enough to vie for the Democratic Wynn's ultra-safe seat. He has eight dogs and six cats; he once tried to pose nude in *Playgirl* magazine as a way of raising funds; and in two previous outings against Wynn he won less than 15 percent of the vote. Kimble, in other words, is just a bump in Wynn's road to a fifth term. The real interest in the story is as the latest sign of revolt in the ranks of silent political wifehood. It seems that when politicians divorce these days, a wife who has hoed the long row of political marriage is ever more inclined to go out with a bang.

A little over a year ago, Pat Fordice, then first lady of Mississippi, was (very sweetly) hanging her governor-husband, Kirk Fordice, out to dry, by publicly declining to vacate the governor's mansion so that he could marry his mistress. And last spring we had Donna Hanover, on the steps of Gracie Mansion, delivering the death blow to Rudy Giuliani's Senate campaign by confirming that his affairs were the reason their marriage was ending. Last month, Marianne Gingrich earned a reported $275,000 for a book proposal promising to relate the saga of her marriage to Newt: hard-earned money indeed.

These auguries are like the early frames of one of those children's dramas—*Mrs. Frisby and the Rats of NIMH*, perhaps—in which lab animals band together to escape from their tormentors. In fact, the phenomenon of the Explosive Political Wife is just one more sign that the entire role of political wife is on its last legs, victim of our dawning awareness that it's a social construct that has outlived its relevance by a good thirty years.

The Wife always served three purposes in politics, at least two of which are now moot. The first was to warrant the husband's basic normality as a family man—that he was just like voters. But increasingly, the man with a single long-term marriage and a helpmeet whose career is to support his career is becoming a rarity; why should voters want to see this vanishing ideal mirrored in their politicians? The second role was to assert his reliability, or morality. (He seems happily married, she sticks with him, ergo he's not a cad.) But in the post-Clinton era, this function not only seems passé, it seems, after Hillary Clinton's long, ambiguous service as her husband's enabler, positively suspect. (Don't be fooled by The Kiss, Al and Tipper Gore's famed clinch before his convention speech last month, which is the exception that proves the rule. Only the man who wants to succeed Bill Clinton has to offer what will henceforth be seen as icky, staged demonstrations of intimacy.) Finally, political wives—especially on the Republican side—have served as guarantors of their husbands' essential niceness, or political moderation. Barbara Bush always allowed people to believe she was liberal on abortion rights and that perhaps therefore her husband was too; she talked so fervently about literacy and Head Start that it was easy to forget to notice how little interest George Bush had in domestic social policy. This function—though theoretically one that wives can still perform—is the least constructive one of all.

In almost any campaign you may still see the wife in the skirted blue or red suit, the sensible pumps, accepting her wrist corsage from the 4-H Club winner. But, behind its impregnable smiles and circle pins, the entire institution has been slowly crumbling. Increasingly, politicians' wives have jobs of their own or, cleanest of all, careers that have absolutely nothing to do with politics. Another reason political wifehood is dying is that men are now trying to be political spouses, too, and they can't stand it. Bob Dole, you'll recall, endured it for about five minutes before he undermined his wife's presidential campaign by carrying on about his admiration for her rival, John McCain.

No matter how many times you see Laura Bush read to a child on the evening news this year, the traditional political wife is an endangered species. May she rest in peace. Some time, in the not-too-distant future, we will acknowledge the passing of her role with the same amazement we felt at the fall of the Berlin Wall, crashing down so easily after standing for decades as an unbreachable certainty. Boy, we'll think; that sucker wasn't as strong as it looked.

—September 1, 2000

THE WIDOW'S MANDATE

It's possible to feel a reluctant admiration for the summary way that Missouri Democrats have drafted Jean Carnahan to kind-of-sort-of become their candidate for the U.S. Senate. After her husband, Governor Mel Carnahan, was killed last week en route to a campaign event in the crash of a small plane piloted by his son, the state party found itself in the awkward position of having no time to replace him in his race against Republican Senator John Ashcroft. So the new governor, Roger Wilson, has urged voters to cast their ballots for the late governor, promising to appoint his widow to the seat if the deceased wins the election.

If the plan seems—as Missouri Republicans have loudly charged—a little on the tricky side, one can rationalize that it avoids an even less democratic outcome: Had party activists done nothing, then Carnahan's untimely death would have disenfranchised all of the state's Democratic voters.

So why does the whole thing make me queasy? One clue is the casuistry that has ruled the state's debate over the process. While a dead man can't hold office, some legal scholars say, he has every right to *run* for office. Ah, but he has to meet the usual eligibility requirements, counter others, and a dead man may not be an American citizen. When your state's best legal minds are debating such questions, it might be a sign that something is amiss.

But more than that, the governor's announcement violates my visceral wish that we'd move beyond the age of the Widow Gambit. If we can draw any lesson from Hillary Clinton's explosive passage across the national scene, it is that women who earn and wield power second-hand, by virtue of their roles as wives, only complicate our slow awakening to women's true capacities. It is no criticism of Jean Carnahan to find something dispiriting in the ease with which we can still reach for a female seat-warmer. Time was, a politician's widow was appointed to fill out his term, or—in the case of a House member—drafted to run in a special election after his death, by whatever political machine had backed the dead man. A widow was thought to be reassuring to the voter (like any good wife, she would think whatever he had thought, right?), but easily controlled by the men behind the scenes, and easily shoved aside once the men had arrived at a worthy (male) successor. In practice, these women weren't always so easy to displace. But the very notion of the "widow's mandate," as it was once known, is an artifact of a time when women mostly couldn't and didn't seek political power directly.

Six of the first thirteen female U.S. senators took this route to power, and a seventh, Margaret Chase Smith, started her congressional career filling out the House term of her late husband. By contrast, only one of the nine women now serving in the U.S. Senate began her political career after a bereavement, and that was in the distant past. (Olympia Snowe, of Maine, first ran for her state's legislature to succeed her husband, who died in a car crash in 1973; she has since amassed a long, estimable record as a moderate Republican House member and senator.)

It's entirely possible that Jean Carnahan—who has signaled that she may be willing to take the seat, but has not officially decided—would make a good senator.* Raising four children while seamlessly supporting a career politician may be a life of such rigor as to prepare a woman for almost anything. But ask yourself why Governor Wilson seized on her. Only a wife possesses the desirable quality of empty vessel, into which the voter can pour whatever sentiment he or she held for the deceased. Only a wife holds the anodyne promise that she can capitalize on the voter's fondness for her husband, while remaining a vague enough figure that her appointment cannot offend.

But perhaps the Carnahan story touches on a more primal uneasiness, for what it says about the implacable nature of our politics. What a thing to ask of a woman who has just lost her husband of forty-six years, and

* She won the Senate seat that November, then lost it in 2002.

one of her children, in a violent accident. Put yourself in her shoes: You can pick up your husband's all-consuming work—which you may love as the cause for which he died, or hate as the thing that killed him or, since you are human, both—or you can refuse, walking away from everything he worked for. Take your time: You have a couple of days to think it over.

It is one of the glories of our form of government that its wheels grind on, even in the face of death and disaster. But it may be the shame of our politics that its practitioners are so very nimble at making the best of our losses.

—October 27, 2000

URIAH HEEP
GOES TO WASHINGTON

"Be among the most humble people in Washington," White House chief of staff Andy Card told a meeting of prospective White House staffers the week before President George W. Bush's inauguration. With that, he nailed down the signature conceit of the new administration: its flamboyant humility.

Bush lauds it as a personal quality: "I hope I'm viewed as a humble person that is not judgmental," he said shortly before taking office. If he gets out of line, he said in a TV interview, his wife Laura "keeps me humble." He favors humility as a foreign policy: "We will have a foreign policy that is humble but strong," he likes to say. He also believes in humility as a governing style: "I expect each of you, as an official of this administration, to be an example of humility and decency and fairness," the new president told his senior staff on his first working day in office.

In theory, it's hard to find fault with these instructions. Only why do we hear so much bragging about the humility of an administration that is supposed to be too humble to brag? Not since Dickens painted the indelible figure of Uriah Heep, David Copperfield's self-abasing tormentor, have we seen such showy modesty. ("I'm a very 'umble person," runs Heep's constant refrain.)

At the end of Bush's first week in office, it was clear that all party loyalists had received their talking points containing the recipe for humble pie. Bush's wooing of the old bulls in Congress "shows a humility and a grand management style," said House majority whip Tom DeLay, that well-known connoisseur of the gentler virtues. "I think there is an under-standing and humility and perspective that has not existed in any other administration," an unnamed Bush adviser (humbly) told the *New York Times*. It brings to mind the great old story about an encounter between Moshe Dayan and Edward R. Murrow, in which Dayan repeatedly tried to praise some of the legendary CBS newsman's greatest broadcasts. At each point, Murrow turned aside the praise, graciously disclaiming the achievement or giving credit to others. Finally, after his third try, Dayan threw up his hands, saying, "Don't be so modest. You're not that good."

How did the Bush administration come to choose humility as its signal virtue? It flows from several sources. One is the aw-shucks posture of the entitled Wasp. Families like the Bushes fill their children's silver spoons with rigorous self-abnegation. In this way, those born to privilege learn to mask the nasty truth of their great advantages in life. Another source, per-haps the one that comes closest to making humility a true concern of the new president, is religious tradition.

But in the political realm, humility chic is above all an artifact of the bitter election that just ended. Bush received stinging criticism, you'll recall, for his first responses to the Florida standoff, which were to act as if his election was already a done deal. After those early missteps, Bush and his staff began to underline his humility at every turn. He declared himself "honored and humbled" when Secretary of State Katherine Har-ris certified him as the winner of the Florida vote while Al Gore was still contesting the result. "I think Gov. Bush has asked us to be humble, to be gracious," said his spokeswoman, Karen Hughes. Bush would now pro-ceed with choosing a cabinet, said Card. "But he's doing it responsibly. There's no arrogance. He's doing it with humility." When Bush decided what personal effects to bring to Washington from Texas, humble and gracious made the cut. Spokesman Ari Fleischer told reporters, two days before the inauguration, that Bush was looking forward to the next few days with "a mixture of graciousness, of humility and opportunity."

It's a big job to keep things humble. Fortunately, Bush chose a chief of staff who specializes in the forms of political humility. A *New York Times* profile that followed Andy Card's designation contained the wonderful sentence, "Mr. Card prides himself on his humility." And so he does: "I'm thrilled, honored, appropriate in my humility," Card truckled to the *Times*. It is not very difficult to be seen as humble when you are following a man like Bill Clinton in office. It is greeted as miraculous that Bush arrives on time for meetings; congressmen are sobbing with gratitude over having their phone calls promptly returned by the White House. But being "among the most humble people in Washington" is not, when you think about it, a very hard standard to meet. And all the showy modesty in the world tells us precisely nothing about the mystery of the hour, which is what the Bush administration will actually do. "I am not fond of professions of humility," Copperfield finally tells Heep, "or professions of anything else."

—January 31, 2001

RUN FOR YOUR LIFE

I was cocooned in a white Toyota, blasting up I–95. Past Baltimore, past Philadelphia. Sadness had sent me back to the cigarettes I had given up a decade ago, and—strangely—to gobbling Smarties, those tiny pastel-colored candies rolled in cellophane. I was going north, as I had the week before and would the week after, to watch both of my parents die, seven weeks apart.

I forgave myself easily for most of my reactions to the grief of that spring, which was almost three years ago. But beneath the thick, dark jelly in which that whole period of my life was suspended, there was a guilty, insistent little pleasure. For along with everything else, my scrambling, solitary trips between my home in Washington, DC, and my parents' homes in New Jersey brought me an escape from my own life: from a two-year-old and a five-year-old; from the endless bargaining over time (I'll be home at six on Tuesday if you'll do it Thursday) that is the two-career couple's lot in parenthood; from the sensible, responsible woman, full of ballast, that I'd somehow become in eight years of marriage. The simple fact of being alone, bound for the town of my girlhood, had a shocking sweetness.

In hindsight, though, the only thing that seems odd is my surprise at this tiny pleasure. I have since come to believe that even in the best of marriages, in the most devoted of mothers, there lurks a thirst for solitude, the fantasy of escape.

"One weekend a month, totally alone," a friend says dreamily, the way a child talks about Christmas. Another friend has a small sideline in real estate, buying and renting out apartments. She does it for the income. But "somewhere," she says, "tucked away in the back of my mind, is the fantasy that if one of them were vacant, I could go and live there. I could have a dollhouse of my own."

Women's fiction teems with characters who act on the fantasy of flight, from the best-seller *Divine Secrets of the Ya-Ya Sisterhood*—in which the most flamboyant character runs out of the house early one morning, wearing only lingerie under her cashmere coat, to have a nervous breakdown in a hotel—to Anne Tyler's *Ladder of Years*, in which a woman stalks off the beach during an argument with her husband and simply disappears for a whole new life in a town down the road. "The most surprising number of women," a policeman tells the vanished woman's family, "seem to take it into their heads to walk out during family vacations."

The fantasy is itself our secret refuge, the part of ourselves we manage to hold out above the water rising around us, the way an infantryman knows to keep his rifle dry as he fords the river. It is the box of chocolates the Victorian lady kept under her sofa; it is the sullen flame at which we warm our chapped martyr's hands. It is the passive-aggressive last resort of the outwardly pliant servant who is secretly pissing into the punchbowl. And sometimes we do escape. Time by ourselves is a treasure we sneak or steal in the furtive interstices of married life. When our husbands are out of town on business, when we are out of town on business, between the errands we have to run. Haven't you seen her at your local Starbucks, the fortyish woman alone in the corner, nursing her latte and her 1,000-yard stare?

It goes without saying, I hope it does, that this is not about loving, or not loving, our families. It's about the vast difference between who we were and the women we are slowly becoming, and the insistent, half-glimpsed hunch that if only we could stop and think, or *something*, these selves might negotiate a more deliberate bond.

I remember that as a teenager I pitied my mother because she had to stay up so late putting the house in order. Now, of course, I know that the time was precious to her: time to be alone, to bring the world around her to the order it never had when those she loved were there. Now I *am* her.

"I like to stop at 7-Eleven on my way home," confesses a friend, "and get one of those really horrible biscuit-and-sausage things and put it in the microwave, and go and eat it in the car, in the dark, and no one knows where I am."

So what if, a new book asks, we took this fantasy seriously? What if we actually escaped—without resentment, without the mulish air of the aggrieved, without apology?

What if we just went away for a while?

The Marriage Sabbatical: The Journey that Brings You Home, was written by St. Louis journalist Cheryl Jarvis. Part memoir, part gentle polemic, part report on the adventures of fifty-five women she interviewed, Jarvis's book proposes that married women should consider leaving home for some pre-arranged period to undertake an experience—study, or travel, or physical rigor, or contemplation—that will sharpen their sense of themselves as people distinct from their husbands and families.

The definition of a marriage sabbatical is vague: It might be three weeks, or it might be—as in the case of a woman who left at fifty to pursue a lifelong dream of joining the Peace Corps—two years. "A five-week leave for one woman can be a more difficult and transformative act than a five-month leave for another," Jarvis writes. One woman went off by herself for six months to read great books; others took summer months off to teach or study in Europe. One left home to study for the federal bar exam; one grieved the death of a child by walking the Appalachian Trail. Jarvis herself left home to spend three months at writers' colonies.

What all these women had in common was the intention to return to their husbands and families at the end of the adventure, after a specified period of time. "No woman I interviewed was *leaving* her husband," Jarvis writes, "any more than professors on sabbatical are *leaving* the universities where they teach." The sabbaticals Jarvis recommends are emphatically not about having affairs. Some husbands and wives worry about the possibility that temptation could strike either of them while they are apart, Jarvis acknowledges. But the experience is aimed at escaping from everyone else's expectations. "This thought that women are all off to have affairs, which is the most common [reaction] I encountered," she says, "it's the last thing they want."

It's hardly radical, almost forty years after Betty Friedan published *The Feminine Mystique*, to note that women still sometimes lose themselves in marriage, that women still do most of the caretaking in life, that decades of juggling kids and home and cooking and work can fracture one's attention span past the point of easy repair. A time away in which to focus on building one's own intellectual or emotional or spiritual muscles is a fairly commonsensical response to those insights. More common sense: "Today's messages promoting stricter divorce laws and a return to the traditional model for marriage focus on making it more difficult to divorce," Jarvis writes. "Why not make it easier to stay married?"

As Jarvis admits, her book is the tip of an iceberg. This is why it may be bracing even to women whose children, like mine, are too young to make a sabbatical an immediately realistic option. Because, of course, Jarvis is tangling with the biggest questions of marriage: How much can you court risk and change, and still avail yourself of the wordless security that marriage offers? What would it feel like to be alone? Who would you be without your spouse in your life? And, of course: How much do you use your spouse or family as excuses for not tackling the challenges you might otherwise choose?

Jarvis is a tall, thin woman with a gorgeous face: green eyes, lips that have the pillowy architecture of a complicated window treatment, and the bone structure of a genetic lottery winner. She looks a decade younger than her fifty-three years. Raised in St. Louis, married fresh out of Duke University at twenty-one, a mother at twenty-four, she had never been away from her husband for longer than a week when she began to dream of a sabbatical.

> Think about that—one week for yourself, where you don't have to think about anybody: where you have to be, who you have to drive, what does your husband want to do tonight? Did he have a bad day? All the things that you think about. One week that I didn't have that, in 22 years.

Jarvis's career has been something of a patchwork: intermittent years of freelance writing, five years at home with her two sons, stints at two St. Louis publications, a tour of duty as a producer for the *Sally Jessy Raphael Show*. Presently she teaches freelance writing and mass communications at Washington University and Webster University. As if to illustrate the shattered female attention span, Jarvis describes these jobs in a rambling, distracted series of anecdotes that yields to a sharp, articulate enthusiasm once she fixes on the subject of her book. "The question is, why don't we think we can do both?" Jarvis asks. That is, have the traditional joys of marriage and family and also the self-sovereignty the women's movement promised. "Because obviously there are women who do. And there are women for whom [that balance] is very natural."

It is curious, when you think about it, that even after decades of social revolution we have no cultural models of women who get to have it both ways—who get to leave and also return. Think about movies: "In *Fatal Attraction*," Jarvis writes,

> when the wife leaves for the weekend, all hell breaks loose. Her husband commits adultery with a woman so deranged that she stalks him, terrorizes his family, and finally ends up in their bathtub, murdered by the wife whose absence started it all. In *Thelma & Louise*, Thelma leaves her husband to go on a two-day road trip and ends up driving off the edge of the Grand Canyon. If women who leave home aren't punished, it's a sure thing they're not coming back.

Yet there have always been women who took marriage sabbaticals; they just went under respectable cover. In the Middle Ages they went on religious retreats in convents. In the Victorian era they got vague but socially sanctioned "illnesses"—hysteria, anxiety, neurasthenia—that sent them on sea voyages or to sanitariums or to take water cures. "No wonder [these illnesses] were overdiagnosed," Jarvis writes. "Getting sick was one of the few acceptable ways women could get time for themselves."

Among the prominent women who have built marriage sabbaticals into their lives are Anne Morrow Lindbergh, who traveled every year to her island refuge in Florida, where she wrote her best-sellers; Georgia O'Keeffe, who spent summers painting in New Mexico while her husband, Alfred Stieglitz, remained in New York; and Amelia Earhart, who spent a month away from her husband every year to teach at Purdue University. Earhart wrote her groom a letter, upon marriage, explaining that "I may have to keep some place where I can go to be myself now and then, for I cannot guarantee to endure at all times the confinements of even an attractive cage."

Considering this rich history, it is striking how hard it felt to Jarvis even to raise the questions she addresses in her book. "I think that her book is a real dissonant idea," says Jarvis's husband, Jim, a soft-spoken therapist who specializes in sports psychology.

It causes you to think about things that aren't necessarily comfortable, on a number of levels. From "Is my marriage good?" to "Am I fulfilling my purpose as a person?" to "Could I survive three months on my own?" Those are all not easy questions. . . . This book will stir up a lot of fear in people.

Jarvis and her husband both encountered what could only be called hostility when they told people the subject of the book she was working on. "I'll never forget this one man," Jarvis says. "He looked at me, and his eyes just kind of turned gray—I mean really slate. And he looked at me and he said, 'You're not writing about marriage. You're writing about *divorce.*'"

There are, of course, husbands to whom the idea is outrageous. Chris, the woman who went to Africa for two years with the Peace Corps, met furious opposition from her husband, David, although he was an Air Force officer who had spent many rotations overseas. "To David, Chris's decision to be away from home felt unfair and arbitrary," Jarvis writes.

Where in their marriage contract was it written that with good behavior she'd get a two-year stint in the Peace Corps? This wasn't his idea of marriage and until now had not been *their* idea of marriage. . . . The old saying comes to mind: Women enter marriage with the expectation that their husbands will change; men enter marriage with the expectation that their wives will never change.

Jarvis's husband admits to having had worries about her sabbatical: "Your mind starts to spin, and you think, Gee, maybe she'll like being away so much that she won't want to come back." And Jarvis, who talked with the husbands of more than half of her subjects, came away appreciating their reservations. Sometimes, if the husband is the chief breadwinner, there is envy or anger at the woman's freedom. Also, "it's generally harder for a man when his wife leaves than the other way around," she writes, "because for many men their wives are their only confidantes." Almost all the couples she considered found the sabbatical changed the marriage, for both husband and wife, in ways large and small. For every husband who discovered he could braid his daughter's hair and cope with the loneliness caused by his wife's departure, there was another who came to an unwelcome recognition of how dependent he was on his wife. "I learned I was more insecure than I thought I was," says Peter, whose wife left their home in Alaska to get a degree in social work 3,000 miles away.

"I felt I was at a scary disadvantage, that she didn't need me as much as I needed her." Yet Peter supported his wife's sabbatical, as did many other men Jarvis interviewed. "I discovered men who gave their wives two-month dream trips as birthday gifts," Jarvis writes, "helped them research distant schools and programs, studied up on the countries they'd be living in, typed their itineraries, bought their sleeping bags, loaded their cars, and drove them to their destinations."

For most couples, Jarvis believes, the biggest danger lies in wives' bowing too easily to their husbands' reservations. The husband who wins such a battle may be the one who ultimately loses the marital war, becoming the object of his wife's resentment. "The man who handles it best," Jarvis writes, "doesn't take it personally."

Much harder, of course, is the question of children. Most of the women featured in the book either had no children or, like Jarvis, launched their adventures after their children were grown. But some did leave kids as well as husbands. One left her husband and three children every summer to teach overseas, starting when the children were preschoolers. Another, a mother who cared for her two daughters full time, agonized about leaving them, at seven and eleven, for two months' self-renewal. "I kept asking myself," this mother told Jarvis, "'Is it okay for me to be doing this as their mother? To be leaving them alone?' What I had to remember was that I wasn't leaving them alone. They had a father they adored who was willing to take on the responsibility."

Jarvis has many brave words for mothers who might want to think about leaving:

> There are no dictates here, no "acceptable" age to leave a child, no "okay" time to be away, no black and white, right and wrong. There is only a woman's soul-searching. . . . When a mother leaves home out of enlightened self-interest with a willing father on the scene, her children will see a disruption in family life, but they will also see an egalitarian model for parenting. They will see a mother who is not a "perfect" caretaker, but they will also see a mother who is a separate person with an emotional life of her own and interests beyond their care.

But this is, of course, where the whole happy notion becomes much, much more difficult to embrace. I can't imagine leaving my children, now five and seven, for longer than four or five nights—and I do it for that long, on business, only when I can tell myself the stern voice of duty demands it. (And if it happens to be heaven to find myself alone in a nice hotel room, with room service on the way and a long, hot bath in store, well, that's just a lucky byproduct I get to enjoy.) What, though, if my children were nine and eleven, and a month-long research trip beckoned? I found it by turns invigorating and terrifying to be invited to consider the possibility—even to think of myself as someone who *could* consider it.

"A child's memories of his mother's absence tend to be memories of his father's presence," Jarvis writes. "No matter how close or enmeshed the family, women return with the realization that they can extricate themselves from everyone and nothing falls apart. Every mother I interviewed made the same discovery and every mother was surprised by it: 'I realized they got along fine without me.'"

Yet Jarvis herself never left home until her children had. Putting her nice ideas about equal parenting into action is a giant step for which few women are prepared. Still, she does us a service in stripping away the pretty notion that there is some bright line dividing the realm in which we are always needed from the day when we will be entirely free. It can only be good for us to be wondering, along the way, how much of our children's need of us is actually our need of them—and to attend to how much we are putting aside or giving away, and whether it is more than we can afford.

The Marriage Sabbatical suffers a little from the lingo of self-improvement and personal growth. It would be easy to mistake it for a pity party, urging women (women rich enough) to treat themselves to the vacations their endless chores have deprived them of. But at its heart is a certain tough-minded recognition that, for all our complaints about the caretaking we do, we also use our duties as excuses. *I can't. He won't let me. I'm too busy. The kids need me.* Maybe he won't, and maybe you are, and maybe they do. But you also know what she's talking about. "A woman will always sacrifice herself if you give her the opportunity," W. Somerset Maugham once wrote. "It's her favorite form of self-indulgence."

"I'm not sure [family responsibilities] get in the way so much as that you reach for them to get in the way," says my friend Mary Beth. "When you get down to saying, 'What am I going to do for the second half of my life?' that's enough to send you to the grocery store with a really long list." My friend Bonnie recently found herself saying,

"I have so much work to do. But I can't do it until I clean under the refrigerator." So we do—we do hide behind our lists in a lot of ways. I know that a lot of the background noise is there because I put it there. But it's still there, now.

This is the most interesting—and the most threatening—part of the invitation to take our escape fantasies seriously, to dredge them to the surface and study their lineaments respectfully.

I came away feeling that Jarvis underrated, a little, both the danger and the difficulty involved in reengineering marriage. Every settled union contains a deal that is Dumbo's magic feather, the unspoken knot of custom we rely on to hold us aloft. Mess with it, and we might indeed find that our marital contraptions fly along anyway, borne high by our strengths and by more conscious, more explicit choices. But we don't know that, any of us, until we try it, and some marriages respond to change with a sickening thud.

But still, what choice do we have? If we stopped letting off the wishful steam of our hungrier selves in furtive gusts, in hilarious asides, in angry gestures, in alluring books, we might be left with some real desire. We might even have a hope of acting on it in the time we have left. "Yes," says Bonnie. "You need to lock yourself in a room somewhere. Take a look at that pile of straw, see what kind of gold you can spin from it. Or you die wondering, I guess."

—February 2001

A WOMAN'S PLACE IS AT THE BAR

Ever on the alert for social shifts among the power elite, the *New York Times* pointed out the other day that this is the year in which women entering law school may, for the first time, outnumber men. Last year women made up 49.4 percent of first-year law students—up from 4 percent in a mere forty years—and this year women applicants passed the magic 50 percent mark.

The *Times* drafted a number of learned observers to speculate on the meaning of it all: Perhaps the atmosphere of law schools will become more "teamlike"; perhaps women will at last become judges and law professors in the same numbers as men; perhaps the hierarchical, competitive world of the major law firms will become more flexible and welcoming to employees' family lives. (Perhaps pigs will fly.) Carol Gilligan, Harvard professor and chief swami of the school of thought that women promote an inherently more sensitive, more "related" way of thinking, speculates that, given the law's history as a training ground for positions in government and business, women lawyers may soon be in a position to transform the very structure of society.

But the most interesting comment in the article came from one Deborah Rhode, a Stanford law school professor who worries that the law may become a "pink-collar ghetto," like other professions that have traditionally welcomed women.

This is the bad news? Let's color in this picture a bit further:

On K Street, clients will start asking their high-paid lawyers to fetch them a cup of coffee. We'll have a National Lawyer's Day, on which clients will be encouraged to send their lawyers a patronizing floral tribute—maybe even take them out to lunch, to let them know they're an important part of the team.

As the status of lawyers declines, so, of course, will the status of what they produce. (Just ask anyone who works in preschool education.) So members of Congress will lose interest in the blandishments of lobbyists. Though come to think of it, Congress will probably be a pink-collar ghetto too, full of striving young members who ran for office to escape the stigma of having settled for law school, only to discover that women are flooding into politics, too.

And once the legal profession is completely overrun, men will begin to leave it in droves. As the status of their hitherto valuable degrees from Harvard and Yale declines, they will be forced to turn to some of the few other white-collar endeavors that welcome ambitious liberal-arts majors: teaching, perhaps, or social work. Before we know it, they'll be opening day-care centers, where they will hire women in junior positions (to serve snacks and wash paintbrushes) but assert that women aren't cut out to put in the long hours required to make it to the top of the profession. The really high-status jobs, like leading Circle Time and singing the alphabet, will be strictly male preserves.

Supreme Court justices (female, of course) will occasionally hire male clerks, young men so dedicated to the law that they're willing to live with the stigma of doing women's work. When these young men go to cocktail parties, they will get lots of noisy approbation from cutthroat fellow partygoers—men in alpha-male professions like nursing—who snicker at them behind their backs.

Of course, all the women lawyers will protest that their work is more important than men are willing to admit. It might not pay as well as teaching elementary school, but that doesn't mean it should be devalued. Of course not, the men will say. And while you're up, honey, could you write me a brief?

Once we have finished ruining law for the boys, we can turn our attention to other professions: Won't it be fun when Wall Street is a pink-collar ghetto? And corporate management? Fortune 500 companies will draft a few token men to round out their boards of directors, but men will never accept slots on low-status assignments like the boards' compensation committees, which will have the responsibility of deciding whether the CEO's birthday should be celebrated at Bennigan's or the Olive Garden.

If we succeed in chasing men out of enough of their old domains, then one day men won't even run for president. But as first husbands they'll decorate the White House Christmas tree with all appropriate swagger, and take up important social causes like changing the designated hitter rule.

Eventually, though, we will run out of important male endeavors to undermine. We may just have to settle for equality in the end, and the freedom to act like Margaret Thatcher if we want to, and like Carol Gilligan if we don't. When that day comes, perhaps my daughter will explain to her children that she went to law school because, well, in the old days, that was one of the few careers that really welcomed women. I could live with that.

—April 4, 2001

MOMMY AT HER DESK

It seems fitting, on the eve of the ninth annual Take Our Daughters to Work Day, that we're seeing a little uptick in working-mother news. The National Institute of Child Health and Human Development has released yet another chapter in its long-running study of the effect of child care on kids, ambiguously suggesting that too much time (amount unspecified, of course) in child care may make youngsters more aggressive. And Massachusetts is having a lively debate about whether it's good, or bad, or indeed anyone's business that its new acting governor is seven months pregnant with twins.

We batten on news stories like these, we working mothers, anxious for even a frightful communal mirror of our ceaseless internal debates. Yet none of our public language for debating these issues—the antiseptic talk of "work-life balance," of quality time and flextime and part-time—really touches or describes the persistent, private kernel of doubt and remorse that almost forty years of social change have left pretty much intact.

So I write, today, in praise of maternal guilt.

After my first child, my son, was born, I thought that one day I would figure out The Answer: that once I had found the perfect child-care provider, and worked out the perfect schedule, and then got used to the perfect strangeness of this new life, it would all stop looking like conflict and begin to feel like fullness. It took me about two years to give up on finding the holy grail of perfect balance; for as long as I had both work and children, I finally realized, my task was not to figure out the one answer but to learn how to live with the knowledge that in pursuing my work, I am in some degree acting selfishly. Not in the high-stakes terms of how my children will turn out, or whether they will thrive, but in the intimate sense that they sometimes yearn for me when I am not there. Guilt, I now think, is the tribute that autonomy pays to love.

Today I think of working-mother ambivalence as a long, low corridor that we (at least those of us who have the luxury of choosing) walk down for as long as our children are young. Some women find exits from it: "I have to work" is the first exit, and for many women it's even true. "Something (higher-quality child care? government subsidies? more caring corporations?) should and shall be done to make this conflict subside," runs the legend over another exit door. "It's better (more stimulating, more socializing) for my child to be in day care," says a third. A fourth explains that this is all just politics and personal choices: Where is it written, outside the culture that indoctrinates us, that mothers are so essential to their children? The biggest, most alluring exit of all, of course, is the one that says you're a better mother for doing whatever it is that will fulfill you in the larger world.

But, though I see partial relief behind some of these doors, none of them wholly works for me. I am with Nora Ephron, who summed it up with words to the effect that any child would rather have his or her mother in the next room undergoing a nervous breakdown than in Hawaii feeling ecstatic.

Last week my daughter came home with a "book" she'd written at preschool. It had only one page, which said, "This is my mommy at her desk," and showed a purple me superimposed on a yellow rectangle. Now the happy, affirming, Take-My-Daughter-to-Work response to this gift would be to think it wonderful that my five-year-old has a picture of womanhood that incorporates a life at work. But most days I am more inclined to see this artwork pessimistically, as a protest: Here is Mommy, always at her desk. What I do at that desk feels as necessary to me as food or air, so I go on doing it, with the knowledge that some of the time spent there is time I could also have chosen to spend giving my children something they dearly wish for. All I know, eight years into motherhood, is that I have a better chance of not blowing it in the big ways if I make these incremental choices with my eyes open.

So, by all means, take your daughter to work. Show her how plausible it is that she could be a scientist, an architect, a marine biologist. But some day, when she's old enough, you must also tell her the truth, which is that, compared to the complexity of doing right by those you love, being a brain surgeon is the easy part.

—April 25, 2001

LIAR, LIAR

He was a good friend amid the early miseries of college life, though he had
that willed eccentricity in which smart, awkward freshmen sometimes
armor themselves. I got to know him by typing his papers, seventy-five
cents a page. He introduced me to olives stuffed with almonds, and to
chilled vodka. He had a precious single room and a bathtub, where I took
long, soaking refuge from my mob of roommates while he chatted to me
from the other side of the door.

I understood very little of what I typed for him because his major was
an abstruse one. But it wasn't hard to see that he was a brilliant guy. The
stars in his field approached him at conferences to discuss his research
with him, he told me with a becoming wonder. But I loved him as much
for his warmth as for his brains. You could tell him anything, and he listened intently. Among all the flitting friendships one tries on at eighteen
or nineteen, I knew this boy was the genuine article.

So I thought of him when I read about the eminent biographer and history professor Joseph Ellis, who stands accused of concocting a series of
puzzling lies about his past. Why would a man who has won the Pulitzer
Prize and the National Book Award for his biographies of the Founding
Fathers make up stories about having served in Vietnam, exaggerate his
role in the civil rights and peace movements, invent a winning touchdown
for a high school football team to which he never belonged? Before Ellis
issued a statement confirming the *Boston Globe*'s account of his lies about

Vietnam, his colleagues raced to his defense. "The idea that Joe Ellis would claim to have done something that he didn't do doesn't hold up," a colleague of five years protested. "He's one of the smartest people I know, and wouldn't have a reason to lie."

But this is where analysis of Ellis's history will baffle us all. The kind of lying with which he has been charged has nothing to do with reason. It is something different from simple resume-padding, or fabrication for an otherwise unreachable goal. We will look in vain for a simple explanation of why a man so accomplished would stoop to little lies of self-aggrandizement.

I know this because my own friend turned out to be a habitual and helpless liar. He lied to me about his family. About his mother's death. About his studies. Eventually, once his friends began comparing notes, he was confronted with these pointless lies. And he had an explanation of sorts, reaching back to the ways that lying had served him in the strange family structure of his early years. His reasons made a crude, shrink-by-numbers kind of sense; they may even have been true. But more than two decades later, I really don't have the faintest purchase on what made my friend tell the tales he did.

We like to think—our culture has trained us to think—that the human psyche is ultimately transparent. Neurosis leads us astray, to be sure, but along well-beaten paths that can now be eliminated, or at least illuminated, by our understanding. People with glitches in their psyches either get better or they get worse, says the *Popular Mechanics* view of the human machine. They get help or they don't, and if they don't, their compulsions get the better of them.

But every now and then, a stranger truth brushes against us in the dark. When I ended the friendship, I told myself it was because I could never trust my friend again. But now I think it had as much to do with my fear of how well he functioned. My friend went on to attend an Ivy League medical school; he married a wonderful woman. All I could take away from his odd, wounding friendship was a respect for the final opaqueness of my fellows.

Mount Holyoke College, where Ellis has taught for twenty-nine years, reacted to the allegations about him with a reflexive loyalty. Now that Ellis has confirmed the central charge in the *Globe*'s story, administrators will have to face more squarely the fact that he made a habit of lying wholesale to the students he was trusted to teach. It doesn't speak well of the college that this possibility wasn't immediately taken seriously. But it's not that hard to understand, really, the shock of finding that the bare mystery of human character has tenure in your midst.

—June 20, 2001

THE HEART-FULL DODGER

More than one observer of George W. Bush's developing political style has noticed his striking use of rhetoric that touches on matters of heart and soul. *National Review* Editor Rich Lowry, writing in last Sunday's *Washington Post*, was only the latest to remark on the forty-third president's "essentially Clintonian" tendency to drag into various policy debates his assessments of others' good natures—or his own.

The president's most recent and controversial excursion into the touchy-feely sciences was his confident inventory of Russian President Vladimir Putin's character. "I looked the man in the eye. I found him to be very straightforward and trustworthy," the president reported, to the alarm of his conservative mates. "I was able to get a sense of his soul."

Pundits offer various reasonable explanations for Bush's reliance on the language of feeling and spirituality: On a political level, he is said to be trying to soften his party's sometimes flinty public image; on a personal level, he is speaking as a deeply religious man, in a vernacular that borrows from both his church and his victory over alcohol, and as someone whose own strength lies in one-on-one charm and persuasion. And all of these explanations seem to hold some partial truth. But the Putin episode—because it finally brought his dewy philosophy to a subject where its application seemed so wildly inappropriate—opens the door to a further explanation: Isn't it possible that Bush's resort to protestations of feeling is also a form of camouflage, a way of ducking intimidating questions?

This is a bit of stonewalling wisdom known to C students since time immemorial: When a tough question presents itself, there are few more effective ways to evade it than to answer a different question entirely. And in an age whose politics are steeped in bathos, in the importance of the personal, there is no more socially acceptable form of evasion than a display of manly vulnerability. What Bush's supporters like to see as the terse, Gary Cooper-esque sentiments of a plainspoken man may in fact be the terse, Eddie Haskell-ish evasions of an unreflective one.

Think back: Bush's talk of the heart does tend to crop up in moments that put him on the spot. Asked in a Republican primary debate what philosopher had influenced him most, Bush replied, "Christ, because he changed my heart." Full stop. And while this answer kicked off a furious debate over whether this was an inappropriate injection of religion into the campaign, it did get him past the perilous topic of whether he had read anything in his life that had stuck to him.

In last fall's debates with Vice President Al Gore, Bush constantly fell back on assurances of his own good intentions and purity of motive. When Gore attacked his record, as governor of Texas, in providing health insurance for women and children, Bush protested, "You can quote all the numbers you want, but I'm telling you, we care about our people in Texas. . . . If he's trying to allege that I'm a hardhearted person and I don't care about children, he's absolutely wrong." Here, again, was the invitation to admire his heart in lieu of examining his head.

In a long interview with Peggy Noonan after his encounter with Putin, Bush recounted his meeting with the Russian president: He had told Putin, he said, that "It's negative to think about blowing each other up. That's not a positive thought. That's a Cold War thought. That's a thought when people were enemies with each other." This level of geopolitical analysis seems to point to the possibility that Bush's soul-talk, in his joint news conference with Putin, was designed to steer him past the more challenging shoals of discussing bilateral diplomacy.

Conservatives love to decry the mushy, "values-oriented," standards-free educational habits that the '60s supposedly loosed upon the land. So it is a delicious irony that they have elected a president who is so inclined to fall back on the marshy counsels of emotion. In so many other ways— his scorn for the protesters who surrounded him at Yale, his coat-and-tie-in-the-Oval-Office ethos of respect—Bush is a man consciously at odds with his own generation. But in this one way, in his easy claims for the primacy of the heart, he is the genial boomer personified, ever ready to flash a feeling in place of a fact.

—*July 4, 2001*

A WORKING MOM'S COMEDY

If you could buy stock in a book, I would stake all my savings on the success of Allison Pearson's new novel, *I Don't Know How She Does It: The Life of Kate Reddy, Working Mother*. Here, at last, is the definitive social comedy of working motherhood. The interesting question is why it took a British writer to bring it to American bookstores.

We meet Kate, time-starved mother of two, standing in her kitchen late at night artfully "distressing" the store-bought pies she plans to pass off as her own at the next day's school bake sale. A hedge-fund manager who masters the markets on four continents, she abases herself before her children's nanny (secretly nicknamed Pol Pot) and dreads "the intricate sequence of snubs and punishments" her five-year-old daughter metes out in retaliation for any business trip. She adores her job, yearns for home, and sometimes thinks of her recent life as "five years of walking around in a lead suit of sleeplessness."

Kate ponders the mysteries of the two-income marriage, such as the touching optimism embodied in her husband's gift of erotic underwear "for a wife who, since the birth of her first child, has come to the nuptial bed in a Gap XXXL T-shirt with a dachshund motif." And why is it, she wonders, that no matter who brings in what salary, it is always the mother who holds in her head the full delicate ecosystem of the family's life? "They could give you good jobs and maternity leave, but until they programmed a man to notice you were out of toilet paper the project was doomed." When a friend of Kate's dies, she leaves behind for her husband a twenty-page memo titled "Your Family: How it Works!"

This sublimely feline novel at last plugs a puzzling hole in our fiction: Where, I have often wondered, is the new literature of the women you see stealing away from their clients between dinner and dessert to croon lullabies over their cell phones in the ladies' room? Women have never had a larger voice in the writing and buying of hardcover fiction than they do today, yet the nexus of work and child-rearing remains a nearly blank page. Of recent popular hits, only *The Nanny Diaries* goes anywhere near this territory. And that was a book that had it both ways in the Mommy Wars, delicately making its Bad Mother character a wealthy New Yorker who neither works nor cares for her child.

So why did it take a Brit to invent Kate Reddy? Simply put, it's hard to imagine the American writer who could have cast aside her defensiveness long enough to make this subject so funny—or so sad. On this side of the Atlantic we still observe the social fiction that women work only and always because they have to; if we pretend to have no choice, then we can pretend not to feel guilty. But beneath all that denial we feel far too culpable to write passages as unblinking as this one: "For once," Kate relates, "I drop Emily off at school myself. . . . Em is thrilled to have me there with the other mummies; she parades me before her friends like a show horse, patting my rump and pointing out my good features. 'My mummy's lovely and tall, isn't she?'"

There is another reason why this mordant book had to be imported. American women—can-do daughters of their country's optimism—still secretly nourish a poignant hope that there is An Answer to the dilemma of work and family. On a personal level, and as a matter of social policy, we often seem to be waiting for the No-Fault Fairy to come and explain at last how our deepest conflict can be managed away. (Perhaps if we called it "blending" rather than "juggling"? What if we told ourselves that day care improves the infant immune system?) This endless quest entails an earnestness too deep for satire.

All great fiction is about something eternal; to write a good book about the conflict is to acknowledge that it is here to stay. And even in its saddest passages, *I Don't Know How She Does It* declines to decide whether its heroine's frantic life is more apt to break her back or her heart. The novel does have one real flaw, but of course you have already guessed what it is. The author couldn't quite find a satisfying ending.

—October 2, 2002

A WOMAN WHO KNEW HER DUE

I have a memory of Mary McGrory sweeping into the *Washington Post*'s newsroom in a wide-brimmed black wool hat that brought to mind a bull-fighter's gear. Her clothes were always a magical combination of the suit-able and the attention-getting—the finest soft wools and silks; capes, scarves, dramatic contrasts of red and white and black. It's possible, I must grudgingly admit, that my fancy added the dramatic hat. If so, it is only because it was so easy to see through Mary's great gentility to the heart of a buccaneer.

Mary, who died this week at eighty-five, was a lady; she was a dame; she was the Katharine Hepburn of journalism, extending her art to the fullest on her very own terms. Her face had an openness, almost an innocence, that seemed improbable, even suspect, in a pro who had watched the sport of Washington for such a long time. But when you came to know her you saw it was both entirely real *and* a part of her method. She also had a beau-tiful voice, with faultless diction and perfect round vowels, and that was part of the charge of any encounter with her: that lulling, low alto always purred the unexpected into your ear.

What a boring observation it is, then, that she was a trailblazer for all us younger women who take for granted our places in the newsroom. That gray cliché never began to encompass her greatest and subtlest contribu-tion, which was the distinctively feminine way she went about her job. When Ellen Goodman and Anna Quindlen were still in diapers, Mary wrote intimately, long before anyone else did: rarely about herself, but in a human voice, both quirky and blunt, that valued the sidelong glance, the intuitive connection and above all her own ear and eye. While other columnists still hurled their thunderbolts from Mount Olympus, Mary's self-confidence propelled a wholly new political prose: a soufflé of surpassing grace packed with raisins of brutal insight.

And watching her work the newsroom was a lesson of its own, a thing of beauty. While harried reporters bustled past her, Mary drifted from desk to desk in what seemed to be aimless, sociable circles. "Did you *see that?*" she would ask, about some important hearing she had just covered (for which most of us had, of course, stayed in our chairs and watched on C-SPAN). Or, "Oh, that *awful man*," about a witness (or for that matter, a president) she couldn't abide.

She always made you feel as if you were the one person she had been pining to discuss the topic with. But in the midst of this breeze-shooting you found yourself telling her about a lunch you'd had with a member of the relevant committee staff two weeks ago, or something you'd heard secondhand from someone you trusted in the White House, or the best idea you'd had in three weeks.

She was completely competitive and extraordinarily kind. When I came to work at the *Post* in 1986, she wrote me a warm message of welcome, saying, in effect (and without rancor): Never mind all those noisy men in the newsroom—they're all bark and no bite. When I wrote something she liked, I would find in my mailbox a beautifully wrought note signed *Your Fan, MM*. I can't emphasize enough what a rarity this made her among the newsroom's tenured stars.

But it is also true, as noted in her obituaries, that she had a queenly expectation of deference. At a small luncheon a dozen years ago, Mary made some pronouncement—the way journalists do, in the presence of both food and other journalists—about the news of the day. (Gennifer Flowers had just thrown her grenade into Bill Clinton's primary campaign, and it pained Mary beyond endurance that The Woman In Question spelled her first name with a "G." I don't think her opinion of Clinton ever really recovered.) When I began to contribute a follow-up thought, Mary intoned—quite sternly—"*I wasn't finished speaking.*" But one took not the least offense, because there was something so gorgeous, in this irretrievably masculine town, about a woman who knew her due. Washington is a place, and public policy a profession, that attract huge numbers of people who are seeking a mask in place of a self. Here, where rank and title still matter so much, and where power and worth are borrowed by association, you can't throw a stone without striking someone who has gravitated here out of some fear (or lack) of singularity.

In the past, the hidden self has been even more crucial—more second nature—to women than to men. To be a woman in a man's town you had to be more careful, make yet a paler impression, than the Brooks Brothers suits all around you. For years we wore, as Randall Jarrell wrote in his classic poem "The Woman at the Washington Zoo," "this print of mine, that has kept its color/Alive through so many cleanings; this dull null/Navy I wear to work, and wear from work, and so/To my bed, so to my grave, with no/Complaints, no comments: neither from my chief,/The Deputy Chief Assistant, nor his chief—Only I complain. . . . "

Mary showed that you could be not only forgiven but rewarded for shedding that dreary disguise. Talent, Mary taught us, was the ultimate get-out-of-jail-free card; but there was no divining the difference between Mary's talent and her ease at being indelibly herself. To our beds, to our graves, there is really no divining that difference for any of us, and what a gift it was to watch a woman who lived that truth.

—April 25, 2004

PART 3

TIME AND CHANCE

HIT BY LIGHTNING:
A CANCER MEMOIR

The beast first showed its face benignly, in the late-June warmth of a California swimming pool, and it would take me more than a year to know it for what it was. Willie and I were lolling happily in the sunny shallow end of my in-laws' pool when he—then only seven—said, "Mommy, you're getting thinner."

It was true, I realized with some pleasure. Those intractable ten or fifteen pounds that had settled in over the course of two pregnancies: hadn't they seemed, lately, to be melting away? I had never gained enough weight to think about trying very hard to lose it, except for sporadic, failed commitments to the health club. But I'd carried—for so many years I hardly noticed it—an unpleasant sensation of being more cushiony than I wanted to be. And now, without trying, I'd lost at least five pounds, perhaps even eight.

I suppose I fell into the smug assumption that I had magically restored the lucky metabolism of my twenties and thirties, when it had been easy for me to carry between 110 and 120 pounds on a frame of 5' 6". In the months before Willie's observation I'd been working harder, and more happily, than I'd done in years—burning more fuel through later nights and busier days. I'd also been smoking, an old habit I'd fallen into again, two years earlier, bouncing back and forth between quitting and then succumbing, working up to something like eight cigarettes a day.

Of course Willie noticed it first, I now think: Children major in the study of their mothers, and Willie has the elder child's umbilical awareness of me. But how is it that I didn't even question a weight loss striking enough for a child to speak up about? I was too happy enjoying this unexpected gift to question it even briefly: The American woman's yearning for thinness is so deeply a part of me that it never crossed my mind that a weight loss could herald something other than good fortune.

As it happened, I took up running about a month later, in concert with quitting smoking for good. Although I've been athletic in the past—team sports and tennis through high school and college—I'd always loathed running, hated the smugness and visible good feeling of people who did it. But now, for some reason, I was able to push past those first awful weeks of getting winded ten minutes into the run, past the shin splints, until somehow I crested the hill, on whose other side running became easy, or at least pleasurable: a necessary part of my day. Within months I loved it, and found myself keeping a journal, recording my mileage and speed, the weather and the odd happening on one of my familiar trails. I had three basic routes I ran near my house, and by the end of the summer I was running about four miles a day, at least five days a week. I was trying to move up from twenty miles a week to twenty-five.

And with all that exercise, I found I could eat pretty much anything I wanted without worrying about my weight. So more weight melted away, and the steady weight loss that might have warned me something was going badly wrong disguised itself instead as the reward for all those pounding steps I was taking through the chill of early fall, the sting of winter, the beauty of spring's beginning. I went from around 126 pounds, in the spring of 2000, to about 109 a year later.

Somewhere in there my period became irregular—first it was late, then it stopped altogether. Well, I'd heard of this: Women who exercise heavily sometimes do become amenorrheic. I discussed it with my gynecologist in January, and he agreed it was no real cause for alarm. He checked my hormone levels and found I definitely hadn't hit perimenopause, but what I most remember about that visit is the amazed approval with which he commented on the good shape I was in.

Around that time—I can't pinpoint exactly when—I began to have hot flashes, almost unnoticeable at first, gradually increasing in intensity. Well, I said to myself, I must be perimenopausal after all; a gynecologist friend told me that hormone levels can fluctuate so much that the test my doctor had done wasn't necessarily the last word on the subject.

Then one day in April I was lying on my back, talking idly on the telephone (strangely, I don't remember to whom), and running my hand up and down my now deliciously scrawny stomach. And just like that I felt it: a mass, about the size of a small apricot, on the lower right side of my abdomen. My mind swung sharply into focus: *Have I ever felt this thing before, this lump? Well, who knows, maybe this is a part of my anatomy I was just never aware of before—I always had a little layer of fat between my skin and the mysteries of the innards.* Maybe there was some part of the intestine that felt that way, and I had just never been thin enough to palpate it before.

You know how you've always wondered about it: Would you notice if you had a sudden lump? Would you be sensible enough to do something about it? How would your mind react? For all of us, those wonderings have a luxuriantly melodramatic quality. Because surely that isn't really how it works, you don't just stumble on the fact that you have a lethal cancer while you're gabbing on the phone like a teenager. Surely you can't have a death sentence just lying there, so close to the surface, without being in some other way aware of it.

I thought about calling my doctor, but then remembered that I had a full check-up scheduled in about three weeks anyway: I would bring it up then. In the intervening weeks I often reached down to find this odd bump: sometimes it wasn't there, and at other times it was. Once, I even thought it had moved—could I possibly be feeling it three inches up and two inches to the left, nearly underneath my belly button? Surely not. This must be just another sign that I was imagining things.

In fact, the mass hadn't moved. That lumpy area I felt briefly under my belly button was an entirely different metastatic tumor, one of the five big ones that had by now invaded my abdomen and pelvis. And still I thought that my biggest problem was a bronchitis I picked up toward the end of April and just couldn't shake.

Checkup day came. I had been seeing the same doctor for at least a decade, a small, faintly prissy, dry-humored man who was part of a booming practice in a good part of town. I'd chosen him casually, foolishly, at a time in my life when having a general practitioner didn't seem like a very important decision: He was the doctor of my then-boyfriend's boss (a boss the boyfriend—later my husband—didn't even like). For most of the past decade, almost all my health care had taken me to the office of my obstetrician, the man who delivered my two babies. To him I felt infinitely bonded. And he had tested my health so vigilantly, as befit a mother who had her first baby at thirty-five, that I hadn't really seen the need, for years, for a general check-up.

So this doctor I was seeing now had never had to see me through anything serious. But he had always handled what little I brought to him with sympathy and dispatch; I had a mild liking for him.

To begin the checkup, he ushered me into his office, fully clothed, to talk; my file in front of him, he showed that he'd boned up pretty well on me before my arrival. He could have passed a pop quiz about my job, number of children, and so forth. I told him about all of it: the stopped periods, the hot flashes, the fact that I could intermittently feel a mass in my belly. But I also told him what seemed most true to me: that overall I felt healthier than I'd been in years. I was running, I wasn't smoking, I'd stopped having the chronic sinus infections that had plagued me for years.

Right off the bat, Dr. Generalist advised me to press the matter of hot flashes, and of the vanished period, with my gynecologist. No Hormones Handled Here. Then he ushered me into his examining room next door, with the standard instruction to dress in a flimsy robe while he stepped out of the room. He inspected me in all the typical ways, then told me to get back in my clothes and step back into his office. I had to remind him that I had reported a strange lump in my abdomen. So he had me lie back down, and felt all around that area. No mass. He got me to feel there too; it was one of those times when I couldn't feel it.

"I would think," he said,

> that what you're feeling is stool that's moving through your bowel. What you're feeling is a loop of intestine or something where the stool is stuck for a while. That's why sometimes it's there and sometimes it's not. The *bad* things don't come and go; the bad things only come and stay.

He could send me off for a lot of expensive tests, he said, but there really wasn't any point in going to that trouble and expense because I was so obviously a perfectly healthy patient. He would call when my labs came back.

He called me, a week or so later, to report that all my lab tests looked great, with one minor exception: My calcium level was high—not the "good calcium" he had pressed on me, in pill form, as standard practice for a woman reaching middle age, but the "bad calcium" that circulates in the blood. It was just an anomaly, not alarming; I should come back in three months and repeat the count. At the time, I was in Seattle with my husband, on a business trip, and the doctor's report came in the form of a message on my voice mail. I never even called him back to discuss those results; he was so casual about them, and he repeated all the same information in a letter mailed to me the following week: Healthy healthy healthy.

Looking back, I know I was uneasy even after I got this clean bill of health. Sometimes I felt what seemed like a flicker of movement in my belly, and got the oddest feeling that I might be pregnant. At one point, I even bought a home pregnancy test and furtively took it in a stall in the ladies' room in the little mall that housed the pharmacy. I felt ridiculous, at forty-three, sneaking off to take a pregnancy test like an anxious highschooler; and I felt ridiculous to myself, even to be suspecting pregnancy—especially since I hadn't had a period for at least six months. That I even did it is a measure of how loudly my unconscious was screaming that something was seriously amiss in my body. But the doctor's reassurances were enough to turn off those klaxons just at the time when they should have been sounding most loudly. Every now and then, the mass in my abdomen actually stuck out when I lay on my back; once, I looked down to see my stomach distinctly tilted high on the right side, much lower on the left. I was at some pains never to point this out to my husband.

Finally, on the last Friday night in June 2001, I had a huge hot flash while my husband was tickling my back, in bed. Suddenly I was drenched; I could feel that his fingers could no longer slide easily along the skin of my back. He turned to me, astonished: "What *is* this?" he asked. "You're *covered* in sweat."

It was as if someone had finally given me permission to notice fully what was happening inside me. I made an appointment with my gynecologist—the earliest one I could get was the next week, on Thursday, July 5—and began deliberately noticing how overwhelming the hot flashes had gotten. For a while now, I realized, I had been clinging to the left side of the mattress at night, hoping to avoid any contact with my husband's warm flesh. Now that I paid close attention, I realized they were coming fifteen or twenty times a day, sweeping over and through me and leaving me sheathed in a layer of sweat. They came when I ran, making my joyous morning run a tedious slog that must be gotten through; they came when I sat still. They exceeded anything that had been described to me as the gradual coming of menopause. This was more like walking into a wall. On both Monday and Tuesday of that week, I remember, I stopped about two miles into my morning run; simply stopped, despite the freshness of the morning and the beauty of the path I usually cut through the gardened streets of Takoma Park. Any runner knows the feeling of having to push past the body's observation that it might be more fun to walk slowly home and pop open a beer (just keep putting one foot in front of the other), but this was something different, like an override system I could no longer ignore. It said: stop. It said, this is a body that can no longer afford to run.

My gynecologist's office is way, way out in the long exurban belt stretching westward from DC, where his practice was previously located. I had long since meant to find a new gynecologist, but I was lazy and also bonded to him because he had delivered both my kids, and so I continued to make the long trek to his alienating, boxy building—one of those addresses in five digits, ending in the word "highway"—in the middle of a fast-developing nowhere.

He was running late that afternoon, so it was probably after five when he finally called me into his office. We traded the chit-chat of near-friends, the usual gossip about people we both knew; we talked about what gynecologist I should start seeing in the district. Finally, we got down to it. I told him about the hot flashes, and about the lump I was feeling in my abdomen. "Yup, you're in menopause," he said somewhat brusquely. "We can start giving you hormones. But first let's check out that lump you say you're feeling."

We went back into the examining room where he keeps his ultrasound equipment. He'd given me dozens of quick exams with it over my child-bearing years. I hopped up on the table and he slapped on some of the chilly goo they apply to your belly, to make the ultrasound mouse slide over your skin, and almost immediately he stopped: "There," he said. "Yeah, there's something here." He looked at it a bit more, very briefly, then started snapping off his gloves. His face looked as neutral as he could possibly make it, which alarmed me instantly. "Just so you know," he said quickly, "it's probably fibroids. I'm not thinking cancer, but I am thinking surgery. So get dressed and come on back to my office, and I'll explain."

We sat back down on either side of his desk. But before we talked, he called out to his receptionist, who was just packing up for the evening. "Before you go," he said, "I need you to book her an ultrasound and a CT scan. Tomorrow, if possible."

I told Pat he was scaring me: What was all this speed about, if he wasn't thinking cancer?

"Well," he said, "I'm pretty sure it's not—I'll explain why in a minute—but I hate to have something like this hanging over a weekend. I want to know for sure what we're dealing with."

He went on to explain that he'd seen what looked like a fairly large growth on my ovary, but that it didn't look like ovarian cancer: Its consistency was different. (Here, he drew me a picture on the back of a piece of scrap paper.) He explained that fibroids can sometimes be removed with surgery but that very often they grew back, even worse than before. His own typical recommendation, for a woman who was done having babies, he said, was a hysterectomy.

"Does this have anything to do with my hot flashes?" I asked.

"No, not a thing, in all probability. You just happen to be starting menopause too."

Finally I felt on the verge of tears. When I left, I sat in the car to collect myself, boggling at the thought of losing my uterus at the age of forty-three. I didn't even call my husband on my cell phone. I just wanted to calm down and get home and then seek the sanctuary of his sympathy. The next morning, Pat's office called to say they had scored a formal ultrasound examination at three in the afternoon, in a DC radiology practice I'd visited from time to time before. When I got there, Pat's nurse told me, they would give me an appointment—probably early the next week—to come back for a CT-scan.

I told my husband I didn't need him to come to the sonogram: It would probably only give a clearer picture of what Pat's ultrasound had already told us, I assumed. There's nothing painful or difficult about a sonogram, and I didn't want to haul Tim out of work twice; I knew I'd want him with me for the CT scan later.

That was a bad decision.

I remember waiting endlessly at the desk for the receptionist to finish a peckish, convoluted phone conversation with the manager of the garage downstairs, about why she'd been billed wrong for that month's parking. She talked on and on ("Yes, I *know* that's what I owe for each month, but I already paid you for both June and July"), with zero self-consciousness about keeping a patient standing there at the desk. There was a sign on her desk that instructed one to sign in and then take a seat, but of course I needed to talk to her about scheduling a CT scan. She kept flicking her hand at me and trying to shoo me toward a chair, then pointing at the sign. I just waited.

Finally I told her why I was standing there: Um, Cat-scan . . . the Doctor's office told me . . . as soon as possible. . . . ."

"What are you?" she said. A puzzled silence. "I mean, what kind are you?"

"Well, um, they're looking at something in my pelvis—"

"Oh, body," she said, her scowl regathering. "We are really, really booked on bodies." She started to flip through her appointment book. I stood there, trying to radiate as palatable a combination of charm and distress as I could manage. "Well, I'll talk to the doctor," she finally mumbled. "Ask me again when your sonogram's done. We *might* be able to do Monday morning, 11 o'clock."

When my father was under treatment for cancer, which put him in and out of various hospitals for five years, I used to roll my eyes at the way he ingratiated himself with all the staff. You could walk into intensive care and he'd be there, his face wan against the pillow, but with his usual charming, modest smile ready for everyone. He would introduce his nurse, and tell you where she was born and how her sister wrote romance novels, and that her brother was on a track and field scholarship at the State University of New York.

Part and parcel, I thought, of his lifelong campaign to be loved by everyone he met. He had always put more energy into captivating strangers than anyone else I knew.

But I learned right away, when I went for this very first test, how wrong I'd been. As a patient, you come to feel that you need *everyone*—from the chairman of the oncology service at a major cancer center down to the least-paid clerk in the admissions department—to like you. Some of them may have the power to save your life. Others have the power to make you comfortable in the middle of the night, or to steer away from you the nurse-in-training who is still just learning to insert IVs, or to squeeze you in for a test you might otherwise wait days for.

I was discovering this truth on my back, while the ultrasound technician guided her wand through the chilly gel she had squeezed onto my belly. She was a friendly young woman with a Spanish accent of some kind, and her job was to get an accurate picture of what was going on in my pelvis while divulging the least information possible to the anxious patient. My job was to find out as much as I could, as quickly as I could.

So there I am: "Gosh, Friday afternoon . . . have you had a long week? . . . How long have you been working in ultrasound. . . . Oh! Is that my ovary there, really? Ah, so you're taking pictures now . . . uh-huh. . . . Gee, that must be the growth my gynecologist was talking about."

Under this onslaught of nice-ness, the technician begins to think aloud a bit. Yes, she is seeing a growth. But usually fibroids, which grow from the outside of the uterus, move in concert with it: Poke the uterus and the growth will move too. This growth seemed to be independent of the uterus.

Is it a mild chill I'm feeling, or a mild thrill? I am still reeling at the thought that I might have a hysterectomy at forty-three; perhaps I am thinking it would at least be fun to have something more interesting than a fibroid?

But if there is a tinge of that interest, it vanishes when she speaks again: "Huh. Here's another one." And another. Suddenly, we are seeing three strange round plants that yield to a mild shove, but don't behave like anything she's ever seen before. She is doubly skeptical now about the fibroid theory. My gynecologist had examined me in detail the previous January, so much of what we're looking at has to have grown within six months. Fibroids, she says, don't grow nearly that fast.

"Is that, um, more like something that could be coming from the colon?" I ask.

"Could be," she says.

I am surprised that she is so forthcoming, but soon see that it is of little use to me: She is looking at something she's never seen before. She summons the doctor—the chief radiologist in the practice—who in turn summons a younger colleague she is training. They all crowd around the machine in fascination.

Again, we do the poking-the-uterus exercise. We try the trans-vaginal sonography wand. Their mystification has begun to make me seriously frightened. I begin to question the doctor very directly. She is quite kind. She really can't say what she's seeing, she says. It could be something attached more to the intestine or the colon than to anything in the reproductive tract. We will probably not know without performing a CT scan. All the while, the technician is photographing the growths from every possible angle.

It almost seems an afterthought—the indulgence of a hunch—when the doctor turns to the technician and says, "Trying moving up, yes, to the navel or so." I can still remember the feel of the equipment casually gliding up toward my navel, and then a sudden, palpable tension in the air. For immediately, another large growth—one even bigger than the three below—looms into view.

This is the moment when I know for certain that I have cancer. Without even looking very hard, this exam has been turning up mysterious blobs in every quarter. I go very still as the doctor begins directing the technician to turn here, look there. Her voice has dropped almost to a whisper, and I don't want to distract her with my anxious questions: I can hold them long enough for her to find out what I need to know.

But then I hear one of them mumble to the other, "You see there? There is some ascites . . ." and I feel panic wash through me. Along with my sisters, I nursed my mother through her death from liver disease, and I know that ascites is the fluid that collects around the liver when it is badly diseased.

"Are you finding something on my liver, too?" I croak.

"Yes, something, we're not sure what," says the doctor, pressing a sympathetic hand to my shoulder. And then suddenly I'm aware that they've made a decision to stop this exam. What's the point in finding more? They've found out enough to know that they need the more subtle diagnostic view of a CT scan. The sonographer is putting away her equipment; the young trainee has left the room. The doctor is still with me.

"Is there a case to be made against my freaking out now?" I ask.

Well, yes, replies the doctor. There's a lot we don't know; there's a lot we need to find out; it could be a great range of different things, some of which would be better than others.

"But then let me ask you this way," I press. "Do you know of anything other than cancer that could give rise to the number of growths we just saw? Could it be anything benign?"

"Well, no," she says. "Not that I'm aware of. But we'll be sure to work you in Monday morning for a CT scan, and then we'll know a lot more. I'm going to call your doctor now, and then I assume you'd like to talk to him after me?"

She shows me to a private office to wait; she will let me know when I should pick up the phone there. In the meantime, I choose a free phone line and dial my husband's cell phone. I have caught him somewhere on the street. There is a huge noise behind him; he can barely hear me.

"I need you—" I begin, barely in control of my voice. "I need you to get in a cab and come to the Foxhall medical building."

This is what he says: "Okay." He doesn't say, "What's wrong?" He doesn't ask, "What did the test show?" It is my first glimpse of the miraculous generosity that will help me get through everything that is about to happen. He can tell how tenuous my control is; he can tell that I need him; he has agreed without speech to hold the anxiety of knowing nothing more for the twenty minutes it will take him to get there.

After this, I talk briefly with my gynecologist on the phone. Pat's first words are, "What time's your CT scan? I'm going to cancel all my Monday morning appointments and come to your scan." I have never heard of a doctor coming to a CAT scan before this. It foretells the huge seams of good fortune that will run through the black rock of the next three years. There is nothing like having a doctor who really cares about you—who can cut through the inhuman pace of medical time, which usually leaves patients begging to hear their test results, waiting too many days for an appointment, at a loss until the conveyor belt brings along the next hurried intervention. Pat is one of the doctors who is willing to break the rules: Here is my cell phone number, call me any time this weekend. We will figure out together what to do on Monday.

Somehow, my husband and I stagger through the weekend. Every hour or so one of us steals away to a computer to re- or mis-diagnose for the fourteenth time. The truth is we know for sure I have some kind of cancer, and that any cancer that has metastasized is bad; and that that is all we will know for a few more days.

In a stroke of uncannily bad timing, we have scheduled to receive a new au pair that Saturday night, a complete stranger from the Czech Republic. We've never had an au pair before, but with both our kids now in school full time, we need only part-time care. The State Department bills it as a cultural exchange program, and yuppies like us get away with paying a third of what we'd have to pay anyone else. There is, of course, room and board thrown in. But whatever you do, it's a roll of the dice: I have friends who had wonderful au pairs with whom they've formed lifelong friendships, and others who felt they'd merely acquired another child, one who could sulk in three languages.

So off Tim goes on Saturday night to the airport, and home he comes with a tall, doe-eyed, beautiful young woman with severely-cut short hair and an aura of incapacitating shyness. Her English is not quite as good as we had thought in our brief telephone conversations with her. My first thought: Oh, she's lovely. My second: God, who's going to be her mother for the next twelve months? Making cheerful conversation with her. And is Prague a beautiful city? I've always heard it is (CANCER). Yes, my in-laws went there on vacation a few years ago and (CANCER) were just knocked out by (CANCER) it.

By Sunday afternoon, I am in tears over the impossibility of it all: the demands of getting dinner on the table, answering the needs of a five-year-old and an eight-year-old, smiling stiffly at this needy stranger. Finally Tim bundles all of them into a car, without me, to do some "sightseeing" for Veronika's edification. At the Lincoln Memorial, as Alice and Willie deliberate over the items on offer in the gift shop, Tim takes her aside and tells her the truth, as far as we know it.

Finally, Monday comes. After the CT scan, Pat takes me directly to the hospital to get prodded by his favorite surgeon, whom I'll call Dr. Goodguy. ("The surgeon I'd take my own family to," Pat says.) In the examining room, Dr. Goodguy frowns over my films, palpates my abdomen, interviews me, and schedules me for both an MRI that afternoon and a biopsy two days later. I finally think to ask how big all these growths are. Several oranges and even one grapefruit, Dr. Goodguy says; my first inkling that citrus metaphor is essential to cancer treatment.

Being a patient requires that you master the Zen of living in hospital time, tuning out as much as possible, while also demanding a constant vigilance, because some people really will screw up your treatment if you're not paying strict attention. When I go for my MRI, the technician—a lovely, smiling man with a very uncertain command of English—seems very vague about what, exactly, he's supposed to be examining. I insist that he call Dr. Goodguy's office.

Pat and Dr. Goodguy have been scratching their heads. What could possibly grow so fast, and so widely? Probably—maybe—lymphoma. They keep telling me this—this would be the good news, because lymphomas are increasingly treatable. My gynecologist friend Laura has told me the same thing over the weekend. My psychotherapist nods at the wisdom of this off-the-cuff prognosis. I find myself on the point of hysterical laughter. How many more people, I wonder, are going to tell me, *Congratulations! You've got lymphoma!!*

By Thursday afternoon this is no longer funny. I've had a biopsy the previous day, and Dr. Goodguy calls about 3 PM. He has a Very Serious Doctor Voice on, and jumps right in: "Well, this isn't good. It's not lymphoma. Your pathology report shows that your tumor is consistent with hepatoma, which is, uh, which is liver cancer." Already I am struggling: Does "consistent with" mean they think that but they don't really know it? No, those are just scientific weasel words they use in pathology reports. (A pathologist, I will learn, would look at your nose and report that it is consistent with a breathing apparatus.)

I know this diagnosis is very, very bad. Liver cancer is one of the possibilities I've researched in my compulsive tours of the Internet over the weekend, so I already know it's one of the worst things you can have. Still, I say to the doctor, "Well, how bad is that?"

"I won't avoid it. It's very serious."
"And it would presumably be bad news that it's already created other tumors around my body?"
"Yes. Yes, that is a bad sign."

A lovely man, who's doing a hard job with a patient he's just met three days before. There are at least five large metastases of the cancer in my pelvis and abdomen, and the mother ship—a tumor the size of a navel orange—straddles the channel where the major venous and arterial structures run in and out of the liver, swallowing up most of the hepatic veins and also surrounding and infiltrating my inferior vena cava, where the tumor tissue has climbed almost into my heart. Tumors so widespread automatically "stage" my cancer at IV(b). There is no V, and there is no (c).

When I hang up the phone I call Tim and tell him. We make it as clinical a conversation as possible, because otherwise there will be so much feeling it might stand in the way of acting. He is on his way home, right away.

I call my friend Liz and tell her. I tell her some of the statistics—that as I read the data, I may be dead by Christmas. Liz almost always says the perfect thing, from the heart, and now she says the two things I most need to hear. The first is "I want you to know that whatever happens, I will be with you the whole way."

The second is, "And you know that all of us—but this is my promise—we will all work to keep you alive in your children's minds." Now tears are pouring down my cheeks, and they feel good.

The drama of discovery and diagnosis happened so long ago, and has been followed by so many drastic plot twists, that it feels to me like ancient history. But I've noticed that almost everyone I talk to is very curious to know those details. Whenever the whim of disease takes me into the view of a new doctor or nurse, we fall into the standard, boring rhythm of summarizing history and condition (when diagnosed, at what stage; what treatments have been administered since, with what results). If the person I'm talking to is young and relatively inexperienced, I may find myself more schooled in this procedure even than she or he is. But there always comes a moment when their professionalism suddenly drops, their clipboards drift to their sides, and they say, "Uhn, how—Do you mind if I ask you how you happened to find out you had cancer?" I realize at these times that they are asking as fellow humans, not too much younger than I am, and their fascination is the same as everyone else's: Could this happen to me? How would I know? What would that feel like?

We have all indulged this curiosity, haven't we? What would I do if I suddenly found I had a short time to live. . . . What would it be like to sit in a doctor's office and hear a death sentence? I had entertained those fantasies just like the next person. So when it actually happened, I felt weirdly like an actor in a melodrama. I had—and still sometimes have—the feeling that I was doing, or had done, something faintly self-dramatizing: something a bit too attention-getting. (I was raised by people who had a horror of melodrama, but that's another part of the story.)

In two months I will mark the year 3 B.T.—my third year of Borrowed Time. (Or, as I think of it on my best days, Bonus Time.) When I was diagnosed with Stage IV(b) liver cancer in early July of 2001, every doctor was at great pains to make clear to me that this was a death sentence. Unless you find liver cancer early enough to have a surgeon cut out the primary tumor before it spreads, you have little chance of parole. The five-year survival rate for those who can't have surgery is less than one percent; my cancer had spread so widely that I was facing a prognosis of somewhere between three and six months. I was forty-three; my children were five and eight.

Liver cancer is so untreatable because chemotherapy has little effect. There are other localized treatments that can slow the growth of the main

tumor, or tumors, in the liver (they pump chemo through an artery directly into the tumor and block the exits; they ablate them with radio frequen-
cy waves; they freeze them, or they install localized chemo pumps to blast
them). But if the cancer has spread, the medical textbooks say, there is no
therapy that can stop it, or even slow it down much. Chemo has about a
25 percent to 30 percent chance of having any impact, and even then it
will almost always be a small and transient one: a slight and temporary
shrinkage, a short pause in the cancer's growth; a check on metastases that
can add to the patient's pain.

But, for some reasons I know and others I don't, my body—with the
help of six hospitals, dozens of drugs, a teeming multitude of smart doctors and nurses, and a heroically stubborn husband—has mounted a
miraculous resistance. As seriously fucked cancer patients go, I am an
astonishingly healthy woman.

I live at least two different lives. In the background, usually, is the
knowledge that for all my good fortune so far, I will still die of this disease. This is where I wage the physical fight, which is, to say the least, a
deeply unpleasant process. And, beyond the concrete challenges of needles
and mouth sores and barf basins and barium, it has thrown me on a roller
coaster that sometimes clatters up a hill, giving me a more hopeful, more
distant view than I'd expected, and at other times plunges faster and farther than I think I can endure. Even when you know the plunge is coming—it's in the nature of a roller coaster, after all, and you know that you
disembark on the bottom and not the top—even then, it comes with some
element of fresh despair.

I've hated roller coasters all my life.

But in the foreground is regular existence: love the kids, buy them new
shoes, enjoy their burgeoning wit; get some writing done, plan vacations
with Tim, have coffee with my friends. Having found myself faced with
that old bull-session question (What would you do if you found out you
had a year to live?), I learned that a woman with children has the privilege
or duty of bypassing the existential. What you do, if you have little kids,
is lead as normal a life as possible, only with more pancakes.

This is the realm of life in which I make intensely practical decisions—
almost, these three years on, without thinking about it. When we bought
a new car last fall, I chose it, bargained for it, and paid for it with the last
of an old retirement account my father had left me. And then I registered
it only in my husband's name—because who needs the hassles over title if

he decides to sell it later? When an old crown at the back of my lower right jaw began to disintegrate last summer, I looked at my dentist, whose fastidiousness I have relied on for almost 20 years, and said, Jeff, look: I'm doing okay right now but I've got every reason to think it would be foolish to sink four thousand dollars into, um, infrastructure at this point. Is there anything sort of half-assed and inexpensive we could do, just to get by?

Sometimes I feel immortal: Whatever happens to me now, I've earned the knowledge some people never gain, that my span is finite and I still have the chance to rise and rise to life's generosity. But at other times I feel trapped, cursed by my specific awareness of the guillotine poised above my neck. At those times I resent you—or the seven other people at dinner with me, or my husband deep in sleep beside me—for the fact that you may never even catch sight of the blade assigned to you.

Sometimes I simply feel horror, that most elementary thing. The irreducible fear, for me, is the fantasy that I will by some mistake be imprisoned in my body after dying. As a child I never enjoyed a minute of any campfire stories of the buried-alive genre. And, even without *that* unwelcome and vivid fear in my mind, I can't find any way around the horror of being left alone down there in the dark, picked apart by processes about which I'm a little bit squeamish even when they're just fertilizing my day lilies. Intellectually, I know it won't matter to me in the slightest. But my most primal fear is that somehow my consciousness will be carelessly left behind among my remains.

There's cremation, of course, the determined housekeeper's way around the thought of decomposition. But here, too—what about mistakes? I see the flames licking up around my feet as the simple box slides smooth into the oven. (I don't even know, of course, if you go in feet-first; I think I got that from a James Bond movie.*) I feel the scouring pain of being killed, as opposed to simply dying.

But of course I am already being killed, by one of nature's most common blunders. And these blunt fears are easily deconstructed as a form of denial: If I'm stuck alive in my coffin, well, that will in some sense override the final fact of my death, no? I can see these dread-filled fantasies as the wishes they are: that I really can stay in this body I love; that my consciousness really will run on past my death; that I won't just . . . die.

* *Diamonds Are Forever* (1971)

There are a million lesser fears, of course. The largest category concerns my children, and weighs both the trivial and the serious. I fear that my Alice will never really learn to wear tights (you'd think, from watching my husband try to help her into them on the rare occasion when he's asked, that he'd been asked to perform a breech birth of twin colts at the peak of a blizzard). That no one will ever really brush her fine, long hair all the way through, so that she will display a perpetual bird's nest at the back of her neck. (And—what? People will say her slatternly mother should have drummed better Hair Care into her family's minds before selfishly dying of cancer?) That no one will ever put up curtains in my dining room, the way I've been meaning to for the last three years.

Deeper: Who will talk to my darling girl when she gets her period? Will my son sustain that sweet enthusiasm he seems to beam most often at me? There are days I can't look at them—literally, not a single time—without wondering what it would do to them to grow up without a mother. What if they can't remember what I was like? What if they remember, and grieve, all the time?

What if they don't?

But even this obvious stuff, the dread and sorrow, make up a falsely simple picture. Sometimes, early on, death was a great dark lozenge that sat bittersweet on my tongue for hours at a time, and I savored the things I'd avoid forever. I'll never have to pay taxes, I thought, or go to the Department of Motor Vehicles. I won't have to see my children through the worst parts of adolescence. I won't have to be human, in fact, with all the error and loss and love and inadequacy that come with the job.

I won't have to get old.

It says a lot about the power of denial that I could so automatically seek (and find!) the silver lining that might come with dying of cancer at forty-three. For good and ill, I no longer think that way. The passage of time has brought me the unlikely ability to work, simultaneously, at facing my death and loving my life.

Often it is lonely work. And I have nothing happy to impart about the likelihood that I will have to take chemotherapy for the rest of my life—nothing, except that I should be so lucky. But I am now, after a long struggle, surprisingly happy in the crooked, sturdy little shelter I've built in the wastes of Cancerland. Here, my family has lovingly adapted to our awful tumble in fortune. And here, I nurture a garden of eleven or twelve different varieties of hope, including the cramped, faint, strangely apologetic hope that having already done the impossible, I will somehow attain the unattainable cure.

Our first stop, after I receive my diagnosis, is the office of my G.P., the one who missed all the signs and symptoms of my disease. We're not feeling especially confident in his skills, but he might have ideas about treatment, and he can at least perform the service of doing a full set of blood tests. (Weeks later, when I send him a form asking him to forward records to my new G.P., he will go through his files to figure out where and whether he might have missed something. Turns out that when he stamped me A–1 healthy he was, in fact, reading the blood test results of someone else entirely. Oops. When he finally found my results, they showed that my liver function tests were wildly inflated—something that would have alarmed even him had he noticed them at the time.)

As we are driving over to Dr. Generalist, Tim turns to me at a stop light and says: "I just want you to know. I'm going to be a total prick." What he means by this is that there is no log he won't roll, no connection he won't tap, no pull he won't use. Tim is a man—a fellow journalist—who would rather swallow gravel than use a job title to get a good table at a restaurant.

But, within an hour of hearing the bad news, he has scored me an appointment early the next Monday at Memorial Sloan-Kettering Cancer Center (MSKCC) in New York City, one of the country's most eminent cancer treatment centers. Tim has done this by the simple expedient of calling Harold Varmus, president and chief executive officer of MSKCC, with whom we'd formed a warm but very tangential friendship when he was in Washington running the National Institutes for Health during the Clinton administration. Harold wasn't in the office at the time, so Tim announced to whatever assistant answered the phone that he was a dear friend of Harold's and needed immediate help. The assistant lined up the necessary appointments immediately. (When finally Harold learned that we had so shamelessly exploited his name, he showed nothing but concern over me, and promised that their entire hepatobiliary team would be available to look me over.)

These are the kinds of appointments, I was to learn, that some people wait weeks or even months for. I say that not in the spirit of a boast, only as a reminder that in this way as in most others, medicine is unfair—rationed in fundamentally irrational ways. But when your own time comes, you will pull pretty much every string available to get what you need.

By the next morning—it is still only the day after my diagnosis—I have a noon appointment with the top-most G.I. oncologist available at Johns Hopkins University Medical Center, which is in Baltimore, a little less than an hour from our house. Hopkins is, of course, also famous for its excellence in cancer. This conquest of the appointment book is the doing of Graydon Carter, the editor of *Vanity Fair*, who, when I first called him responded by unleashing the magazine's best researcher to find the names of the top five liver guys in the country. He called me back and left a message on my machine, saying, "Look, this is going to sound like a very crass thing to say, but I'm really good at getting people into hospitals. Call me if you need any help. Call me." I didn't doubt it for a moment, and called him back to ask if he could solicit the help of his good friend Mike Bloomberg (then still a mere media baron, not yet the mayor of New York) to get me an appointment at Hopkins. I knew, from reading Bloomberg's autobiography, that he had given millions to the medical center there and that he was chairman of the hospital's board of trustees. Within the hour I got a call from Bloomberg's office telling me who my contact at Hopkins would be (a staff member of the "development," i.e., fundraising, department) and to call him right away.

We've also got an appointment at the National Cancer Institute (NCI) for later the following week. I don't really remember how that one came about, but it is further reassurance that we're touching all the bases, hearing about the very latest treatments.

So I had all the appointments I needed, and a husband who did yeoman leg work running from place to place getting copies of MRIs and CT scans and pathologist's reports and blood tests. If speed was needed in my case, I was well on my way to a record pace.

Just one problem: All this moving and shaking, driving to Baltimore and flying to New York, took us to the very same brick wall. In strode the doctor (usually trailing a retinue of students) to meet me, ask me a little about the onset of my disease. Out he went with my films under his arm, to look at them in privacy. In he came, quietly, his pace slowed and his face grim. He said some version of what the oncologist at Hopkins said: "I couldn't believe—I just told my colleague after we first met you, 'there is no way she looks sick enough to have this degree of disease. Someone blew this diagnosis.' Then I looked at this MRI."

It fell to the man at Hopkins to be the first to tell us just how bad my situation was. But they all said more or less the same thing: The Hopkins doc did it while focusing intently on the shape of his cuticles, turning them in and then splaying them forward like a bride showing off her new rock. (Later, we would hear on the oncology grapevine that he has regular manicures.) Another did it while holding my hand and looking sweetly into my face. "My dear," this one said, "you're in desperate trouble." One did it in the midst of a completely impenetrable lecture on the chemistry of chemotherapy. One did it with a look of panic on his face. That was the one at NCI, who turned out to look like a first-year med student—here our due diligence had simply run out of gas. Inevitably, we called him Doogie Howser. Doogie sprinted from the room and came back with a phalanx of doctors in military uniforms who proceeded to try to sell me on a phase I clinical trial from which I couldn't possibly profit.

What it boiled down to was: We have nothing to do for you. You can't have surgery, because there's so much disease outside the liver. You certainly can't have a transplant—they'll never give a liver to someone who's had extra-hepatic disease; it's against all the rules. You're not a good candidate for any of the newer interventional strategies, and we can't do radiation because we'd destroy too much viable liver tissue. All we can do is chemotherapy, and to be honest, we really don't expect much in the way of results.

The first time we heard this lecture, at Hopkins, we stepped blinking into the sunshine of a hot July day. "I need to take a walk," I told my husband, and we set off in the direction of Baltimore's Fell's Point neighborhood. Before long, I wanted to sit and talk. The only place we could find to sit was the concrete staircase of a public library. We sat there to absorb what we'd just heard.

"Maybe," said Tim, "the doctors at Sloan-Kettering will have something different to say."

"I doubt it," I said, out of the certainty of my Internet travels and the doctor's unambiguous pessimism. This pretty much set the pattern Tim and I would follow for the coming months: He took care of the hope, and I took care of getting ready to die.

"If this is as bad as it sounds," I told him now, "I don't want to end my life in some hospital barfing in the name of science. I mean it: I want to be realistic about what's happening to me."

* * *

The days fractured into lurching, indelible moments and odd details that stuck. The way the Sloan-Kettering waiting room—lush with Rockefeller-funded orchids and a splashing water sculpture—had nice rows of seats whose armrests were attached with Velcro, so you could tear them away when you needed to sit and sob in your husband's arms. The black-and-white bumper sticker on the glass door of an East Side coffee shop we stopped into while killing time before an appointment: THIS IS REALLY HAPPENING, it said, in what felt like a message nailed there just for my eyes.

For the first ten days or so, I had a necessary composure. I got to, and through, all those appointments. I went to my desk and got together a filing system for all the names and information that were flooding into our life. I knew I wanted to keep it together while we decided what we were going to tell the children.

But after our discouraging visit to Sloan-Kettering, I could feel the dam getting close to flood tide. We decided to stay in New York an extra night or two to take advantage of the hospital's offer of a PET scan, which might identify new tumors, or spot the regression of old ones, more quickly than a CT scan. The doctors there had suggested that a "baseline" PET scan might help us figure out a little quicker than otherwise whether whatever chemotherapy regimen we ultimately chose was working for me.

As we sat in that plush waiting room making this decision, it came to me that I couldn't bear to continue staying with the dear old friends who had put us up the night before. They were contemporaries of my parents and very dear to me—Sheila Smith is, in fact, my godmother—but I couldn't face talking to anyone about this latest news, or having to be in the least bit socially adept.

Tim, who knows me so well, put his arm around me and said, "Let's not think about money. Where do you want to go?" I brightened for a moment. There might not be any treatments out there that would work for me, but, by God, New York had some fine hotels. "Mmmm. . . . The Peninsula?" So off we went to the land of high thread counts and long baths with a TV screen just above the taps.

It's amazing how you can distract yourself in the midst of such a dramatic experience—because you can't believe such awful news 24 hours a day. So I surrendered to the pleasure of a great hotel for about a day. I had my hair washed and blow-dried, and received a pedicure in the Peninsula salon. (I still remember sitting there staring, staring at all the colors of polish I could pick from. It took on the crazy proportions of an important decision: A docile sort of peach? A very feminine light pink, which might acknowledge surrender? Hell no: I chose a violent red, brighter than fire engines, bright as lollipops.)

Then, feeling beautiful, I actually danced around the room when Tim was out, my CD headphones blasting Carly Simon in my ears. When I was done I looked out the window of our room on the eighth floor, down all those hard surfaces to the tarmac of Fifth Avenue, and wondered what it would feel like just to jump. Would it be better or worse than what I was stepping into?

That night, finally, the dam broke. I was lying in bed with Tim when I realized it was all true: I was dying. Soon I would be dead. No one else would be in it with me. I would be the one in the bed, and when the hospice nurse stopped by, my dearest loves would retreat to the hallway and swap impressions—separated from me already. Even while still alive, I would leave their party. I lay under those wonderful sheets and felt cold to the bone. I began to cry, loud, then louder. I shouted my terror. I sobbed with my entire rib cage. Tim held me while I heaved it out this way, a titanic purging. I was so loud that I wondered why no one called the police to say there was a woman getting murdered across the hall. It felt good to let go, but that feeling was little. It was dwarfed by the recognition I had just allowed in.

We came to think of my cancer not just as a disease but also as a locale. Cancerland is the place where at least one of us is often depressed: It is as if my husband and I hand the job back and forth without comment, the way most couples do about child-minding or being the Saturday chauffeur. Some of the time I have been so sunk in the sadness of believing I'm going to die soon—not to mention the aggressions of chemotherapy—that I have slept most of the day and at 6 PM sent my fairy double downstairs to handle evenings with the kids, dinner, putting them to bed.

At other times, Tim is so tired of all he shoulders, and so preoccupied with a vision of grief—no, of grief combined with the prospect of handling alone everything from tax preparation to school applications to his daughter's puberty—that he is almost unreachable. We don't have to be actively *thinking* about the wild uncertainty of our future together to be pulled by its undertow. Sometimes, when either of us comes out of it and manages briefly to raise from the ocean floor the graceful wreck of our old, normal life, we can be happy for days or weeks or even a month. And then that very happiness begins to make us depressed, because certainly we are repressing something too powerful to stay contained for long. Wearily, we climb again into our cramped lifeboat.

I try to remember that I'm one of the luckiest cancer patients in America, by dint of good medical insurance, great contacts who gained me access to the best of the best among doctors, an amazing support system of friends and family, and the brains and drive to be a smart and demanding medical consumer, which is one of the very hardest things I've ever done. I'm quite sure that if I were among the 43 million of my fellow Americans who had no health insurance—let alone really good insurance—I'd be dead already. As it is, I never see a hospital bill that hasn't already been paid. And there is no co-payment on the many medications I've taken. Which is fortunate: One of them—the Neupogen with which I inject myself every day for a week after chemo to boost my bone marrow's production of white cells—costs about $20,000 a year.

For me, time is the only currency that truly counts any more. I have weathered days of wretchedness and pain without a whimper, only to come unglued when some little glitch suddenly turns up to meddle with the way I had planned to use some unit of time: that this half-hour, and the contents I had planned to pour into it, are now lost to me forever seems an insupportable unfairness. Because, of course, any old unit of time can suddenly morph into a bloated metaphor for the rest of your time on earth, for how little you may have and how little you may control it.

At the time I was diagnosed, I felt that I had just learned about the elasticity of time: After struggling for years with a self-critical ambivalence over what and how I should write, I had somehow found a deeply satisfying well from which to draw. My time, my body, my energy—they all felt infinitely expansive, as if hard work enabled me to work even more and harder; as if I suddenly had the gift of forging time for everything. Too much work? I could stay up all night. And taking time with the people I loved only made room for more love.

Now, I can do absolutely nothing to stretch my available time. Time is cement, it is rock. And it is stolen and stolen and stolen by treatment: Something like two-fifths of the time, when I am on the far side of the chemo moon, I don't feel up to doing (or at least planning) anything. I have to work in time to get CT scans (there goes half a day) and a weekly blood draw and appointments with doctors. Even on good days, I need four or five hours of extra rest.

You have time for only so many cups of coffee with friends before your next round of chemo; if you have half your old energy, there are only so many intimate friendships you can maintain, only so many new ones you can explore. Most of the time, for the past three years, even my good days have given me energy to do only one Big Thing: lunch with a friend; writing a column; a movie with the kids. Choose, choose, choose. I find myself on the phone with someone I'd love to see, and then I look at my calendar and find that realistically, my next episode of unscheduled Free Play is going to be five weeks off, on the far side of my next treatment; and even then there will really only be a total of about seven hours I can assign before the next treatment. I am forced to admit that in this cramped context, I don't actually want to spend two of these hours with the person I'm talking to. These forced choices make one of the biggest losses of sickness.

But on the other side of this coin is a gift. I think cancer brings to most people a new freedom to act on the understanding that their time is important. My editor at the *Washington Post* told me, when I first got sick, that after his mother recovered from cancer his parents literally never went anywhere they didn't want to. If you have ever told yourself, breezily, that life is too short to spend any of it with your childhood neighbor's annoying husband, those words now take on the gleeful raiment of simple fact. The knowledge that time's expenditure is important, that it is up to you, is one of the headiest freedoms you will ever feel.

Today nothing, beyond the demands of being a patient and a parent, is obligatory. If I hate being forced to choose, it is also true that nearly everything in my life now is chosen.

Some of my choices surprise me. One afternoon—a blowy day in early spring, the first day when the sun actually seemed to outpower the wind— I ducked a meeting people were counting on me to come to, and I didn't lie or apologize for my reasons, because the most pressing thing I could possibly do that afternoon was plant something purple in that little spot next to the garden gate, the one I'd been thinking about for two years.

Time, I now understand, used to be a shallow concept to me. There was the time you occupied, sometimes anxiously, in the present (a deadline in three hours; a dentist's appointment for which you were ten minutes late); there was your inarticulate sense of time's grander passage, and the way it changes with age.

Now, time has levels and levels of meaning. For example, I have clung for a year and a half to a friend's observation that young children experience time in a different way from adults. Since a month can seem an eternity to a child, then every month I manage to live might later teem with meaning and memory to my children. This totem is all I need during times when my pockets are otherwise empty of wisdom or strength.

Since I was diagnosed, I have had an eternity of time—at least six times as much as I was supposed to have—and sometimes I think that all of that time has been gilded with my knowledge of its value. At other moments, I think sadly of how much of the past three years have been wasted by the boredom and exhaustion and enforced stillness of treatment.

We arrived at last at the office of the preeminent gastrointestinal oncologist in Washington, DC, whom I will call Dr. Liver. We had been warned away from the hospital where he was based—in part by former employees we'd met in other hospitals, who had said, "Whatever you do, don't go there. It's a mess." Administratively, they meant. But it turns out that you don't really have that much choice if you want to get treated in the Washington area. This ran against my assumptions, but there it was.

We sat for a while in the pleasant waiting room of the hospital's cancer clinic. Then a nurse led us to a tiny examining room. And about forty-five minutes later, in swept Dr. Liver with a retinue of two—a nurse and a "Fellow" (as I learned later, this is a full-fledged doctor who comes to the hospital for a time to be trained in oncology). Because the room was so tiny, with only two chairs, Dr. Liver stood. He was a tall, southern presence, with fair skin and very light blond hair with a tint of red.

Dr. Liver had looked at my MRI already, and, I imagined, had made a series of binary decisions. Will she live? (Yes/no ... No.) Will she die soon? (Yes/no ... Yes.) Is her situation so desperate that I should convey this with all possible, brutal force? (Yes/no ... Yes.) Should I bother to learn her name? (Yes/no ... No.)

He began by shaking his head. "How much do you know about what's going on?" he asked. As he spoke, he leaned against the examining table and towered over us. (For the next two years, I made a point of perching on the examining table for the duration of every appointment, to match his height—until one day I realized he had for a long time been sitting down in a chair for our meetings.)

We assured him we'd already been to five doctors: We knew how bad it was.

Dr. Liver nodded. Good: We didn't have to have The Conversation.

"So," he said, "you know your only real treatment option is chemotherapy. And even that is unlikely to do much good."

We talked about various chemotherapies I might try. He wanted to try a fairly standard combination of adriamycin and taxotere.

"But we have a trial—," he said; words I would hear him say again and again in the future. "A trial, where we're using those drugs but testing a new regimen of the agent we give you *after* the chemo to keep your white count up."

"So the trial part," I said, "wouldn't actually be doing anything toward treating the cancer."

"Nope," he said.

"Can I get those drugs outside of the trial, just as a regular patient?"

"Well. Sure. But I'll get you the consent form to read over, just in case. Think about what you want to do and call us when you're ready."

His voice and body language were beginning to hint that our meeting was coming to a close. One day I would come to respect and be grateful for his frankness, and discover an unsuspected well of kindness and compassion; but for the moment he had the air of a breezy pessimist: not the easiest personality type for someone with a death sentence to enjoy.

"What," I asked, "are we shooting for here? I mean, what would you consider a success?"

"Well you know," he said,

this is mostly palliative care. If we didn't do any chemo, you'd begin to have some very unpleasant symptoms soon. So I guess we'd be hitting a single if it acted enough to make you comfortable for a while. A double would be if it actually shrank your tumors some. And a triple—which is very unlikely—would be if we were still standing here six months from now talking about what to do next.

Apparently a home run was not an option.

Tim asked whether we couldn't consider some far-out experimental treatment—something way back in the pipeline, which we might attain through a compassionate-use policy at some drug company yet to be identified. "No. There's not a chance," Dr. Liver answered bluntly. "This is Washington. Everyone thinks they can be the exception. But the lists for the kind of treatment you're talking about are ten thousand long."

Finally, we had the obligatory conversation about how I could have gotten this cancer. "You've got no cirrhosis," he said wonderingly, ticking off the potential causes on his fingers. "You've got no hepatitis. It's wild that you look so healthy."

So how do you think I got it? I asked.

"Lady," he said, "you got hit by lightning."

My biggest fear was that death would snatch me right away. An oncologist at Sloan-Kettering had mentioned, parenthetically, that the tumor in my vena cava could give birth at any time to a blood clot, causing a fast death by way of pulmonary embolism. The tumor was too close to the heart for them to consider installing a filter that would prevent this. It would be "rational," he said, in answer to our questions, to make it a policy for me not to drive anywhere with the children in the car.

I knew, too, that the disease outside my liver had grown with incredible speed. Only a couple of weeks after diagnosis, I began having symptoms—including stomach pain bad enough to hospitalize me for two days. After watching my father's five-year battle with cancer, I was aware that a cascade of side effects could begin at any time, some of them fatal.

I wasn't ready, I said to friends. Not in the way I could be ready in, oh, three or four months. Perhaps I was kidding myself in imagining that I could compose myself if only I had a little time. But I think not entirely. I had watched my parents die three years earlier, seven weeks apart—my mother, ironically, of liver disease, and my father of an invasive cancer of unknown origin. I had a pretty good idea, I thought, of what was coming.

But from almost the first instant, my terror and grief were tinged with an odd relief. I was so lucky, I thought, that this was happening to me as late as forty-three, not in my thirties or my twenties. If I died soon there would be some things I'd regret not having done, and I would feel fathomless anguish at leaving my children so young. But I had a powerful sense that, for my own part, I had had every chance to flourish. I had a loving marriage. I'd known the sweet, rock-breaking, irreplaceable labor of parenthood, and would leave two marvelous beings in my place. I had known rapture, and adventure, and rest. I knew what it was to love my work. I had deep, hard-won friendships, and diverse, widespread friendships of less intensity.

I was surrounded by love.

All this knowledge brought a certain calm. I knew, intuitively, that I would have felt more panicked, more frantic, in the years when I was still growing into my adulthood. For I had had the chance to become the person it was in me to be. Nor did I waste any time wondering why. Why me? It was obvious that this was no more or less than a piece of horrible bad luck. Until then my life had been, in the big ways, one long run of good luck. Only a moral idiot could feel entitled, in the midst of such a life, to a complete exemption from bad fortune.

So now my death—as a given—dominated my relationships with all of those close to me: With my two dear, dear older sisters, to whom I was doubly bonded by the shared ordeal of helping my mother die, and with my stepmother—a contemporary of mine, who had seen my father through his five ferocious years of survival. With my best friends—who spoiled and cosseted and fed and sat with me, rounding up great brigades of clucking acquaintances to bring us dinners, saying just the right thing, and never turning aside my need to talk: especially my need to talk about when, not if. My friend Liz even went out to look over the local residential hospice, to help me work through my practical concerns about whether, with children so young, I was entitled to die at home.

Above all, of course, death saturated my life with my children—Willie, then eight, and Alice, then five. I don't think death (as opposed to illness) dominated their view of me, but it certainly barged its cackling way into my heart and mind during even the simplest of family interchanges. After talking to friends and reading several books, Tim and I had decided to handle the matter openly with them: We told them that I had cancer, and what kind. We told them about chemotherapy, and how it would make me seem even sicker than I looked then. We emphasized that they couldn't catch cancer, and had nothing to do with causing it.

Beyond that, we would answer with honesty any question they asked, but wouldn't step ahead of them in forcing their knowledge of just how bad things were. When the timing of my death revealed itself, then we would have to tell them. Above all, I wanted to spare them the loss of their childhood to a constant vigilance: If they knew we would talk to them honestly, they wouldn't have to put all their energy into figuring out at every turn what new distress was agitating the air around them. Neither of them, at first, chose to ask the $64,000 question. But I couldn't lay eyes on them without seeing them swallowed by the shadow of devastation to come.

Notice, though, that I don't include my husband among those to whom my death was an imminent fact. From the moment of diagnosis, Tim rolled up his sleeves and went to work. In this way, we divided the work of assimilating our nightmare. I addressed myself to death; he held a practical insistence on life. It was the best possible thing he could have done for me, although it often separated us at the time. It could make me crazy, lying awake on the left side of the bed, wanting to talk about death, while Tim lay awake on the right side trying to figure out the next five moves he had to make to keep me alive, and then beyond that, to find the magic bullet in which I did not believe.

But I never thought of refusing treatment. For one thing, it was obvious that I owed my children any shot at reprieve, no matter how improbable. Also, my doctors said that even the slim prospect of mitigation was worth a try. And so Tim and I drifted into a tacit, provisional agreement to act as if. . . . As if, while I began chemotherapy, I were in some genuine suspense about the outcome.

Yet it made me furious any time someone tried to cheer me up by reciting the happy tale of a sister-in-law's cousin who had liver cancer but now he's eighty and he hasn't been troubled by it in forty years. I wanted to scream, DON'T YOU KNOW HOW SICK I AM? I knew, of course, how narcissistic and self-dramatizing this sounded. Still, it enraged me when anyone said, *Aaanh, what do doctors know? They don't know everything.* I was working so hard to accept my death: I felt abandoned, evaded, when someone insisted that I would live.

That was a deeper anger than the irritation I felt at the people—some of them important figures in my life—who had memorably inappropriate reactions. I can't count the times I've been asked what psychological affliction made me invite this cancer. My favorite *New Yorker* cartoon, now taped above my desk, shows two ducks talking in a pond. One of them is telling the other: "Maybe you should ask yourself why you're inviting all this duck hunting into your life right now."

Another woman sent me a card to "congratulate" me on my "cancer journey," and quoted Joseph Campbell to the effect that in order to achieve the life you deserved, you had to give up the life you had planned. *Screw you*, I thought. *You* give up the life *you* had planned.

And a former mentor insisted on explaining the entire cosmic plan: According to Teilhard de Chardin, she said, we are not human beings having a spiritual experience, we are spiritual beings having a human experience, and so now I had taken on this cancer because I had evolved to the point that I could ascend to the next level, where her Aunt Shirley was already hanging out. But I would also get to somehow swoosh down and visit my family and check out how they were doing. It was painful to hear such an admired friend explain this, with no humility or scintilla of doubt, but finally it became funny when she began sending me books on the same theme: I never got past a single glance into pages that couched the words "life" and "death" in quotation marks.

You know how common wisdom insists, in answer to the awkward feelings that always accompany sickness and death, that there's really no wrong thing to say? This is entirely false. Around the same time I started treatment, my friend Mike revealed to all his friends that he had been dealing for some years with Parkinson's Disease. We began a competition, by email, to see who could compile the most appalling reactions.

I found my best ones in hospitals, among doctors and nurses who seemed unacquainted with—or terrified of—fear and death; who were constantly holding up the garlic of their difference from me, to ward me off even as they pretended to minister to me. There was the nurse who hissed at me, with inexplicable ire, *"You have a very bad disease, you know."* There was the nurse's aide at Georgetown University Hospital who trudged into my room one morning, heaved a great sigh, and said, "I tell you, I hate working the oncology floor. It's so *depressing.*" Her aunt had died of cancer, she said, and, *"Boy,* is that an awful disease."

At least her oddball gloom was right out there on the surface. Perhaps worst of all was the nurse in the chemo infusion ward, with whom I fell into conversation to while away my seventh hour of chemotherapy on a gray day in late December. We talked idly about vacations we'd like to take some day. "Oh well," she said, putting down my chart and stretching kittenishly on her way out the door, "I have all the time in the world."

At the start of this struggle, with one shining exception, no one in a white coat ever uttered a single humble word; a single doubt; a single suggestion that surprises happen in medicine, and I might hold out a distant hope of doing better than the norm. It was as if any flickering hope I held might set fire to the floor, forcing them to stamp and stamp until they had blown it out. I see, of course, the reasons why oncology might make you a pessimist (or might attract pessimists in the first place): Ninety percent of Dr. Liver's patients die, so why would it be anything but painful for him to watch false hope lighting the eyes of a young-ish mother who had children the same ages as his own? But, until very recently, understanding didn't mitigate my anger. Is it so much to ask that a doctor, while telling the truth, might at least refrain from lashing his patients with the rage of his impotence?

The great exception among the scythe-bearers was Jerome Groopman, MD, the hematologist-oncologist-researcher who writes medical articles for the *New Yorker* and holds an endowed chair at Harvard Medical School. I knew of Jerry by reputation, and was lucky enough to have several mutual friends and acquaintances in journalism who put us in touch. When my husband called him and described the specifics of my case, Jerry said, "We're going to have to manufacture a miracle." He made it sound eminently possible. And while I never formally became his patient, he became our guide, sherpa, adviser-in-chief—teaching us the secret handshakes, describing the tests we should insist on and the drugs we should ask about, shaking out of his pockets at several turning points the specialists that my other doctors thought there was no point in pursuing. He never denied the reality of my disease, but took the unusual attitude that *until shown otherwise*, any patient entering treatment had at least the right to hope for the best.

But while Jerry's bracing advice would revive my courage at many turns, I had bought deeply into the pessimism of the doctors treating me. We think our culture lauds the stubborn survivor, the one who says, "I will beat this cancer" and then promptly wins the *Tour de France*. But the truth is that there is a staggering vulnerability in asserting one's right to hope. Even most of the doctors who have, from time to time, promoted my optimism tend to wash their hands of it as soon as some procedure or potion fails to pan out. So I have carried what hope I have as a furtive prize.

This attitude was driven, too, by what I brought to the fight. I grew up in a house where there was a premium on being wised-up to impending disapproval or disappointment; and there was punishment by contempt for any blatant display of innocence or hopeful desire. It was all too easy for me to feel shamed in the blast of medicine's certainty. If I carried hope from the start, I did it in secret, hiding it like an illegitimate child of a century past. I hid it even from myself.

It is in my personality, anyway, to linger on the dark side, sniffing under every rock, determined to know the worst that may happen. Not to be caught by surprise. I was raised in a family full of lies—a rich, entertaining, well-elaborated fivesome that flashed with competition and triangles and changing alliances. If your sister was becoming anorexic, no one mentioned it. When your father's ubiquitous assistant came along on family vacations year after year, and sat at picnics with him thigh-to-thigh, no one named the strangeness of it. That my parents divided me and my sisters up between themselves and schooled us in scorn for the other team: that was *certainly* never acknowledged. But it married me for life to the inconvenient argument, the longing to know what was real.

Hence, even when my prospects for recovery or remission have looked best, there has always been one face of my being that was turned toward the likelihood of death—keeping in touch with it, convinced that denying it any entry would weaken me in ways I couldn't afford. Forced into a corner, I'll choose truth over hope any day.

I worried, of course, that I was dooming myself. Americans are so steeped in the message that we are what we think, and that a positive attitude can banish disease. (You'd be amazed how many people need to believe that only losers die of cancer.) Was my realism going to shoot down any possibility of help? Superstitiously, I wondered.

But it turns out that hope is a more supple blessing than I had imagined. From the start, even as my brain was wrestling with death, my body enacted some innate hope that I have learned is simply a part of my being. Chemotherapy would knock me into a passive misery for days. And then—depending on which formula I was taking at the time—a day would come when I would wake up feeling energetic and happy and very much like a normal person. Whether the bad time I had just had lasted five days or five weeks, some inner voice eventually said—and still says— Never mind. Today is a ravishing day, and I will put on a short skirt and high heels and see how much of the future I can inhale.

On the morning of my first chemotherapy, Dr. Liver dictated notes that closed with this fragmentary, misspelled sentence: "It is to be hoped, . . . unlikel that we will get a second chance."

Two chemo cycles later, I had a CT scan that showed dramatic shrinkage in all my tumors—shrinkage by as much as one half. Dr. Liver actually hugged me, and hinted that it was not impossible I might be a "complete responder." The first thing you learn when you get cancer is that the disease you've always thought of as 90 or 100 precise conditions is in fact hundreds of different diseases, which shade into each other all along the spectrum. And I turned out to have some mysterious fluke, a bit of biological filigree in the make-up of my tumors, that rendered them far better targets than I'd had any right to expect.

I went right out and bought four bottles of champagne, and invited our eight dearest friends to the house for a party. It was a beautiful September night and we all ate pizza on the front porch. The kids were thrilled by the energy of it all, without quite understanding it. (After all, I still had cancer, didn't I? And they hadn't known how firmly I had felt sealed in my coffin before now.) It was as if a door far across a dark room had opened a small crack, admitting brilliant light from a hallway: It was still a long, long shot, I knew, but now at least I had something to drive toward. A possible opening, where before there had been none.

I became a professional patient. And all my doctors learned my name.

—*May 2004*

TELLING THE REAL, REAL TRUTH

Both my kids ask in the same week, with the faultless sensor for parental vulnerability that is bundled into every child's operating system. Alice, at six, has probably found her curiosity on the playground; Willie, a scientist at eight, is hard at work on the dubious physics of reindeer travel. But in their separate ways, both pursue the matter with prosecutorial zeal: Mommy, isn't Santa really you?

It would be hard to overstate how much I want to evade the question. Their faces hold such tension as they ask, such a desire to be wrong. But really my dismay is rooted in practice: They are catching me at a time when I'm fed up with telling them the truth.

The common wisdom about how to discuss cancer with your children says, above all, that you should be honest. And so we have tried to be: When will you get better, Mommy? (I don't know, but I'm working on it as hard as I can.) Will it be this year? (No, not this year.) If you don't get better this year, you'll definitely get better next year, right? (We hope so, but not definitely.) To turn your children loose in the same uncertainty that wakes you at four in the morning feels exactly like cruelty. But amid all the available advice, the piece that makes the most visceral sense to me is the proposition that kids shouldn't have to be vigilant, sentenced constantly to seek out the particulars of a danger they're dimly aware of.

Yet the moments when one of them asks me direct questions about my survival are easily among the most anxious of my life. I have rehearsed all the good counsel on how to answer in a way that blends realism with hope, truth with optimism—letting their questions guide us; stressing the good news of how my treatment is going, while never flatly denying the real possibility of failure. But I often feel false as I do it: As so many parents have discovered in discussing September 11 with their kids, it feels hugely unnatural to express true uncertainty about something vital to a child's sense of safety. I suspect I project equivocation instead, and imagine that, in my daughter's head, it is instantly boiled down to a baffling essence: On the one hand, on the other hand. Mommy's getting better, Mommy might die. The tension of it probably matches the bipolar strangeness of having a mother in chemotherapy, wan and exhausted one week, full of energy the next.

Their hunger for the truth is palpable. There are days when they ask me constant, minor questions on unrelated matters, queries that seem designed to triple-check the calibrations of their crucial inner polygraphs. Where before I would have told a tiny lie to ease my daughter past a difficult moment—*No, I didn't hear when your brother just said out loud what you got me for Christmas*—I know this will no longer fly. She follows up too fiercely: "Is that the real, real truth you're telling me?"

So when they press me on the subject of Santa, I know it for the test it is. It seems such a huge, sad sacrifice, this consigning of the fantasy of Christmas to the cause of security. More than ever, I wish they would settle for the wormy playbook of parental good cheer. (What do *you* think? Well, some people think Santa's real, and some people don't!) But finally I square myself to the task, and ask them: What do they hope the answer is? They both hope Santa is real. I tell them the truth anyway.

Their disappointment brings me all the familiar sadness and reflexive guilt. But it turns out that hard things do get easier with practice. Because next I find myself saying, with an ease that surprises me, that we can have it both ways: We can know what we know but also pretend he's real, and then he'll come on Christmas for as many years as we want him to.

Alice decides on the spot that Santa's nonexistence is no bar to his bringing her a Barbie Grand Hotel this year. Willie savors the adult-flavored chance to clear up some of the ancillary mysteries (yes, Mom and Dad eat the Oreos you leave out for Santa, but the carrots go back in the fridge). But the next day he goes back to talking about whether Santa will fill a stocking for the cat.

If this had been a normal year, I couldn't have asserted, with such authority, that it is feasible to live two possibilities at once. Facing down the Santa issue reminds me that every time I step up to one of those big, choking questions about the future, my anxiety eventually turns to relief. You can almost see the children choose which parts they can take on right now, which to jettison. And then off they run, in search of the rich oblivion of SpongeBob and baseball. I hope, as they go, that somewhere in them another little muscle of trust has been fed. That is the best safety I have to offer right now.

—*December 13, 2001*

THE RANDOM DEATH OF
OUR SENSE OF EASE

A cancer patient learns to see them coming, the ones who want to ask you (or tell you) just how you managed to give yourself this illness, and why you have failed so far to cure it. It is your toxic anger. It is what you eat, or fail to eat. It is your neglect of your third chakra, or your stubborn refusal to take coffee enemas. They would never be so foolish.

These conversations have given me a new, if irritated, respect for the human animal's drive to explain away the random fact of bad fortune. And I've found them helpful in groping to answer the question my son asked immediately when the sniper attacks* began: Why does *this* series of killings have everyone so upset? It saddened me, to say the least, that he was trying at the age of nine to fix the murders into some larger context of more quotidian mayhem. But I was also fascinated by his quick intuition that these killings have a special power to tamper with our core sense of safety.

Sudden death always threatens to strip away our illusions that we have some dominion over fate. But this killer seems especially frightening for his apparent determination to mirror, in the randomness of his acts, the brute impartiality of death itself. When someone is picking off victims with the implacable dispassion of nature, we can't tell ourselves, "Oh, she

---

* In 2002, John Allen Muhammed and Lee Boyd Malvo killed ten randomly-chosen people in the Washington area, using a rifle hidden inside the trunk of a Chevrolet Caprice.

walked home from the Subway after dark in the wrong neighborhood."
Or: "Well, he smoked for twenty-five years." Or even: "She always did
drive too fast." Any of the stories we tell ourselves, in other words, to set
ourselves apart from the dead. These shootings insist on reminding us that
even if we buy our next tank of gas unscathed, any Thursday can bring the
slip in the shower, the crash on the interstate, the look on the technician's
face when she sees the bad shadow on the film.

It is only human, our desire to tell ourselves that death is an ugly relative who need never be invited to dinner. But, of course, it doesn't stand
up to scrutiny, and this is just what our sniper has forced on us. Suddenly
we have to perform consciously all the little calculations we are always
making to appease the fates. And there is something shaming about being
caught in the act. Did anyone see me scuttle from the door of the grocery
store to the safety of my car? Will people think I'm crazy if I don't let my
child go to baseball practice? If I do? What is my gut belief about the laws
of probability, and how much more vulnerable do I make myself if I expose
my magical thinking to the cold light of day?

I have no evidence of this, beyond what my heart tells me. But I also
think a part of our horror and fear is how legible this killer feels to us. The
awful shrewdness of the way this person has gone about scaring us invites
us to puzzle over his acts—and, in doing so, to join him. We are trying so
hard to parse the hunter's cruelty that for minutes at a time we step into
his shoes: What does he want? How does he decide? What does he see
when he waits for someone to stand still in his sights? If we are perfectly
honest, there is relief in standing for those moments at his end of the gun.
None of us is very different from my gentle son, who responds by model-
ing small fingers in the shape of a weapon and shooting at everything
around him, making secretive, muffled sounds of explosion in the back of
his mouth.

When he asked me why everyone is so upset by these particular crimes,
I found myself wading hip deep into the concept of motive, and its apparent absence here. I dragged the conversation back out of this swamp as
quickly as I could. (The fact that killers usually have reasons, however bad,
for what they do: Is that the most or the least comforting thing a nine-
year-old could hear?) But I knew, too, that his question led straight to the
heart of the matter. What we really labor to keep from our children is the
same bitter knowledge that their elders avoid: not that people get killed by
strangers, or that there are too many guns in our world, or that madness

never sleeps, but that there is no logic at all to some of the worst blows that life metes out. Time and chance happen to us all, darling boy, and even grown-ups can bear it only a little bit at a time.

—October 11, 2002

THE DOCTOR FACTOR

At long last, the revelation I've been waiting for: the reason why—beyond the prospect of epic, McGovernesque defeat—I feel so uneasy about Howard Dean.

The man is a doctor. This is the least-examined chapter of his career. But suddenly it all makes sense: Where else but in medicine do you find men and women who never admit a mistake? Who talk more than they listen, and feel entitled to withhold crucial information? Whose lack of tact in matters of life and death might disqualify them for any other field?

As it happens, I've spent almost two decades observing politicians, whom on balance I quite like, and more recent years observing doctors, who. . . . Well, let's just say that mine is a grudge tenderly nurtured over two-and-a-half years of illness, encompassing roughly thirty-two doctors in six hospitals, plus scores of the medical students, fellows, interns, and residents in whom we can see the doctor in larval form.

A doctor who has told you one thing at Appointment A might propose an entirely different course of action at Meeting B. Fair enough—*except for the pretense that nothing has changed*. It is the very rare doctor who will say, "I've changed my mind," or, "Sorry, I was wrong when I said X at our last meeting." Usually, what he said last time has simply become . . . inoperative.

Now let's turn the clock back to September, and watch Dean answer George Stephanopoulos on *This Week* about his 180-degree turn, over the years, on the North American Free Trade Agreement:

GS: On NAFTA, you used to be a very strong supporter of NAFTA.

HD: George, you're doing it again. I supported NAFTA and wrote a letter to President Clinton in 1992 supporting NAFTA. That's different than you used to be a very strong supporter of NAFTA.

GS: You were a strong supporter of NAFTA.

HD: I supported NAFTA. Where do you get this I'm a strong supporter of NAFTA? I didn't do anything about it. I didn't vote on it. I didn't march down the street demanding NAFTA. I simply wrote a letter supporting NAFTA.

Dean was not in the least abashed that he had described himself on the same show, eight years earlier, as "a very strong supporter of NAFTA."

Now, we patients rarely dare to have such pugnacious dialogue with our doctors. George Stephanopoulos doesn't have to wear one of those demoralizing gowns with all the confusing snaps, and if you're sick you have more important things to do during your tiny portions of face time than bicker with your doctor. (A disclaimer: Naturally, all the doctors who are *presently* treating and advising me are paragons of sagacity and compassion, nothing at all like the men and women I am so broadly lampooning. You know who you are.)

The odd thing is that most of Dean's unacknowledged shifts in position are of the kind any other half-good politician, with some vaporous wording, could explain away in his sleep. But, even when Dean makes what is clearly a blunder, it takes him days to make the apology that a rival campaign would instinctively produce before the next news cycle.

Which brings me to the irrationally strong impulse, shared by doctors and politicians, to hoard information. Consider the high-handed way Dean has tried to shield great portions of his gubernatorial records. Similarly, doctors seem bent on ensuring that you not read the runic scribblings they have made in your chart. During one hospital stay, as I sat in a wheelchair outside Radiology waiting to be pushed back to my room, I began idly flipping through my chart. A young female doctor-in-training I had never seen before stopped in front of me and said, "You know, you really shouldn't be reading your chart." I thanked her for her advice and continued reading. She repeated her admonition. I explained that I was forty-three and couldn't possibly read anything worse there than I had already been told by five real doctors. Upon which she actually *wrested* it from my grasp. (From this I learned always to go to a stall in the ladies' room when I want to read my chart.)

Finally, let's turn to what newspapers delicately title "the temperament question." Dean's been called arrogant, angry, condescending, prickly. He has gotten this far by playing his chesty irritability as a sign of honesty and integrity.

But I have enough brusque, irritable doctors in my life without sending one to the White House. My most memorable brushes have been with an eminent surgeon whose method is to stride into the examining room two hours late, pat your hand, pronounce your certain death if he can't perform an operation on you, and then snap at your husband to stop taking notes, he can't *possibly* follow the complexity of the doctor's thinking. Dr. X swats away questions like flies. He spends five precious minutes swearing at the wall-mounted phone, which decades of surgical experience have not equipped him to operate, and then finally pronounces that he can't perform the surgery. "Unless you want me to. But there's a 50–50 chance I would kill you."

Why is it, I ask my husband on the way home, that I'm the one who's sick, but they're the ones who are allowed to have the big, operatic personalities?

I have the same concern about Dean. Why should Democrats choose to stand around all spring and summer holding their breath against the moment when Dean says something arrogant or impolitic? We're the ones who are supposed to be allowed to go on with our temperamental little lives, while our major-party nominees are the poor chumps who have agreed to adhere to the rigid, Ken-doll theater of politics.

And so I bring to my assessment of this year's Democratic candidates one requirement that never crossed my mind before. First, do no harm.

—*December 31, 2003*

THE HALLOWEEN OF MY DREAMS

I was the one who insisted on the body glitter. Normally, you understand, I am a mother who pulls her daughter's shirt down and tucks it into her waistband every morning to keep her from showing her navel to the whole third grade. I make her scrub the supposedly water-soluble unicorn tattoos off her cheeks before she goes to school. I court her wrath by refusing to buy the kids' fashions that seem designed to clothe tiny hookers.

But after all, this was Halloween, the holiday that celebrates license. (A fifth KitKat bar after 9 PM? Why not?) Alice was determined to be a rock star, and I was happy to help her. Simple enough.

Yet my joy in conspiring with her felt so *big*. Usually I'm not much of a Halloween enthusiast, not since I was thirteen or so. For a while, having children of my own brought me a new version of the old childhood thrill. One year Will came home from preschool and told me he'd learned about a new Halloween creature, one that lurches through the night swathed in flapping bandages.

"Oh," I said casually. "What's it called?"

"The MOMMIES!" he announced, with much more excitement than dismay.

But my delight lasted for only a few years before I returned to thinking of Halloween as just a silly, gaudy night that strains at symbolism—the floozy among the family of big holidays. I thought, for a while, that I had simply buckled under the demands of Costume Hell. ("I want to be a computer, but also my feet will be, like, a robot, and you can make me a head with glowing red eyes and a voice like Darth Vader.") But that explanation has become less and less convincing: At eleven and almost-nine, after all, the kids have more and more fun making their own costumes, with minimal help. Really, I think that I'm just not one of those people who easily climbs into fantasy and achieves flight.

Recently, after my dear cousin Sally spent a night guarding my sleep in the hospital, we talked about the one part of the experience I remembered as clearly as she. When I'd finally taken aboard enough pain medicine to dull the effects of the procedure I'd just been through, I'd said clearly, out of my cloud of Dilaudid, "I love all these random thoughts. All my life I've worked so hard to get words and sentences into line. They had to have a *point*. I love floating along on all these random thoughts."

It made me hugely sad to see that my escapes from the taskmistress of literalism are still so rare and hard-won. And in the days before this Halloween, it was especially hard for me to avoid interpreting its elements too bluntly. If you have cancer, if you've had it for a while, at some point you start really *seeing* all those skulls and skeletons and Styrofoam headstones, all those children in hooded capes, bearing scythes on their little shoulders.

So how could I explain the euphoria of the forty-five minutes Alice and I spent in her bedroom, colluding over her hair, giggling at her faux-leather, deeply fringed bell-bottoms? The pleasure of watching her strap on those awful silver platform shoes, like something I wore in 1973?

Because Alice was getting picked up to join friends for trick-or-treating, I kept my eye on the clock, and shooed her into the bathroom just in time to add make-up: grown-up lipstick, a layer of shimmery lip gloss over that, and an overall, emphatic scribble, on her neck and face, with the body-glitter crayon. Every other day of the year, any mother knows that glitter is the work of Satan, but last Sunday it lit her skin with a dew of every color.

We could hear her friends pull up to the curb. As her momentum carried her to the top of the stairs, Alice looked back and tossed me a radiant smile. She had become my glimmering girl: She looked like a rock star. She looked like a teenager. She looked absolutely stunning. She thundered down the stairs in those shoes, and as the front door slammed behind her, it came to me—what fantasy I had finally, easily entered this Halloween.

I'd just seen Alice leave for her prom, or her first real date. I'd cheated time, flipping the calendar five or six years into the future. The character I'd played was the fifty-two-year-old mother I will probably never be.

It was effortless.

—November 3, 2004

Editor's Note: A month after Marjorie wrote this, her oncologist concluded that there was no further treatment to recommend. Marjorie died, at home, on January 16, 2005, three days after her forty-seventh birthday.

ACKNOWLEDGMENTS

At the time of Marjorie's death, a few people observed that, amid the many injustices of her loss, one could be righted: she left behind no anthology of her writings. One of these people was Peter Osnos, publisher and chief executive of PublicAffairs. My first thanks go to Peter for initiating this project and lending it his wisdom and his zest. At PublicAffairs I am also indebted to the skillful editor assigned to this book, Lindsay Jones, and to Nina D'Amario, Lisa Kaufman, Robert Kimzey, Jaime Leifer, Clive Priddle, Melissa Raymond, and Gene Taft. For their help with the production of this book, I thank Lisa Teman, Janet Tingey, Jeff Georgeson, and Robert Swanson. Marjorie's agent, Andrew Wylie, and his associates Lisa Halliday, Margot Kaminski, and Katherine Marino handled the business end with their usual panache, and they provided helpful guidance on editorial matters as well.

Many friends and family members rallied to assist in the assembling of this book. David Von Drehle and Jacob Weisberg kindly served as go-betweens to Peter and Andrew during the difficult first weeks after Marjorie's death. Patsy Noah (my sister) and Veronika Jiranova (Will and Alice's nanny) patiently retyped into Marjorie's old computer a great deal of published material that couldn't be retrieved electronically. Mark Feeney, Ann Hulbert, and Bob Thompson reviewed the manuscript in its entirety, and Dana Stevens gave a close read to parts of the book that had not previously been edited for publication. Also helpful in getting this project across the finish line were David Atkins, Bill Barol, Philip Bartolf,

David Corn, Matthew Cooper, Jason DeParle, Abby Frankson, Peter Ginna, Paul Glastris, Bonnie Goldstein, James Grady, Jerome Groopman, Rachel Halterman, Bruce Handy at *Vanity Fair*, Susan Hewitt, Russell James at the Washington Post Writers Group, Elizabeth Kastor, Mickey Kaus, Charles Lane, Paul Leonard, Phillip Longman, Bob Lyford at the *Washington Post*, Ruth Marcus, John McPhee, John Mintz, Marie Monrad, Jim Naughton, Robert and Marian Noah (my parents), Peter and Paula Noah (my brother and sister-in-law), Meghan O'Rourke, Charles Peters, David Plotz, Wistar Rawls (Marjorie's sister), Thomas E. and Mary Kay Ricks, Robin Rue (Marjorie's stepmother), Jack Shafer, Alan Shearer at the Washington Post Writers Group, Clifford M. Sloan, Jeffrey Stern, Laura Stone, Jill Timmons, Kathleen and David Townsend, Anne and Rosina Williams (Marjorie's sisters), Sally and Susan Williams (Marjorie's cousins), Diane Willkens, Meaghan Wolff at the *Washington Post*, Robert Wright, and Emily Yoffe. When she heard that Marjorie had died, Marjorie's childhood friend, the singer-songwriter Mary Chapin Carpenter, sat down and composed a beautiful tribute titled "Love Goes On," and while preparing this volume I listened to the song countless times for solace and inspiration. I thank her for writing and performing it.

I now turn to the difficult task of trying to identify the people Marjorie would want to thank. She'd likely start with the many people who granted her interviews while she was reporting the profiles and essays collected here. The ones who spoke on the record are readily identifiable in the text; those who didn't must remain anonymous (and in most cases are unknown to me). My familiarity with the cast of characters who participated in conceiving and editing these pieces is incomplete, so I apologize in advance to the many former bosses and colleagues I'm about to overlook.

At the *Washington Post*, Editorial Page Editor Fred Hiatt saw an op-ed columnist in Marjorie before Marjorie herself did. After she fell ill, he was a font of moral and other support, and somehow managed to extract some of the best writing of Marjorie's career. A decade earlier, Bob Thompson, who shared Marjorie's skepticism about Washington's official culture, helped her learn to express it in long-form magazine profiles. Other bosses who guided Marjorie at the *Post* included Benjamin C. Bradlee, Leonard Downie, Sandy Flickner, Donald Graham, Mary Hadar, Robert Kaiser (the man most responsible for hiring Marjorie to the national staff when she had zero experience in journalism), Ken Ikenberry, Gene Weingarten, and Tom Wilkinson. The colleagues at the *Post* who helped Marjorie learn the ropes in a more general way included—but were by no means limited to—Henry Allen, Rick Atkinson, Dan Balz, the late Ann Devroy, the late Mary McGrory, and Sally Quinn.

At *Vanity Fair,* Graydon Carter oversaw nearly all of Marjorie's pieces, demonstrating an uncanny instinct for whom to profile and when. His steadfastness after Marjorie got sick extended well beyond the isolated example Marjorie writes of in "Hit By Lightning," and, if fully document-ed, would ruin his reputation as a 21st-century Walter Burns. Other important influences at *Vanity Fair* include Judy Bachrach, Tina Brown (who hired Marjorie), Bryan Burrough, Klara Glowczewska, Bruce Handy, Wayne Lawson, Dee Dee Myers, Maureen Orth, Elise O'Shaugh-nessy, and Sally Bedell Smith. Marjorie felt particular gratitude to *Vanity Fair*'s amazingly resourceful fact-checking team.

At *Talk*: Tina Brown, Tucker Carlson, Robert B. Wallace, and Tom Watson.

At *Slate*: Jodi Kantor, Michael Kinsley, Cyrus Krohn, Judith Shulevitz, and June Thomas.

At the *Washington Monthly:* James Bennet, Katherine Boo, Charles Peters, and Alexandra Starr.

At *U.S. News & World Report*: James Fallows, Marianne Lavelle, Har-rison Rainie, and Steven Waldman.

Generous friends helped our family in a thousand ways during Mar-jorie's illness. But there are so many of them—including just about every name that's appeared in these acknowledgments so far—that merely list-ing them would require publication of an entire separate volume. Instead, I'll thank the doctors who tended most assiduously to Marjorie's body and her spirit. First among these is John Marshall, whose dedication as a physician is matched, we came to see, by a deep well of empathy. Other doctors who (literally) kept Marjorie alive during the writing of this book include Damian P. Alagia, Letitia Clark, Ross Donehower, Stephen Hersh, Jane Ingham, Roger Jenkins, David Kelsen, Virginia Townsend LeBaron, David Patterson, Martin Paul, Andrew Tyler Putnam, Stephen H. Shere, and Keith Stuart. Jerome Groopman was never officially Mar-jorie's doctor, but he guided us through the medical labyrinth with shrewdness, compassion, and the gift of hope. I don't know what we would have done without him.

Marjorie's deceased parents, Alan and Beverly Williams, stand first among those whose contributions to her life's work are large but indirect.

Next would be Marjorie's dearest friends over the course of her lifetime: the late Julie Browder, Beth Frerking, and Vicky Stein. Others include Robert Barnett, Juliana Capois, Monique DuPree, Stephen "Felix" Mantell, Alice Mayhew, Debbie Moses, Daniel Okrent, Sheila and the late Corlies Smith, Willa and the late William Stackpole, Mary Sulerud, and Abigail Wiebenson. Marjorie would want to extend special thanks to Joni Evans, her boss at Simon & Schuster, for teaching her how to be a grown-up. Marjorie would also—I hope this doesn't sound weird—want to thank the people with whom she participated for two decades in group psychotherapy; they were as important to her, in some ways, as her own family. Finally, Marjorie would want to thank our children, Will and Alice. And she'd want to thank me.

You're welcome, my love. Thank you for spending your life with me. I will miss you every day of mine.

RIGHTS AND PERMISSIONS

INDEX

PublicAffairs is a publishing house founded in 1997. It is a tribute to the standards, values, and flair of three persons who have served as mentors to countless reporters, writers, editors, and book people of all kinds, including me.

I.F. STONE, proprietor of *I. F. Stone's Weekly*, combined a commitment to the First Amendment with entrepreneurial zeal and reporting skill and became one of the great independent journalists in American history. At the age of eighty, Izzy published *The Trial of Socrates*, which was a national bestseller. He wrote the book after he taught himself ancient Greek.

BENJAMIN C. BRADLEE was for nearly thirty years the charismatic editorial leader of *The Washington Post*. It was Ben who gave the *Post* the range and courage to pursue such historic issues as Watergate. He supported his reporters with a tenacity that made them fearless and it is no accident that so many became authors of influential, best-selling books.

ROBERT L. BERNSTEIN, the chief executive of Random House for more than a quarter century, guided one of the nation's premier publishing houses. Bob was personally responsible for many books of political dissent and argument that challenged tyranny around the globe. He is also the founder and longtime chair of Human Rights Watch, one of the most respected human rights organizations in the world.

For fifty years, the banner of Public Affairs Press was carried by its owner Morris B. Schnapper, who published Gandhi, Nasser, Toynbee, Truman, and about 1,500 other authors. In 1983, Schnapper was described by *The Washington Post* as "a redoubtable gadfly." His legacy will endure in the books to come.

Peter Osnos, *Founder and Editor-at-Large*